Cornell Studies in Security Affairs

edited by Robert J. Art *and* Robert Jervis

Deterrence and Strategic Culture

CHINESE-AMERICAN CONFRONTATIONS,

1949–1958

SHU GUANG ZHANG

Cornell University Press

ITHACA AND LONDON

International Standard Book Number 0-8014-2751-7
Library of Congress Catalog Card Number 92-52777
Printed in the United States of America
*Librarians: Library of Congress cataloging information
appears on the last page of the book.*
⊖ The paper in this book meets the minimum requirements of
the American National Standard for Information Sciences—
Permanence of Paper for Printed Library Materials, ANSI Z39.48-1984.

To my mother, father, and sister

Contents

[vii]

Maps

Acknowledgments

Many people generously supported the writing of this book, but some contributors deserve special thanks. I owe an especially large debt of gratitude to John Lewis Gaddis, who has guided my study of American diplomatic history, encouraged my exploration of the theory of international relations, and worked closely with me in preparing this book. He has urged me to think carefully and pushed me to clean up my prose. Professor Gaddis read my manuscript at different stages and did a great amount of editing. I have been very fortunate to work with him. I also thank other history professors at Ohio University, especially Charles C. Alexander, Alonzo L. Hamby, Donald A. Jordan, Steven M. Miner, and Robert H. Whealey, who have stimulated my thinking.

This book is based heavily on the Chinese materials that have only recently become available. I am deeply grateful to those friends who assisted me in assessing the materials in Beijing, Nanjing, and Shanghai. A two-year dissertation fellowship in international peace and security from the John D. and Catherine T. MacArthur Foundation and Social Science Research Council financed the research and writing. An honorary postdoctoral fellowship from the Contemporary History Institute, Ohio University, helped me revise the manuscript. John J. Mearsheimer at the University of Chicago and Steven M. Goldstein at Smith College taught me how to approach issues of international security and Sino-American relations. Warren I. Cohen, Richard Ned Lebow, Janice Gross Stein, and Nancy B. Tucker read an early draft of this book. Robert Art spent generous amounts of time reading the manuscript and offered important criticism.

Writing this book in my second language would have been impossible without the help of American friends, especially George Barnes, Hugh M. Culbertson, Gifford B. Doxsee, Mary K. Jordan, Donna Stone, and Gerald Stone. Their friendship and assistance are much appreciated.

My wife, Chen Ni, has contributed to this book in a unique but indispensable way. Her expertise in mass communications has broadened the horizon of my knowledge; her love, care, and tolerance have helped me overcome constant frustrations during the writing.

An earlier and shorter version of Chapter 2 was published in the January 1990 issue of the journal *Chinese Historians*.

Chinese personal names, place names, and sources are given, with a few exceptions, in *pinyin*.

S. G. Z.

Athens, Ohio

Abbreviations

In preparing this book I have cited several collections of documents and materials. I have used the following abbreviations when citing frequently used sources. Full citations are given in the bibliography.

DDZGHGY	Dangdai Zhongguo Series. *Dangdai Zhongguo Hegongye.*
DDZGHJ	——. *Dangdai Zhongguo Haijun.*
DDZGJSGZ	——. *Dangdai Zhongguo Jundui De Junshi Gongzhuo.*
DDZGKJ	——. *Dangdai Zhongguo Kongjun.*
DDZGWJ	——. *Dangdai Zhongguo Waijiao.*
DWGXWJ	Editorial Division of *Shijie Zhishi. Zhonghua Renmin Gongheguo Duiwai Guanxi Wenjian Ji.*
FRUS	U.S. Department of State. *Foreign Relations of the United States.*
JFJZS	Division of Military History, Chinese Academy of Military Sciences. *Zhongguo Renmin Jiefangjun Zhan Shi.* Vol. 3.
JGYLMWG	Mao Zedong. *Jianguo Yilai Mao Zedong Wengao.*
KMYCZZ	Dangdai Zhongguo Series. *Kangmei Yuanchao Zhanzheng.*
MJSWXNBB	Mao Zedong. *Mao Zedong Junshi Wenxuan—Niebuban.*
MSXWS	——. *Mao Zedong Sixiang Wansui.*
PJSWX	Peng Dehuai. *Peng Dehaui Junshi Wenxuan.*
SWM	Mao Tse-tung. *Selected Works of Mao Tse-tung.* Vol. 4.
SWZ	Zhou Enlai. *Zhou Enlai Xuanji.*
ZYJZS	Division of Military History, Chinese Academy of Military Sciences. *Zhongguo Renmin Zhiyuanjun Kangmei Yuanchao Zhan Shi.*

Deterrence and Strategic Culture

[1]

Mutual Deterrence and Standard Models

This book is about Chinese-American conflicts between 1949 and 1958. From an international security perspective, it offers an explanation of the actual and potential military confrontations between the People's Republic of China (PRC) and the United States by focusing on the deterrent relationship between the two nations. Moreover, it attempts to reconcile deterrence theory with historical evidence.

I

Why do Sino-American relations during this period have anything to do with the problem of deterrence? My answer is simple: deterrence as a strategy was a predominant theme in the policy assumptions and objectives of both the PRC and the United States. The available archival sources make it clear that as conflicts arose, deterrence became a main objective. Each state sought to persuade the other, by demonstrating military capability and political resolve, not to initiate actions perceived as threatening; each sought to assure that the benefits the other anticipated would not justify the attendant costs and risks. This pattern of crisis behavior fits well into both our theoretical and our practical understanding of deterrence.[1]

---

1. For traditional studies of deterrence, see, for example, Robert E. Osgood, *Limited War: The Challenge to American Strategy* (Chicago, 1956); Bernard Brodie, *Strategy in the Missile Age* (Princeton, 1959); Daniel Ellsberg, "The Crude Analysis of Strategic Choice," *American Economic Review* 21 (May 1961): 472–78; Thomas C. Schelling, *The Strategy of Conflict* (Cambridge, Mass., 1960) and *Arms and Influence* (New Haven, 1966); Glenn

Deterrence theory is the most impressive theoretical achievement of international security studies to date, but it can be invoked too easily and, too often to explain too much. The Sino-American deterrent relationship was subtle and complex, little has as yet been written about it, and contemporary deterrence theorists have difficulty explaining it in several respects:

First, the relationship was one in which the two countries applied deterrence against each other, often simultaneously but without knowing what the other was doing. Standard deterrence theory assumes that in any deterrent situation there is an aggressor who seeks to challenge the status quo and a defender who wants to maintain it.

A rational aggressor will pursue attainable goals through available means and only when anticipated gains outweigh estimated costs. A rational defender will confront the aggressor with a credible prospect of unacceptably high costs of aggression.[2]

Here we have not an aggressor and a defender, but two defenders. Both China and the United States perceived the other as the aggressor state attempting to overturn the status quo, always ready to expand its sphere of influence at the expense of its opposite number. As a result, both relied on deterrence rationality to influence the other's behavior. In retrospect, we can see that neither state had the aggressive intentions that the other so consistently attributed to it. There is no evidence that the United States sought to expand its sphere of influence in Asia by attacking the Chinese mainland, nor is there any indication that Beijing authorities ever sought to eliminate U.S. influence by encroaching on the non-communist countries in the region. Each side misjudged the other, both in the short and long term. How does this kind of mutual misjudgment occur? How does misperceiving an adversary's intentions, and thus exaggerating the external threat, lead

---

Snyder, *Deterrence and Defense* (Princeton, 1961); and Bruce Russett, "Pearl Harbor: Deterrence Theory and Decision Theory," *Journal of Peace Research* no. 2 (1967): 89–105. For the reviews of deterrence literature, see Richard A. Brody, "Deterrence Strategy: An Annotated Bibliography," *Journal of Conflict Resolution* 4 (December 1960): 443–57, and Robert Jervis, "Deterrence Theory Revisited," *World Politics* 31 (January 1979): 289–324.

2. Most of the works mentioned in note 1 have followed this argument in one way or another. For a traditional treatment of the nation as a unitary actor capable of making calculated and rational choices, see, for example, William W. Kaufmann, "Limited War," in *Military Policy and National Security*, ed. William W. Kaufmann (Princeton, 1956). A good overview in this regard is Patrick M. Morgan, *Deterrence: A Conceptual Analysis*, 2d ed. (Beverly Hills, Calif., 1983). For recent rational deterrence debate, see Christopher H. Achen and Duncan Snidal, "Rational Deterrence Theory and Comparative Case Studies," *World Politics* 4 (January 1989): 143–69; Alexander L. George and Richard Smoke, "Deterrence and Foreign Policy," ibid., pp. 170–82; Robert Jervis, "Rational Deterrence: Theory and Evidence," ibid., pp. 183–207; and Richard Ned Lebow and Janice Gross Stein, "Rational Deterrence Theory: I Think, Therefore I Deter," ibid., pp. 208–24.

two countries into a mutual-deterrence situation? Deterrence theory does not answer these questions.

Second, Sino-American relations were in constant flux throughout this decade. Little in the existing body of deterrence literature deals with a situation extending over such a span of time. Standard deterrence theory tends to regard deterrent situations as single instances and to assume that deterrence ends once military conflict begins. It is difficult for deterrence theorists to explain how two countries without a common border—in fact, separated by a considerable geographic distance—so frequently slipped into crisis and hostilities. During the period 1949-58, there were seven such instances in three main arenas—the Korean peninsula, Indochina, and the Taiwan Strait—where each side sought to deter the other. How did these individual crises come to reinforce each other to form a continuous deterrent relationship? This question, too, remains unanswered.

Third, standard deterrence theory has difficulty explaining the mixed means both states deployed to achieve deterrence. There are generally assumed to be three types of deterrence: strategic, extended, and conventional. The first, *strategic* deterrence, involves nuclear confrontations between superpowers; the second, *extended* deterrence, refers to attempts by one superpower to deter local or limited crises by threatening to launch nuclear strikes in response to conventional attack.[3] Although still relatively underdeveloped theoretically, the third, *conventional* deterrence, applies to situations in which non-nuclear forces face each other on a large battlefield. "Guerrilla conflict" or "episodes dominated by naval and air warfare" are deliberately excluded.[4]

Each type of deterrence tends to rely, in theory, on a single category of counterthreat. But the history of Sino-American relations in the

---

3. Extended deterrence theory is still underdeveloped. Prominent treatments include Alexander L. George and Richard Smoke, *Deterrence in American Foreign Policy: Theory and Practice* (New York, 1974); Richard K. Betts, *Nuclear Blackmail and Nuclear Balance* (Washington, D.C., 1987); Paul Hugh and Bruce Russett, "What Makes Deterrence Work? Cases from 1900 to 1980," *World Politics* 36 (January 1984): 496–526, "Deterrence Failure and Crisis Escalation," *International Studies Quarterly* 32 (May 1988): 29–45, and "Testing Deterrence Theory: Rigor Makes a Difference," *World Politics* 42 (July 1990): 466–501; and Paul K. Huth, *Extended Deterrence and the Prevention of War* (New Haven, 1988) and "Extended Deterrence and the Outbreak of War," *American Political Science Review* 82 (Spring 1988): 423–43. Also see Stephen J. Cimbala, *Extended Deterrence: The United States and NATO Europe* (Lexington, Mass., 1987), pp. 7–28, and 197–218.

4. See John J. Mearsheimer, *Conventional Deterrence* (Ithaca, N.Y., 1983), chaps. 1–3. For other studies of conventional deterrence, see Samuel Huntington, "Conventional Deterrence and Conventional Retaliation in Europe," *International Security* 8 (Winter 1983–84): 32–56; John Lepingwell, "The Laws of Combat? Lanchester Reexamined," ibid., 12 (Summer 1987): 89–127; Richard K. Betts, "Conventional Deterrence: Predictive Uncertainty and Policy Confidence," *World Politics* 37 (January 1985): 153–79; and Jonathan Shimshoni, *Israel and Conventional Deterrence* (Ithaca, N.Y., 1988).

1950s suggests that both sides applied a mixture of means. The United States threatened nuclear retaliation, conventional military action by naval and air forces, collective efforts with allies, and diplomatic intimidation. The PRC also relied on mixed counterthreats, including its own conventional military force, the Sino-Soviet military alliance, and Soviet nuclear retaliation. And finally, China decided to build its own nuclear weapons to reinforce deterrence. Neither Beijing nor Washington relied on any one form of deterrence as today's international security theorists suggest. How did the policymakers formulate counterthreats? Why did they not adhere to a specific type of counterthreat? There is no succinct answer in the existing body of deterrence literature.

A fourth, particularly acute problem with contemporary deterrence theory is the absence of cross-cultural comparison. National styles of strategic thinking may reflect cultural differences, but standard deterrence theory does not acknowledge the possibility of such differences. In accord with the rational-choice models, deterrence theory simply assumes a common understanding of deterrence. The defender possesses some prize that the initiator covets. If, as Christopher Achen and Duncan Snidal put it, "the initiator believes it likely that the option to retaliate actually exists (the defender has the military means to retaliate after an attack and is politically free to do so) and the defender would find retaliation in his interests if the prize is threatened," then the initiator who attacks will be worse off than one who does not, and the initiator will not attack.[5] Thus under rational-choice theory, the success of deterrence turns on the defender's credibility.

But reality is often inconsistent with the argument that as long as deterrent threats are credible, meaningful, and communicable, adversaries will retreat. China and the United States are two nations of distinctively different cultures. The Chinese and the Americans may well calculate prizes and interests, threats and counterthreats, costs and gains, failures and successes, weaknesses and strengths, declaratory policies and actual behavior differently. Deterrents may not mean the same thing in Beijing and Washington. If this is true, to what extent did such differences shape Sino-American confrontations? Contemporary deterrence literature cannot say.[6]

5. Achen and Snidal, "Rational Deterrence Theory and Comparative Case Studies," p. 151. Also see Joseph S. Nye, Jr., and Sean M. Lynn-Jones, "International Security Studies: A Report of the Conference on the State of the Field," *International Security* 12 (Spring 1988): 11.
6. For studies of Sino-American deterrence, see Allen S. Whiting, *The Chinese Calculus of Deterrence* (Ann Arbor, 1975) and *China Crosses the Yalu: The Decision to Enter the Korean War* (New York, 1960), and George and Smoke, *Deterrence in American Foreign Policy*.

Two main phases distinguish a deterrent encounter: the perception of an external threat, and the formulation and execution of a counter-response. To date, the counterresponse has received the lion's share of scholarly attention. The standard argument is that decision makers are rational actors and are not likely to misperceive external threats, but that a great danger arises if a "potential" aggressor believes that the status quo power is weak in capability and resolve. Therefore, deterrence theorists regard credibility as essential to deterrence. The search for credibility, most nuclear deterrence theorists find, has taken various forms: counterforce or countervalue targeting; mutual assured destruction; strategic invulnerability; enhanced command, control, and communication facilities; offensive versus defensive priorities; and the like.[7] The point, however, is how to make counterthreats potent enough to force an opponent to conclude that it is not in its self-interest to encroach on a defender's interests.

Critics of this argument assert that rational-choice theorists take the perception of external threats for granted. As they point out, decision makers do not always perceive an adversary's intentions correctly or adequately. Cognitive motivation and distortion, leadership style and personality, domestic political difficulties, bureaucratic competition, military intelligence failures and information processing problems, and ideological differences can all produce misperceptions. These non-rational factors can weaken the effect of deterrence and thus enhance the risk of war.[8]

These, however, are largely one-sided studies. J. H. Kalicki, *The Pattern of Sino-American Crises: Political and Military Interactions in the 1950s* (New York, 1975), and Melvin Gurtov and Byong-Moo Huang, *China under Threat: The Politics of Strategy and Diplomacy* (Baltimore, 1980), are good studies of Sino-American crisis relations in the 1950s.

7. Some of the most important works are Brodie, *Strategy in the Missile Age;* Herman Kahn, *On Thermonuclear War* (Princeton, 1960); Snyder, *Deterrence and Defense;* Morton Kaplan, "The Calculus of Nuclear Deterrence," *World Politics* 11 (Fall 1958): 20–43; and Albert Wohlstetter, "The Delicate Balance of Terror," *Foreign Affairs* 37 (January 1959): 211–34. For recent works, see John D. Steinbruner, "National Security and the Concept of Strategic Stability," *Journal of Conflict Resolution* 22 (September 1978):411–28; Jack S. Levy, "The Offensive-Defensive Balance of Military Technology: A Theoretical and Historical Analysis," *International Studies Quarterly* 28 (June 1984): 219–38; Scott Sagan, "1914 Revisited: Allies, Offense, and Instability," *International Security* 12 (Fall 1987): 151–75; Charles Glaser, "Why Even Good Defenses May Be Bad," ibid., 9 (Fall 1984); Bruce G. Blair, *Strategic Command and Control: Redefining the Nuclear Threat* (Washington, D.C., 1985); Paul J. Bracken, *The Command and Control of Nuclear Forces* (New Haven, 1983); and Morton H. Halperin, *Nuclear Fallacy: Dispelling the Myth of Nulear Strategy* (Cambridge, Mass., 1987).

8. See Richard E. Neustadt and Ernest R. May, *Thinking in Time: The Uses of History for Decision-Makers* (New York, 1986), pp. 34–38, and 212–31; John D. Steinbruner, *The Cybernetic Theory of Decision* (Princeton, 1974), pp. 1–150; Ole R. Holsti, *Crisis, Escalation,*

Neither rational-choice nor misreperception theorists provide a complete analytic model for understanding deterrence. The first group digs deeper and deeper into credibility-of-commitment issues, but pays little attention to the problem of threat perception. The second group identifies the sources of misperception, but disregards the process of deterrence. Both focus on finding out why deterrence fails—in order to hypothesize how it could succeed. Neither pays enough attention to identifying how and under what conditions a bilateral deterrent relationship evolves.

To portray a mutual deterrence relationship, a broader conceptual framework is undoubtedly needed. Such a framework would have to cover both the perception of external threat and the actual operation of deterrence strategy in a cross-cultural context to discover the origins of the relationship in order to find out what really happened when each state misperceived the other's intentions and organized strategies to deal with them.

How does one state come to identify another as an adversary or a potential aggressor? Why do policymakers suddenly feel that their nation's security interests are threatened? These things do not happen out of pure imagination or intuition. Decision makers look for identifiable indicators, both objective and subjective, of an opponent's hostile intentions. Such indicators fall into four categories.

Conflicting Security Interests. The determination to protect a nation grows out of an understanding of national security interests and the extent to which these interests conflict with those of another nation over a certain geographical area. Thus policymakers would consider: Do we have vital security interests in that area? How much do we value our interests, if at all? Does any other state have interests there too? Are there conflicts of interest between us and the other states involved? How much does the conflict matter to our overall security? How is our opponent likely to deal with the conflicts? Policymakers, in short, identify adversary intentions in terms of their own interests.

Matrix of Power Potentials. Knowing that intentions are closely associated with capabilities, decision makers look for indications of an

War (Montreal, 1977), pp. 7–26, and 81–142; Robert Jervis, *Perception and Misperception in International Politics* (Princeton, 1976), pp. 58–111, and 319–409; Robert Jervis, ed., *Dominoes and Bandwagons: Strategic Beliefs and Great Power Competition in the Eurasian Rimland* (New York, 1991); Richard Ned Lebow, *Between Peace and War* (Baltimore, 1981), pp. 101–232; Robert Jervis, Richard Ned Lebow, and Janice Gross Stein, *Psychology and Deterrence* (Baltimore, 1985), pp. 13–34, 35–60, and 125–80; Robert Jervis, Richard Ned Lebow, and Janice Gross Stein, "Beyond Deterrence," *Journal of Social Issues* 43 (Winter 1987): 27–41, and "Deterrence: The Elusive Dependent Variable," *World Politics* 42 (April 1990): 336–69; Arthur A. Stein, "When Misperception Matters," ibid., 34 (July 1982): 505–26; and Jack S. Levy, "Misperception and the Cause of War," ibid., 36 (October 1983): 79–99.

[6]

opponent's power as a means of determining whether the opponent has hostile intentions. These include an opponent's military capability (conventional force ratio, weaponry, logistic quality and quantity) and strategic potential (economic proficiency, technological advancement, strategic resources, geographical position, military bases, and military alliance relationship). After assessing these factors, decision makers ask: Why does such a nation deploy such weapons? Why does it build military bases? Why does it form such alliances with our potential adversaries?

Nature of Adversary Decision Making. Conventional decision theory finds that one's decision making shapes crisis-management behavior. But it can also be argued that decision makers are no less significantly affected by their understanding of an opponent's decision making. In international affairs, decision makers often consider: Who is making decisions in that country? What is its political system? What kind of ideology will affect decision making and to what extent? Does the government have political support either at home or from its allies to act as it intends to?

Military Intangibles. Decision makers, particularly military strategists, often identify an opponent's intentions by looking at its military establishment. They examine the opponent's military doctrines, strategic planning, combat experience, and morale levels, the quality of military intelligence, and even the leadership styles of individual commanders. In particular, strategists stress the importance of finding correlations between an adversary's strategic planning and military organization on the one hand, and its belligerent intentions and actions on the other.

If policymakers perceive a threat, how do they then calculate and implement deterrence strategy? As Alexander George and Richard Smoke put it, this may involve "delicate judgments to balance the relative advantages and disadvantages of different and somewhat incommensurable options—political, diplomatic, economic, and in the end, military."[9] A great deal has already been written about the intricacies of the credibility-of-commitment issue, but a broader analysis of how decision makers decide upon and implement deterrence strategy at different levels is still needed. Such an analysis must include six elements that guide the execution of deterrence strategy.

Weighing Costs versus Gains. Policymakers must assess the advantages and disadvantages of countering a perceived threat. They must determine the appropriate response to a perceived challenge and how "expensive" that response should be allowed to become in terms

---

9. George and Smoke, *Deterrence in American Foreign Policy,* p. 64.

of resources consumed or other opportunities foregone. Very often, decision makers tend to differentiate between short-term and long-term benefits and costs when evaluating the expected outcomes of deterrence.

Availability of Counterthreats. The credibility of one's deterrence commitment is first of all determined by the availability of sufficient military and strategic means to persuade an opponent to give up its intentions. The power to punish an aggressor, not the power to deny him success, makes up the counterthreat. Therefore, policymakers must evaluate military and strategic capabilities such as combat force ratios, quality and quantity of weaponry, effectiveness of military operations, advanced military technology, and strategic resources to answer the question "Do we actually have the means to do what we need to do?"

Willingness to Take Risks. Are decision makers politically free to execute military counterthreats if deterrence fails? Even if one state possesses sufficient means to punish, its deterrence will fail if its opponent believes that its leaders lack the political will to exercise that capability. Decision makers, therefore, have to consider whether their choice of responses to perceived challenges will be supported both at home and by allies, and how much support or restraint they will get when a decision has to be made to risk a war if deterrence has not succeeded. Moreover, they have to assure the opponent that they have the political resolve to react if the opponent initiates military action.

Credibility of Warning and Signaling. Conventional deterrence theory has sufficiently stressed the importance of communicating one's deterrent intent in a credible way. Decision makers must take into account whether their counterthreats are communicable to an adversary and whether or not they are meaningful. In order to achieve credibility, they also have to consider on what occasions they should release warnings and through what channels.

Timing. It has never been easy for policymakers to determine the best time to implement deterrence, because no one wants to respond too soon or too late. Especially when external threats appear uncertain or actually in a state of development, policymakers must determine exactly when to execute military threats and when to send out warning messages.

Flexibility. Military counterthreats in response to a perceived challenge may not be the only way to impress an opponent. Flexible diplomacy as well as tough deterrence may be required. Therefore, the "hardness" of deterrence may depend upon how much policymakers consider it necessary to leave themselves another option besides military threat.

[8]

These aspects of threat identification and deterrence organization provide a broad frame of reference for evaluating deterrence situations. That framework will, in particular, help to establish how the Chinese-American deterrent relationship evolved and developed from 1949 to 1958. To recount what happened, I intend to probe into how each side's misunderstandings of the motives and actions of the other paved the way to conflict and crisis; how the conflict of interests, rooted in the Cold War context, furnished and reinforced the misperceptions; and how cultural differences concerning national security and, more important, ignorance of these differences on the part of each state's policymakers caused and enhanced the likelihood of military conflict.

III

This book is an interdisciplinary effort to reconcile deterrence theory with history. It does not aim at deducing concepts, or theories from historical "illustrations," but attempts to depict the problem of deterrence as much as possible on the basis of detailed historical evidence. Its principal data bases are the primary and secondary sources available both in the United States and China.

American materials are much more abundant and systematically arranged than are the Chinese. Government documents, memoranda, intelligence assessments, personal papers, and oral history records of both the Truman and the Eisenhower administrations are available in the National Archives, the presidential libraries, and many university manuscript collections. A large amount of material concerning U.S. China policy in 1955–58 has recently been declassified.[10]

The accessibility of Chinese sources has been and remains a big problem. Thanks to the "Open Door" policy of the Chinese government, however, new and reliable materials concerning PRC policy toward the United States during the 1949–58 period have been released. These sources fall into four categories. First, several official collections have been published that cite classified documents including telegrams, correspondence, and minutes of the meetings of the central leadership of the Chinese Communist Party (CCP). The Chinese Social

10. Although I largely relied on U.S. Department of State, *Foreign Relations of the United States (FRUS)*, I also made use of the National Archives (both Diplomatic and Modern Military Branches), Seeley Mudd Library, Princeton University (John Foster Dulles Papers, H. Alexander Smith Papers, and Karl Rankin Papers), and Butler Library at Columbia University (Wellington Koo Collection). I also used the John Foster Dulles Papers and Dwight D. Eisenhower Papers at the Eisenhower Library.

Science Publishing House's Dangdai Zhongguo [China Today] Series produced several important documentary collections such as *Dangdai Zhongguo Haijun* [China Today: The People's Navy], *Dangdai Zhongguo Hegongye* [China Today: Nuclear Industry], and *Dangdai Zhongguo Waijiao* [China Today: Diplomacy] in 1987, *Dangdai Zhongguo Kongjun* [China Today: Air Force] and two volumes of *Dangdai Zhongguo Jundui De Junshi Gongzhuo* [China Today: The Military Affairs of the Chinese Army] in 1989, and *Kangmei Yuanchao Zhangzheng* [China Today: The War to Resist U.S. Aggression and Aid Korea] in 1990. The Division of Military History of Chinese Military Science Academy released *Zhongguo Renmin Jiefangjun Zhan Shi* [The War History of the People's Liberation Army], vol. 3, in 1987 and *Zhongguo Renmin Zhiyuanjun Kangmei Yuanchao Zhan Shi* [The War History of the Chinese People's Volunteers in the War to Resist the United States and Assist Korea] in 1988. The Division of Central Archives and Manuscripts published *Zhu De Nianpu* [The Chronicle of Zhu De] in 1986 and *Zhou Enlai Nianpu: 1898–1949* [The Chronicle of Zhou Enlai] in 1989.

Second, several important personal memoirs by those who were involved in decision making at the time have now appeared. It is interesting that some of these memoirs were undertaken not only on the basis of personal papers or records, as is usually the case in the West. Rather, they were researched and written by teams of designated academics with specially permitted access to still-classified documents. These sources include memoirs of such military leaders as Marshal Peng Dehuai (commander-in-chief of the Chinese People's Volunteers [CPV] in Korea and first PRC minister of national defense), Marshal Nie Rongzhen (acting chief of staff and vice-premier in charge of nuclear weapons), Marshal Xu Xiangqian (chief of staff and minister of national defense), Xiao Jingguang (commander of the Navy), Hong Xuezhi (deputy commander of the CPV in Korea in charge of logistics), Yang Dezhi (deputy commander of the CPV in charge of combat operations), Du Ping (director of the CPV Political Department), and such senior diplomats as Wu Xiuquan (deputy minister of foreign affairs in charge of East European affairs), Liu Xiao (ambassador to Moscow), Wang Bingnan (China's main negotiator at the Sino-American talks in Warsaw), Shi Zhe (Mao's interpreter in Moscow), and Chai Chengwen (one of China's main negotiators in the Panmunjom truce negotiation).

Third, there is an increasing number of publications by Chinese scholars on Sino-American relations during this period. Many of them are very well researched and contain many useful insights; some are based on classified documents and first-person interviews. Most of these articles appear in *Shijie Lishi* [World History], *Shijie Zhishi*

[World Knowledge], *Wenxian Yu Yanjiu* [Materials and Studies], *Zhonggong Dangshi Yanjiu* [Studies of CCP History], *Dangshi Zhengji Tongxun* [Newsletter of Collected CCP History Materials], *Junshi Lishi* [Military History], *Junshi Shilin* [Studies of Military History], and *Ren Wu* [Individual Biography].

Fourth, and most important, the Division of Central Archives and Manuscripts is compiling *Jianguo Yilai Mao Zedong Wengao* [Mao Zedong's Manuscripts since the Foundation of the PRC] and has completed five volumes to date. The first volume (issued in 1987) covers the period September 1949–December 1950. The second (1988) and third (1989) volumes contain documents from 1951 and 1952, and Mao's manuscripts from 1953 to 1955 are collected in the fourth (1990) and fifth (1991) volumes. These are collections of Mao's correspondence with Stalin, Kim Il-sung, and Ho Chi Minh, Mao's memoranda to other CCP leaders, and his drafted instructions (on behalf of the CCP Central Committee and the Central Military Commission) to field military commanders and regional authorities. These volumes, printed from the original copies of Mao's papers (which remain classified at the CCP Central Archives), are restricted as quasi-classified documents. Moreover, the Division of Central Archives and Manuscripts has recently published selected works of Zhou Enlai, Liu Shaoqi, Zhu De, Chen Yun, Peng Dehuai, Li Xiannian, Wang Jiaxiang, Peng Zhen, and Zhang Wentian, which contain many new and useful materials. With this new information on both the American and Chinese sides, a systematic archival study of Sino-American relations from 1949 to 1958 is possible for the first time.[11]

This book is an analysis of seven incidents that illustrate the mutual deterrence relationship between the PRC and the United States during the period 1949–58. Chapter 2 deals with the origins of Sino-American confrontation in 1949–50, when Chinese Communist leaders decided

11. During my tenure at Ohio University, I twice visited China for research. My most recent trip (September–October 1988) was very productive. First, I collected almost all recent publications of personal memoirs and studies about PRC policy toward the United States in the 1950s. Second, I visited some important historical museums, such as Zhongguo Geming Lishi Bowu Guan [Chinese Revolutionary Historical Museum], Beijing; Zhongguo Renmin Jiefangjun Junshi Bowu Guan [PLA Military Museum], Beijing; Shanghai Danganguan [Shanghai Archives]; and Dier Lishi Danganguang [Second Historical Archives], Nanjing. While in China, I also went through some of the important newspapers, journals, and official publications from the period. Third, I had several interviews with those who were involved in Beijing policy making and analysis and those who had access to classified CCP documents. (Because of current political sensitivity, I will not mention their names. They will be cited as off-the-record interviews). I also listened to oral history tapes of interviews with important persons such as Liu Chun (PRC ambassador to Laos), Ma Lie (personal secretary to Zhou Enlai), and He Fang (personal secretary to Zhang Wentian, vice-minister of foreign affairs), collected by the Institute of American Studies at the Chinese Academy of Social Science.

to execute a deterrence strategy against possible U.S. military intervention, and the Truman administration reformulated America's commitments in the Far East. Chapter 3 focuses on Washington's decision, at the outbreak of the Korean War in June 1950, to dispatch the Seventh Fleet to the Taiwan Strait, and how Beijing responded. Chapter 4 covers the Korean War from the summer of 1950 to the spring of 1951 and deals with why the UN/U.S. forces crossed the thirty-eighth parallel and marched toward the Yalu River, and why and how Chinese forces intervened. As the Korean War became a military stalemate in 1951–53, both China and the United States sought a cease-fire. Chapter 5 shows how each pursued this objective and how a truce finally developed. As soon as the conflict in Korea came to a halt, both states shifted their attention to Indochina, and both were concerned about the possibility of the other's intervention in that area. Chapter 6 examines how the two countries coped with each other in Indochina between the fall of 1953 and the spring of 1954. After the Geneva settlements in 1954, the Korean peninsula and Indochina began to calm down but tension in the Taiwan Strait started to grow. Twice in the next four years (1954–55 and 1958), the People's Liberation Army shelled the offshore islands held by the Nationalists. Chapters 7 and 8 treat each of these crises, with a focus on why Beijing initiated action and how Washington responded. Finally, a concluding chapter summarizes the origins, evolution, and development of Sino-American mutual deterrent relations during this period.

This book contributes to international security studies in several ways. First it exploits newly available materials and thereby sheds fresh light on the Cold War in Asia. Second, it examines the origins of a mutual deterrent relationship, thereby expanding the scope of deterrence theory. Third, it calls attention to the importance of historical evidence in strategic studies. Finally, it employs a cross-cultural approach that I hope will encourage the development of "strategic culture" studies.

[2]

The Establishment of the
Battleground, 1948–1950

By the end of 1948, the Chinese Communist leaders had become more confident than ever that their final victory over the Kuomintang (KMT) would occur soon. Over the past three years of civil war the enemy front had crumbled completely; however, they perceived the danger of U.S. armed intervention on the KMT's behalf. How did the Chinese Communists develop this perception? What did they do to encounter this perceived threat? How did American officials view a Communist China? What was the Truman administration's policy toward a Communist regime in that country?

I

In his New Year's message for 1949, Mao Zedong proclaimed that "public opinion the world over, including the entire imperialist press, no longer disputes the certainty of the country-wide victory of the Chinese People's War of Liberation."[1] Mao's optimism was in part based on his contrasting the military strength of the CCP with that of the KMT. The People's Liberation Army (PLA) had finally achieved numerical superiority. Mao's statistics suggested that the whole of the KMT's armed forces—army, navy, air force, regulars and irregulars, combat troops, and men in the rear service establishment—numbered only some 2,040,000, whereas the PLA had increased in total strength to more than 4,000,000 men. "Thus, [said Mao] the numerical superiority

1. Mao Zedong, "Carry the Revolution through to the End," 31 December 1948, in *SWM* 4:301.

[13]

long enjoyed by the Kuomintang army had rapidly turned into inferiority."[2] The PLA had gone through a fundamental changes in weaponry and organization. For the first time, it has its own artillery and engineer corps. And, even though the PLA still lacked aircraft and tanks, Mao believed that "once it has formed an artillery and engineer corps superior to the one of the Kuomintang army, the defensive system of the Kuomintang [will] appear negligible by contrast." Also from November 1948 to January 1949, it had added four field armies—each composed of two to four army groups—to its order of battle. These changes enhanced PLA's ability to wage mobile and positional war. The PLA had a much higher level of morale than the KMT. The rate at which the PLA destroyed KMT troops had recently accelerated. From July to December 1948, according to Mao Zedong, "The number of enemy divisions entirely wiped out was fifteen more than the grand total for the previous two years."[3] A nation-wide victory seemed imminent.

Optimism about final victory did not lessen the CCP leadership's sensitivity to the threat of possible U.S. military intervention to save the KMT. Ever since fighting between the CCP and the KMT had resumed in 1946, Mao Zedong and other leaders had worried that the United States might enter the civil war on Chiang Kai-shek's behalf. As early as July 1947, the Secretariat of the CCP Central Committee, including Mao, Liu Shaoqi, Zhou Enlai, Zhu De, and Ren Bishi, met at Xiao He, in Shanxi, to assess America's China policy. They agreed at the meeting that the United States was withdrawing its commitment to the KMT and was not even active in providing military aid; that with its strategic focus on Europe, the United States was conducting a general defensive policy in Asia; and that U.S. policy toward China was therefore in transition and development was still uncertain.[4] The findings seemed to be encouraging.

Two years later, however, the CCP leaders had reached a new consensus that the U.S. government might change its policy of simply backing the KMT to one of undertaking both direct and indirect intervention to save Chiang. This conclusion was clearly stated in a CCP Central Committee document, drafted by Mao, of 8 January 1949, entitled "The Current Situation and Our Tasks in 1949." Assessing the military situation, Mao asserted that Chiang's rule was doomed unless

2. Mao Zedong, "The Momentous Change in China's Military Situation," 14 November 1948, in *SWM* 4:287–88. Also see *JFJZS*, pp. 231–32.

3. Mao, "Carry the Revolution through to the End," p. 301.

4. Tian Weiben, "The Meeting at Xiao He, July 1947," *Dangshi Zhengji Tongxun*, July 1987, pp. 21–24. Also see the minutes of the Xiao He meeting, 21 July 1947, in *Zhou Enlai Nianpu, 1898–1949*, ed. Division of Central Archives and Manuscripts (Beijing, 1989), pp. 740–41.

the United States rescued it. He then warned of the possibility that "the United States would send armed forces to occupy some of China's coastal cities and directly fight against us" and that it "might throw in its own forces to blockade China's ports." Further, Mao believed that even if the United States did not intervene directly, it would surely try to undermine the CCP's rule through sabotage, espionage, and political infiltration. Since "the imperialists will not change their nature in near future," Mao urged, "the entire Party should take [these] possibilities into full consideration" while carrying out its tasks for 1949.[5]

This seemed to be a major change in Mao's perceptions of U.S. China policy. It was not an unexpected change given the CCP's general framework for evaluating external threats and its leaders' understanding of the cold war situation. These leaders became more certain than ever before that the United States was likely to challenge their victory. Mao reminded the party in January 1949 that "we have always taken into our considerations the possibilities of American imperialist armed intervention." While assessing "the possible trends of current situation" in the same month, Zhou Enlai also pointed out that "there exists a possibility of U.S. military intervention, but we are fully prepared."[6]

Why were the CCP leaders so concerned with the possibility of U.S. military intervention? How did their perception of this threat evolve? One answer has to do with Mao's concept of an "intermediate zone," which was based on his understanding of the Cold War. The central argument was that although the United States and the Soviet Union were confronting each other, they were separated by "a vast zone which includes many capitalist, colonial and semi-colonial countries in Europe, Asia, and Africa." Mao calculated that "before the U.S. reactionaries have subjugated these countries, an attack on the Soviet Union is out of the question."[7] Thus, for Mao, the Cold War was defined as the period during which the United States would fight for this vast intermediate zone. General war with the USSR would come *only* *after* the United States had consolidated its hold on countries within the zone. Since any anti-American or pro-Soviet forces within the zone

5. CCP Central Committee document, drafted by Mao Zedong, "The Current Situation and Our Tasks in 1949," 8 January 1949. The complete text is printed in *Wenxian Yu Yanjiu*, October 1984, pp. 1–3.

6. Ibid., p. 2; Zhou Enlai, "Report on the Current Situation," 16 January 1949, in *Zhou Enlai Nianpu*, p. 808.

7. Mao Zedong, "Talks with the American Correspondent Anna Louise Strong," August 1946, in *SWM* 4:99. Also see Lu Dingyi, "The Explanation of Several Basic Questions concerning the Post–World War II International Situation," *Jiefang Ribao*, 4 January 1947, p. 1. (Lu was a senior CCP official in charge of political propaganda, and now we know that Mao himself drafted this article.)

would weaken, in one way or another, American capabilities for fighting the Russians, the United States would have to wipe out those forces first. As Mao had explained in August 1946:

In the Pacific, the United States now controls areas larger than all the former British sphere of influence there put together; it controls Japan, the part of China under KMT rule, half of Korea, and the South Pacific. It has long controlled Central and South America. It seeks also to control the whole British Empire and Western Europe. Using various pretexts, the United States is making large-scale military arrangements and setting up military bases in many countries. . . . True these military bases are directed against the Soviet Union. At present, however, it is not the Soviet Union but the countries in which these military bases are created [that] are the first to suffer U.S. aggression.[8]

To the CCP leadership, Mao's "intermediate zone" argument made sense. Indeed, Chinese officials regarded the Truman Doctrine, the Marshall Plan, the rehabilitation of Germany and Japan, the U.S. occupation of South Korea, and especially, U.S. military assistance to the KMT and the stationing of U.S. Marines along China's coast as strong evidence of a struggle for this "intermediate zone."[9]

Mao's understanding of Washington intentions had been shaped by his political and ideological views. As a Marxist-Leninist, Mao saw U.S. foreign policy as characteristic of imperial capitalism faced with shrinking domestic and foreign markets. Mao warned that the United States was "sitting on a volcano." This situation, he predicted, would drive the American imperialists to "draw up a plan for enslaving the world, to run Europe, Asia, and other parts of the world like wild beasts."[10] Mao and other CCP leaders also believed that the U.S. government was counterrevolutionary by nature because of its record of intervening on behalf of reactionaries. Important instances included Frederick Townsend Ward's "Ever-Victorious Army," which assisted the falling Qing (Ching) regime against the Taiping uprising in 1860–63, participation in the Western intervention against the Chinese Boxer rebellion in 1900–1901, and more important, military intervention against the Bolshevik Revolution in Russia in 1918–19. As Hu Sheng, a senior CCP political analyst, pointed out in 1949, "We have to be aware that the imperialist interventions [against revolutions]

8. Mao, "Talks with the American Correspondent Anna Louise Strong," p. 99.

9. Lu Dingyi, "The Explanation of Severai Basic Questions concerning the Post–World War II International Situation," p. 1. Also see the telegram, CCP Central Committee to Liu Ningyi, 21 March 1948, cited in *Zhou Enlai Nianpu*, p. 767.

10. Mao Zedong, "The Present Situation and Our Tasks," 25 December 1947, in SWM 4:172.

China: Provinces and major cities

always follow the same pattern: supplying the reactionaries with material assistance first, then imposing diplomatic isolation, and at last, possibly starting armed blockade or direct intervention."[11] Therefore, a CCP Central Committee policy directive drafted by Zhou Enlai on 24 March 1948 stated that "the essence of our anti-American imperialism is to prevent American imperialists from colonizing China and to overthrow American imperialist rule in China."[12]

The CCP leaders distrusted the U.S. China policy, which affected their assessment of the U.S. threat. They had not had much experience in dealing with the Americans, but from those few occasions where contacts had taken place, they had felt cheated and humiliated. The Marshall mission of 1946, they at first believed, had been intended to mediate China's civil war impartially, but its actions had been anything but impartial. George Marshall allowed the KMT to move two infantry armies to northeast China in April 1946 with the help of the U.S. Air Force while he persuaded the CCP to evacuate from Siping and Changchun, promising a cease-fire. Marshall had Chiang Kai-shek flown to Shengyang to command the KMT troops against the CCP in Marshall's own plane, but at the same time he asked the Chinese Communist leaders to continue negotiations with the Nationalists. "The policy of the U.S. Government," Mao asserted, "is to use the so-called mediation as a smoke screen for strengthening Chiang in every way and suppressing the democratic forces in China through Chiang Kai-shek's policy of slaughter so as to reduce China virtually to a U.S. colony." Moreover, in the light of continuing American military and economic aid to the KMT, the CCP leadership concluded that to expect America to remain neutral was only wishful thinking. U.S. aid, Mao pointed out, would certainly "enable him [Chiang] to wage a civil war on an unprecedented scale."[13] Mao concluded regretfully: "[Since]

11. Mao Zedong, "Cast away Illusion, Prepare for Struggle," 14 August 1949, in *SWM* 4:425–26. Hu Sheng, "The Foreign Relations of the Taiping Heavenly Kingdom and Capitalism," *Xue Xi*, September 1949, p. 21. Hu was a CCP senior theoretician and worked very closely with the top leaders. Ke Bainian, "How the Soviet Union Struggled with Imperialism in the Initial Period after the October Revolution," *Xue Xi*, November 1949, pp. 12–14. Ke was then working in the CCP Foreign Affairs Commission and became the first director of the Asian Affairs Division of the Ministry of Foreign Affairs in February 1950. Ward, an American from Massachusetts, actually was paid by the Qing (Ching) government to lead a local corps of foreign-officered mercenary at Shanghai. Ward trained four thousand men and won more than one hundred engagements against the Taiping Forces, hence the name "Ever-Victorious Army" given his troops. Ward died in 1862. See Jonathan D. Spence, *The Search For Modern China* (New York, 1990), p. 177.

12. Telegram, CCP Central Committee to the Commanders of the Third Field Army, Rao Shushi and Chen Yi, 24 March 1948, in *Zhou Enlai Nianpu*, p. 767.

13. Mao Zedong, "The Truth about U.S. 'Mediation' and the Future Civil War in China," 29 September 1946, in *SWM* 4:109.

it was the first time we had dealt with the U.S. imperialists, we did not have much experience. As a result, we were taken in. Now with the experience we won't be cheated again." Zhou Enlai also asserted in late 1946 that after dealing with Marshall, "we have found out that the real intention of the United States is to dominate China alone." As he put it, Washington could "no longer play the game of fraud [*pian ju*]."[14]

Soviet warnings of possible U.S. military actions in China formed another important element in the CCP's perception of external threats. In order to develop a better understanding with Moscow, in April 1948 Mao planned a trip to the Sino-Russian border hoping to meet Joseph Stalin there in person. But Stalin abruptly rejected the proposal and replied that since the CCP was facing a "critical turning-point," it would be better for Mao to stay on the spot. Instead, he proposed sending a representative to China if necessary. Stalin explicitly advised Mao that everything—including possible foreign interventions—should be taken into full consideration.[15] Through Gao Gang, one of the top CCP leaders whom the Kremlin trusted, Moscow also warned several times during this period that if the CCP crossed the Yangtze River to defeat the KMT, the United States and other western powers might intervene militarily. If that occurred, the Russians stressed, the Soviet Union would not be able to provide any assistance because of the danger of provoking a general war between the USSR and the United States in the Far East.[16] Further, on 10 January 1949, when the Communist forces were gathering at the northern bank of the Yangtze River, Stalin forwarded a letter from KMT foreign minister Wang Shijie asking the Soviet leader to arbitrate the CCP–KMT dispute. Implying his willingness to do so, Stalin showed his concern that the United States might intervene "with its armed forces or navy against the Chinese People's Liberation Army."[17] That was not all. Anastas Mikoyan, Stalin's personal representative to the CCP, arrived at Xibaipo, Hebei province, then the CCP headquarters, on 31 January 1949. He told the Chinese leaders that Stalin had instructed him to "bring ears with him only." But he reminded the Chinese to watch for

14. Mao's remark was cited in He Di, "The Development of the CCP's Policy toward the United States, 1945–1949," *Lishi Yanjiu* June 1987, pp. 17–18. Also see Zhou Enlai to the CCP Central Committee, 31 August 1946, in *Zhou Enlai Nianpu*, p. 688, and Zhou's speech at the CCP Central leadership meeting, 21 November 1946, ibid., p. 706.

15. Shi Zhe, "With Chairman Mao in the Soviet Union," *Ren Wu*, May 1988, pp. 6–7 [hereafter cited as *Shi Zhe Memoirs*].

16. Off-the-record interviews.

17. Letter, Stalin to the CCP Central Committee, 10 January 1949, cited in Yu Zhan and Zhang Guangyou, "On Whether Stalin Ever Persuaded Us Not to Cross the Yangtze River," in *Xinzhongguo Waijiao Fengyun*, ed. Division of Diplomatic History, Ministry of Foreign Affairs (Beijing, 1990), p. 19.

possible changes in the international situation.[18] As a result, the CCP leaders were strongly impressed with the view that Stalin was worried about the United States seizing the opportunity in China to act more vigorously against the Soviet Union either in the Far East or elsewhere.

Moreover, Chinese Communist leaders believe that they clearly saw some objective indicators of hostile U.S. intentions. One particular concern, as Mao told the CCP Central Committee in January 1949, was that the United States was "fostering the forces of aggression in Japan." He noted that General Douglas MacArthur had rehabilitated political and military personalities implicated in criminal acts against China, revised the policy of breaking up Japanese industry, canceled reparations shipments, and suppressed progressive forces seeking demilitarization. Even less tolerable was the fact that Washington paid no attention to the CCP's call for the early conclusion of a peace treaty that would bring the American occupation in Japan to an end, thus removing the excuse for U.S. troops to stay there. The Chinese press therefore kept asking why the United States was trying to militarize Japan.[19]

The CCP leaders were also concerned with the activities of U.S. military forces in China. "U.S. naval, ground, and air forces," Mao asserted in August, "did participate in the war in China." As he noted:

> There were U.S. navel bases in Tsingtao [Qingdao], Shanghai, and Taiwan. U.S. troops were stationed in Peiping [Beijing], Tientsin [Tianjin], Tangshan, Chinwangtao [Qinghuangdao], Tsingtao, Shanghai and Nanking [Nanjing]. The U.S. air force controlled all of China's airspace and took aerial photographs of all China's strategic area for military maps. At the town of Anping near Peiping, at Chiutai near Changchun, at Tangshan and in the Eastern Shantung [Shandong] Peninsula, U.S. troops and other military personnel clashed with the People's Liberation Army and on several occasions were captured. Chennault's air fleet took an extensive part in the civil war. Besides transporting troops for Chiang Kai-shek, the U.S. air force bombed and sank the cruiser Chungking, which had mutinied against the Kuomintang.

Mao believed that "all these were acts of direct participation in the war, although they fell short of an open declaration of war and were not large in scale, and although the principal method of U.S. aggression was the large supply of money, munitions, and advisers to help

18. Division of CCP Central Archives and Manuscripts, ed., *Zhou Enlai Zhuang, 1898–1949* (Beijing, 1989), pp. 742–43. Also see *Shi Zhe Memoirs*, p. 6, and Bo Yibo, *Ruogan Zhongda Juece yu Shijian de Huigu*, vol. 1 (Beijing, 1991), pp. 36–37 [hereafter cited as *Bo Yibo Memoirs*].

19. Mao Zedong, "Statement on the Present Situation," 16 January 1949, in *SWM* 4:316; New China News Agency (NCNA), *Daily News Release*, 26 April 1949, p. 3, 19 May 1949, p. 21, 21 June 1949, p. 2, 22 June 1949, pp. 2–3, and 27 June 1949, p. 1.

Chiang Kai-shek fight the civil war."[20] Especially when PLA intelligence noticed "the sudden increase of [U.S.] marine activities in Qingdao" in the late spring of 1949, the CCP leader showed an immediate concern, thinking not that the United States had entered the war on the side of the KMT, but that it had always been on the side of the KMT and had now decided to take an active role.[21]

Even in late 1949, when immediate U.S. military action seemed less likely, the Chinese Communist leaders were stressing the hostile intentions of the United States over the long term—if not the short. Mao explained in August that it was the "objective situation in China and the rest of the world, and not . . . any lack of desire on the part of the Truman-Marshall group, the ruling clique of U.S. imperialism, to launch direct aggression against China" that had prevented direct U.S. intervention in the Chinese civil war. In his view, the United States had placed China as a top priority in its efforts to control the "intermediate zone," because, "China, the center of gravity in Asia, is a large country with a population of 475 million; [thus] by seizing China, the United States would possess all of Asia. With its Asian front consolidated, U.S. imperialism could concentrate its forces on attacking Europe." The United States would never cease its pursuit of this long-term objective, Mao insisted, "make trouble, fail, make trouble again, fail again till their doom; that is the logic of the imperialists and all the reactionaries the world over in dealing with the people's course. They will never go against this logic."[22] The CCP's assessment of the possibility of U.S. military intervention had gone from "no immediate threat" to "imminent." They felt that the U.S. attitude toward the PRC would be "long-term hostility." CCP leaders consistently regarded the United States as an actual challenger to their rule in China. How, then, did they attempt to cope with the perceived challenge?

II

Available evidence leaves no doubt that deterrence—discouraging the United States from intervening directly or even indirectly both in the short and long run—had been a primary objective of the Chinese

20. Mao Zedong, "Farewell, Leighton Stuart," 18 August 1949 in *SWM* 4:434. As early as 1946, Zhou Enlai protested in his talks with Stuart that "to support Chiang Kai-shek, the United States has in fact stationed its troops [in China] and provided ammunition and financial assistance [to Chiang]" (minutes of Zhou-Stuart talks, 6 August 1946, in *Zhou Enlai Nianpu*, p. 685).

21. He Di, "The Development of the CCP's Policy toward the United States, 1945–1949," p. 21.

22. Mao, "Farewell, Leighton Stuart, p. 433, and "Cast away Illusion, Prepare for Struggle," p. 428.

Communists since early 1949. Three actions by the CCP indicate this clearly: (1) the deployment of a larger conventional force to China's coastal area than was actually needed to destroy the KMT rearguard during the Yangtze River crossing in February-May; (2) the proclamation in June 1949 that a new Chinese government would "lean" toward the Soviet Union; and (3) the formation of Sino-Soviet military alliance in July 1949–February 1950.

Mao Zedong insisted in his New Year's message for 1949 that his party and army should "unswervingly persist in overthrowing imperialism, feudalism, and bureaucratic-capitalism in China."[23] But how could that be accomplished without provoking American imperialist intervention? Mao had his solution. He told the Party's Central Politburo on 9 January 1949, that "the greater the Chinese people's revolutionary strength and the more resolute our stance [against the United States], the less likely direct U.S. military intervention will be." Mao even predicted that, faced with CCP's vigorous counteractions, Washington might be compelled to "decrease its economic and military aid to the KMT or disengage from the [civil] war."[24] A determined show of military strength and political resolve would work for both deterrence and compellence, Mao thought, without clearly differentiating the two.

It is important to note that Mao believed in worst-case assumptions: one could hope for the best but should prepare for the worst. The worst outcome of a Sino-American confrontation would be a general war. Mao, however, was optimistic about China's counterthreat when he contrasted strategic strengths and weaknesses on both sides. First, geography would favor the Chinese if the United States invaded. "China is a vast country," he noted, " 'When the east is still dark, the west is lit up; when night falls in the south, the day breaks in the north.' Hence, one need not worry about whether there is room enough to move around [for mobile operations]." Believing in an old Chinese saying "As long as the green mountains are there, one need not worry about firewood," Mao asserted that "even though some of our territory may be lost, we shall still have plenty of room for maneuver and thus be able to promote and await domestic progress, international support, and the internal disintegration of the enemy."[25] With a fresh memory of how the Japanese had failed to conquer China, Mao understood that geography would be China's first ally in defeating foreign invaders.

23. Mao, "Carry the Revolution through to the End," p. 302.
24. CCP Central Committee, "The Current Situation and Our Tasks in 1949," p. 3.
25. Mao Zedong, "On Protracted War," May 1938, in *Selected Military Writings of Mao Tse-tung* (Beijing, 1963), pp. 197 and 255.

[22]

Second, China would have superiority in numbers over the United States if a war were to start on the mainland. The peasants, 80 percent of the population, could easily be mobilized to fight against foreign invasions. To Mao, these millions of souls were a formidable deterrent that made any plan to attack China "unrealistic." Believing that the United States only had 11,000 troops along China's coast and a few thousand in reserve elsewhere in the Far East, the Chinese leaders claimed that at worst the United States might be able to control some of China's coastal cities—but not the whole country.[26] Even if the Americans have technological superiority, Mao believed, aircraft, tanks, artillery, and even atomic bombs were no better than "paper tigers" compared to a vast human sea. A war in China would be determined not "by any weapons but by the people who operate them."[27]

Third, China would enjoy much better morale than the United States. The CCP leadership believed that a war against reactionaries and foreign invasion was by all means a just war, and a just war would have the full support of the masses. This had proven to be true in the fighting against the KMT, which Mao analyzed as a struggle "in which the United States supplies the money and guns and Chiang Kai-shek supplies the men. . . . It does no good to the reactionaries but causes the Chinese people to hate imperialism, and compels them to bring their revolutionary spirit into full play." Mao thought that the strong xenophobia in China could be further exploited to the CCP's benefit.[28] But it would be a different case for the U.S. government. "To start a war," Mao calculated, "the U.S. reactionaries must first attack the American people, . . . at present, the actual significance of the U.S. slogan of waging an anti-Soviet war is the opposition of the American people."[29] Moreover, the United States, as a strong power, would be afraid of "losing face" in a war with China. "If they fight us," Liu Shaoqi, one of CCP's top leaders, explained in early 1948, "and if we capture their troops and wipe out a few thousand of their forces, what could they do? If they withdraw, they will lose face; if they keep fighting they can not afford it."[30]

Fourth, the Chinese could always fight a protracted war. Such a protracted-war strategy would work, as Mao put it, when "tactically

26. See Ren Bishi's speech to the CCP Politburo, 13 September 1948, cited in "Ren Bishi," in *Jiefangjun Jiangling Zhuan*, ed. "Xinghou Liaoyuan" Editorial Division, vol. 1 (Beijing, 1984), p. 152.

27. Mao, "Cast away Illusion, Prepare for Struggle," p. 427, and "Talks with the American Correspondent Anna Louise Strong," p. 100.

28. Mao, "Cast away Illusion, Prepare for Struggle," p. 426.

29. Mao, "Talks with the American Correspondent Anna Louise Strong," pp. 98–99.

30. Liu Shaoqi, "Address to the Students of the Marxist-Leninist Institute," March 1949, in *Liu Shaoqi Xuanji*, vol. 2 (Beijing, 1985), pp. 408–9.

the enemy is strong but strategically he is weak." The United States, like Japan, enjoyed superiority in weapons but was in a unfavorable position in terms of geography, human resources, and morale. Moreover, at the operational level, "retreat and luring the enemy deep into [the interior areas] and striking [it] with one fist" had been how the PLA had defeated more powerful Japanese and Nationalist forces. With the PLA increasingly improving its equipment and combat mobility, Mao believed that protracted-war strategy would succeed according to his expectations.[31]

At the beginning of 1949, the CCP leaders began to prepare militarily and psychologically for possible U.S. intervention. At the CCP Central Politburo meeting in December of 1948, the participants had predicted that if the United States wanted to intervene at the moment that the PLA crossed the Yangtze, it would probably launch a surprise attack against either Qingdao or Yantai, two seaport cities in Shandong province. How, then, should the CCP respond? The Politburo decided that the CCP forces should retreat at Qingdao but counterattack immediately at Yantai, because the loss of Yantai would render the PLA's southern offensive strategically more difficult.[32] Primarily for this reason, the party's Central Military Commission (CMC)—chaired by Mao—ordered both the Second and the Third Field Armies, a total of more than one million soldiers, to deploy along the northern bank of the Yangtze by the end of March 1949. And for the first time, the CMC established a combined front command commission. It was headed by Deng Xiaoping and was to direct both field armies.[33]

The crossing of the Yangtze began on April 23, and the PLA took Nanjing, the Nationalist capital within twenty-four hours. There was no sign of U.S. intervention. The CCP leadership, however, did not relax its vigilance. On 23 May, when the PLA finished encircling Shanghai, the CMC instructed Deng Xiaoping in a telegram that the main task of the Second Field Army remained that of "preparing for U.S. possible military action while assisting the Third Field Army for the Shanghai campaign." For this purpose, "the main bulk of the Second Field Army should gather in the areas of Southern Anhui, Eastern Jiangxi, and Western Zhejiang, and prepare to move to Southwest China only after the possibility of imperialist intervention dimin-

31. See Mao, "On Protracted War," pp. 187–262; "Concentrate a Superior Force to Destroy the Enemy Forces One by One," 16 September 1946, in *Selected Military Writings of Mao Tse-tung*, pp. 313–18; and "Carry the Revolution through to the End," pp. 301–2.

32. PLA commander-in-general Zhu De was seriously concerned about Qingdao. At the combat operations meeting at PLA headquarters, 16 October 1948, Zhu stressed that "we shall not plan any military action against Qingdao because there are American troops there" (Zhu De, *Zu Dhe Xuanji* [Anhui, 1983], p. 244).

33. The CMC instruction is cited in *JFJZS*, p. 322.

ishes." Moreover, the CMC informed Deng that to coordinate the Second Field Army's mission, "the Twentieth Group Army under the direct commander of the Central Military Commission, is to be sent to the northern China coastal area—possibly near Tianjin—in case of imperialists' armed intervention." To strengthen the Second Field Army's position, the CMC had earlier decided to dispatch the Twelfth Group Army of the Fourth Field Army to cross the Yangtze River ahead of schedule.[34] The CMC explicitly stressed deterrence as a major objective of these arrangements: "With [such preparations] we can *dissuade* the United States from realizing its ambition of armed intervention [in China]."[35]

The PLA occupied Shanghai on 27 May, but U.S. Marines in Qingdao and Shanghai did not react. Obviously, the likelihood of U.S. military intervention seemed to be small. But it is interesting to note that the CCP top leaders did not think that they were overreacting. They were almost certain that the preparation of counterthreats had so far worked. As soon as the Shanghai campaign was over, the CMC issued a new directive to all the PLA commanders, entitled "Instructions on How to Prepare for Imperialist Intervention against the Chinese Revolution." The directive stated:

> The main aspect of [our] measures is that our field armies will continue eliminating the remaining KMT forces so as to deprive the imperialists of their running dogs on the Chinese mainland; . . .
>
> Second, [we should try our best] to achieve economic self-reliance in case of sea blockade of our coastal line by the imperialists; . . .
>
> Third, [we will continue] to deploy sufficient troops in North and East China in order to prevent the U.S. naval force from coordinating with the remaining KMT ground forces to attack us from behind.[36]

Meanwhile, the CCP leadership cautioned against any mistakes that might give the United States cause to respond vigorously. Between March and May, the party issued a number of instructions to the lower authorities that appropriate measures must be taken to avoid provoking the foreigners in China. On 25 April, Zhou Enlai in particular instructed Deng Xiaoping that the lives and property of the American and British in Nanjing "shall be by all means protected; we should see to it that these foreigners will not get humiliated, and we need not

34. CMC telegram 23 May 1949, in *JFJZS*, p. 308. Also see telegram, CMC to the commanders of the Fourth Field Army, Lin Biao, and Luo Ronghuan, 19 February 1949, in *Zhou Enlai Nianpu*, p. 814.

35. *JFJZS*, p. 355 [emphasis added].

36. CMC instruction, "How to Prepare for Imperialist Intervention against the Chinese Revolution," 28 May 1949, in *JFJZS*, p. 320.

register them." As a Chinese historian has noted, "the idea was to avoid a direct confrontation with western powers and not to give them any pretext to interfere in China's internal affairs."[37]

The next but more important step was Huang Hua's secret mission of 13 May–2 July 1949 to meet U.S. ambassador John Leighton Stuart in Nanjing. Huang was the director of the Foreign Affairs Division of the CCP Nanjing authority, but was acting on instructions from the CCP top leaders, Zhou Enlai in particular. Huang was directed by the Central Committee to spend more time listening to what Stuart would have to say rather than talking; to repeat Li Tao's statement of 30 April that "any foreign governments wishing to establish diplomatic relation with us must cease its tie with the remnant KMT and withdraw its forces from China" if Stuart mentioned the possibility of establishing diplomatic relations; and not to reject out of hand suggestions that Stuart continue his ambassadorship in China or revisions to Sino-American trade treaties.[38]

There is reason to believe that the primary purpose of Huang's mission was to probe U.S. intentions toward the CCP and a future Communist China. When Nanjing fell to the PLA, almost all the foreign embassies, including the Soviet, moved to Guangzhou (Canton) with the KMT government, but Stuart and the American embassy remained. The CCP leaders, particularly Mao, felt puzzled. They urgently needed firsthand information about U.S. intentions, especially since the PLA was soon to attack Shanghai, which was likely to trigger foreign intervention. It was no coincidence that Huang's mission was authorized by CCP top leaders only two weeks before the scheduled attack on Shanghai. At no point did the CCP leaders consider establishing diplomatic relations with the United States during this period. The CCP Central Committee's line on that issue had been determined in March: "As for the question of seeking recognition from the western capitalist countries, we should not be in a hurry to deal with it now, and need not to be in hurry to consider it even for a fairly long period after our country-wide victory."[39]

37. Telegram, Zhou to the General Front Command Commission, 25 April 1949, in *Zhou Enlai Nianpu*, p. 824; Chen Xiaolu, "China's U.S. Policy, 1949–1955," in *Sino-American Relations, 1945–1955: A Joint Reassessment of a Critical Decade*, ed. Harry Harding and Yuan Ming (Wilmington, Del., 1989), p. 186.

38. Huang Hua, "My Contacts with Leighton Stuart in the Early Days after the Liberation of Nanjing," in *Xinzhongguo Waijiao Fengyun*, pp. 22–31. When I interviewed Wang Bingnan, who then worked in the Foreign Affairs Commission, on 14 October 1988, Wang confirmed the instructions to Huang Hua.

39. Mao Zedong, "Report to the Second Plenary Session of the Seventh Central Committee of the CCP," 5 March 1949, in *SWM* 4:370–71. Also see Warren I. Cohen, "Conversations with Chinese Friends: Zhou Enlai's Associates Reflect on Chinese-American

During the Nanjing and Shanghai campaigns, U.S. forces in China were actually in the process of retreating from China. The marines withdrew from Qingdao at the CCP's request shortly after the battle for Nanjing; the U.S. gunboats moved from Shanghai to Wusong Kou right after Shanghai fell to the Communists. Huang Hua was explicitly informed by Stuart that "there were no American warships beyond Wusong Kou."[40] Nevertheless, the prospect of no immediate U.S. military action did not change the CCP's belief in long-term U.S. hostility toward a Communist regime in China. Meeting a group of senior CCP cadres and intellectuals returning from Hong Kong on 12 May, Mao asked how the British had reacted to the PLA's sinking of British gunboat *Ziying Hao (Amethyst)* in the Yangtze River in that same month. After being told that the British had no vigorous reaction, Mao commented that Britain as an old imperialist power was more sophisticated but "the United States as a new imperialist country is much less predictable."[41]

What, then, could the CCP possibly do to inhibit U.S. hostility toward a new China? Based on his understanding of the postwar world, Mao saw that the primary confrontation was between the Soviet Union and the United States. In order to prevent the United States from invading China in the future, Mao calculated that his new regime would have to identify itself with the Soviet Union. Such an identification would not be easy, however, for Moscow's attitude toward Mao's CCP was a mixture of suspicion and indifference. The CCP leadership knew that Stalin, afraid that Mao was another Tito, was particularly skeptical.[42] In an attempt to eliminate Stalin's distrust, the Communist leaders decided in May to dispatch a secret mission to Moscow. Liu Shaoqi and Zhou Enlai, assisted by Wang Jiaxiang, were in charge of the preparations. Two months later, Liu led a five-person delegation to Moscow. Secretary of the CCP Northeastern Bureau Gao Gang, the closest friend of the Kremlin, was also asked to joint the group. In

Relations in the 1940s and the Korean War," *Diplomatic History* 11 (Summer 1987): 287–88. Cohen found out in his interview with Huang that the CCP leaders "were not looking for friendly relations. They had at best one concern: to forestall a major American intervention which might rescue the Guomindang at the eleventh hour, cheating them of their impending victory" (ibid., p. 288).

40. Chen Xiaolu, "China's U.S. Policy, 1949–1955," p. 186. Also see Zhang Baijia, "Comments on the Seminar on the History of Sino-American Relations, 1945–1955," *Lishi Yanjiu,* June 1987, pp. 40–41.

41. Xia Yan, "From Hong Kong to Shanghai," *Renmin Wenxue,* January 1988, pp. 46–47. Xia attended the meeting with Mao and, in September 1949, was placed in charge of political propaganda in Shanghai by the CCP Central Committee.

42. Steven Goldstein, "Communist Chinese Policy toward the United States: Opportunities and Constraints, 1945–1950," in *Uncertain Years: Chinese-American Relations, 1947–1950,* ed. Dorothy Borg and Waldo Heinrichs (New York, 1980), p. 253.

Moscow, Liu met with Stalin and his top aides on four occasions. At these meetings, Liu reported back that Stalin made three important points: First, the Soviet Union had not offered as much help to the Chinese Communists as it should have and even "hampered your revolution to some extent. . . . because we did not know China very well." For this, Stalin apologized. Second, the victorious CCP, should immediately establish its government, otherwise "the foreigners would take the chance to intervene, probably in collective efforts." Third, the world revolution is now moving eastward and, therefore, the Chinese comrades should be prepared to assume more responsibility [for carrying the revolution]. This is our wish from the bottom of our hearts." Concerning military assistance, Stalin explicitly promised that the Soviet Union would help the CCP build a modern air force.[43] In early August, Moscow signed an agreement that Russia would sell 434 military aircraft to China and send 878 specialists to train CCP pilots and ground personnel.[44]

Liu's mission seemed to have been an unexpected success. Apparently, Stalin had changed his attitude toward the CCP; he had even admitted the errors that he had made. Still, the Chinese leaders felt that Stalin was ambivalent about how to support a new Chinese government. They were certain that Stalin and other Soviet leaders could not have dissolved their suspicions so quickly and so easily. Moreover, the issue of the relationship with the Soviet Union was complicated when a group of pro-CCP "democrats" in China appealed for keeping a distance from the Russians but accommodating the West. People like Zhang Naiqi and Luo Longji were few in number, but politically important to the CCP's "United Front." Besides, their views would affect both the general public and the Party itself. Under these circumstances, Mao decided to move swiftly. On the eve of the Party's twenty-eighth anniversary (30 June 1949), Mao made his "lean-to-one-side" speech, and released it to the public the next day. For the first time, the CCP proclaimed that it would *only* lean to the side of the Soviet Union and not to any others.[45]

Mao's announcement was directed at three different audiences. The first was, of course, the Kremlin leadership. By acknowledging the Soviet Union as the center of the world Communist movement, by expressing admiration for Stalin as the leader of "peace-loving" peoples,

43. *Shi Zhe Memoirs*, pp. 8–10.
44. *DDZGKJ*, p. 58.
45. Mao Zedong, "On the People's Democratic Dictatorship," *Renmin Ribao*, 1 July 1949, p. 1. Zhang and Luo among others, as representatives of non-communists in China, expected to share rule with the CCP. Zhang, in particular, had hoped to use his connections with the West as a bargaining chip for the position of foreign affairs minister. Also see *Bo Yibo Memoirs*, pp. 38–39.

and by confirming the CCP's deference to Moscow, Mao expected his announcement to please the Soviet leaders greatly and help eliminate their long-held suspicions. Second, Mao wanted both the "democratic individuals" and the "moderates" within the Party to be aware that any inclination toward the West would go nowhere in China. This message was even more explicitly conveyed when Mao one month later launched the "Five Commentaries on the U.S. White Paper" campaign. The pro-West tendency of the "democratic individuals," he told the Party and the people, would only serve the interests of an American conspiracy aimed a political infiltration within China.[46] Then, Mao also—probably more eagerly—wanted to tell Washington that the CCP was openly and firmly incorporating itself to the Soviet-led, anti-imperialist camp. "Only if we draw a clear line between reactionaries and revolutionaries," he explained in the speech, "[and] heighten our will to fight and crush the enemy's arrogance, can we isolate, . . . vanquish, or supersede them." Mao meant, a senior Chinese diplomat recalls, to demonstrate that the CCP would "not show the slightest timidity in front of a wild beast."[47]

The CCP leadership now seemed to be ready to move further. The Central Committee decided in early September that it was time for Mao to visit Moscow and talk with Stalin in person. Even if Mao felt the same way, however, he was not sure how much the Kremlin would be able to meet CCP demands, and how his visit should proceed. In order to probe Stalin's intentions, on 9 November 1949 Mao sent a telegram to Wang Jiaxiang, the CCP representative in Moscow, that instructed him to ask Stalin if he would want Zhou Enlai to accompany Mao to Moscow. Mao hoped that if Stalin let Zhou, the CCP's best negotiator, come with him, that would indicate the Kremlin's intention to achieve something substantial.[48] Probably because of Mao's ambivalence or Moscow's reluctance, Mao left China for Russia in early December, but without Zhou Enlai.

Even though Mao departed with a sense of uncertainty, his welcome in Moscow was splendidly cordial. Upon his arrival, Stalin and almost all of the Soviet top leaders held a state banquet in Mao's honor. The Soviet leader once again apologized, this time in front of all the attendees, for the mistakes that he had made and told Mao, "now that

46. Mao drafted the five articles as his commentaries on the White Paper during this period. See especially "Cast away Illusion, Prepare for Struggle," p. 428. For analysis on the commentaries, see, for example, Tang Tsou, *America's Failure in China, 1941–1950* (Chicago, 1963), pp. 510–11.

47. Mao, "On the People's Democratic Dictatorship," p. 1; Wang Bingnan, October, 1988, Beijing (oral history).

48. Telegram, Mao to Wang Jiaxiang, "On Chairman Mao's Visit to the Soviet Union," 9 November 1949, in *JGYLMWG* 1:131.

you are a winner, and as a winner, no criticism should be imposed on you."[49] Then Stalin asked what the Soviet Union could do to help the Chinese comrades, inquiring what Mao really wanted from his trip. It is interesting that Mao did not choose to answer Stalin directly. "For this trip," Mao replied, "we expect to create something that should not only look nice but taste delicious." Mao actually meant to achieve a substantial Sino-Soviet relationship, but his Chinese-style metaphor was so ambiguous that when it was translated into Russian, no one understood what it really meant. Shi Zhe, the main translator present, recalls that Lavrenti Beria even could not help laughing at it, but "Stalin was very serious and kept asking Mao to clarify it," which he did not.[50]

For the next two weeks Mao remained patiently ambivalent concerning his real intentions in Moscow. Stalin acted sincerely ready to offer whatever Mao wanted. In a short meeting as well as three telephone calls, all made by Stalin himself, he repeatedly urged Mao to express directly what he wanted. But Mao was still beating around the bush, insisting that Zhou Enlai should come to Moscow and that Zhou would present the whole package.[51] Mao also conveyed his ambivalence to the Soviet public. He told the Tass News Agency on 1 January 1950 that "the length of my stay in the Soviet Union will largely depend on the time actually needed to settle the issues concerning the interests of the People's Republic of China." He never mentioned a word about what these interests were or how to settle them.[52]

The Kremlin appeared to have run out of patience. One the day after Mao's comments to Tass, Mikoyan and Vyacheslav Molotov informed him that Stalin had authorized them to talk with Mao about the possible results of the visit. Beginning to see that his hosts were sincere, Mao listed three possible alternative outcomes:

(1) We may sign a friendship and military alliance treaty as well as new economic cooperation agreements, [so as] to settle the Sino-Soviet relationship on the basis of these new treaties. In this case, Zhou must come to Moscow. (2) We may sign an informal agreement to set some general guidelines for the future Sino-Soviet relationship. (3) We may just sign a communique to confirm the friendly relationship between the two countries. In cases (2) and (3), Zhou need not come.

Mao was impressed when Molotov and Mikoyan said, "we will do the first." Mao wasted no time. He dispatched a telegram to Beijing on the

49. *Shi Zhe Memoirs*, p. 13.
50. Ibid.
51. Ibid., p. 14.
52. "Chairman Mao in Moscow," *Xinhua Yuebao*, January 1950, p. 579.

same day, in which he reported his meeting with Molotov and Mikoyan and asked Zhou to leave China for Moscow in five days. But Mao still did not seem to be in a hurry because he wanted Zhou to "take the train not an airplane."[53]

Once the Soviets agreed to establish a military alliance, Mao expected serious and comprehensive negotiations over the future Sino-Soviet relationship. In his 5 January telegram to the CCP Central Committee, he wrote, "We must prepare fully for the coming negotiations [with the Soviets], which should include all the issues that concern our Central Committee. Now that negotiations are to be formal, we should proceed by all possible means and should make all our positions clear [to the Soviets]."[54]

When the negotiations started, the Soviets did not seem to be willing to accommodate all the Chinese demands. Zhou had great difficulty obtaining a clear commitment from the Soviet Union to assist China if it was invaded, a point he regarded as key to an alliance treaty. The first Soviet-drafted version of the treaty stated that if one side was invaded by a third party, the other side "is supposed to offer assistance." To Zhou, this was not strong enough because it did not make clear the binding liability of a military alliance. He tried everything to get a clarified version. The phrase "is supposed to" [*de yi*] was finally changed to "must devote all its efforts" [*jiejin quanli*]. This change took quite a time, but the Chinese were happy with the final text, which stated that "if one side is attacked by a third party, the other side must devote all its efforts to provide military and other assistance."[55] Mao had explicitly instructed Zhou to secure a treaty "the basic spirit of [which] should be to prevent Japan and its ally [the United States] from invading China" and which China "will be able to use . . . as a big political asset to deal with imperialist countries in the world."[56] This he had done.

In addition to the Soviet long-term commitment to China's security, the Chinese leaders expected to incorporate military forces directly into China's national defense, at least for a short period. In Dalian (Dairen) and Lushun (Port Arthur), the Soviet armed forces had been stationed at military bases since the end of World War II. Although the Chinese wanted the Russians to go home eventually, they wished the

53. Telegram, Mao to the CCP Central Committee, "On Zhou's Participation in Moscow Negotiations," 2 and 3 January 1950, in *JGYLMWG* 1:211.

54. Telegram, Mao to the CCP Central Committee, 5 January 1950, in *JGYLMWG* 1:215.

55. Wu Xiuquan, *Zhai Waijiaobu Banian de Jingli: 1950.1–1958.10* (Beijing, 1983), pp. 8–9 [hereafter cited as *Wu Xiuquan Memoirs*].

56. Telegram, Mao to the CCP Central Committee, 2 January 1950, in *JGYLMWG* 1:213. Also see *Bo Yibo Memoirs*, pp. 40–42.

Red Army to stay until "things get a little quieter in the Pacific." At China's request, the Soviets arranged to leave troops in those bases until the end of 1952, the projected date for a final peace treaty with Japan.[57] Moreover, during Mao's stay in Moscow, Nie Rongzhen, acting chief of staff of the PLA, telegraphed Mao, asking if Moscow could help defend China's coastal cities against KMT air raids. This was agreed to immediately. One Soviet air force division arrived in Shanghai between February and March 1950 and was immediately deployed to defend that city.[58] Moscow also agreed to send a fairly large number of Soviet military advisers and professionals to assist the "regularization and modernization" of the People's Liberation Army. A large group arrived in China in early 1950, and Nie put most of them in the high positions of PLA command.[59]

Concerning economic assistance, the CCP leaders were not disappointed either. The Soviet Union agreed to provide 300 million rubles in loans over five years at only one percent per annum. That was what Mao had originally expected. He could have asked for more, but as he told the CCP Central Committee on 3 January 1950, "It will be appropriate for our own sake not to borrow too much in [the] next few years."[60] Probably Mao believed that the loans were debts and that debts ought to be paid back sooner or later, but he was also aware of— and disliked—the Soviet reluctance to provide economic assistance.[61]

Mao and the other leaders were on the whole satisfied with the outcome of the Sino-Soviet negotiations. Much more important than anything else was the creation of a means for long-term deterrence against the United States. Mao told the Central People's Government Council, which was considering the ratification of the Sino-Soviet alliance treaty, that "since the foundation of the People's government, one of its significant achievements is the signing of the alliance treaty. [Since] the imperialists still exist in the world, we therefore need friends and allies. . . . Now that the treaty has confirmed the friendship of the Soviet Union and formed the alliance relationship, we will thus have someone who will lend a hand if the imperialists prepare to invade us."[62] By this time, the CCP leaders should have felt much more re-

57. *Wu Xiuquan Memoirs*, p. 10.

58. Nie Rongzhen, *Nie Rongzhen Hui Yi Lu* (Beijing, 1984), 3:729 [hereafter *Nie Rongzhen Memoirs*]. Also see *DDZGKJ*, p. 78.

59. *Nie Rongzhen Memoirs*, p. 730. Nie was in charge of assigning and arranging positions for the Soviet military advisers.

60. Telegram, Mao to the CCP Central Committee, 3 January 1950, in *JGYLMWG* 1:213.

61. *Shi Zhe Memoirs*, p. 17.

62. Mao Zedong's speech at the sixth meeting of the Central People's Government Council, 11 April 1950, in *JGYLMWG* 1:291.

laxed than before. But did they accurately perceive the threat of the United States? To what extent was the challenge they perceived from America real?

III

Since the failure of the Marshall mission in 1946, the Truman administration had never entirely disengaged from the civil war in China: it continued, willingly or unwillingly, to assist Chiang Kai-shek. By early 1949, KMT efforts to eliminate the Communists had faltered. As George F. Kennan, director of the Policy Planning Staff (PPS) in the State Department, predicted in November 1948, the disappearance of Chiang's government was "only a matter of time, and nothing that we can realistically hope to do will save it."[63] This prospect immediately raised two major questions. Would a Communist government in China threaten U.S. security interests in the Asia-Pacific region? And if it would, what could the United States possibly do about it?

President Truman, as an American historian has put it, was "kept only marginally informed and rarely intervened, even though he reserved final authority" concerning the making of policy in China. It was in the National Security Council (NSC), the Joint Chiefs of Staff (JCS), the Division of the Far Eastern Affairs, and the PPS of the State Department that the China policy was mostly discussed.[64] This was the key circle of decision making, even though pressures from both houses of the U.S. Congress played an important role from time to time.

Washington officials tended to see China's strategic importance in the Cold War context, much as they did when crises occurred elsewhere. Their primary question was to what extent a Communist government in China would enhance the Soviet strategic position in the Far East. Military and civilian officials had different answers to that question. The NSC staff appeared to believe that the Soviet objective in Asia was to establish influence over China first, then over Southeast Asia, and finally over the whole Asia-Pacific area. NSC 6, dated 26 March 1948, pointed out that for the Soviets, China was military significant "because of its (a) geographic position and (b) tremendous man power." The document further suggested that "China's propinquity to Southeast Asia means that if the Chinese Communists take

---

63. PPS 45, George F. Kennan to the secretary of state (George C. Marshall), "U.S. Policy toward China in Light of the Current Situation," 26 November 1948, in *FRUS: 1948*, 8:214.

64. Nancy Bernkopf Tucker, *Patterns in the Dust: Chinese-American Relations and the Recognition Controversy, 1949–1950* (New York, 1983), pp. 174–75.

over all China, they would in turn probably strengthen the communist movements in Indochina, Burma, and other areas further south."[65]

Military strategists were convinced that the Communist movement in China was part of a long-range Soviet campaign in Asia that was clearly in conflict with U.S. interests. The Joint Chiefs of Staff had predicted in June 1947 that China would eventually belong to the Soviet sphere of influence. To them, the CCP was a tool for expanding Soviet military positions from North Korea, Port Arthur, and Mongolia into Manchuria and further south and east. They stressed in August 1948 that "Soviet expansionist aims and long-range objectives are being furthered in China by the military operations of the Chinese communists." They agreed with the NSC that Soviet expansionist intentions in China "are clearly incompatible with United States security."[66]

If Washington officials were not certain as to just how a Soviet-dominated China would jeopardize U.S. military positions in the Far East, Douglas MacArthur, commander-in-chief of U.S. Far East Armed Forces, envisioned the threat more specifically. Talking with Fayette J. Flexer, counselor to the U.S. Embassy in the Philippines while en route to Washington in December 1948, MacArthur "needed no urging" to express his deep concerns about the vulnerability of the U.S. lines of defense in the Far East. To him, the situation had changed for the worse when Manchuria fell to the Communists, and had continued to decline as the Communists drove down the coast of China. MacArthur's conviction was based on his calculations of both U.S. and Soviet military strength in the Far East. The Soviet Union, he thought, could not mount any amphibious offensive against U.S. defensive lines in the Western Pacific from ports within its own territory for fifty years, because of the fact that "its most easterly war plants [were] concentrated in the Urals and its dependence for transport placed in a single-track Trans-Siberian railway." But with the Communist advance southward, MacArthur saw that advantages were about to shift to the Soviets. Even worse was the fact that, unwilling to provide funds for airfield construction in Japan, Washington had begun transferring

65. NSC 6, "The Position of the U.S. Regarding Short-term Assistance to China," 26 March 1948, in *FRUS: 1948*, 8:44–45.

66. SM-8388, JCS to the State-War-Navy Coordinating Committee, "Study of the Military Aspects of U.S. policy toward China," 9 June 1947, in *FRUS:1947*, 7:838–42; JCS to the secretary of defense, 5 August 1948, enclosed in NSC 22/1, "Possible Courses of Actions for the U.S. with Respect to the Critical Situation in China," 6 August 1948, in *FRUS: 1948*, 8:133. These views were stressed in NSC 37, "Strategic Importance of Formosa," 7 December 1948, in *FRUS: 1949*, 9:262, and NSC 48/1, "The Position of the United States with Respect to Asia," 23 December 1949, in *United States–Vietnam Relations, 1945–1967, U.S. Department of Defense* (Washington, D.C., 1971), book 7-8, pp. 225–284.

a bomber group from Okinawa to Europe and a squadron of fighters from Guam to the Canal Zone. The general explicitly warned that "the fighting strength in the Pacific was less than on the day of Pearl Harbor," and that the fall of China to the Communists would enhance the Soviet capability of launching serious amphibious attacks from Asiatic ports.[67]

State Department officials also felt that a Communist victory in China would be devastating to U.S. security interests, but they tended to emphasize the political, ideological, and psychological implications. Kennan argued in February 1948, that since all of the Asiatic peoples were faced with necessity of adapting to the impact of modern technology, "it is not only possible, but probable, that in the course of this process, many peoples will fall, for varying periods, under the influence of Moscow, whose ideology has a greater lure for such peoples."[68] A PPS analysis pointed out in September that it was the political advantage—not the economic or the military-strategic benefits—of a China ruled by the Communists that had attracted the Kremlin. Although the Soviets coveted the natural resources of Manchuria and north China, the PPS report reasoned, the Kremlin regarded "the bulk of China proper as a vast poorhouse, responsibility for which is to be avoided." The Kremlin would at best "regard Manchuria and Sinkiang as gaps in the buffer defense zone" or possibly as an avenue of attack on the USSR by a third power. Therefore, the only advantage to the Soviets of a Communist victory in China would be a stronger political offensive against the rest of East Asia. "In positive terms," the PPS assessment explained, "China is worth having because capture of it would represent an impressive political victory and more practically, acquisition of a broad human glacis from which to mount a political offensive against the rest of East Asia."[69]

In trying to understand the nature of CCP policy, American officials debated whether the Chinese Communists were real communists or potential Titos. The Joint Chiefs explicitly pointed out that although the CCP did not always follow the normal pattern of Communist operations employed in other countries, it had merely adjusted its techniques to fit the conditions of the rural and agrarian China. The Chinese Communists, they asserted, were "motivated by the same basic totalitarian and anti-democratic policies as were the Communist

67. Memorandum of conversation with MacArthur by Fayette J. Flexer, 6 December 1948, in *FRUS: 1949*, 9:263–65.
68. PPS 23, "Review of Current Trends in U.S. Foreign Policy," 24 February 1948, in *FRUS: 1949*, 1:524–25.
69. PPS 39, "To Review and Define United States Policy Toward China," 7 September 1948, in *FRUS: 1948*, 8:146.

parties in other countries."[70] The NSC staff concurred. Tito's Yugoslavian Communist Party had broken with the Kremlin in June of 1948, but the NSC did not expect the same happening in China in the foreseeable future. Even if it did happen, it would make no big difference: an independent Communist China would not necessarily be friendly to the United States. Once a Communist government was established in China, the NSC anticipated, it would have tremendous difficulties reconstructing the economy and the society of a devastated China. They concluded in February 1949 that Mao and his party would "remain hostile to the United States for an indeterminate time as long as the CCP is in control."[71]

With this State Department officials did not agree. They believed that even if China became a Communist state, the Kremlin would not necessarily be able to control it or direct it to implement Soviet objectives in Asia in the foreseeable future. In September 1948 Kennan pointed out that "Moscow faces a considerable task in seeking to bring the Chinese Communists under its complete control, if for no other reason than that Mao Tse-tung had been entrenched in power for nearly ten times the length of time that Tito has." He argued that ideology was not strong enough to bind foreign communists to Russia nor was it a substitute for Soviet control of a foreign state's party, secret police, and armed forces. "To the old conspirators of the Kremlin," Kennan explained, "the questions to ask about any foreign communist party are: who controls the party apparatus; who controls the secret police; who controls the armed forces; does the foreign leader love power more than he fears the Kremlin?" The State Department generally accepted Kennan's view, and even anticipated in November 1949 that "great strains will develop between Peiping and Moscow. These strains would not only work to our advantage but would contribute to the desired end of permitting China to develop its own life independently rather than as a Russian satellite."[72] Nevertheless, the State Department did not overrule the military in this matter.

Another way of identifying threats was to calculate power potentials, primarily in terms of industrial warmaking capability. It is interesting that the military and the civilians did not differ very much on this point. They all maintained that Japan, not China, had the highest

70. SM-8388, JCS to the State-War-Navy Coordinating Committee, 9 June 1947, p. 840.
71. NSC 34, 13 October 1948, U.S. National Security Council Records, Modern Military Records Branch, National Archives; NSC 34/2, 28 February 1949, ibid. For more NSC analysis on the possibility of splitting the CCP from Moscow's dominance, see David Allan Mayers, *Cracking the Monolith: U.S. Policy against the Sino-Soviet Alliance, 1949–1955* (Baton Rouge, 1986), pp. 25, 28–29, and 38–39.
72. PPS 39, 17 September 1948, p. 148; For State Department consensus on this point, see memorandum by Charlton Ogburn, Jr., 2 November 1949, in *FRUS: 1949,* 9:160–61.

power potential in Asia. Arguing that there existed only five vital power centers in the world—the United States, the Soviet Union, Great Britain, the Rhine Valley, and Japan—Kennan in November 1948 had deemphasized the strategic importance of even a China under Communist control. "There is little likelihood," he asserted, "that the Communists could develop and exploit [China's] *resources* in a manner seriously dangerous to the security interests of this country."[73] The JCS agreed with Kennan and argued that "the inability of the USSR to rapidly extend the lines of communications, base development operations, and military and political control through the vast area of Siberia and into the Communist-dominated China appears to preclude military exploitation of this area, to our detriment, in the immediate future."[74]

Later in 1949, this assessment was incorporated into NSC 48/1, a comprehensive NSC study of Asian policy. The document confirmed that the strategic importance of Japan—not China—was due to "its industrious, aggressive population, providing a large pool of trained manpower, its integrated internal communications systems with a demonstrated potential for an efficient merchant marine, its already developed industrial base and its strategic position." Therefore, it predicted, Japan was the place which the Soviet Union would be inspired to control because it would "add measurably to the warmaking potential of the USSR."[75]

Despite these differences, Washington policy planners had reached a consensus by late 1949. They all accepted that China alone, under Communist control, would not enhance the Soviet capability of undertaking military aggression on the basis of Asia's strategic potential unless the Communists controlled Japan as well. Therefore, the fall of China to the Communists should not necessarily result in an immediate threat to U.S. security interests in the Asia-Pacific area, at least in the foreseeable future. Nevertheless, it is interesting to note that this policy consensus was based on the prospect of no immediate threat if China fell to communism. No one doubted that Communist rule in China would be devastating to U.S. interests in the long run. And no one denied that the Communist control of China would promote Soviet expansionist objectives in the Far East.

73. PPS 39/1, "U.S. Policy toward China," 23 November 1948, in *FRUS: 1948*, 8:208–11 [emphasis added].
74. JSPC 877/72, "The Impact of Current Far Eastern Development on War Emergency Planning," 14 September 1949, cited in John Lewis Gaddis, *The Long Peace: Inquiries into the History of the Cold War* (New York, 1987), p. 78.
75. NSC 48/1, 23 December 1949, pp. 254–55.

Given these threat assessments, Washington strategic planners pro-posed a general line to guide U.S. policy toward China. "The current concept of strategy in the event of war with the USSR," NSC 48/1 de-termined in late 1949, "is to conduct a strategic offensive in the 'West' and a strategic defensive in the 'East.' "[76] But with regard to China, the National Security Council had earlier recognized that the U.S. long-term objective would be "the furtherance of a stable, independent and unified China which is friendly to the United States and capable of be-coming an effective *barrier* to possible Soviet aggression in the Far East." To this end, the NSC stressed that "the most important objective which is practical to pursue in the short run is the *prevention* of com-plete communist control of China."[77] How could these objectives be accomplished?

With a strong sense of pessimism growing out of U.S. inability to in-fluence overall events in China, State Department officials consistently supported a policy of disengagement from the Chinese civil war. Prob-ably under the influence of the Secretary of State George C. Marshall and his disillusionment resulting from the failure of his mission, Ken-nan strongly advocated in February 1948 that the administration should "liquidate as rapidly as possible our unsound commitment in China and recover vis-à-vis that country, a position of detachment and freedom of action." To him, the administration was "greatly overex-tended in our thinking about what we can accomplish, and should ac-complish, in that area." Later that year, Kennan even more explicitly pointed out that "in the present situation in China, the tide is against us and we need the freedom to talk, or perhaps even to lie at anchor until we are quite sure of our bearings."[78] The State Department found it easy to talk but difficult to put such a policy into effect. Although aware of the rationale for staying out of the civil war, Marshall had to placate the "China bloc" in Congress by continuing economic and mil-itary assistance to the KMT in 1948 to keep congressional support for his European Recovery Program. Dean G. Acheson, upon becoming secretary of state in January 1949, let the policy continue without any change. As a result, the Truman administration did not disengage from its involvement in China's internal conflict.[79]

76. Ibid., pp. 255–56.
77. NSC 6, 26 March 1948, pp. 44–45 [emphasis added].
78. PPS 23, 24 February 1948, p. 525; PPS 39, 17 September 1948, p. 150. For State Department pessimism, see Gaddis, *The Long Peace*, p. 75.
79. Gaddis, *The Long Peace*, p. 75.

Even though the United States never ceased providing economic assistance to the KMT, there is no evidence that the administration was prepared to intervene with its armed forces— either ground troops or naval and air forces—on behalf of the KMT. U.S. Marines had landed at Qingdao on 11 October 1945, replacing the Japanese. By late 1948, the U.S. Navy maintained fewer than four thousand on shore with minimal (approximately sixteen fighters) air support. Their main mission was to protect American lives and property.[80] As early as May 1948, Vice-Admiral Oscar C. Badger, the commander of U.S. naval forces in the Western Pacific, informed Washington of an imminent Chinese communist attack on Qingdao, and proposed to "assist Nationalist forces in defense of city and essential suburban facilities." He requested "prompt reinforcement amounting to doubling Marine Force presently available." But in considering Badger's suggestion, W. Walton Butterworth, director of the Office of Far Eastern Affairs, felt it desirable to "take precautionary measures toward phasing out." He explained that "if it might be necessary to evacuate Tsingtao, it would be in our interest to act gradually rather than abruptly and dramatically." Secretary of Defense James V. Forrestal agreed, and suggested making emergency plans to withdraw U.S. forces from Qingdao and redeploy them "to [a] more tenable position further south in China or withdraw from China entirely should the situation so require." Secretary of State Marshall accepted Forrestal's suggestion but stressed that U.S. forces there "should avoid participation in hostilities between the Nationalists and Communists."[81] In January 1949, the State Department and the Department of the Navy agreed that shore activities of the U.S. armed forces at Qingdao should be reduced. Also in early May, Acheson informed Ambassador Stuart in China that, assuming Shanghai fell soon, "all ships and activities of U.S. Navy in Tsingtao would be withdrawn at the time of Communist capture of Shanghai." Acheson explained to Stuart that since "withdrawal would be none the less inescapable, . . . it would be too embarrassing to withdraw under the request of the Communists."[82]

80. Rear Admiral C. W. Styer, Office of the Chief of Naval Operations, to W. Walton Butterworth, 8 January 1948, in *FRUS: 1948*, 8:308; William T. Turner, consul general at Qingdao, to John Leighton Stuart, 24 September 1948, ibid., p. 322; Arthur R. Ringwalt to W. Walton Butterworth, 24 March 1948, ibid., p. 109.

81. Oscar C. Badger to the chief of naval operations, 3 March 1948, in *FRUS: 1948*, 8:310–11; Butterworth to Marshall, 21 May 1948, ibid., p. 313; Forrestal to the NSC, 28 May 1948, ibid., pp. 316–17.

82. Memorandum of understanding between the acting secretary of state (Robert M Lovett) and the secretary of the Navy (Forrestal), 21 January 1949, in *FRUS: 1949*, 9:1199; Acheson to Stuart, 13 May 1949, ibid., p. 1205.

And in fact, no source suggests that Washington's withdrawal took place under pressure from CCP forces.

At the same time, much more attention in Washington was directed toward formulating an overall strategic conception and a defense system for the entire Far Eastern area. The primary concern was to determine, given the increasing influence of the Soviet Union on the Asian mainland, given the limited resources of the United States for a global commitment, and also given the conviction that Japan would be of vital strategic importance in the area, what the United States could possibly do to deter the Communists from further challenging U.S. security interests in the long run.

The idea of a "defensive perimeter" in the Western Pacific became the predominantly accepted solution. Kennan had pointed out in February 1948 that U.S. influence in the Far East should be "primarily military and economic." He asserted that an American security system in that region should be based on "what parts of the Pacific and Far Eastern world are absolutely vital to our security." In his view, Japan and the Philippines would be "the corner-stones of such a Pacific security system."[83] In March, Kennan clarified his view on a defensive perimeter: "Okinawa would be made the center of our offensive striking power in the western Pacific area. It would constitute the central and most advanced point of a U-shaped U.S. security zone embracing the Aleutians, the Ryukyus, the former Japanese mandated islands, and of course Guam." The objective of such a defense system, Kennan stressed, was "to *prevent* the assembly and launching [of] any amphibious forces from any mainland ports in the east-central or northeast Asia [with our] Okinawa-based air power plus our advanced naval power." To operate under this system, he suggested, the U.S. Navy should "continue to *show* the flag actively in the entire Western Pacific area, make frequent visits to Japanese and Philippines ports along the line of present policy in the Mediterranean." He concluded that given the availability of U.S. military capability in the Western Pacific, this would be the best way of "*frustrating*" the long-term objectives of the Soviets on the Asian mainland.[84]

As he stressed in his overall containment strategy, Kennan thought that the United States should also make political and economic efforts to strengthen its outposts in the region. He insisted that Japan, despite its vital strategic significance, was the most vulnerable as far as its political stability and economic recovery were concerned. After he visited Japan in March 1948, Kennan found that none of U.S. activities there

83. PPS 23, 24 February 1948, p. 525.
84. Kennan to the secretary of state, 14 March 1948, in *FRUS: 1948*, 1:533–35 [emphasis added].

"has any particular relationship to our long-term strategic problems. We have formulated no definite objectives with respect to the military security of Japan in the post-treaty period." Any social and economic chaos and internal instability in Japan, in his view, would induce the Kremlin to seek expanding its influence there.[85] In the months following his visit to Japan, Kennan vigorously opposed U.S. occupation policies in Japan, including the purges, reparations, and war crimes trials. Nothing of this kind should continue, he thought, because that would "operate against the stability of Japanese society" and would stand in the path of the "prime objective," which was economic recovery. Otherwise, however, Kennan did not see any reason to rearm Japan or build military bases on the Japanese main islands provided that no other power made any effort to obtain strategic facilities on them. Moreover, from 1949 until June 1950, Washington was encouraging Japanese trade with the People's Republic of China. Secretary of State Dean Acheson still considered trade as a means of attracting a Communist China away from the Kremlin. Indeed, U.S. trade policy was even more liberal toward China than toward the Soviet Union.[86]

Late that year, General MacArthur came up with almost the same outline of a defense system as Kennan had proposed. He wanted to include the Aleutians, Midway, Okinawa, the Philippines, Australia, New Zealand, and the British and Dutch islands in the Southwest Pacific. From a military point of view, MacArthur argued that Okinawa was a "spearhead," which would be under "immediate and constant threat and would be untenable or dangerously undefendable." But with such a defense system, the general stressed, any attempted amphibious operation from northeastern Asian ports would be *discouraged*, because "American troops on these off-shore islands would serve as a trip wire."[87] The Joint Chiefs concurred in MacArthur's design in June 1949. "The ultimate minimum US position in the Far East vis-à-vis the USSR," they reasoned, "requires at least our present degree of control of the Asian offshore chain. In the event of war, the island chain would constitute in effect a system of strong outposts for our strategic position." The Joint Chiefs, however, recognized that the system "would

85. Ibid., pp. 531–32.
86. Michael Schaller summarizes Kennan's view in his *American Occupation of Japan: The Origins of the Cold War in Asia* (New York, 1985), pp. 126–27. Also see Warren I. Cohen, "China in Japanese-American Relations," in *The United States and Japan in the Postwar World*, ed. Akira Iriye and Warren I. Cohen (Lexington, Ky., 1989), pp. 36–37.
87. Memorandum of a conversation with MacArthur by Kennan, 5 March 1948, enclosed in PPS 28, "Recommendations with Respect to U.S. Policy toward Japan," 25 March 1948, in *FRUS: 1948*, 6:700–701,, and 703. Also see Flexer's memorandum of a conversation with MacArthur, 6 December 1948, pp. 263–65. For additional analysis, see Gaddis, *The Long Peace*, p. 74.

have only limited offensive value." They asserted that "Japan's capability for self-defense must be developed against the time when it may be determined by the Soviets that overt aggression by them or their satellites is their only means for gaining control over Japan." Enhancing U.S. military strength in Japan, the Chiefs believed, "would contribute importantly to military operations against the Soviets in Asia, thus forcing the USSR to fight on the Asiatic front as well as elsewhere."[88]

The NSC synthesized the concept of a defensive perimeter in December 1949. First, it recognized that if a successful defense was to be constructed against future Soviet aggression in the Far East, the United States would have to maintain a minimum military position in Asia. Second, this minimum position would consist of at least the present U.S. military position in the islands just off the coast of Asia and would ensure its denial to the Communists in the event of war. Third, this island chain, including Japan, the Ryukyus, and the Philippines, represented a "US first line of defense as well as offense from which the United States could seek to reduce the areas of Communist control, using whatever means available without using sizable military forces." Fourth, the chain would also permit the United States to control the main lines of communications necessary to American strategic development of the important sections of Asia.[89] This strategy seemed to have met the requirement of committing minimum resources to curtail further Soviet advance in the area.

Meanwhile, however, an important concern was with how the American public might respond to this low-risk policy. It is interesting to note that there existed a strong pressure for rearming Japan and including Taiwan—the last place Chaing could sustain his rule—within the U.S. defensive perimeter. The *New York Times* and the *Washington Post* repeatedly argued that the U.S. military should stay in Japan for an indefinite period or rearm Japan. In the summer of 1949, these newspapers told American readers that the Soviets were planning to construct a new Communist "Co-Prosperity Sphere," and warned that "if Southeast Asia goes, Japan should not prove to be a difficult target [for the Russians] unless American troops are to hold Japan indefinitely by brute force."[90] In late 1949, the so-called China bloc in Congress, ranging from Senator Pat McCarran (D-Nevada) to Senator William F. Knowland (R-California), and Senator H. Alexander Smith

88. NSC 49, "Strategic Evaluation of United States Security Needs in Japan," 9 June 1949, in *FRUS: 1949*, 7:774–75.
89. NSC 48/1, 23 December 1949, p. 257.
90. *New York Times*, 4 May 1949; *Washington Post*, 22, 24, and 29 August and 18 September 1949.

(R-New Jersey), shifted their pressure for the continuation of material assistance to the KMT to the inclusion of Taiwan into the U.S. defense system and incorporated this issue into their political attack on the Truman administration.[91] Amid this political heat, it was hardly possible for the Democratic administration to accommodate its political opponents at home. The voices of its critics distorted the real intentions of the U.S. government.

At the same time, Mao Zedong's visit to Moscow and the prospect of a Sino-Soviet military alliance made it urgent that the United States announce its policy concerning its security interests in the Asian-Pacific area. As soon as Mao arrived in Moscow on 16 December 1949, Ambassador Alan S. Kirk reported that the primary purpose of Mao's visit was to sign "mutual assistance (military) pacts." O. Edmund Clubb, consul general in Peiping, [Beijing], suggested that the CCP leadership was anxious to secure a military alliance with the Soviet Union, because the "Chinese have always preferred others to do their fighting with big powers." Clubb further pointed out on 31 December 1949 that Mao and Stalin would make arrangements including "(1) Chinese and USSR would be allied in event of war; (2) Besides troops, . . . Chinese to furnish 5 million workers as manpower; (3) Transport to be placed under Soviet supervision, supported by railway guards and (4) Interior Department also to be under Soviet supervision."[92]

Dean Acheson finally announced the U.S. policy of a "defensive perimeter" in the Asia-Pacific region to the public on 12 January 1950. In his speech to National Press Club, he outlined the perimeter primarily as it had been designated in NSC 48/1, two weeks earlier: neither Taiwan nor South Korea were included, nor were any plans announced to rearm Japan.[93] It might have been inappropriate to tell an adversary the exact intentions of the United States, given that maintaining the ambivalence of one's strategic intentions is sometimes better deterrence. It might also have been necessary to send out signals of a firm U.S. commitment to its interests in the area in case the enemy was planning to challenge them. Although no evidence indicates that Acheson intended his defensive perimeter speech as deterrence, announcing the scope of U.S. defensive commitments might have the effect of avoiding miscalculation by the Communists.

91. Memorandum of a conversation with Senators Knowland and Smith by Acheson, 5 January 1950, in *FRUS: 1950*, 6:258–63.

92. Kirk to the secretary of state, 18 December 1949, in *FRUS:1949*, 8:637–38; Clubb to the secretary of state, 23 December 1949, ibid., pp. 643–45; Clubb to the secretary of state, 31 December 1949, ibid., p. 651.

93. Acheson's speech at the National Press Club, 12 January 1950, in *Department of State Bulletin*, U.S. Department of State, 23 January 1950, p. 116.

The period 1948–49 marked the beginning of the confrontation between the People's Republic of China and the United States. Both the CCP and the Truman administration believed it adequately understood the intentions of its potential adversary and made its decisions accordingly. In retrospect, however, it seems clear there existed gaps of understanding on both sides.

The CCP did not have a full and correct understanding of U.S. intentions toward its rule in China. They believed that the United States, because of its rivalry with the Soviet Union, would not tolerate a Communist regime in China. One big problem was that the CCP exaggerated U.S. strategic interests in the Far East. Mao's "intermediate zone" concept was in fact inadequate to the Cold War situation and rather misleading in predicting the future of the U.S.–USSR relationship. The CCP leaders' desire for quick political control in China and their revolutionary zeal for national liberation and independence further complicated this conceptual framework. For instance, the presence of no more than four thousand U.S. troops in Qingdao—although the CCP believed there were altogether 11,000 in Qingdao, Shanghai, and Taiwan—should not have been seen as a big threat. But anxiety to get rid of all foreign forces in China led CCP leaders to overreact. Even worse was their lack of information about the U.S.'s China policy. Because they knew little about the pluralistic nature of the U.S. political system, the CCP often took congressional pronouncements as reflections of Truman administration policy. Not having many sources of information—except Tass—most CCP analysts rested U.S. policy on citations from American and western newspapers obtained either in Hong Kong or in Warsaw.[94]

The CCP victory in the Chinese civil war forced American policymakers to consider whether Communist rule in that country would threaten U.S. security interests. In their assessment, as with crises elsewhere, U.S. officials primarily examined Soviet objectives and actual and potential Soviet roles in China. They concluded that since the Soviets had political expansionist aims in the Far East, a Communist China would be detrimental to U.S. interests in the long run; but that since the CCP leaders were nationalistic Communists and would resist Soviet dominance, a CCP government in China would not endanger U.S. security in that region in the short run. This perception was based more on deduction than on an adequate understanding of Soviet far eastern policy, and particularly the CCP-Soviet relationship. The belief

94. Off-the-record interviews.

that Stalin would seize every chance to expand Soviet influence in Asia at the expense of the United States was too simple. And the terms "Kremlin-inspired" and "Moscow-directed" were not an appropriate frame of reference within which to understand the CCP-Soviet relationship. Mao's determination to pull Moscow behind him was easily underestimated, and the CCP's alliance arrangements with the Soviet Union, designed for defense and deterrence, were likely to be mistaken as being for offense and aggression. The policy consensus based upon this reasoning would prove vulnerable later. Regarding Europe, not Asia, as its strategic focus, the Truman administration did not want its effort, attention, and resources diverted elsewhere. But the Democratic administration had great difficulty dealing with domestic politics. It could hardly avoid strident public voices calling for a strong U.S. commitment in Asia. Particularly misleading were the appeals for unleashing Japan by rearming it and saving Chiang's rule by supporting its resistance to the Communists; these reinforced the CCP leadership's suspicion and fear of hostile U.S. intentions regarding a new China.

Taking the adversary's hostility for granted, both sides ended up with the same strategy: to deter the other side's aggressiveness by establishing military counterthreats. Nevertheless, the mutual deterrent relationship that evolved was an odd one. First, the CCP primarily targeted the United States, which, in turn, focused on the Soviet Union, for the United States did not believe a Communist China alone would threaten its security even though Mao's "lean-over-to-the-Soviet-Union" policy and consequent Sino-Soviet military alliance did worry the Truman administration. Second, since neither side was sure of when and how its perceived adversary would take military action, uncertainty determined the nature of deterrence strategy; that is, policymakers on both sides had to design their commitments on a worst-case assumption. This was hardly difficult for Mao. With a keen understanding of Chinese strategic tradition, he believed and apparently admired the old teachings that "deeds speak louder than words," "one pair of strong fists cannot match two pairs of weak fists," and "the best strategy is to force enemy into retreat without actually fighting."

Neither China nor the United States had any clear idea of what the perceived opponent would do next, even though neither doubted the other side's hostile intentions. This circumstance laid out a potential battleground for further confrontations, particularly when unexpected crises occurred.

[3]

The Origins of the Taiwan Question, September 1949–August 1950

It became apparent in late 1948 that the KMT could not hold the mainland and that Taiwan would be a last refuge for the Nationalists. The military situation clearly indicated that the CCP forces would soon drive the KMT remnants to the island and would continue their pursuit until they finally eliminated the Nationalists. U.S. strategists began to consider whether Chinese Communist control over Taiwan would threaten national security in the Western Pacific, and if it would, what the United States could do to prevent the fall of Taiwan. For Beijing authorities, any U.S. military action to protect the KMT remnants in Taiwan would delay final victory over the Nationalists. How did the CCP leaders assess U.S. policy toward Taiwan? What did they do in response?

I

A primary concern of Washington officials was to what extent Taiwan was strategically important to the United States. The Joint Chiefs of Staffs had asserted in November 1948 that should Taiwan fall into the hands of the Chinese Communists, "the strategic implications to the security of the United States would be seriously unfavorable." Taiwan, the JCS calculated, would be of great military value to the United States in the event of future war with the Soviet Union. Since the fall of Chinese mainland to the Communists would prevent the United States from using China's strategically valuable areas—including air bases, harbors, and coastal railroad terminals—Taiwan's value would be enhanced "as a wartime base capable of use for staging troops, strategic air operations, and control of adjacent shipping routes." Communist Chinese control of Taiwan, they asserted, would undoubtedly benefit the Soviets, who would not only be in a position to dominate the sea routes between Japan and Malaya, but would also gain "a greatly improved . . . capability of extending . . . control to the Ryukyus and the Philippines." Taiwan was also a major source of food and other raw materials for Japan. Its loss, the JCS concluded, "would quite possibly be a decisive factor as to whether Japan would prove to be more of a liability than a potential asset under war conditions."[1]

General Douglas MacArthur agreed with the Joint Chiefs, but approached the question in more strictly operational terms. He was concerned that a Communist-controlled Taiwan would threaten the entire Western Pacific. In a conversation with Fayette J. Flexer, counselor to the U.S. Embassy in the Philippines, on 7 December 1948, MacArthur said "vehemently" that "to permit the access of an unfriendly power to Taiwan would be to invite rupture of our whole defense line in the Far East."[2] Two months later, the general explained that "Formosa was astride the line of communications between Okinawa and the Philippines, and that it outflanked our position on Okinawa and, in the hands of the Chinese Communists, broke through the island wall which we must have along the Asiatic 'littorals' in order to maintain in a strategic sense a defensive line in the Western Pacific."[3] Aides to the Far East Command also saw Taiwan as an important part of the U.S. defense in East Asia. William J. Sebald, the acting political adviser in Japan, regarded "the line [of] Japan-Formosa-Philippines" as where "United States objectives in the cold war with Soviet Russia envisage a containment of the Soviets along the perimeter of Soviet influence." Major General Charles A. Willoughby, assistant chief of staff to MacArthur, explicitly argued in September 1949, that Taiwan was within "the Main Line of resistance, . . . namely, the holding of positions through the island chain of Japan, the Ryukyu Islands and the Philippines."[4]

State Department officials accepted the Joint Chiefs' conclusion that "it is in our strategic interest that Formosa be denied to communists." They, however, did not see any immediate danger from a Communist-controlled Taiwan. They did not see how Taiwan might fall to the

1. JCS to the secretary of defense, James V. Forrestal, included in NSC 37, "The Strategic Importance of Formosa," 1 December 1948, in *FRUS: 1949*, 9:262.

2. Memorandum of a conversation with MacArthur by Fayette J. Flexer, counselor of the U.S. Embassy in the Philippines, 7 December 1948, in *FRUS: 1949*, 9:263–64.

3. Memorandum of a conversation with MacArthur by Max M. Bishop, 16 February 1949, in *FRUS: 1949*, 7:656–57.

4. William J. Sebald to the secretary of state, 29 August 1949, in *FRUS: 1949*, 7:835; Sebald to the secretary of state, 9 September 1949, ibid., p. 857.

Communists in the next few years, and more important, how the Soviets might use it militarily against the United States. The threat to Taiwan did not lie in a Communist amphibious invasion from the mainland, they asserted, but rather in "the classic communist technique of infiltration, agitation and mass revolt, and . . . the classic Chinese technique of a deal at the top"—implying that the KMT might make a deal with the CCP over Taiwan.[5] Reports from China indicated that the CCP, anticipating conflict with the United States should it attack Taiwan, would not resort to military means in the near future. Observers on the mainland noted that Mao Zedong's "agitation re[garding] Formosa" was due to his sensitivity to any American role in defending the island. The Communists "demand its prompt restoration to Chinese, i.e., communist sovereignty," and regarded "complete withdrawal [of] all U.S. Naval military forces from China and China waters including Taiwan [as a] prerequisite to [diplomatic] relations." But U.S. officials predicted that the Chinese Communists "would probably not proceed immediately to launch an attack on Taiwan," because they "seemed [to] feel [that] USA would somehow assist [the] Nationalists [to] hold Formosa" and a military action "might involve them in conflict with the United States."[6] None of this meant, of course, that State Department officials rejected the assertion that a Communist-controlled Taiwan would endanger U.S. security interests in the long run, particularly in the event of war with the USSR.

In February 1949 the National Security Council concluded that since U.S. "military capabilities in the Western Pacific must rest primarily on the control of sea lanes and the maintenance of strategic air potential from strategically tenable island positions . . . [e]nemy control of Formosa would seriously jeopardize our capabilities in these respects." Should Taiwan fall to the Communists, the NSC further asserted, it would prove "a major contribution to enemy's capabilities."[7] The administration thus achieved a consensus that the fall of Taiwan to "an administration . . . susceptible of exploitation by Kremlin-directed

5. The acting secretary of state (Robert M. Lovett) to President Truman, 14 January 1949, in *FRUS: 1949*, 9:266; NSC 37/1, "The Position of the US with Respect to Formosa," 19 January 1949, ibid., pp. 271–72.

6. O. Edmund Clubb to Dean Acheson, 29 June 1949, in *FRUS: 1949*, 8:398–99; Walter McConaughy to Acheson, 25 August 1949, ibid., pp. 507–8; Clubb to Acheson, 31 August 1949, ibid., p. 514; LaRue R. Lutkins, vice-consul at Kunming, to Acheson, 2 September 1949, ibid., pp. 516–17; and Robert C. Strong to Acheson, 21 October 1949, ibid., pp. 555–56.

7. NSC 37/3, "The Strategic Importance of Formosa," 11 February 1949, in *FRUS: 1949*, 9:284–86; NSC 37/5, "Supplementary Measures with Respect to Formosa," 1 March 1949, ibid., pp. 290–91; NSC 37/7, "The Position of the United States with Respect to Formosa," 22 August 1949, ibid., pp. 376–78.

communists" would threaten U.S. military positions in the Far East. The next question then was, as Acheson raised it in March, whether Taiwan was "so great a *prize* that we are justified in risking *a show of force*" to deter the Chinese Communist from seizing it.[8]

It is interesting that U.S. military strategists explicitly opposed defending Taiwan by force. The JCS did not value Taiwan as a "vital U.S. interests" requiring a U.S. military establishment. Pointing out a clear distinction with another island, they asserted that "Iceland is directly vital to our national security while the importance of Formosa cannot be said to be in that category." Besides, "the current disparity between our military strength and our many global obligations . . . makes it inadvisable to undertake the employment of armed force in Formosa, for this might lead to the necessity for relatively major effort there, even making it impossible then to meet more important emergencies elsewhere." They acknowledged, however, that Taiwan's strategic importance was "great," and argued that, when "unfavorable diplomatic repercussion[s] might result from undue resort to what might be termed a show of force, . . . diplomatic risks and difficulties are thus justified." They therefore suggested that "some forms of military support should be made available now" by the "stationing of minor numbers of fleet units at a suitable Formosan port or ports, with such shore activity . . . as may be necessary for maintenance and air communication and for the recreation of personnel."[9]

State Department officials clearly saw "evident [political] disadvantages in establishing U.S. naval forces on Taiwan." In a memorandum dates 14 December 1948 the State Department concluded that political difficulties would render a show of military force in Taiwan highly risky. One concern was that if the United States sent forces to Taiwan, it would "cause mainland Chinese to flee to Taiwan in large numbers in the belief that they would be protected by the U.S. Navy." The additional influx of Chinese refugees "could only increase the burden on the island's economy and exacerbate the present Taiwanese hatred of mainland Chinese." The resulting disorder, the officials anticipated, might pave the way for Communist infiltration and a Communist-inspired uprising, and consequently, "facilitate rather than prevent the spread of Communism in the island." Another problem was that the stationing of U.S. forces in Taiwan would lend "credence to Communist charges that we are preparing to detach the island from China."

---

8. NSC 37, 1 December p. 201; statement by Acheson to the NSC, enclosed in Sidney W. Souers to the NSC, 3 March 1949, in *FRUS: 1949*, 9:295 [emphasis added].

9. JCS to Forrestal, 10 February 1949, enclosed in NSC 37/3, 11 February 1949, p. 285.

The Communists would "seize the opportunity thus presented to charge us with imperialistic and predatory designs upon Taiwan."[10]

Secretary of State Acheson firmly stood for nonmilitary means to prevent the fall of Taiwan. In March 1949, he made it clear to the National Security Council that "a show of military force in Formosa . . . would impair the efficacy of what we are trying to do through diplomatic and economic means." The presence of U.S. forces there, Acheson asserted, would raise "the spectre of an American-created irredentist issue just at the time we shall be seeking to exploit the genuinely Soviet-created irredentist issue in Manchuria and Sinkiang." Besides, he calculated, "given the tactics employed by the Communists in seizing power, the use of our military power, short of complete blockade and occupation, will be ineffective to prevent Communist control of Formosa." It is interesting that Acheson anticipated that nonmilitary measures might not guarantee a denial of Taiwan and that military force might be called for in the future. Nevertheless, he insisted: "If we are to intervene militarily on the island, we shall, in all possibility, do so in concert with likeminded powers, . . . and with the proclaimed intention of satisfying the legitimate demand of the indigenous Formosans for self-determination either under a UN trusteeship or through independence."[11]

The National Security Council adopted Acheson's views. It recognized that sending troops to Taiwan would be both a diplomatic and a political mistake. The NSC stressed: "A show of military strength would be of dubious efficacy in preventing Communist agitation and infiltration or secret negotiations between communist emissaries and Nationalist commanders on Formosa. A show of military strength would have serious political repercussions throughout China; it might create an irredentist issue." So the NSC decided not to station U.S. forces in Taiwan. But it noted that "this conclusion is without prejudice to a reexamination of the possible course of action should developments on Formosa so justify."[12]

What, then, did the administration prefer as nonmilitary measures? The State Department strongly recommended secretly supporting the Taiwanese separatist movement, which would deny the island to *both* the Chinese Communists and the Chinese Nationalists.[13] The National

10. State Department memorandum, enclosed in the memorandum from the acting secretary of state to Sidney W. Souers, NSC 14 December 1948, in *FRUS: 1948*, 7:340–41.
11. Acheson's statement to the NSC, enclosed in Souers to the NSC, 3 March 1949, pp. 295–96.
12. NSC 37/5, 1 March 1949, pp. 290–92.
13. NSC 37/1, 7 January 1949, pp. 272–74. Acheson wanted to conceal U.S. support to the Taiwanese separatists. See Souers to the NSC, 3 March 1949, p. 295.

Security Council and President Harry S. Truman approved such a plan in February 1949 and Secretary of State Acheson directed Livingston Merchant, then counselor to the U.S. Embassy in Nanjing, to contact Chen Cheng, the KMT governor of Taiwan, with instructions to discourage the further influx of KMT refugees and to encourage Taiwanese participation in the government through a promise of U.S. economic aid.[14] No one in Washington, however, was certain that such an effort would deny Taiwan to the CCP without running the risk of offending nationalistic sentiment in China. And curiously, no one questioned how Chen Cheng, a close friend of Chiang, could be persuaded to betray the KMT.

By late spring, the situation in Taiwan had changed dramatically. The sudden transportation of an estimated 300,000 KMT troops to the island rendered the question of an independent Taiwan moot. Donald D. Edgar, the U.S. consul at Taipei, reported from Taiwan in April that the mainland Nationalists there had a "widespread . . . fear that we have imperialistic design on [the] Island." He saw "nothing to be gained and much to be lost by approaching Governor Chen [Cheng]." In May, Merchant informed Acheson that the strategy of seeking an independent regime in Taiwan was going nowhere. Since Nationalist domination of Taiwan seemed to be a fait accompli, the U.S. policy of promoting autonomy had become irrelevant. It therefore became apparent that it was necessary to reconsider U.S. policy on Taiwan.[15]

Now a main concern was whether the new situation in Taiwan would justify a show of military force. George F. Kennan regarded immediate military action as desirable. In a PPS draft paper of July 1949, he pointed out that "Formosan separatism is the only concept which has sufficient grass roots appeal to resist communism." He argued that the United States should now "announce the temporary unilateral reassertion of authority over the island on the grounds that subsequent events had invalidated all the assumptions underlying the Cairo Declaration and that the U.S. intervention was required by the interests of stability in the Pacific as well as by the inhabitants of the islands." What Kennan wanted was to remove "the Chinese force and many of the Chinese refugees by force [back] to the mainland." He claimed that if his arguments "were to be adopted and carried through with sufficient resolution, speed, ruthlessness, and self-assurance, the way

14. NSC 37/4, "The Current Position of the US with Respect to Formosa," 18 February 1949, in *FRUS: 1949*, 9:288–89; Acheson to Livingston Merchant, 14 February 1949, ibid., pp. 287–88. For further analysis, see Gaddis, *The Long Peace*, p. 81.

15. Stuart to Acheson, 23 March 1949 in *FRUS: 1949*, 9:302–3; Edgar to Acheson, 11 April 1949, ibid., pp. 313–14; Merchant to Acheson, 4 May 1949, ibid., pp. 324–25; Donald D. Edgar to Acheson, 4 May 1949, ibid., pp. 324–26; State Department to Souers, 4 August 1949, ibid., pp. 369–71.

Theodore Roosevelt might have done it, it would be not only successful but would [also] have an *electrifying effect* in the country and
throughout the Far East." If the president and the administration felt
as strongly as he did, Kennan argued "that our situation in the Far
East will not permit further inaction, . . . then my personal view is
that we should take the plunge."[16]

Ambassador John Leighton Stuart in China also urged that Washington should consider a new course of action. "We could have," he
noted in June 1949, "included Taiwan in SCAP [Supreme Command,
Allied Power in Japan] or even claimed it as our share of postwar settlement as USSR did with Sakhalin and Kuriles, to say nothing of
Manchuria."[17] It seems that MacArthur liked the idea of temporarily
incorporating Taiwan into his defense responsibilities. Although he
did not believe that the U.S. should occupy the island, the general
pointed out in November that " 'by hook and crook' we must keep it
out of Communist hands." His "hook and crook" formula was that
"rather than permit Formosa to go to the Communists, it would be better to return it to Japan."[18]

Meanwhile, supporters of Chiang Kai-shek in Congress openly appealed for immediate U.S. action to defend Taiwan. In October, Senator H. Alexander Smith, an influential Republican member of the
Senate Foreign Relations Committee, visited Taiwan. After he returned, he vigorously urged the administration to prevent its fall. In
December, Senator William F. Knowland—often called the "senator
for Formosa"—also visited Taiwan and called for the dispatch of a military mission to the island. At the same time, Senator Robert A. Taft
and former president Herbert Hoover explicitly advised the administration to deploy U.S. naval units there.[19]

The JCS, however, reiterated in August 1949 that "the strategic importance of Formosa does not justify overt military action." They made
it clear that the United States should not establish military forces on
the island even "in the event that diplomatic and economic steps prove
unsuccessful to prevent Communist domination, [and] so long as the
present disparity between our military strength and our global obliga-

16. PPS 53, "U.S. Policy Toward Formosa and the Pescadors," memorandum by Kennan, canceled on 6 July 1949 (a note stated that the view would be submitted by Kennan
in a personal memorandum), in *FRUS: 1949*, 9:356–59 [emphasis added].

17. Stuart to Acheson, 6 June 1949 in *FRUS: 1949*, 8:751.

18. Memorandum by Robert A. Fearey of the Office of Northeast Asian Affairs, 2 November 1949, in *FRUS: 1949*, 8:894.

19. Gaddis, *The Long Peace*, pp. 82–83. Also see Robert M. Blum, *Drawing the Line: The
Origins of the American Containment Policy in East Asia* (New York, 1982), pp. 178–79.

tion exists."[20] But they suggested in December that some military measures, "short of the dispatch of a major force," should be undertaken to support "U.S. political, economic and psychological measures now under way." These measures would include "a modest well-directed, and closely supervised program of military aid to the anti-Communist government in Taiwan." To this end, they proposed to direct MacArthur "with the assistance of the commander, the 7th Task Fleet, to make an immediate survey of the nature and extent of the military assistance required in Formosa in order to hold Formosa against attack."[21] Chairman of Joint Chiefs of Staff Omar N. Bradley did not regard the JCS positions as inconsistent. He reminded Acheson on 29 December of an earlier proposal to station a minor naval force in Taiwan and to provide military assistance to the Nationalists. This recent JCS recommendation, Bradley stressed, was "based on the existence of funds under Section 307 of the Military Assistance Act" enacted on 6 October 1949.[22]

State Department officials insisted on nonmilitary means to prevent the fall of Taiwan. Acheson particularly stressed that a show of force on the island would generate an outcome politically unfavorable to U.S. policy toward China as a whole. At a State Department meeting in September, the Secretary of State doubted the feasibility of Kennan's proposal for immediate action on the grounds that it would "nullify our effort to exploit Chinese irredentist sentiment with respect to the Soviet action in the North [China]." In early November, Acheson secured a consensus in the State Department that "we should not seek to detach Formosa from the Communist-controlled mainland either by the application of force or by seeking jurisdiction over the island through a trusteeship arrangement on behalf of Formosan self-government."[23]

Communist Chinese forces advanced toward the southeastern coast of China in late 1949; an attack on Taiwan seemed inevitable. The State Department began preparing to accept a possible loss of Taiwan. A "Policy Information Paper—Formosa" proposed on 23 December that

20. JCS to Johnson, 17 August 1949, enclosed in NSC 37/7, 22 August 1949, p. 377.

21. JCS to Johnson, 23 December 1949, enclosed in NSC 37/9, "Possible United States Military Action toward Taiwan Not Involving Major Military Force," 27 December 1949, in *FRUS: 1949*, 9:460–61.

22. Memorandum by Acheson, 29 December 1949, in *FRUS: 1949*, 9:464.

23. Report by Charles Yost to Jessup, 16 September 1949, in *FRUS: 1949*, 7:1204–07; NSC 37/8, "The Position of the United States with Respect to Formosa," 6 October 1949, ibid., pp. 392–97; memorandum by Charlton Ogburn, Jr., "Decisions Reached by Consensus at the Meeting with the Secretary and the Consultants of the Far East," 2 November 1949, ibid., p. 161.

the administration should make it clear to the public that "Formosa is exclusively the responsibility of the Chinese Government." Late that month, Acheson tried to persuade the Joint Chiefs that, since the political price was too high to pay for protecting Taiwan, "it was better to let Formosa go for political reasons." On 5 January 1950, Acheson also tried to convince Senators Smith and Knowland that Taiwan was of insufficient strategic importance to require U.S. military protection. He urged them to accept that the United States could do nothing to prevent the fall of the island.[24]

Acheson finally had Truman's endorsement of the State Department position. The president announced on 5 January 1950, "The U.S. has no predatory designs on Formosa. . . . The U.S. has no desire to obtain special rights or privileges or to establish military bases on Formosa at this time. Nor does it have any intention of utilizing its armed forces to interfere in the present situation." Acheson further clarified this policy at a press conference on that day. It is interesting that he explained the phrase "at this time" as "a recognition of the fact that, in the likely and unhappy event that our forces might be attacked in the Far East, the U.S. must be completely free to take whatever action in whatever area is necessary for its own security."[25]

Obviously, U.S. Taiwan policy was consistent with U.S. strategic thinking toward the Far East at that time. Washington officials generally believed that since the Soviet Union would not challenge U.S. security interests militarily in the near future, a Communist-controlled Taiwan would be at worst a long-term threat to U.S. security. It could only endanger U.S. interests in the event of war if the Soviets were able to use it. To deter such a long-term and uncertain threat, U.S. strategists understood, a show of military strength in Taiwan would entail too many political risks and difficulties. Acheson explained on 29 December that it would first involve "U.S. prestige in another failure for all to see," and then "risk giving the Soviets a chance of bringing us before the [UN] Security Council." The United States, therefore, could not pay the price when "there does not appear to be demonstrated a claim that the loss of Formosa really breaches our defense."[26] But if unexpected changes occurred, what would the United States do with Taiwan?

24. "Policy Information Paper—Formosa," 23 December 1949, in *Military Status in the Far East*, U.S. Senate (Washington, D.C., 1951), p. 668; memorandum by Acheson, 29 December 1949, pp. 463–67; memorandum by Acheson, 5 January 1950, in *FRUS: 1950*, 6:258–63.

25. U.S. Department of State, *Department of State Bulletin*, 16 January 1950, pp. 79 and 81.

26. Memorandum by Acheson, 29 December 1949, pp. 465–67.

Six months after the Truman-Acheson proclamation that the United States would not occupy or defend Taiwan, Truman decided to announce publicly on 27 June 1950 that his administration would send the U.S. Seventh Fleet to the Taiwan Strait to prevent both an attack on Taiwan from the mainland and an attack from Taiwan against the mainland.[27] This was one of the first actions the administration undertook after the outbreak of the Korean War. Such a dramatic change of U.S. policy, as Senator H. Alexander Smith explained on the next day, was "God-guided" for the purpose of saving Chiang Kai-shek.[28] Nevertheless, a more careful examination of U.S. policy considerations in the spring of 1950 would suggest that other elements were of far more immediate significance.

U.S. threat perception changed in the spring of 1950. As Truman pointed out, "The attack upon Korea makes it plain beyond all doubt that Communism has passed beyond the use of subversion to conquer independent nations and will now use armed invasion and war. In these circumstances, the occupation of Formosa by Communist forces would be a *direct threat* to the security of the Pacific area and to United States forces performing their lawful and necessary functions in that area."[29] This was a shift in Washington's thinking on the Soviet threat in general and Taiwan in particular. What had made this change possible?

One element was the conviction that the Soviet Union had become more likely to apply military force—not just economic or political pressure—to further its expansion. Paul H. Nitze, who had replaced George F. Kennan as the director of the Policy Planning Staff at the beginning of 1950, was the main advocate of this assessment. Nitze did not accept Kennan's assertion that the Soviet threats would be primarily political and economic in character. Why did Nitze perceive imminent military threats from the Soviet Union?

First, Nitze based his perception on the idea of "soft-spots" in the Soviet-American strategic confrontation. He explained in February that the USSR was consolidating its previous gains in some areas, especially Western Europe. But recent Soviet moves, particularly in the Far East, demonstrated that the Soviets had started to look into "soft spots" and to seize "every opportunity to move into a vacuum area or to exploit completely the momentum of a successful development."

27. *FRUS: 1950*, 7:202–3.
28. H. Alexander Smith Diary, 28 June 1950, Smith Papers, Box 282, Seeley Mudd Library, Princeton University; also cited in Gaddis, *The Long Peace*, p. 87.
29. Statement issued by the president, 27 June 1950, pp. 202–3 [emphasis added].

The "soft spots," in Nitze's view, included "Indochina, Berlin, Austria, Korea," all areas where the U.S. deterrent was weak, and where opportunities existed for Soviet expansion.[30]

Second, historical precedents, Nitze maintained, were by no means sufficient to judge the nature of Soviet policymaking. He argued at a PPS meeting in February that "some of the basic elements of Communist dogma no longer hold." He asserted that the Soviets no longer believed "that the communist bastion has infinite time in which to achieve its purpose, that capitalist nations carry within themselves the seeds of their own destruction which require watering but not planting by the Soviet Union, that the Red Army is [to be] used only when a revolutionary atmosphere makes the situation right for the coup de grace." Nitze concluded that "there appears no reason to assume that the USSR will in the future necessarily make a sharp distinction between 'military aggression' and measures short of military aggression." He also argued that Moscow's faith in the inevitable collapse of capitalism was not a passive faith in automatic historical evolution but "a messianic faith that not only spurs the USSR to assist the transformation of the Marxist blueprint into reality, but also gives the Soviet leaders a sense of confidence that in whatever particular course they follow they are riding the wave of the future."[31]

Third, Nitze believed that the Kremlin had recently become more confident because of the increase of its strategic power. Early in February, he pointed out that "[the Soviet Union] has developed an A bomb; it has achieved the prewar level of production and offered solid economic successes; [and] it has made progress in consolidating its control of the European satellites." The Nitze-directed study, NSC 68, submitted on 7 April 1950, presented a detailed and systematic calculation of Soviet military, economic, and political capabilities. The drafters of the document explicitly believed in a correlation between Soviet aggressive intentions and the increase of Soviet strategic capabilities.[32]

Fourth, Nitze asserted that the present U.S. strategy of containment, which was strategically defensive in the East and offensive in the West, might mislead the Kremlin concerning U.S. intentions. He bluntly warned in NSC 68 that "in the content of present polarization of power between the U.S. and the USSR, a defeat of free institutions anywhere is a defeat everywhere." The implication was that a military strategy of

30. Study by Nitze, "Recent Soviet Moves—Conclusion," 8 February 1950, in *FRUS: 1950*, 1:146–47.

31. Record of the eighth meeting (1950) of the Policy Planning Staff, 2 February 1950, in *FRUS: 1950*, 1:142–43; Nitze, "Recent Soviet Moves," p. 145.

32. Nitze, "Recent Soviet Moves," p. 146. Also see NSC 68, 7 April 1950, in *FRUS: 1950*, 1:248–53.

defending selected strong points, especially the offshore defensive perimeter, would no longer be able to deter the Russians from overt military action in the areas excluded from the defense system.[33]

Other American officials besides Nitze were increasingly concerned about the possibility of a Soviet-occupied Taiwan. Early in the spring of 1950, Walter P. McConaughy, consul general in Shanghai, reported that the Soviet Union would provide the Chinese Communists with "Taiwan invasion equipment (mainly planes)." Retired admiral Charles M. Cooke, then living in Taiwan, repeatedly supplied Mac-Arthur and Admiral Forrest S. Sherman, chief of naval operations, with information regarding a Soviet Air Force buildup along the China coast. In early May, he explicitly pointed out that "if Formosa is lost to the [Chinese] Communists, which means to the Russians, [it] means further the setting up of a Russian jet plane air strength in Formosa." To him, this meant that "World War III sooner or later becomes inevitable." McConaughy also noted in June that there were already three thousand Soviets who had arrived in the Shanghai area by April, and that about half of them were "military, consisting for the most part of air force personnel, including the crews and technicians requisite to ground installations." With "widespread Soviet aid to the Chinese Communists," U.S. military observers in the Far East anticipated, "the chances for a successful defense of Taiwan are very slight."[34] The Far East Command, too, seemed to be concerned about Taiwan. In his memorandum to the Joint Chiefs on 29 May, MacArthur pointed out: "In the event of war between the United States and the USSR, Formosa's value to the Communists is the equivalent of an unsinkable aircraft carrier and submarine tender, ideally located to accomplish Soviet strategy as well as to checkmate the offensive capabilities of the central and southern positions of the FEC [Far Eastern Command] front line."[35]

Meanwhile, concerns about an immediate Chinese Communist attack on Taiwan were mounting in Washington. A CIA intelligence report of 22 March estimated that the PRC possessed the capability to seize Taiwan in 1950, and "would probably do so during the period of June–December." Robert C. Strong, chargé d'affaires at Shanghai, pointed out in April that Chinese Communist attack on Taiwan would

---

33. NSC 68, 7 April 1950, pp. 288, and 237–39. Also see John Lewis Gaddis, *Strategies of Containment: A Critical Appraisal of Postwar American National Security Policy* (New York, 1982), p. 91.

34. McConaughy to Acheson, 21 January 1950, in *FRUS: 1950*, 6:291; Cooke to Mac-Arthur, 2 May 1950, cited in Gaddis, *The Long Peace*, p. 86; memorandum by Ogburn, 2 June 1950, in *FRUS: 1950*, 6:355; Rusk to Acheson, 26 April 1950, ibid., p. 333.

35. MacArthur to the Department of the Army, 29 May 1950, cited in Gaddis, *The Long Peace*, p. 86.

be more likely in the coming "August weather . . . until the end of typhoon season in late October or November." He noted that the PLA would be able to transport the invading forces "in variety of powered vessels from good-sized steamers to coastal vessels to river vessels, LSTs and landing craft of their own construction, protected by [their] own naval vessels and aircraft." In following month, Strong even warned that a PLA attack on the island would come between 15 June and the end of July. Secretary of Defense Louis Johnson also showed keen concern. He noticed that during June, the PLA had increased its strength opposite Taiwan from "slightly more than 40,000 to approximately 156,000, backed by a force of some 300,000 additional troops."[36]

Washington officials evidently believed that the Soviets might start their military challenges to "soft spots" in the Far East and that Taiwan might be one such "spot" on the Soviet list. How could the United States prevent the Communists from taking military action? One answer was to strengthen American deterrence immediately. On the concluding section of NSC 68, Nitze suggested that "the U.S. must substantially increase general air, ground, and sea strength, atomic capabilities, and air and civilian defenses to *deter* war and to provide reasonable assurance, in the event of war, that it could survive the initial blow and go on to the eventual attainment of its objectives."[37] It seems that Acheson accepted Nitze's proposition. From February to May, the secretary of state spoke on several occasions to the American public, repeatedly elaborating the theme that an increase of American deterrent strength was badly needed to persuade the Soviets not to challenge the status quo. "What we expected to achieve by the creation of strength throughout the free world—military, economic and political—to replace the inviting weak spots offered to Soviet probing," Acheson asserted, "was to diminish further the possibility of war, [and] to prevent 'settlements by default' to Soviet pressures." He claimed that actions were much more important than words. Acheson, though, made no indication of what the United States would specifically do to enhance military deterrence in Taiwan.[38]

To deter the anticipated invasion, John Foster Dulles, a prominent Republican spokesman on foreign policy and then a special consultant to Acheson on the Japanese peace treaty, proposed to establish a U.S.

36. ORE 75-50, CIA Reappraisal of Formosa, 20 March 1950, enclosed in Rusk to Acheson, 17 April 1950, in *FRUS: 1950*, 6:330; Strong to Acheson, 27 April 1950, ibid., p. 337; Strong to Acheson, 17 May 1950, ibid., p. 340; U.S. Senate, *The Military Situation in the Far East* (Washington, D.C., 1951), pt. 4, p. 2621.

37. NSC 68, 7 April 1950, pp. 287–88 [emphasis added].

38. Dean Acheson, *Present at the Creation: My Years in the State Department* (New York, 1969), pp. 378–81.

military presence on Taiwan. He pointed out in May that "if our conduct indicates a continuing disposition to fall back and allow doubtful areas to fall under Soviet Communist control," the Unites States would lose its credibility to deter the Soviet Communist expansion in that area. For him, further inaction in Taiwan "will be everywhere interpreted that we are making another retreat because we do not dare to risk war." Therefore, "we [should] quickly take a dramatic and strong stand that shows our confidence and resolution." Dulles calculated that it was within U.S. power to take a strong stand in Taiwan, because "it is not subject to the immediate influence of Soviet land power. It is close to our naval and air power. It is occupied by the remnants of the non-Communists who have traditionally been our friends and allies. . . . It is greatly menaced by a joint Chinese-Russian expedition in formation." Dean Rusk, then assistant secretary of state for Far Eastern affairs, fully concurred with Dulles. On 30 May, he reminded State Department Far Eastern specialists that both "world and domestic opinion are unhappy with the lack of forthright American action in Taiwan." To him, the island "presents a plausible place to 'draw the line.' "[39]

Apparently, both Dulles and Rusk had weighed the risks of U.S. military action in Taiwan. They thought that a strong U.S. stand would have political complications with American and world opinion, as well as with the Chinese Nationalists in Taiwan, and probably would also stir up irredentist sentiment in China. They believed that a show of U.S. military force there could "slightly" increase the risk of war with the Soviets. How to avoid these risks? Dulles's solution was to announce the "neutralization" of the Taiwan Strait by the U.S. Navy. In his 18 May memorandum he argued that the United States should make it known to the public that "it would neutralize Formosa, not permitting it either to be taken by the Communists or to be used as a base of military operations against the mainland, that is the decision which we would certainly maintain, short of open war by the Soviet Union." By doing so, Dulles asserted, all the calculated political and military risks would be only of a "secondary" importance. Rusk had earlier proposed to go through UN "trusteeship." His formula was that Chiang should be invited to appeal for U.S. responsibility, and the United States would then back the appeal and, as Rusk put it, "ready the fleet to prevent any assumed attack on Formosa while the move for

39. Memorandum by Dulles, 18 May 1950, in *FRUS: 1950*, 1:314–16; Rusk to Acheson, 30 May 1950, enclosed in Howe to W. Park Armstrong, special assistant to Acheson for intelligence and research, 31 May 1950, ibid., 6:347–51. (In his memorandum Rusk quotes Dulles's 18 May memorandum verbatim.)

trusteeship was pending." But by the end of May, Rusk had dropped this plan and endorsed Dulles's neutralization proposal.[40]

By June 1950, it seems that administration officials felt it imperative that the United States do something vigorous to deny Taiwan to the Communists. As General MacArthur asserted on 14 June, "There can be no doubt but that the eventual fate of Formosa rests with the U.S."[41] But nobody was certain when it would be appropriate to take such a strong stand. The Korean War, which broke out suddenly on June 25, erased any doubts. It was then clear to Washington officials that the "Russians" were activating their military challenges. On that day, the Estimates Group of the Office of Intelligence Research issued a special report on Soviet intentions in the Korean conflict. It pointed out that the Soviets sought (1) to test the U.S. resolve, (2) to eliminate the U.S. salient in Korea in order to deny the United States a dry-land staging area for an "attack on either Soviet Far Eastern territories or China," and (3) to discourage the Japanese from aligning themselves with the United States.[42] On that same day, Acheson locked himself in his office for an hour or two, giving serious "thought" to the situation. He concluded that the North Korean attack was an open challenge to the Korean status quo, which was "an area of great importance to the security of . . . occupied Japan." To retreat before this challenge, he believed, "would be highly destructive of the power and the prestige of the United States." Acheson later explained, "By prestige, I mean the shadow cast by power, which is of great deterrence importance."[43]

In assessing the Korean situation, Washington policymakers repeatedly raised the Taiwan question in meetings at the Blair House on 25, 26, and 27 June. Secretary of Defense Johnson insisted that relatively the security of the U.S. was more affected by Formosa than Korea. At the 25 June meeting, JCS chairman Bradley read MacArthur's memorandum of 14 June, which identified Taiwan as the target of the next Soviet-directed aggression. Answering Truman's query about the Soviet Air Force in the Far East, General Hoyt S. Vandenberg, chief of staff of the U.S. Air Force, pointed out that "a considerable number of Russian jets are already based on Shanghai," implying that the Chinese Communists might use these jets in their assault on Taiwan. Linking the Taiwan question with the Korean conflict, administration officials all agreed that the United States should immediately show

40. Rusk to Acheson, 30 May 1950, pp. 348–49.

41. MacArthur to the JCS, 14 June 1950, enclosed in Sebald to Acheson, 22 June 1950, in *FRUS: 1950*, 6:366–67.

42. Intelligence Estimate by the Estimate Group, Office of Intelligence Research, 25 June 1950, in *FRUS: 1950*, 7:148–54.

43. Acheson, *Present at the Creation*, p. 405.

military force in Taiwan. Acheson, following the Dulles-Rusk plan, proposed dispatching the Seventh Fleet to neutralize the Strait, preventing either a Chinese Communist attack on the island or a Chinese Nationalist attack on the mainland.[44] Truman approved this action, announced it publicly on 27 June and ordered the dispatch of the fleet to the Strait under MacArthur's command three days later.[45] By these actions, Washington clearly sought to establish explicit deterrence in the Taiwan Strait.

It is important to note that U.S. strategists had different expectations concerning the role of the Seventh Fleet. Kennan, who had resigned but continued to advise Acheson on an informal basis, stressed that deterrence would largely depend on the fleet's fighting capability. In two memoranda to Acheson he argued that the Seventh Fleet should be capable of defending Taiwan without Nationalist support for two reasons: First, according to Kennan's sources, the Chinese Communist threat to attack Taiwan was imminent. The Communists had great concentrations of shipping along the coast opposite Taiwan; they had recently appointed their best generals to command there; and the typhoon season was approaching, providing an incentive for the PLA to speed up its amphibious operations. Second, the Chinese Nationalists in Taiwan, in Kennan's judgment, were totally unreliable. He saw Chiang continuing to treat his armed forces as the key to his own political interests rather than to the best interests of the defense of the island. Chiang's forces would be incapable of any effective resistance if any sizable PLA force succeeded in landing. For Kennan, the fleet, to be a credible deterrent, should show its readiness for counterattack. But as he complained in a memo to Acheson, "[I] cannot learn that we have any surface vessels whatever in the Formosa Strait or in the immediate vicinity," and "our own reconnaissance" was in an "inadequate status." Kennan thus urged Acheson to bring this situation to Truman's attention, and also proposed that "we must consider demanding [from] the Generalissimo [Chiang] an entirely different arrangement which would give us adequate control over his forces" in defending Taiwan.[46]

Military strategists undoubtedly expected the fleet to be fully deployed as a military threat. The Joint Chiefs proposed in late July that it should be permitted to assist the Chinese Nationalists in taking preventive action against the mainland. They calculated that "the success-

44. Memorandum by Jessup, 25 June 1950, in *FRUS: 1950*, 7:151–59.
45. JCS to MacArthur, 29 June 1950, in *FRUS: 1950*, 7:240–41.
46. Kennan to Acheson, 17 July 1950, Department of State (SD) Decimal Files, Record Group (RG) 59, Box 4258, 7.94A.5/7–1750, Diplomatic Branch, National Archives; Kennan to Acheson, 24 July 1950, ibid., SD7.94A.5/7–2450.

ful accomplishment of the mission assigned to the 7th Fleet and the denial of Formosa to the Communists is seriously hazarded by Chinese Communist capabilities" unless the United States would "permit the National Government to employ its military forces in defensive measures to prevent Communist amphibious concentrations directed against Formosa or the Pescadores." The Chiefs added, "such measures should include attacks on such concentrations and mining of those mainland water areas from which such an [amphibious] assault would be staged." Secretary of Defense Johnson concurred and urged Acheson to submit the proposal to Truman.[47] MacArthur "regretted" but "accepted" the recommendation. He was convinced that the Seventh Fleet, together with American air power—the aircraft under his own command, and especially, those based in Okinawa and the Philippines—could eventually destroy any Chinese Communist troops attempting to invade Taiwan.[48]

Acheson, however, insisted that the fleet was to neutralize the Strait and not to provoke another conflict. He asserted that deploying the fleet would simply function as a symbol of U.S. commitment to the defense of Taiwan. Thus, the deterrent effect of the Seventh Fleet, in his view, depended more on its announced mission than on its strength or even its actual presence in the Strait.[49] Acheson strongly opposed permitting or supporting KMT air strikes on the Communist Chinese troop concentrations and military installations, regarding it as "unacceptable from a foreign policy point of view." He reminded Secretary of Defense Johnson on 31 July that "we are not at war with Communist China nor do we wish to become involved in hostilities with Chinese Communist forces." He was particularly concerned that "our commitment may already be greater than our present capabilities; the action recommended would extend our involvement." Even worse, Acheson asserted, was the possibility that a preventive action would provoke a Chinese Communist attack on Taiwan. Citing an intelligence estimate of 27 July that "there is no *reliable* information that an attack on Taiwan is imminent," Acheson believed that "the action recommended would convert the risk into a certainty."[50]

Despite these efforts, the Truman administration had great difficulty avoiding the appearance of partiality in the Chinese civil war. On 29

47. JCS to Johnson 28 July 1950, enclosed in Johnson to Acheson, 29 July 1950, in *FRUS: 1950*, 6:401.
48. Memorandum of conversations with MacArthur by W. Averell Harriman, 6–8 August 1950, in *FRUS: 1950*, 6:429. Also see Johnson to Acheson, 29 July 1950, p. 401. Johnson noted that MacArthur "completely concurred with the recommendation."
49. Acheson to the embassy in China [Taiwan], 8 November 1950, in *FRUS: 1950*, 6:552.
50. Acheson to Johnson, 31 July 1950, in *FRUS: 1950*, 6:402–3 [emphasis in original].

June, KMT ambassador V. K. Wellington Koo informed the State Department that more than twenty unidentified U.S. planes had flown over Taiwan's military installations and caused the Nationalist Air Force to scramble. Koo requested establishment of a liaison group between the U.S. Seventh Fleet and the KMT Air Force. On 17 July, the Nationalists also asked Washington to permit KMT reconnaissance flights along the mainland coast. The administration could hardly turn down these requests.[51] In August Truman, indeed, had to approve dispatching a military mission to survey Nationalist capabilities and material needs for the defense of Taiwan. Later that month, he allocated to the Department of Defense the sum of $14,344,500 to be used for military aid to Taiwan.[52] During MacArthur's visit to Taiwan on 31 July, a joint announcement between the general and Chiang was released to the public, implying that MacArthur had made military arrangements with Chiang. Taipei hailed MacArthur's visit as a step toward the abandonment of U.S. neutrality in the Taiwan Strait.[53]

The administration also had difficulty in securing the cooperation of allies—especially Britain—with its Taiwan policy. Talks with the British began on 10 August 1950, primarily focusing on two issues: U.S. military action in the Taiwan Strait and a multilateral settlement of Taiwan's status through the United Nations. The British supported the interposition of the Seventh Fleet and U.S. military aid to Taiwan because of their fear that the Korean conflict might expand to Hong Kong.[54] But British officials disagreed with the U.S. proposal for a UN plebiscite on Taiwan. They thought it was impractical, for it would invariably risk a forcible resistance from the Nationalists. In their judgment, as long as the crisis continued to exist in the Taiwan area, military neutralization by the United States alone should be maintained.[55] Finally, the two governments reached a compromise: to create a UN commission to investigate the Taiwan problem that would submit its recommendation to the UN General Assembly.[56] Indeed, the

51. Memorandum of conversation with Koo [Ambassador] by Fulton Freeman, 29 June 1950, Decimal Files, SD794A.00/6–2950; Acheson to Johnson, 31 July 1950, pp. 404–5.

52. NSC 37/10, "Immediate US Courses of Action with Respect to Formosa," 3 August 1950, in *FRUS: 1950*, 6:413–14; Truman to Acheson, 25 August 1950, ibid., p. 414 n. 4.

53. Political Report on Formosa, 1 November 1950, Karl Lott Rankin Papers, Box 14, Chiang Kai-shek file, Seeley Mudd Library, Princeton University; Strong to Acheson, 4 August 1950, *FRUS: 1950*, 6:417–18.

54. Memorandum from Warren Matthews to Acheson, 30 August 1950, Decimal Files, SD794A.00/8–3050.

55. Telegram for Warren R. Austin (U.S. ambassador to the UN), 29 August 1950, Decimal Files, SD794A.00/8–2950; memorandum by Merchant, 29 August 1950, ibid., SD611.94/8–2950.

56. Memorandum by Matthews, 30 August 1950, Decimal Files, SD794A.00/8–3052. This was also a main proposal of the draft resolution for the UN session.

administration had to admit that its attempt to seek a multilateral settlement on Taiwan to back up its military action of denying the island to the Communists had turned out to be fruitless.[57]

In spite of—or in response to—U.S. military action in the Taiwan Strait, there was no sign of immediate attack from the mainland. But at no point did the Truman administration consider moving the fleet out of the Strait as the Korean War intensified. The status of Taiwan was left uncertain and no one realized at that time that it would remain that way for decades to come.

III

Did the interposition of the Seventh Fleet deter the People's Republic from attacking Taiwan? The answer largely depends on the answers to several other related questions: How much strategic importance had Taiwan assumed for the CCP? How did the CCP perceive U.S. intentions regarding Taiwan? Had the PLA prepared to attack Taiwan? What were the actual prospects of giving the Soviets military base rights on Taiwan if the PRC took it? And how did Beijing react to U.S. neutralization of the Taiwan Strait?

As early as the spring of 1949, the CCP leadership had begun considering the importance of Taiwan. It is important to note that it consistently stressed two main themes: First, that the United States, faced with failure in China, would seek to bring the island within its sphere of influence in order to have it as a stepping-stone for a future invasion of China. Second, that the KMT, foreseeing its eventual defeat on the mainland, would by all means try to turn the island into its final stronghold under U.S. military protection in order to gain breathing time for its own return in the future. *Xinhua* (New China)—the CCP's official news agency—first elaborated these two themes on 15 March 1949, and repeatedly stressed them throughout the summer of 1950.[58] The Chinese Communists clearly understood that either possibility would forestall their final victory over the Nationalists.

How did the CCP leaders develop such a position? They assumed that Taiwan was strategically important to the United States. The CCP noticed in March 1949 that Truman had endorsed a proposal of the National Security Council to build a defense system linking Taiwan and

---

57. Jessup minutes, Acheson–Sir Oliver Franks conversation, 7 December 1950, in *FRUS: 1950*, 6:1452–53, and 1455–56.

58. Xinhua News Agency, "The Chinese People Must Liberate Taiwan," *Xinhua Yuebao*, 15 March 1949, p. 43, and "Carry on Our Fighting to Taiwan and Liberate the Taiwanese People," ibid., 4 September 1949, p.4; and Wang Mingzhi, "Taiwan Is Chinese People's Taiwan," ibid., p. 45.

Hainan—another major island in South China Sea—"at all costs" and that Washington had already started the "extensive preparations" to this end.[59] The reason the United States was building such a defense system, the Chinese Communists believed, was that Washington was seeking not only to encircle China but to resurrect the "Great East Asian Co-prosperity Sphere" of Imperial Japan in a new disguise. The CCP press pointed out that Taiwan, under "imperialist control," would be "an unsinkable aircraft carrier" for U.S. military expansion in the Far East.[60] Chiang' Kai-shek's visit to Manila in July, in their view, was evidence of Washington's attempt to combine Taiwan, South Korea, and the Philippines into an anticommunist Pacific alliance. Such an alliance, the Chinese Communists argued, would be a counterrevolutionary cordon sanitaire under American direction with "Taiwan at the middle of the line extending from Japan in the north to the Philippines in the south, from which it would then extend through Indonesia toward India."[61] The Chinese Communists thus watched closely the Baguio Conference in December 1949, attended by Myron Cowen, the U.S. ambassador to the Philippines, Chen Ziping, Chiang's envoy to Manila, and the Philippines President Elpidio Quirino. The CCP inferred that the conference sought to discuss coordinating plans of defense and the covert shipment of U.S. arms to Taiwan via the Philippines.[62]

The CCP also believed that Washington was ambivalent regarding Taiwan's legal status because it was still looking for a pretext to occupy the island. The CCP press repeatedly pointed out that the Truman administration had cast doubts on the status of Taiwan as Chinese territory. One example was MacArthur's public statement that until Taiwan's status had been determined by a peace treaty with Japan the island was a piece of surrendered Japanese territory, and therefore should be under his jurisdiction as the commander of allied occupation forces in Japan. The CCP leadership saw MacArthur's statement as a U.S. attempt to keep its options open for the future control of Taiwan.[63] The CCP also noted that the United States was promoting the Taiwanese independence movement. Chinese Communist newspapers pointed out in September 1949 that the two brothers known in

59. Wang Mingzhi, "Taiwan Is Chinese People's Taiwan," p. 46.
60. *Dagongbao*, Shanghai edition, 29 August 1949, p. 2. It is still unclear whether the CCP press deliberately echoed MacArthur's use of this phrase or the Chinese Communists thought of it themselves.
61. *Wenhuibao*, Shanghai edition, 10 August 1949, p. 2.
62. *Wenhuibao*, Shanghai edition, 4 January 1950, p. 1.
63. Xinhua News Agency, "The Chinese People Must Liberate Taiwan," p. 43, and "Carry on Our Fighting to Taiwan and Liberate the Taiwanese People," 4 September 1949, p. 44.

the west as Joshua and Thomas Liao, the leaders of the movement, were working under the direction of MacArthur, and that the Truman administration intended to make Chen Cheng, nationalist governor of Taiwan, "Syngman Rhee the Second." The papers claimed that the United States was "conspiring" with such a separatist movement to create another opportunity to take over Taiwan.[64]

The Chinese Communists, indeed, believed that the United States had actually supported KMT offensive activities in the Taiwan area. The CCP propaganda network asserted that Washington was supporting Chiang's resistance along the China coast because it was part of the U.S. economic blockade against the new China. On 20 July 1949, the Chinese Nationalists had proclaimed a naval blockade against shipping to the Communist-controlled areas. Although U.S. merchant vessels were intercepted and held to be in violation of the blockade, the CCP noted, Washington did not object.[65] The CCP also believed that the United States supported indiscriminate bombing raids by the KMT Air Force from Taiwan against Shanghai and other coastal cities. One piece of evidence was that the KMT had used American-supplied aircraft, B-24 "Liberators," in the raids: twelve such bombers were used against Shanghai on 25 January and 6 February 1950. During these raids, a major American-owned electricity plant, the Shanghai Power and Electricity Company, was hit. The CCP reasoned that the KMT had to have had Washington's approval, otherwise it would not have dared to attack American property.[66]

Moreover, reports directly from Communist intelligence sources in Taiwan emphasized that U.S. military activities had greatly increased in the Taiwan area. A report pointed out in September 1949 that the United States had recently undertaken intensified military activities in Taiwan, including: frequent U.S. Air Force visits and overflights "to make geographic surveys of the island"; flights between Taiwan and air bases in the Philippines "to test air movement above the Pacific"; and the buildup of a U.S. air base in Pingdong [P'ing-tung]—a coastal city on Taiwan—occupied by the U.S. Thirteenth Air Corps, where the pilots were undergoing extensive training to conduct air strikes if needed in the Taiwan Strait.[67] Other information indicated in March

64. Xinhua News Agency, "Carry on Our Fighting to Taiwan and Liberate the Taiwanese People," 4 September 1949, p. 44.

65. *Jiefang Ribao* [The Liberation Daily], 27 July 1949, p. 1. Also see Chen Zhaowu, "The U.S. Economic Blockade against China Is Doomed to Failure," *Shijie Zhishi*, 10 March 1951, pp. 5–7.

66. *Wenhuibao*, 10 February 1950, p. 3.

67. Editorial, "How the United States Has Conspired to Invade Taiwan," *Guangming Ribao*, 4 September 1949, reprinted in *Xinhua Yuebao*, September 1949, pp. 46–47.

1950 that the United States had dispatched twenty-five more combat aircraft to Taiwan and was assisting the construction of a new air base in the Zhoushan offshore islands for the purpose of bombing Beijing, Tianjin, Qingdao, Hankou, and Chongqing.[68]

Meanwhile, the CCP noted that the KMT had reorganized its line of resistance along the Southeast China coast in order to be favorably positioned for a future counterattack. The Nationalists had concentrated on building a chain of offshore defenses, within which Zhoushan, Xiamen (Amoy) and Jinmen/Mazu (Quemoy/Matsu), and Hainan formed three strong points. The KMT had already gathered sixty thousand soldiers on Zhoushan, ninety thousand on Xiamen and Jinmen/Mazu, and three-hundred thousand on Hainan. The main purpose, the CCP military calculated, was to "(1) construct an outer defense line off Taiwan, and (2) to retain stepping-stones for a future counteroffensive against the mainland."[69] Therefore, at the end of the Shanghai campaign (late August), the CCP Central Military Commission instructed the Third Field Army Command: "You must begin preparing to move into Fujian [province] immediately so that [we] can seize Fuzhou, Quanzhou, Zhangzhou and other key coastal cities in June and July and then prepare to attack Xiamen." The CMC aimed at wiping out the KMT forces on the offshore islands before these islands became bridgeheads in the event of future counterattack by the KMT and possibly coordinated by the United States.[70]

It is still not clear how much the CCP leaders, particularly Mao Zedong, really believed in an immediate U.S. threat in the Taiwan Strait. But it is fair to argue that they believed that the United States would seize Taiwan to make trouble along the China coast. Shortly after the People's Republic was founded in October 1949, the Beijing regime began preparing to counter this possible challenge. In a telegram of 31 October to the Fourth Field Army commander Lin Biao, Mao pointed out that "the focuses of our national defense are on three areas, centering around Tianjin, Shanghai, and Guangzhou." But he showed keener concern about the Northeast China coast, namely, the Tianjin area. It was not because an attack to that area was more likely, but because, as he explained to Lin, "we only have three [infantry] armies headed by Yang Chengwu and six class-two divisions in that area. If anything serious happens, we do not have enough troops for counterattack."[71]

68. *Wenhuibao*, 2 March 1950, p. 2.
69. See *JFJZS*, pp. 335–36.
70. CMC to the Third Field Army Command, late August 1949, cited in *JFJZS*, p. 336.
71. Telegram, Mao to Lin Biao, "Instructions on Reorganizing the Military Force," 31 October 1949, in *JGYLMWG* 1:106–7.

To counter possible threats to China's coast, Mao wanted immediate military preparations. In mid-October, he ordered the Nineteenth Group Army consisting of three infantry armies totaling 100,000 soldiers to gather in Baoji (a city near Tianjin) as "national defense mobile forces for reinforcement."[72] Meanwhile, he instructed Lin Biao that "after finishing the battles in Guangxi, the Fourth Field Army should dispatch five infantry armies to the Guangzhou area, mainly responsible for the defense of Guangdong and Guangxi [provinces], and should also send three armies to Henan [province] ready to reinforce the North China coast. The rest of the Fourth Field Army should gather at the railway lines of Hunan, Hubei, and Jiangxi [provinces] to be rapidly transported to either South or North China whenever necessary." Mao stressed that "at this point, the Third Field Army is only capable of defending the East China coast, particularly the Shanghai, Hangzhou, and Nanjing areas, [because] part of its force is assigned to preparing for the attack of Taiwan."[73] Moreover, the Central Military Commission decided in early August to form an anti-aircraft artillery army. In a telegram to Moscow on 6 August, the CCP leaders asked for 360 pieces of anti-aircraft artillery and requested the Soviet leaders to ship these guns to China immediately. The CCP leaders also thought it imperative to establish a modern navy and air force. "Our national defense will be consolidated," Mao announced at the opening session of the Chinese People's Political Consultative Conference (CPPCC) on 21 September, "and no imperialist will be allowed to invade our territory again." To this end, he declared, "Our people's armed forces must be preserved and developed with the heroic and tested People's Liberation Army as the foundation. We will not only have a powerful army but also a powerful air force and a powerful navy." In early October, Mao further claimed: "We must build a powerful navy to defend China's coast and effectively prohibit imperialist invasion."[74] Evidently, Mao and other leaders were preoccupied with defending the China coast to demonstrate CCP's readiness to counterattack against any possible military challenges.

There can be no doubt that the PRC intended to attack Taiwan; but not immediately. The PLA, mainly a light infantry army, lacked effective means—in particular, air support—to seize Taiwan. In early July

72. Telegram, Mao to Peng Dehuai, "On Combat Planning in Southeast and Northwest China," 13 October 1949 in *JGYLMWG* 1:54.

73. Telegram, Mao to Lin Biao, 31 October 1949, p. 107.

74. Telegram, CMC to Liu Shaoqi and Wang Jiaxiang in Moscow, 6 August 1949, in *Zhou Enlai Nianpu*, pp. 836–37; telegram, CMC to Liu and Wang, 11 August 1949, ibid., p. 837; Mao's speech at the Plenary Session of the CPPCC, 21 September 1949, in *SWM* 5:7; Mao's instructions to the Naval Command of the East China Military Region, 10 October 1949, in *DDZGHJ*, pp. 38–39.

1949, PLA commander-in-general Zhu De wrote to the CCP Secretariat urging them to accelerate the buildup of the PLA Air Force, which, he argued, would be central to the attack of Taiwan. To this end, he proposed to "send students to the Soviet Union for air force training so that they could be deployed in six months." Mao concurred with Zhu. In his letter to Zhou Enlai on 10 July, he explained: "We must begin planning the liberation of Taiwan. In addition to ground forces, [I think], the attack of Taiwan will mainly rely on an air force. With one of these two forces, the attack will succeed; with both, a complete victory is guaranteed." Mao was, however, aware that "it is unlikely that our air force would overpower the enemy air force in a short period of time (say, one year)." He thus directed that "we should consider sending three to four hundred people [to the Soviet Union] for six to eight months of air force training. Meanwhile, we will purchase one hundred aircraft [from the Soviet Union], which, together with the airplanes we have, will form an attacking force to support the landing operations of our ground forces. [If this plan goes well,] we should expect to seize Taiwan next summer." The CMC made it clear in its 26 July telegram to the Third Field Army Command, which was responsible for the attack of Taiwan, "the construction of an air force must be our top priority . . . so that we can have an air force combat ready in about one year."[75]

At this point, however, the CCP central leadership requested that the Third Field Army concentrate on destroying the KMT remnants on the offshore islands. The field commanders understood that the KMT force alone could not hold out for long. Militarily, the KMT was still in the weaker position. In August 1949, Chiang Kai-shek had already assembled 70,000 to 80,000 ground troops along the Fujian coast. This total would eventually rise to a maximum of 150,000 to 200,000. Chiang had also moved his air and naval forces to Taiwan. The CCP field commanders calculated that the Nationalists had not yet been able to fortify their entire front, and the more quickly the PLA forces advanced to the Southeast China coast, the less likely that the KMT troops would hold. The Third Field Army Command decided in late August 1949 to leave the Eighth Group Army in the Nanjing area and sent the Seventh Group Army to attack the Zhoushan islands of East Zhejiang province, the Tenth Group Army to Fujian, and the Ninth-Group Army consisting of four infantry armies, altogether fifteen

---

75. Zhu De to the CCP Secretariat, early July 1949, in *Zhu De Nianpu*, ed. Division of Central Archives and Manuscripts (Beijing, 1986), p. 330; Mao to Zhou Enlai, 10 July 1949, in *DDZGKJ*, p. 35; CMC to the Fourth Field Army Command, 26 July 1949, ibid., p. 35.

divisions, to the Shanghai area to rest and reorganize for the attack of Taiwan.[76]

The Third Field Army commanders were very optimistic. They believed that the morale of the KMT force was still low, and that a PLA advance would cause a panic that would dissolve the KMT line. They also believed that the KMT still had too many internal political problems to be able to mount a coordinated resistance. Any show of PLA troops would encourage uprisings against Chiang's regime, as had happened on the mainland.[77] Indeed, the Twenty-eighth, Twenty-ninth, and Thirty-first armies of the Tenth Group Army commanded by Ye Fei had won battles one after another in Fujian. They captured Fuzhou, a major KMT coastal naval base, on 17 August, which brought the PLA to a point about 120 nautical miles directly across the Taiwan Strait from Jilong, and breaking in part Taiwan's outer defense.[78] The Tenth Group Army also seized Xiamen—a peninsula in the Taiwan Strait—in mid-October, although with difficulties. Since this was the first test of the PLA's ability to stage a large-scale water-borne assault, its success greatly reinforced military commanders' optimism. They thought the KMT forces were nothing but a group of "scared birds." Group Army Commander Ye paid little attention to the campaign against Jinmen just offshore. Underestimating the enemy's strength, he only assigned seven regiments to that attack. The amphibious operation started on the evening of 24 October and ended in a total defeat with nine thousand PLA soldiers killed or captured by the KMT.[79]

When the news of the defeat reached Beijing, Mao was highly alarmed. A few days later, he himself drafted a report on behalf of the Central Military Commission and addressed it to all the PLA high commanders. "The main causes of the [Jinmen] failure," Mao pointed out, "include the underestimation of our enemy and recklessness. . . . The commanders did not pay enough attention to the preparations nor had an adequate assessment of the enemy's situation." Now that the failure had taught a good lesson, Mao urged, "no other operations against the offshore islands should be launched unless with a full and careful preparation, unless we are absolutely sure of victory." He particularly instructed that all PLA commanders "should now wake up and watch for possible reckless decisions as well as the tendency to

76. *JFJZS*, p. 336; Ye Fei, *Ye Fei Huiyilu* (Beijing, 1988), pp. 585–86 [hereafter *Ye Fei Memoirs*]. (General Ye was the commander of the Tenth Army Group of the Third Field Army.)

77. *Jiefang Ribao*, 29 July 1949, p. 3; *Dagongbao*, 29 August 1949, p. 1; *Jiefang Ribao*, 4 February 1950, p. 2; General Su Yu, first deputy commander of the Third Field Army, proclaimed on that day that the campaign to cross the Taiwan Strait would surely succeed.

78. *JFJZS*, pp. 337–38. Also see *DDZGJSGZ*, 1:222–25.

79. *JFJZS*, pp. 338–42. For Ye Fei's own account, see *Ye Fei Memoirs*, pp. 586–609.

underestimate our enemy, and should tell all our soldiers that our national liberation is not yet over and we shall certainly drive for it in a planned, steadfast, and patient manner."[80] Meanwhile, Mao cabled the CCP East China authorities to call off the scheduled mission of the Tenth Group Army to attack Chaozhou and Shantou, two small offshore islands near Xiamen. Also on 5 December, he stressed to Su Yu, first deputy commander of the Third Field Army, that "the timing of attacking the Zhoushan Islands should only be decided by [the Central Military Commission in] Beijing. It would be better to put it off till next spring." For this reason, he asked Su to come to Beijing for a briefing on the military situation.[81]

Mao then decided to postpone the Hainan campaign to which the Fifteenth Group Army of the Fourth Field Army was assigned. When Lin Biao reported on 10 December that his troops were ready to attack, Mao replied from Moscow that Lin should double-check all the preparations, and that the field commanders should fully study the lesson of the Jinmen failure. "Even though the enemy in Hainan may not be as strong as those in Jinmen," Mao pointed out, "you should by no means underestimate them. . . . I hope that you could talk with Su Yu and obtain the entire essence of his lesson so that we can avoid another Jinmen setback."[82] Probably afraid that the field commanders might not take his warning seriously enough, Mao sent another telegram to Lin Biao on 31 December, stressing once again that "the principle for the Hainan campaign should still be that we have to be absolutely sure of victory before we start attacking, and absolutely free of any hasty and reckless decision." He therefore ordered that "Deng Hua, Lai Chuanzhu, and Hong Xuezhi [the commanders of the Fifteenth Group Army] should go to the front immediately [to assess the situation for themselves]."[83] Mao was pleased when the Fourth Field Army postponed the scheduled attack. On 10 January 1950, he asked the leaders in Beijing to pass his suggestion to Lin Biao that the attack on Hainan should take place no earlier than late spring or early summer, provided that "sufficient motor vessels are constructed."[84]

80. Central Military Commission Report (drafted by Mao), "On the Lesson of the Failure at Jinmen," 29 October 1949, in *JGYLMWG* 1:100–101.

81. Letter, Mao to CCP East China authorities, 25 October 1949, in *JGYLMWG* 1:93; telegram, Mao to Su Yu, "On Designing Courses of Action on Attacking Zhoushan Island," 5 December 1949, ibid., p. 179.

82. Telegram, Mao to Lin Biao, "On Issues of the Amphibious Operations," 18 December 1949, in *JGYLMWG* 1:190–91.

83. Telegram, Mao to Lin Biao, "On the Principles of Attacking Hainan," 31 December 1949, in *JGYLMWG* 1:203.

84. Telegram, Mao to Lin Biao, "On the Problems of the Hainan Campaign," 10 January 1950, in *JGYLMWG* 1:228–29.

Under Mao's pressure, the field commanders took the preparations for the Hainan campaign very seriously. In early February 1950, the commanders met at the South China Military headquarters in Guangzhou to discuss how to better prepare. They agreed to observe the principle of "attempting a secret landing, landing in smaller numbers, and finally a large-scale amphibious landing." The conferees decided to have all the combat troops train intensively for these operations and to have as many motor vessels built as possible. Two months later, the preparations turned out to be very encouraging: both the Fortieth and Forty-third armies had mastered the basic landing technique; altogether 2,100 motor vessels were constructed and manned by six hundred skilled sailors; and more important, two successful secret landings in March had transported more than nine thousand soldiers onto Hainan island. The commanders thought that they would be ready for a final action sometime in April. Satisfied with the preparations, Mao and the Central Military Commission approved the action. The assault on Hainan started as a surprise attack on 16 April, and gained complete control of the island by 1 May after killing thirty-three thousand Nationalists and forcing the rest to retreat to Taiwan.[85]

While the Fourth Field Army was undertaking the Hainan campaign, the Third Field Army intensified its military activities along the Fujian coast. A large number of supply and transportation units were organized, and all the combat units conducted amphibious warfare training day and night. Ten thousand motor launches were under construction.[86] All these activities, however, were aimed to serve two purposes: (1) to tie up the enemy forces in the Fujian area in order to prevent the KMT from reinforcing Hainan; and (2) to further demonstrate the CCP's determination to seize Taiwan and the offshore islands. But no one in the Third Field Army headquarters had any idea of when to attack or whether the objective should be Jinmen again or Taiwan.

When Mao returned from Moscow in the early spring, he did not seem enthusiastic about seizing Taiwan in near future, even though he now had a military alliance with the Soviet Union. There is no evidence that Mao and Stalin made any deal regarding Taiwan. Stalin might even have pressured Mao not to attack Taiwan for fear of a vigorous reaction by the United States. The Soviets did dispatch an air force division to Shanghai in February–March 1950, but only at the re-

85. Minutes of the Guangdong Military Command meeting, early February 1950, cited in *JFJZS*, p. 358; Mao to Lin Biao, 12 February 1950, ibid. For the Hainan campaign, see ibid., pp. 359–62; and for the landing operation of the Fifteenth Group Army, see "Deng Hua," in *Jiefangjun Jiangling Zhuan*, ed. "Xinhuo Liaoyuan" Editorial Division, (Beijing, 1986), 7:26–28.
86. *Jiefang Ribao*, 4, 13, 16, and 19 February 1950.

quest of the Chinese Communists to strengthen that city's defense against KMT air raids. There is no indication that these Soviet jet fighters were to be used offensively, although they could have.[87]

At this time, however, Mao was seeking some other way to resolve the Taiwan problem. It happened that Zhang Zhizhong, a former KMT senior official and then adviser of national security for the People's Republic, had advocated a "peaceful solution." Though its real content is still unknown—perhaps a secret deal between the CCP and the anti-Chiang leaders in the KMT, for instance, Li Zhongren who recently resigned his acting presidency and emigrated to Hong Kong—the proposal evidently attracted Mao's attention because of its "peaceful" nature. In early March, Mao and the Central Party Committee agreed to let Zhang work on his plan. In his 11 March telegram to Zhang, Mao pointed out that "what you are working on is very important as far as our national victory is concerned, and I wish that you would try harder to succeed as early as possible."[88] Late that month, when Zhang wanted to discuss with Mao the details of his plan, Mao immediately ordered Guangzhou authorities to see to it that Zhang "arrived in Beijing quickly and safely."[89]

There is reason to believe that the Chinese Communist leadership decided in the spring of 1950 not to attack Taiwan. It is true that Mao had expected in July 1949 to have an air force ready by the summer of 1950 to support an attack on Taiwan, but there is no indication that the CCP actually set a timetable for the campaign.[90] It seems that the CCP had decided that an attack of Taiwan would be premature and that a large-scale military action against the island would probably provoke a U.S. counterattack either in the Taiwan Strait or elsewhere along the Chinese coast. Beijing therefore decided to settle for quickly eliminating the KMT remnants on the coast in order to gain a better military position to inhibit a potential U.S. threat, and postpone seizing Taiwan until conditions were more favorable. This strong sense of insecurity made the CCP leaders alert to changes in the Far East throughout the spring of 1950.

When the United States announced its intention to send the Seventh Fleet into the Taiwan Strait at the outbreak of the Korean War, Beijing authorities were highly alarmed. On 27 June, Zhou Enlai proclaimed that Washington's objective was to prevent the People's Republic from liberating Taiwan and was an act of aggression that the CCP leadership

---

87. *Nie Rongzhen Memoirs*, pp. 129–30; DDZGKJ, p. 78.
88. Telegram, Mao to Zhang Zhizhong, "On a Peaceful Solution to the Taiwan Problem," 11 March 1950, in *JGYLMWG* 1:271.
89. Telegram, Mao to Zhang Zhizhong, 20 March 1950, *JGYLMWG*, 1:281.
90. Letter, Mao to Zhou Enlai, 10 July, 1949 in *Zhou Enlai Nianpu*, p. 833.

had fully anticipated. He asserted that the United States had insti-
gated Syngman Rhee to initiate the Korean conflict as a *prelude* to
America's grand strategy of controlling Korea, Taiwan, Vietnam, and
the Philippines.[91] On the evening of 28 June, Mao addressed the State
Council, emphasizing the duplicity of Truman's statement of 5 January
1950, which had seemingly disavowed American designs on Taiwan.
He pointed out that the United States had now made an open declaration of its imperialist policy, thereby removing any pretense of non-
interference in Chinese internal affairs. Mao told the State Council that
China should not be intimidated by the U.S. action.[92]

Not trusting the Truman administration, the Chinese Communist
leaders could not believe that U.S. Seventh Fleet intended simply to
neutralize the Taiwan Strait. They could only assume that U.S. military
action in the area was imminent. The Central Military Commission
canceled all Third Field Army preparations to attack Taiwan and requested all the forces along the East China coast move to a completely
defensive posture. The CMC also ordered the Third Field Army to
speed up its combat preparations against the offshore islands still in
the hands of the KMT forces, assuming that U.S.-directed KMT remnants would otherwise use them as stepping-stones for the invasion of
the mainland.[93] As the war in Korea intensified, Mao became more
concerned that the KMT, now directly backed by the U.S. Navy, would
"seize the chance to attack us." On 25 August, he warned both the
Third and Fourth field armies to remain "highly alert, . . . because the
enemy would probably take an amphibious action against the Chaoshan and Hai-Lu-Feng areas." Mao also instructed the commanders to
"improve the [efficiency of] intelligence collection so that we will have
adequate information prior to the enemy's action."[94] By November,
the CMC even ordered the cancellation of preparations for another attack on Jinmen. Mao urged the Third Field Army to "concentrate on
the KMT remnants within Fujian [province] and have them eliminated
in six months."[95]

It is interesting to note that the Beijing authorities had been very
cautious in June and July. They did not even want their propaganda to

91. Editorial Division of *Shijie Zhishi*, ed., *Taiwan Wenti Wenjian Huibian* (Beijing, 1957),
pp. 9–10.

92. *DWGXWJ*, pp. 130–32.

93. CMC instructions, enclosed in deputy commander of the Third Field Army Su Yu
to each Group Army command, mid-July 1950, in *DDZGHJ*, p. 41; *Ye Fei Memoirs*,
pp. 612–13.

94. Telegram, Mao to Deng Zihui and Tan Zheng, commanders of CCP Southwestern
Military Region, "To Prepare for Possible Enemy Attack on the Chaoshan and Hai-Luo-
Feng Areas," 25 August 1950, in *JGYLMWG* 1:480.

95. Telegram, Mao to Ye Fei, November 1950, cited in *Ye Fei Memoirs*, pp. 613–14.

be misleading about their intentions regarding Taiwan. Mao was very much worried when he was told that the CCP press had once announced to the public that the People's Liberation Army would seize Taiwan in 1950. Mao immediately wrote to Hu Qiaomu, his former secretary and then the director of the CCP Press Bureau, asking him to check whether the press had ever said this. He pointedly requested Wu to make sure that "we will only let the public know that we shall liberate Taiwan and Tibet, and we shall never give any exact timetable [for the liberation action]."[96] Moreover, Mao wanted to hide Beijing's intentions with regard to Taiwan "at this critical juncture." On 1 September, he instructed Chen Yi, commander of the East China Military Region and the Third Field Army, that the line of communications between Chen and the CMC should be guaranteed "highly confidential." He told Chen to use cable wires rather than radio for "top secret" reports. "We are getting into a critical situation," Mao stressed, "it is extremely important to keep [our intentions] absolutely secret."[97] Recall that Beijing authorities were also considering intervening in Korea, by ensuring no leak of intelligence to the enemy, Mao probably sought to keep secret the transfer of PLA forces from East China to the Sino-Korean border and at the same time, to keep the enemy guessing at Beijing's Taiwan policy.

Publicly, the leadership of the PRC vigorously opposed the U.S. action in the Taiwan Strait and mobilized Chinese public opinion against this foreign "invasion." On 30 June, Mao and Zhou called upon for a nationwide propaganda campaign to strengthen domestic unity on the assumption that disunity in China would always invite invasions, as China's history had clearly shown.[98] The Beijing government arranged an anti-American rally to be held on 7 July, the thirteenth anniversary of the Japanese invasion of China in 1937. The Chinese government compared U.S. policy toward Taiwan with Japanese. The campaign for domestic unity and against the United States reached its peak when in Beijing on 10 July, forty-two leaders of "mass organizations" announced that they were fully supporting a nationwide mobilization campaign against potential U.S. intervention.[99]

At the same time, the Beijing leaders attempted to mobilize world opinion against U.S. actions in the Taiwan Strait. Zhou Enlai proposed sending a special delegation to the UN to confront the Americans face to face. Mao and the CCP Politburo approved Zhou's proposal in

96. Mao Zedong to Hu Qiaomu, 29 September 1950, in *JGYLMWG* 1:536.
97. Telegram, Mao to Chen Yi, commander of the Third Field Army, 1 September 1950, in *JGYLMWG* 1:494.
98. *Renmin Ribao*, 30 June 1950, p. 1.
99. Ibid., 11 July 1950, p. 1.

August, and the UN Security Council accepted Beijing's request on 9 September. Wu Xiuquan, then vice-minister of foreign affairs, headed the Chinese delegation. As Wu recalls, Mao instructed him to reject any compromise on the Taiwan question and that the delegation was not to show the slightest intimacy with the Americans. Wu arrived in New York via Paris on 24 November, and announced to the world that the imperialists had no chance of "enslaving the Chinese people again."[100]

Communist Chinese leaders never believed that the mission of U.S. Seventh Fleet was only to neutralize the Taiwan Strait, and they clearly understood that the People's Liberation Army would encounter the U.S. Navy should it attack Taiwan. More important, they were inclined to see the U.S. action in the Taiwan Strait not as a defensive act but as a reflection of general U.S. hostility to China. To deter such a threat, Beijing authorities had long been preparing both militarily and psychologically. They sought to build a strong line of defense along the China coast and hoped that such a demonstration of their resolve and readiness would dissuade the United States from carrying out its hostile intentions. Highly alert to potential invasion, the Beijing authorities finally chose to confront the United States in Korea when the war turned against the North Koreans in early September 1950.

IV

The events in Korea rapidly overshadowed the Taiwan question. The PRC and the United States maintained a mutual deterrence relationship based on mutual misunderstanding and miscalculation, which had a great impact on Sino-American conflict in the Taiwan area.

U.S. strategists assessed Taiwan's value mainly in the context of confrontation with the Soviet Union. A Taiwan in the hands of a hostile power would be strategically important, but no one in Washington was sure how soon the allegedly Moscow-directed CCP would attack Taiwan, or how willing the CCP would be to turn the island into a Soviet military base. U.S. assessments of Soviet intentions dramatically changed in the spring of 1950. With the outbreak of the Korean War, the unclear and long-term threat in the Taiwan Strait suddenly appeared certain and imminent. Washington officials believed that Taiwan was the next place (after Korea) where the Communists—without specifying *which* Communists—would challenge the status quo in the Far East. A show of force to deter the perceived challenge therefore

100. *Wu Xiuquan Memoirs*, pp. 36–43.

seemed to be badly needed. This judgment exaggerated Soviet intentions in the Far East and miscalculated Moscow's dominance over CCP Taiwan policy. As a result, Washington officials tended to see Soviet jet fighters stationed in Shanghai—which the Chinese Communist leaders wanted there to defend Shanghai from the KMT air raids—as evidence of Moscow-Beijing military cooperation against Taiwan. And they also took for granted the hypothesis that the CCP would automatically turn Taiwan into a Soviet military base after seizing the island.

Washington's deterrence strategy, too, reflected some miscalculation. In order to prevent the fall of Taiwan, U.S. strategists had long considered the feasibility of showing military strength there. But they were deterred from doing this simply by the anticipation of diplomatic difficulties and by the recognition that U.S. resources were limited. When they thought to promote Taiwan independent of the Chinese both Communist and Nationalist, Washington officials wishfully overestimated separatist strength in Taiwan. When they decided to neutralize Taiwan, they underestimated the difficulties of avoiding further involvement in the Chinese civil conflict on behalf of the KMT. To establish a military threat and at the same time to avoid diplomatic difficulty, however, proved unrealistic, given that the Nationalist supporters in Congress would certainly do their utmost to salvage Chiang in Taiwan, and given that Chiang Kai-shek, envisioning an outbreak of World War III, would do his best to manipulate the United States for the sake of his survival and a possible return to the mainland. That Beijing never believed that the United States would not intervene in the Chinese civil war indicates that Acheson's neutralization policy was simply more wishful thinking. Washington's attempt to create multilateral cooperation to deny Taiwan to the People's Republic was miscalculated, too. Although Britain regarded Taiwan as important because it feared Communist expansion to Hong Kong, the British were not that interested in denying Taiwan to Communist China. Since Britain had already recognized the PRC at the beginning of 1950, London found it difficult to work with the United States to protect the Nationalists in Taiwan.

It is obvious that Beijing was convinced in 1949 and 1950 that the United States was trying to prevent the PLA from seizing Taiwan; however, they did not understand why. They did not see this as a U.S. attempt to build up a better defense line against possible Soviet expansion in the Far East, but rather as part of a scheme to invade first China and then the Soviet Union. Every piece of information about U.S. activity in the Taiwan Strait "proved" aggressive U.S. intentions, which Mao's "intermediate-zone" conception had earlier anticipated. Beijing could neither see the Seventh Fleet as only neutralizing the Taiwan

Strait for defensive purposes nor differentiate U.S. intentions from those of its "running dogs." The attempt to form a Far East Anti-Communist Alliance in 1949 was in fact initiated and promoted by Rhee and Chiang to manipulate U.S. commitment, but there is no evidence that the Truman administration ever incorporated this alliance into its strategic planning.

Beijing leaders, it seems, overreacted to a misperceived threat as well. Seeking a strong defensive position along the China coast, they actually accomplished just the opposite: PLA military assaults on KMT-held offshore islands and military preparations for amphibious operations in effect indicated that the Communist government in China did intend to challenge the status quo. Although actual military conflict did not take place between the PRC and the United States, the pattern of confrontation would have a tremendous impact on Sino-American fighting in Korea. It also created a prelude to the later but more intense conflicts over the Taiwan Strait.

[4]

Military Conflict in Korea, July 1950–January 1951

The Korean War changed dramatically in the latter half of September 1950. Douglas MacArthur's remarkable successes at Inchon and around Seoul had destroyed the organization and cohesiveness of the North Korean army. UN forces were pushing the scattered enemy regiments back into North Korea. By the end of September, the initial objective of the UN Security Council Resolution of 25 June had been attained: The aggressors were repelled from South Korea, and the status quo had been restored. Rather than halt at the Thirty-eighth parallel, the UN forces crossed it in pursuit of the second objective vaguely incorporated in the UN resolution—"to restore international peace and security to the area."[1] But their advance toward the Yalu River stalled, and they were soon forced to retreat by a large Communist Chinese force. Why did the Truman administration decide that UN forces should cross the Thirty-eighth parallel? And why did Beijing authorities decide to send troops across the Yalu?

I

Only a few days after the outbreak of the Korean conflict, U.S. officials were already considering the possibility that the UN troops would have to advance into North Korea. General Richard C. Lindsay, deputy director for strategic planning of the Joint Chiefs of Staff, first

1. D. Clayton James, *The Years of MacArthur: Triumph and Disaster, 1945–1964* (Boston, 1985), 3:486.

proposed this at an NSC staff meeting on 29 June. He argued that General MacArthur should be authorized to cross the Thirty-eighth parallel "if he considered it necessary to the success of his mission."[2]

Military strategists consistently supported the idea of crossing the parallel. They argued that adherence to the status quo after compelling the North Koreans to withdraw from South Korea would be unacceptable both in military and geopolitical terms. The Joints Chiefs called the line "a geographical artificiality violating the natural integrity of a singularly homogeneous nation." Since the parallel was nothing more than "the eastern outpost of the iron curtain," in their view, to halt there would enable the "USSR to re-arm a new striking force for a second attempt. Thus it would still require a very great outlay of funds to reconstruct and secure South Korea." But crossing the parallel, they calculated, would provide "the US and the free world with the first opportunity to displace part of the Soviet orbit"; penetration of the Soviet orbit, short of all-out war, "would disturb the strategic complex which the USSR is organizing between its own Far Eastern territories and the contiguous areas." The Joint Chiefs further argued that "Manchuria, the pivot of that complex outside the USSR, would lose its captive status, for a free and strong Korea could provide an outlet for Manchuria's resources." The Chiefs also saw an "incalculable" psychological significance in unifying Korea. Japan would "see demonstrated a check on Soviet expansion," and then "elements in the Chinese Communist regime . . . might be inclined to question their exclusive dependence on the Kremlin . . . [Beijing] might prefer different arrangements and a new orientation."[3]

How would the Soviets or the Chinese respond if the UN forces crossed the Thirty-eighth parallel? Those who opposed moving into North Korea believed that such a decision would provoke the Soviets into taking military action that would lead to general war. Seeing "ample evidence of the strategic importance to Russia of the Korean peninsula," the Policy Planning Staff argued on 25 July, "it is unlikely that the Kremlin at present would accept the establishment in North Korea of a regime which it could not dominate and control." PPS officials clearly anticipated that UN military action north of the parallel would result in conflict with the USSR or Communist China, and that "the Kremlin might bring about the occupation of North Korea either with its own or with Chinese Communist forces."[4]

2. Minutes, NSC meeting, 29 June 1950, in *FRUS: 1950*, 1:328.

3. Draft memorandum prepared in the Department of Defense, "United States Courses of Action in Korea," 31 July 1950, in *FRUS: 1950*, 7:503–4, and 507–8.

4. Draft memorandum prepared in the Policy Planning Staff, 25 July 1950, in *FRUS: 1950*, 7:469–71.

A CIA report in August reinforced the assessment that "the USSR would regard the invasion of North Korea as a strategic threat to the security of the Soviet Far East." According to this report, "the USSR is now in a high status of readiness for general hostilities, and the Kremlin might well calculate that with U.S. mobilization set in motion, the USSR is better prepared now than it would be later for a test of strength with the United States." Under such circumstance, the CIA predicted, the Kremlin might place its forces on the Thirty-eighth parallel, thus obligating the United States to initiate hostilities against the Soviet army. This situation would put the United States in an unfavorable position. According to the CIA report, "It would alienate most of Asia . . . [and] permit full exploitation of the propaganda theme that the South Koreans under U.S. guidance opened the aggression against the North Koreans." More important, it would "enable the USSR to neutralize and conquer most of Europe and the North East [Asia] before the impact of United States industrial mobilization could be felt upon the defensive capability of those areas." Thus CIA officials strongly opposed the parallel.[5]

Concerned about the Soviet Union's sensitivity to its own borders, George F. Kennan pointed out in that same month that possible Soviet opposition would render UN military operations north of the parallel too risky. "The Soviet leaders," Kennan argued, "must be seriously worried over the proximity of the Korean fighting to their own borders and over the direct damage which can conceivably be done to their military interests by any extension of the area of hostilities." He regarded Soviet strategic interests in the Far East as already "affected by the destruction of industrial installations of military significance in North Korea." He also held that the Kremlin would view an advance into North Korea as a threat to the Port Arthur and the Vladivostok areas, a threat they would enter North Korea to neutralize.[6] John Foster Dulles also opposed any U.S. advance beyond the Thirty-eighth parallel, because it "might involve us much more deeply in a struggle on the Asiatic mainland with Soviet and Chinese communist manpower because of the strategic bearing that the northern part of Korea has toward Port Arthur and Vladivostok."[7]

Other considerations in favor of crossing the parallel, however, outweighed the risk of Soviet counterthreats. Many believed that UN military strength in Korea could deter Soviet military intervention. The National Security Council clearly stated in early July that the Kremlin

5. CIA memorandum, 18 August 1950, in *FRUS: 1950*, 7:601–2.
6. Kennan to Acheson, 8 August 1950, in *FRUS: 1950*, 1:361–64; Kennan to Acheson, 21 August 1950, ibid., 7:623–24.
7. Dulles to Nitze, 1 August 1950, in *FRUS: 1950*, 7:514.

North Korea

would hesitate to commit its own armed forces to action, because they understood that such action might "lead to the outbreak of a new world war."[8] U.S./UN field commander MacArthur maintained in late August that the Soviets had shown no interest in intervening directly in Korea or engaging in a general war with the United States elsewhere.[9] The Joint Chiefs also believed that the Soviets would hesitate because the movement of their forces into North Korea "might be delayed by destruction along the lines of communication in Korea." Potential Soviet action, in their judgment, could be inhibited by "skillful . . . military and political operations in North Korea."[10] The National Security Council then incorporated these ideas in NSC 73/4, dated 25 October: "It has been our estimate that the Kremlin did not intend to engage in a major war and might be deterred from initiating such a war if confronted with sufficient political, economic and military strength."[11]

Another conviction held that the United States should take even the risk of provoking Soviet military action in order to unify Korea. John M. Allison, director of the Office of Northeast Asian Affairs, advocated boldness. As he told Rusk in July, taking a risk was worthwhile, because showing "determination that the aggressors should not go unpunished . . . should have a *salutary effect* upon other areas of tension in the world." But perpetuating the artificial division of Korea, in his view, "would cause the people and army of South Korea to lose what little morale they have left and would run the grave danger of turning them actively against American forces now in Korea." Allison thus concluded: "I fail to see what advantage we gain by a compromise with clear and moral principles and shirking of our duty to make clear once and for all that aggression does not pay."[12]

Administration officials did, indeed, consider the possibility of Chinese military opposition to the movement of the UN forces into North Korea. Regarding China as Russia's largest satellite, American strategists worried that if the United States attempted to challenge the status quo in Korea, Moscow might use its proxy's large army to counter

8. NSC 73, "The Position and Actions of the U.S. with Respect to Possible Soviet Moves in the Light of Korean Situation," 1 July 1950, in *FRUS: 1950*, 1:333.

9. Memorandum by W. Averell Harriman, 20 August 1950, in *FRUS: 1950*, 7:543.

10. Draft memorandum prepared in the Department of Defense, "US Courses of Action in Korea," 31 July 1950, p. 503; Also see the Department of Defense memorandum, 7 August 1950, in *FRUS: 1950*, 7:529.

11. NSC 73/4, "The Position and Actions of the United States with Respect to Possible Future Soviet Moves in the Light of the Korean Situation," 25 August 1950, in *FRUS: 1950*, 1:378.

12. John M. Allison to Rusk, 1 July 1950, in *FRUS: 1950*, 6:272. Rusk noted on his copy of this memorandum, "Agree DR." Allison to Rusk, 15 July 1950, ibid., pp. 393–95; Allison to Nitze, 24 July 1950, ibid., pp. 460–61 [emphasis added].

such a move. At a meeting of NSC consultants on 29 June, Kennan warned that the Chinese Communists should be "carefully watched."[13] Washington officials reasoned that the Chinese Communists might enter the war not because they wanted to do so but because the Soviets would press them to intervene. In early July, the National Security Council had already pointed out that Moscow might use Communist Chinese forces in Korea if the military situation underwent a "rapid alteration."[14] The NSC also cautioned in August that the Soviet Union might involve Chinese military forces in Korea to "secure its eastern flank and lessen the probability that the Soviet may have to fight on two fronts simultaneously."[15] The CIA even suggested that "the Kremlin might welcome the outbreak of hostilities between the U.S. and China, [because it] would thus have an additional opportunity of driving the wedge between the U.S. and its allies."[16]

But when assessing Communist China's own intentions, U.S. strategists simply did not believe that the Chinese would intervene. From their perspective, U.S. actions in Korea did not affect Chinese security interests, and the Chinese leaders would worry more about intentions in Asia if the Russians intervened. "It would be sheer madness for the Chinese to enter the Korean War," Acheson asserted, "when their great problem is with Soviet domination along their northern border."[17] For John Paton Davies of the PPS, it was conceivable that the Chinese Communists would decline "to snatch the [Soviet] chestnut from the fire." Kennan also thought it "doubtful" that Mao would commit any of his own forces to Korea, because "there is no evidence that Moscow has reached any agreements with him envisaging such entry."[18]

Others argued that the Beijing regime would be politically disadvantaged should it intervene in Korea. A CIA estimate on "the threat of full Chinese Communist intervention in Korea," dated 12 October, pointed out that the Chinese Communists "undoubtedly fear the consequences of war with the US." These consequences could include collapse of China's domestic economy under the strain of fighting in Korea, invalidation of its claim on the Chinese seat in the General Assembly and on the Security Council of the UN, increased Soviet inter-

13. Minutes, NSC meeting, 29 June 1950, pp. 325, and 327–29.
14. NSC 73, 1 July 1950, p. 334.
15. NSC 73/4, 25 August 1950, pp. 382–83.
16. CIA memorandum, 18 August 1950, pp. 601–2.
17. Rosemary Foot, *The Wrong War: American Policy and the Dimensions of the Korean Conflict, 1950–1953* (Ithaca, N.Y., 1985), p. 81.
18. Memorandum by John P. Davies, 22 September 1950, in *FRUS: 1950*, 7:753; Kennan to Acheson, 8 August 1950, p. 361.

ference in its internal affairs, and internal disaffection should the intervention fail.[19]

Moreover, U.S. officials did not believe that the Chinese Communists were capable of countering the movement of the UN forces into North Korea. The Joint Intelligence Committee (JIC) suggested in early July that the combat experience of Communist Chinese forces had been primarily based on "hit-and-run" guerrilla tactics, and that their soldiers had never met a "well trained force with high morale equipped with modern weapons." Therefore, the JIC asserted that Chinese Communist military intervention could not effectively forestall the advance of UN forces, even if the Chinese intended to do so.[20] "The Chinese Communist ground forces, currently lacking requisite air and naval support, are capable of intervening effectively," the CIA also estimated, "but not necessarily decisively, in the Korea conflict."[21] For Kennan, the introduction of Chinese Communists troops into Korea was not a frightening prospect; rather, they would place the United States "in a better position to conduct military operations north of the Thirty-eighth parallel," because the United States would then have a legitimate reason to "even bomb [the targets] in Manchuria."[22] The NSC staff echoed this position: "if they [the Chinese] should become engaged in the theater we would have adequate grounds for air and sea attacks on targets in Communist China directly related to the enemy effort in Korea."[23]

Washington officials were further convinced by local reports that Chinese Communist intervention was unlikely. Washington had three main sources of information at this point: Ambassador Alan G. Kirk in Moscow, reporting primarily on Beijing-Moscow connections; Consul General James R. Wilkinson in Hong Kong, reporting on the basis of both covert sources and information leaked from China; and Ambassador Loy W. Henderson in India, passing information supplied by the Indian government from its embassy in Beijing. Kirk wrote in early August that Beijing was not yet solidly tied to the Kremlin, and that even Stalin, as "an old man, . . . would not wish to do anything [in Korea] which might result in [the] destruction [of the] Soviet 'house' which he had constructed." In late September, Kirk advised that Washington should not take seriously the Soviet press summaries of

19. CIA memorandum, "Threat of Full Chinese Communist Intervention in Korea," 12 October 1950, in *FRUS: 1950*, 7:933–34.
20. Joint Intelligence Committee to the JCS, 11 July 1950, cited in Foot, *The Wrong War*, p. 81.
21. CIA memorandum, 12 October 1950, p. 933.
22. Minutes, NSC meeting, 29 June 1950, pp. 327–28.
23. NSC 73, 1 July 1950, p. 334.

Mao's comments on Marshal Zhu De's speech of September 25—stressing the buildup of a strong army to defend China's frontiers—because it would be impossible for Communist China to maintain a large army along its Korean border.[24]

Wilkinson's messages, too, indicated that the Chinese Communists had no real intention of intervening. Zhou Enlai's warning that China would not stand aside should the imperialists invade its neighbor's territory, in Wilkinson's judgment, was primarily to "present [the] Communist Government as [the] champion of Chinese nationalism and [to] solidify public support and belief of its pro-USSR and anti-U.S. policy." In late October, he further reported that "reliable sources informed" him that China would not intervene, because "(a) [the] Chinese are unable to cope with UN air power; (b) UN artillery [is] also greatly superior; and (c) even [if] the USSR provided air support, UN air power could disrupt transportation in China, and make supply problems very difficult."[25]

The information from India also sounded no warning of possible Chinese intervention. In September, Henderson reported that Communist Chinese leaders were not prepared to push China into war in Korea. Mao was merely "anxious to carry non-Communist opinion with him." Apart from strengthening the defense of Manchuria because of its "geographical proximity to conflict," he found, "there is no evidence of military preparations." China had not even taken "elementary precautions against air raids in Peking [Beijing], Tientsin [Tianjin] and Shanghai." Henderson did, indeed, pass along Beijing's verbal warnings of military intervention, which came through K. M. Panikkar, Indian ambassador in Beijing, in late September and early October; however, Panikkar's reliability and thus the credibility of the warnings were repeatedly questioned in Washington.[26]

A few people in the State Department, however, did worry about Chinese intervention in Korea. O. Edmund Clubb, then director of the Office of Chinese Affairs, cautioned in early October that Zhou Enlai's statement to Panikkar might not be a bluff, because "Peking and Moscow might be prepared to risk the danger of WW III." Zhou's "demarche," Clubb warned, "must be regarded as having been made with [the] full knowledge and support of [the] USSR. Moscow and Peiping

24. Alan G. Kirk to Acheson, 1 August 1950, in *FRUS: 1950*, 7:512; Kirk to Acheson, 26 September 1950, ibid., pp. 777–80.

25. James R. Wilkinson to Acheson, 5 September 1950, in *FRUS: 1950*, 7:698–99; Wilkinson to Acheson, 12 September 1950, ibid., pp. 724–25; ibid., p. 1003.

26. Loy W. Henderson to Acheson, 20 September 1950, in *FRUS: 1950*, 7:742 and 743; Henderson to Acheson, 4 October 1950, ibid., pp. 869–73; memorandum by Livingston T. Merchant, 27 September 1950, ibid., pp. 793–94, and 864.

may be prepared to take considerable risks."[27] U. Alexis Johnson of the Office of Northeast Asian Affairs argued that China's threats should not be dismissed as "entirely bluff," and that "it may . . . well [be] worthwhile further to explore the possibility of using entirely ROK forces for the subjugation of North Korea . . . while reducing the grave risk of calling the Chinese bluff."[28]

Acheson was not persuaded. Although admitting that there might be a risk involved in crossing the Thirty-eighth parallel, the secretary of state asserted on October 5 that "a greater risk would be incurred by showing hesitation and timidity." Acheson was not convinced by Beijing's warnings. "The Chinese Communists were themselves taking no risk," as he put it, they could always deny anything said in "their private talks to the Indian Ambassador." If they want to send a warning, then they should do so in a "statement directly to the United Nations or to the Unified Command." He pointed out that if the Chinese "wanted to take in the 'poker game' they would have to *put more on the table* than they had up to the present." Acheson thus stressed that "the only proper course to take was a firm and courageous one, and that we should not be unduly frightened at what was probably a Chinese Communist bluff."[29]

It is important to note that at this time the secretary of state was under pressure in domestic politics. Congressional critics of the Truman-Acheson policy in Asia hailed the outbreak of the Korean War as a great opportunity to reunite Korea, and had frankly shown their readiness to attack any caution regarding such a move. In early July Senator Robert Taft advocated "march[ing] right on over the 38th parallel and at least occupy[ing] the southern part of North Korea." At a 29 September cabinet meeting outlining plans for the November election, Acheson explicitly admitted that the "parallel was to be ignored, and Korea would be used as a stage to prove what Western Democracy can do to help the underprivileged countries of the world."[30]

Some officials in the State Department insisted on using diplomacy to dissuade Beijing from intervening. On 4 October James E. Webb, acting secretary of state, instructed Ambassador Henderson in India to "seek some opportunity . . . to meet Chi[nese] Amb[assador] and put directly to him this Govt's position re Korea." He wanted Henderson to make it clear to the Chinese that they should not "underestimate [the] determination [of the] American people [to] act in full support

27. O. Edmund Clubb to Merchant, 4 October 1950, in *FRUS: 1950*, 7:864–65.
28. U. Alexis Johnson to Rusk, 3 October 1950, in *FRUS: 1950*, 7:848–49.
29. Memorandum by John M. Allison, 4 October 1950, in *FRUS: 1950*, 7:868–69 [emphasis added].
30. Cited in Foot, *The Wrong War*, pp. 69–70.

[of] international peace in [the] Pacific in accordance with decisions approved [by the UN]." While finding it difficult to arrange meetings with the Chinese Ambassador in India, Henderson sought to have the Indian government pass a warning that "if China should intervene in Korea, it would thereby lose any sympathy which it might have from any nations of the free world."[31] For Rusk, diplomatic intimidation appeared to be insufficient to deter Chinese Communist intervention. On 9 October he proposed that the United States should "reserve an attack on the [Yalu River] Dam as a bargaining point in case it came to that pass with the Chinese Communists."[32]

U.S. strategists believed that even if the Chinese meant to intervene, their threat could be countered. A military contingency plan had distinctively expressed this position: In the event of open deployment of major Soviet forces in Korea, "the UN commander should break off the action as rapidly as possible consistent with the orderly withdrawal of his force," but in the event of open deployment of major Chinese Communist forces in Korea, "the US should not permit itself to become engaged in a general war with Communist China, but as long as action by UN military forces offers a reasonable chance of successful resistance, the UN command should continue such action and be authorized to take appropriate air and naval action outside Korea against Communist China." The State Department first considered this proposal on 31 August, the National Security Council then incorporated it in NSC 81/1 on 9 September, and Truman finally approved it on 27 September.[33] It seems that the Truman administration was ready to direct the movement of the UN forces into North Korea regardless of possible Chinese Communist intervention. How did the Beijing authorities assess the Korean situation? How did they decide to respond?

II

The People's Republic, a regime only eight months old, was unprepared for any form of military involvement in Korea. The war came at

---

31. Webb to Henderson, 4 October 1950, in *FRUS: 1950,* 7:875–76; Henderson to Acheson, 6 October 1950, ibid., pp. 886 and 888. The Chinese ambassador to India actually refused to meet Henderson. See Henderson to Acheson, 10 October 1950, ibid., p. 921.

32. Perkins to Clubb, 9 October 1950, in *FRUS: 1950,* 7:916–17.

33. Memorandum prepared in the Department of State, "US Courses of Action as to Korea," 31 August 1950, in *FRUS: 1950,* 7:673; NSC 81, "United States Courses of Action with Respect to Korea," 1 September 1950, ibid., pp. 689–90; NSC 81/1, "United States Courses of Action with Respect to Korea," 9 September 1950, ibid., pp. 717–18, and 793n. [emphasis added].

a time of tremendous domestic problems both in economic reconstruction after a nationwide civil war and in political consolidation involving the removal of the scattered KMT remnants. Despite the fact that the war was unexpected and unwelcomed by Chinese Communist leaders, in the October 1950, they determinedly sent a large army to fight the UN forces in Korea. How did the PRC leadership decide to do so and why? Or more adequately, how did Beijing perceive that China's security interests were threatened? How did the CCP leaders try to deter this perceived threat? And, when deterrence failed to halt the UN forces at the Thirty-eighth parallel, how did the Beijing authorities decide to have the Chinese soldiers cross the Yalu?

Ever since seizing power, the CCP leadership had been quite alert to potential U.S. military threats. It insisted that a war between the new China and the United States was "possible," or perhaps even "unavoidable," because of the inherent contradictions of Sino-American interests in the Cold War. The belief that the United States would, in one way or another, try to smash the Chinese revolution, which was of "world significance following the October Revolution," remained strong through the spring of 1950. Mao explicitly pointed out on 6 June that any counterrevolutionary efforts against China must be "directed from behind the scenes by the imperialists, particularly by U.S. imperialists."[34]

In Beijing's perception of the U.S. threat, a major element was the belief that the United States would attack at three points along China's borders: across the Taiwan Strait, still under KMT control; from French Indochina, where, the CCP leaders believed, Washington supported the French attempt to regain complete control over the region as a step toward an eventual encirclement of China; and over the Korean peninsula. The Chinese leaders suspected that the United States intended to turn the entire peninsula into a staging area for an eventual attack against China or the Soviet Union, or both. The PRC leadership based its defense planning on this assumption. As early as October 1949, Mao had proclaimed that China's defense "must be centered around the areas of Tianjin, Shanghai, and Guangzhou," three strategically important cities along the China coast. Clearly, Chinese Communist leaders wanted to pay special attention to the defense of the northern (Sino-Korean), eastern (the Taiwan Strait), and southern

34. Mao Zedong, "The Chinese People Have Stood Up," 21 September 1949, in *SWM* 4:17; "Don't Hit Out in All Directions" (Part of a speech delivered at the Third Plenary Session of the Seventh Meeting of the Central Committee of CCP, 6 June 1950), ibid., p. 33; and "Fight for a Fundamental Turn for the Better in the Nation's Financial and Economic Situation," 6 June 1950, ibid., p. 27.

(Sino-Indochinese) borders.[35] In the early spring of 1950, the Central Military Commission established a strategic reserve force with the best units of the Fourth Field Army, which it stationed in Henan Province where it could be most promptly dispatched to reinforce any one of these three areas.[36]

Beijing probably accepted North Korea's request for military assistance in its fight for the liberation of the whole of Korea in order to secure the Sino-Korean border. In January 1950, Kim Il-sung sent a secret mission headed by Kim Kwang Hwop to Beijing to appeal for Chinese military assistance. The CCP Central Committee decided to repatriate to North Korea fourteen thousand soldiers of Korean origin who had been recruited into the PLA's Fourth Field Army. Kim requested these troops to be equipped and combat ready immediately. The Central Committee authorized that action on 22 January.[37] Kim may have explained his intentions to the Chinese leaders, but there is no indication of how much the Chinese leaders knew about when the North Koreans would act and how.

Nevertheless, Beijing reacted immediately and vigorously to U.S. intervention in the Korean War. Mao and Zhou warned that the United States not only intended to take action in the Taiwan Strait but also in "Korea, the Philippines, Vietnam and other [Asian] countries."[38] The 26 July edition of *Renmin Ribao* [People's Daily], the CCP's official newspaper, further charged that the Truman administration would intervene in Korea so as "to change it into a gangway of aggression for the United States on the borders of China and the Soviet Union."[39] It seems that the PRC leadership was convinced that long-expected U.S. invasion had begun.

Such a perception of the U.S. threat did not, however, dictate an immediate and full-scale PRC commitment to North Korea. On the contrary, China's initial public reaction demonstrated its caution, watchfulness, and explicitly defensive posture. The *Renmin Ribao* edi-

35. Telegram, Mao to Lin Biao, "On the Military Reorganization of the Fourth Field Army," 31 October 1949, in *JGYLMWG* 1:106–7; Yao Xu, "The Wisdom of Deciding to Resist the United States and Assist Korea," *Tangshi Ziliao Yanjiu*, October 1980, p. 7.

36. Telegram, Mao to Lin Biao, "On the Military Reorganization of the Fourth Field Army," p. 107. Also see Du Ping, *Zhai Zhiyuanjun Zhongbu* (Nanjing, 1989), pp. 7 and 11 [hereafter *Du Ping Memoirs*]. General Du was then director of personnel office of the Fourth Field Army Command and later became director of Political Department of the Thirteenth Group Army Command.

37. *Nie Rongzhen Memoirs*, 3:744. For a detailed description of the Korean soldiers who had fought in China's civil war, see Bruce Cumings, *The Origins of the Korean War*, Vol. 2, *The Roaring of the Cataract, 1947–1950* (Princeton, 1990), pp. 355–64.

38. Mao's comments on Truman's statement of 27 June 1950, *Xinhua Yuebao*, July 1950, p. 525.

39. *Renmin Ribao*, 26 July 1950, pp. 4–5.

torial of 6 July acknowledged that "the Korean people's victory [will] come a bit slower" due to the rapid U.S. military reinforcement of the South Koreans with superior weapons, and "the Korean people can not but prepare to undertake prolonged and more arduous fighting." An article in the *Shijie Zhishi* [World Knowledge], an official journal of the Ministry of Foreign Affairs, on 14 July, also stated that "all peace-loving people . . . will sympathize with the liberation movement of the Korean people, but this does not mean we should enter the war."[40]

But at the same time, the People's Republic began considering military preparations in case China came under direct attack. At Mao's request, Zhou Enlai and Nie Rongzhen, the acting chief of staff, called a national defense meeting of the State Council and the Central Military Commission in Beijing on 7 and 10 July. The meeting involved CCP's major military leaders, including Director of General Political Department Luo Ronghuan, Director of General Logistics Department Yang Lisan, Commander of the Air Force Liu Yalou, Commander of Armored Forces Xu Guangda, Deputy Commander of the Artillery Force Su Jing, Commander of the Railway Engineering Corps Teng Daiyuan, Commander of the Fourth Field Army Lin Biao, Deputy Political Commissar of the Fourth Field Army Tan Zheng, Deputy Commander of the Northeast Military Region Huo Jingnian, and Director of CMC Combat Operations Bureau Li Tao. They reconfirmed the notion that U.S. intervention in Korea was "the first step of the whole U.S. Asian scheme of aggression." They felt an urgent need for an immediate military mobilization, assuming that "one should open an umbrella before it starts to rain." When Mao received the meeting's report, he immediately directed the implementation of the recommended military preparations.[41]

Three days later, the Central Military Commission issued an order entitled "The Decision to Defend the Northeastern Border." This order had three major provisions: It established the Northeast Border Defense Army (NBDA) along the Sino-Korean border, which would include the Thirteenth Group Army (composed of the Thirty-Eighth, Thirty-Ninth, and Fortieth armies) and the Forty-Second Army of the Northeast Military Region, the First, Second, and Eighth artillery divisions, and three anti-aircraft artillery corps, totaling 255,000 men. It created a headquarters with First Deputy Commander of the Third Field Army Su Yu and Deputy Director of the General Political Department Xiao Hua as the commanders-in-general, and former Fifteenth

---

40. Ibid., 6 July 1950, p. 3; *Shijie Zhishi*, 14 July 1950, pp. 11–13.
41. The minutes of this meeting are cited in ZYJZS, pp. 7–8. Also see *DDZGJSGZ* 1:449–50. Letter, Mao to Nie Rongzhen, "My Agreement with the National Security Meeting of 7 July 1950," 7 July 1950, in *JGYLMWG* 1:428.

Group Army commander Deng Hua as the Thirteenth Group Army commander (replacing Huang Yongsheng). It moved the Ninth Group Army stationed in Shanghai and the Nineteenth Group Army in Northwest China to North China as strategic reserves. All the NBDA forces were to gather in the Sino-Korean border towns, including Andong [Dandong], Fengchang, Jian, Tonghua, Liaoyang, Haicheng, Benxi, Tieyuan, and Kaiyuan, by the end of July.[42] In mid-August, Acting Chief of Staff Nie Rongzhen suggested moving the Ninth Army Group, which consisted of fifteen infantry divisions, to North China immediately. Later that month, the Central Military Commission, anticipating engaging U.S. forces, organized four air force corps, three mobile regiments, and eighteen anti-artillery corps, and constructed new field army hospitals capable of accommodating sixty thousand patients in Northeast China (Manchuria).[43]

Between 7 and 11 August, about twenty thousand American and South Korean soldiers attacked the North Korean Sixth Division near Masan in the southeast portion of the Pusan perimeter. The battle ended with the first major UN victory and relieved the Eighth Army's flank.[44] Greatly concerned about this development, Mao anticipated that the Chinese forces would soon have to enter the conflict. He ordered Gao Gang, the commander of the Northeast Military Region, to have the NBDA forces combat ready by early September.[45] On 18 August, Mao requested Gao to see to it that "[the NBDA] commanders should get everything ready at any costs before 30 September."[46]

The Chinese leaders actually foresaw that the military situation would turn against the North Koreans. On 31 August, NBDA field commander Deng Hua, in assessing the prospect of this change, noted:

> The intention of the enemy's counterattack is estimated as follows: first, to land part of its troops on some coastal areas in North Korea for harassing and holding operations, and advance its main forces northward along main highways and railways gradually; second, to make a large-scale landing of its main force on our flank rear areas (Pyongyang or Seoul), and at the same time employ a small force to pin down the [North Korean] People's Army in its present position, in order to attack it from the front and rear simultaneously.

42. CMC instruction, "The Decision to Defend the Northeastern Border," in *ZYJZS*, p. 8.
43. CMC instructions to all PLA commanders, August 1950, in *ZYJZS*, p. 8. Also see *KMYCZZ*, p. 18.
44. Whiting, *China Crosses the Yalu*, p. 71.
45. Telegram, Mao to Gao Gang, "On the Establishment of the Northeast Border Defense Army," 5 August 1950, in *JGYLMWG* 1:454.
46. Telegram, Mao to Gao Gang, 18 August 1950, in *JGYLMWG* 1:469.

Deng further predicted that if his judgment turned out to be true, "the People's Army would be in a very difficult position."[47] Agreeing with Deng, Mao directed the reinforcement of the NBDA. For this purpose, he instructed Song Shilun to move the Ninth Group Army to Jinan, Shandong Province, "no later than the end of October, but to start training and preparations immediately."[48] Meanwhile, Mao explicitly warned Lee San-chok, Kim Il-sung's personal envoy to Beijing, of a UN amphibious attack to cut off the North Korean front. He predicted that the enemy would attack one of the three port cities, including Inchon, along the western coast of North Korea. He then urged him to "tell Comrade Kim Il-sung to prepare for a possible U.S. amphibious assault."[49] MacArthur successfully carried out his Inchon landing and the liberation of Seoul between 11 and 28 September. It is curious that even after Mao had warned him, Kim Il-sung was still surprised by— and poorly prepared for—the UN offensive.

Beijing clearly understood that military preparations alone would not be enough to discourage the United States from invading China. Demonstrating domestic harmony against foreign aggression seemed to be equally important. During the Third Plenary Session of the CCP's Seventh Central Committee in June, Mao asserted that at this critical juncture, "we must convert those among the people who are dissatisfied with us into our supporters. Although the task is fraught with difficulties at present, we must overcome them by any possible means." He proposed that the government should proceed with "proper readjustment in industry and commerce so that factories can resume operations; gain the support of the unemployed; and take measures to assist the independent craftsmen find ways to earn a living."[50] These conciliatory policies, Mao believed, would broaden support for the CCP and promote internal unity.

In addition, the Beijing authorities launched a propaganda campaign against American imperialism to further demonstrate Chinese resolve to confront the United States. *Xue Xi* [Studies], a leading CCP journal of political theory, noted serious popular "fear" or "awe" of the United States throughout the CCP. "There are some people who

47. Deng's estimate is cited in Chen Xiaolu, "China's U.S. Policy, 1949–1955," in Harding and Yuan, eds., *Sino-American Relations, 1945–1955*, p. 188. For the Chinese text of Deng's report, see "Deng Hua," *Jiefangjun Jiangling Zhuan*, in "Xinhuo Liaoyuan" Editorial Division, ed., 7:30–31.

48. Mao's instructions to the commander of the Ninth Group Army, 8 September 1950 in, *JGYLMWG* 1:498. Also see Ye Yumen, *Heixue: Chubing Chaoxian Jishi* (Beijing, 1989), pp. 5–6.

49. Sun Baosheng, "Mao Zedong Anticipated the U.S. Landing at Inchon," *Junshi Shilin*, October 1990, p. 13.

50. Mao, "Don't Hit Out in All Directions," p. 34.

take a fence-sitting attitude toward truth and falsehood," it pointed out in August, "they doubt whether the Soviet-led anti-imperialist and peaceful democratic camp is definitely safeguarding long-lasting peace." The basic objective of this campaign therefore, was to prepare the Chinese public to support potential Chinese involvement in the Korean War when that involvement became unavoidable.[51] Later that month, *Shijie Zhishi* more explicitly stated that "the barbarous action of the American imperialists and their hangers-on in invading Korea not only menaces peace in Asia and the world in general but also seriously threatens the security of China in particular. [Therefore] it is impossible to solve the Korean problem without the participation of its closest neighbor, China." It further explained to the Chinese people that "North Korea's friends are our friends, North Korea's enemy is our enemy; North Korea's defense is our defense, North Korea's victory is our victory."[52] Calling for domestic harmony, on 30 September Zhou Enlai made it clear that "the unity of our nation and our people is so important and so powerful that any imperialist attempt to invade China would be *frightened away by it*."[53]

As the North Korean front collapsed, Beijing watched to see whether the UN forces would cross the parallel. Two weeks after the Inchon-Seoul operations, MacArthur ceremoniously welcomed Syngman Rhee back to Seoul and indicated his support of Rhee's intention to unify the whole of Korea. The South Korean Third Division actually started moving into North Korea on 1 October. The Chinese leaders now believed that it was high time to warn the United States not to follow them. On 24 September, in a protest to the United Nations concerning U.S. air raids on Northeast China, Zhou pointed out that "the flames of war being spread by the United States in the [Far] East are burning more fiercely. If the representation of the majority of states attending the UN General Assembly should continue to play deaf and dumb to these aggressive aims of the United States, they should not escape a share in the responsibility for setting the fires of war in the East."[54]

The next day, Acting Chief of Staff Nie Rongzhen issued a further warning when he spoke to Indian Ambassador Panikkar. Nie clearly stated that China would not "sit back with folded hands and let the Americans come up to the border. . . . We know what we are in for, but at all costs, American aggression has to be stopped." Nie even re-

---

51. Liao Gailong, "Problems of War and Peace," *Xue Xi*, 16 August 1950, pp. 17–22.

52. *Shijie Zhishi*, 26 August 1950, pp. 7–9.

53. Zhou Enlai, "To Fight for Consolidation and Development of Our People," *Renmin Ribao*, 1 October 1950, p. 1 [emphasis added].

54. Cited in Whiting, *China Crosses the Yalu*, p. 107.

marked that "the Americans can bomb us, they can destroy our industries, but they can not defeat us on land. . . . They may even drop
atomic bombs on us. What then? They may kill a few million people.
Without sacrifice, a nation's independence can not be upheld."[55] To reinforce Nie's warning, Zhou called in Panikkar for an urgent meeting
on 2 October, and directly stated that the entry of U.S. forces into
North Korea would compel China to intervene.[56] On 10 October, the
CCP press publicized Zhou's warning as an official statement of the
Ministry of Foreign Affairs. "Now that the American forces are attempting to cross the Thirty-eighth parallel on a grand scale," the *Renmin Ribao* proclaimed, "the Chinese people can not stand idly by."[57]
Using both public and private channels, Beijing leaders believed that
their warning signals would reach Washington.

The Chinese leaders tried to augment their warning with the counterthreat of the Sino-Soviet military alliance. In early October, Beijing
publicized Mao's declaration of the establishment of the Sino-Soviet
Friendship Organization, stressing that "the unity of the Chinese and
Soviet peoples is extremely important. . . . If the two nations can cooperate, the unity of the world is not at all difficult."[58] Song Qingling,
widow of Sun Yat-sen and then vice-chairman of the People's Republic, explained to the public more directly that "the Sino-Soviet friendship is guarding us at present and will guard us in the future as well."
Guo Moruo, the president of the Sino-Soviet Friendship Organization,
also pointed out that "thanks to Marshal Stalin and Chairman Mao
Zedong, we have the splendid Sino-Soviet alliance treaty for our mutual safety. The treaty has consolidated the friendship of the two
nations."[59]

But the Soviet Union was never prepared to intervene to prevent
the UN forces from entering North Korea. Pessimistic about his ability
to save the North Koreans, Stalin asked Beijing in late September
whether China would allow the North Korean government to evacuate to Northeast China and set up an exile regime there, to await a future counteroffensive. Clearly, he was not willing to do anything to
counter the UN advance into North Korea. More interesting, there is

55. Kavalam M. Panikkar, *In Two Chinas: Memoirs of a Diplomat* (London, 1955), p. 108.
For the Chinese text of the Nie-Panikkar talk, see Chai Chengwen, *Banmendian Tanpan*
(Beijing, 1989), p. 74. Chai was then a military attaché in the PRC embassy to Phyongy-
ang, and later became one of Beijing's major negotiators at the Panmunjom truce talks
[hereafter *Chai Chengwen Memoirs*].

56. DDZGWJ, p. 37.

57. "Statement of the Ministry of Foreign Affairs," *Renmin Ribao*, 10 October 1950,
p. 1.

58. *Renmin Ribao*, 7 October 1950, p. 1.

59. Ibid.

no evidence that Stalin ever pressed the Chinese Communists to intervene on Moscow's behalf, or that the Soviets had promised to support a Chinese military intervention.[60]

This, indeed, left Beijing in a difficult position. Without direct Soviet involvement, what could the PRC do if the UN forces moved into North Korea despite Chinese warnings? On 2 October, Mao presided over a Politburo meeting to discuss the crisis. On whether or not to intervene, the Chinese leaders were divided into two camps. Some, including Gao Gang and Lin Biao, opposed entering the Korean War on the grounds that the tasks of rebuilding after civil war were not complete and that the people were not trained or equipped for a modern war. They suggested that it would be wiser merely to deploy defensively along the northern bank of the Yalu River.[61]

Leading the other side, Mao felt that China's security would be directly threatened if the UN forces were allowed to approach the Sino-Korean border. In his view, even if the United States did not attack China immediately it would surely deploy its troops along the Sino-Korean border, thus constituting a grave threat to northeastern China. "How many troops are needed to guard a thousand kilometers of Yalu River?" Mao asked. "We would have to wait there year after year unsure of when the enemy will attack us," he added, and declared that the burden of a passive defense against a long-term U.S. threat would be unacceptable.[62] Peng Dehuai, deputy PLA commander-in-general and commander of the northwest military region, firmly supported Mao's argument. He asserted that even if "we enter the war but are pushed back by the U.S. forces, we would still have the initiative; . . . [and] even if U.S. imperialists force us out of northeastern China, it would only mean that our liberation war would last a few years longer."[63] But if China did not intervene, Peng believed, the People's Republic would encounter even greater problems both domestically and internationally. First, "domestic reactionaries would be encouraged, and the pro-American element would be more actively against us." Second, "should the United States occupy Korea, . . . the Amer-

60. Yao Xu, "The Wisdom of Deciding to Resist the United States and Assist Korea," p. 10. Also see *ZYJZS*, p. 14. Kim Il-sung wrote to Mao in late September requesting Chinese military intervention. The letter is cited in Ye Yumen, *Heixue*, pp. 49–51.

61. Peng Dehuai's address to the CPV high commanders, 14 October 1950, in *PJSWX*, pp. 320–21. Also see Ye Yumen, *Heixue*, pp. 6–48. Lin Biao earlier indicated that it might be better for the North Koreans to fight a guerrilla war in Korea than for the Chinese to intervene on their behalf (*Chai Chengwen Memoirs*, pp. 78–79).

62. Peng Dehuai, *Memoirs of a Chinese Marshal* (Peking, 1984), pp. 422–423 [hereafter cited as *Peng Dehuai Memoirs*]. Also see Ye Yumen, *Heixue*, pp. 47–48.

63. *Peng Dehuai Memoirs*, p. 423.

icans could shift to Vietnam and Burma, making trouble against us everywhere." Moreover, U.S. control of the whole of Korea would not only threaten China's security in the short run, but also "make other nations shift sides toward the American imperialists" in the long run. Third, if China did not react this time, "the United States would be able to rearm Japan, which would then provide more troops, making it more difficult for us to prevent a future foreign invasion."[64]

The Chinese leaders regarded the Soviet attitude toward Chinese intervention as crucial. Without reaching a final decision at the Politburo meeting, Mao telegraphed Stalin on 2 October, informing him that China had decided to send a "People's Volunteer Army" into Korea. "If the Americans occupy the whole of Korea," Mao explained to Stalin, "it would mean complete defeat for Korean revolutionary forces, and American aggressors would become even bolder, to the detriment of the whole East [bloc]." Although he hoped that "American forces and other countries' invading armies would be eliminated or forced to withdraw by the Chinese forces fighting in Korea," Mao anticipated that "we would have to prepare for the U.S. declaration of a general war with China—even if our troops are called volunteers. The United States would at least bomb China's cities and industrial bases, and attack our coastal areas with its naval forces." A worst-case outcome of Chinese intervention, Mao foresaw, would be that "the Chinese forces would fail to annihilate the U.S. troops in substantial numbers but end up in a military stalemate in Korea while America is already openly operating a general war against China and attacking other parts of China." In that case, China might have to fight a two- or three-front war. An additional side effect could be that "China's national and petty bourgeoisie and some other groups would be resentful toward our policy (because they are afraid of war)." Stressing all these difficulties, Mao wished Stalin to understand that Soviet military support would be definitely needed if the Chinese intervened in Korea.[65]

It is still unknown how Stalin responded. The CCP Politburo, however, decided to dispatch troops to Korea on 8 October, the day following the UN resolution authorizing the UN forces to unify Korea. Mao instructed the Thirteenth Group Army together with three artillery divisions "to get ready immediately and to prepare to cross the Yalu River." The Central Military Commission named Peng Dehuai the commander-in-general of the Chinese People's Volunteers (CPV), and assigned Gao Gang to direct logistics, transportation, and other rear

64. Peng's address to the CPV high commanders, 14 October 1950, pp. 322–23.
65. Telegram, Mao to Stalin, "On Our Decisions to Dispatch Military Forces to Korea," 2 October 1950, in *JGYLMWG* 1:539–41.

services.[66] Meanwhile, in informing Kim Il-sung of the CCP Politburo's decision, Mao asked the North Korean leader to send one of his top advisors to Shenyang, the CCP Northeast China headquarters, to coordinate liaison with Peng and Gao.[67] Four days later, Mao also decided to send the Ninth Group Army into Northeast China to back up the Thirteenth once it entered Korea.[68]

It is interesting that Mao still hoped for Soviet military assistance before moving the CPV into North Korea. On 8 October, he sent Zhou Enlai (joined by Lin Biao) to the Soviet Union in hopes of logistical support and air cover for the Chinese ground forces in Korea. Stalin, however, was only willing to "loan" the Chinese munitions and supplies and rejected Beijing's request for Soviet air support. Skeptical of the Chinese capability to match the United States in combat, Stalin also warned the Chinese not to fight any large-scale offensives against the U.S. forces, which, he feared, could potentially trigger a general war.[69] Because of this, Mao informed Peng on 12 October that the decision to enter Korea had been reversed and that the CPV was not to cross the Yalu. He then asked Peng and Gao Gang to fly to Beijing for an emergency meeting.[70] On the same day, Mao canceled the order to move the Ninth Group Army into northeastern China. He told all the commanders that "there is no need to explain either inside or outside the Party [about the sudden change]."[71] The CCP leadership halted the deployment of the Chinese forces, pending a decision on whether China should enter the war even if the Soviets would not assist.

Another Politburo meeting was held in Beijing on 13 October. The Chinese leaders decided to intervene in the Korean War even without Soviet military assistance. Mao informed Zhou in Moscow on the same day that "the result of our Politburo discussion is a unanimous agreement on the soundness of our decision to enter the Korean War." He explained that "such an active policy will benefit not only China, Korea, but also the East and world peace. If we do not enter the war and allow the enemy to approach the Yalu River, the result would be devastating to all of these areas and more so to Northeast China, [because] all our northeastern border defense forces will be tied down there and

66. The order of the Central Military Commission to all commanders of the PLA, "On Establishing the Chinese People's Volunteers," 8 October 1950, in *JGYLMWG* 1:543–44.

67. Telegram, Mao to Kim Il-sung, 8 October 1950, in *JGYLMWG* 1:545.

68. Telegram, Mao to Chen Yi, commander of the Third Field Army, 12 October 1950, in *JGYLMWG* 1:551.

69. For the Zhou-Stalin talks, see Ye Yumen, *Heixue*, pp. 97–116. Also see *Chai Chengwen Memoirs*, p. 83.

70. Telegram, Mao to Peng Dehuai, 12 October 1950, in *JGYLMWG* 1:552.

71. Telegram, Mao to Chen Yi and Rao Shushi, 12 October 1950, in *JGYLMWG* 1:553.

the southern Manchurian power plants would be directly threatened by the enemy."[72]

The Chinese leaders, however, did not intend to provoke a general war with the United States. They did not even plan to engage the UN forces in Korea, but hoped that by having military forces *ready*, China could dissuade the UN forces from occupying North Korea. Peng Dehuai told the CPV high commanders on 14 October that "our entry [into Korea] does not mean a declaration of war with the United States, . . . we are in Korea to support Korean revolutionaries as People's Volunteers."[73] Mao also told Zhou that "during the first phase, we will only engage the South Korean forces, [whom] we are confident we can defeat." In his 14 October telegram to Zhou, noting that "both Comrades Peng and Gao have agreed that we are capable of handling the South Koreans, and [that] they have shared my view that entering the war now is necessary and beneficial to us," Mao further explained that "if we can get all our troops into Korea as soon as possible, . . . there exists a possibility that U.S. and South Korean forces would be *discouraged* from moving northward. In that case, we do not even have to fight at this moment but can wait till the best chance comes." Probably still expecting that Zhou would be able to convince Stalin, Mao told him that "Peng is waiting for your reply in Beijing at this moment."[74]

With or without Soviet approval, on 14 October, Mao ordered all the four infantry armies (twelve divisions) and three artillery divisions of the Thirteenth Group Army to begin crossing the Yalu on 19 October. "Since it will take ten days for all the 260,000 soldiers to be transported over the river," Mao calculated, "the earliest date that our troops can gather in North Korea will be 28 October."[75] As he defined it, the CPV's initial task was to establish a defensive front somewhere north of the line between Pyongyang and Wonsan. "If the enemy does not continue driving northward but stops at the Pyongyang-Wonsan line in the next six months, we will not attack them. . . . Any talk of offensive actions will wait till six months later if by then we are better equipped and have both ground and air superiority over the enemy." Mao even expected that "if our defense line is stabilized and the enemy ceases moving over the Pyongyang-Wonsan line, we will withdraw half of our troops back to China for resupply and training, and

72. Telegram, Mao to Zhou Enlai, "On the Decisions of the Politburo Meeting of 12 October," 13 October 1950, in *JGYLMWG* 1:556.

73. Peng's address to the CPV high commanders, 14 October 1950, p. 322.

74. Telegram, Mao to Zhou Enlai, 14 October 1950, in *JGYLMWG* 1:558–59 [emphasis added].

75. Telegram, Mao to Chen Yi, 14 October 1950, in *JGYLMWG* 1:557; Telegram, Mao to Zhou Enlai, "On the Policies and Guidelines of the CPV in Korea," 14 October 1950, ibid., pp. 560–61.

probably send them back only when we are ready for a large-scale offensive." Mao believed that the CPV would have time to build such a defense line and get better prepared after entering North Korea, because "the U.S. forces are still around the Thirty-eighth parallel at this point, and it would take them months to get to Pyongyang even if they decide to do so and the South Koreans alone would not be able to go too far."[76]

MacArthur's forces advanced northward far more quickly than Mao had anticipated. On 19 October the commanders of the Thirteenth Group Army reported that "the UN forces would probably intercept the CPV before it would reach its defensive positions."[77] Mao concluded that an immediate engagement with the enemy was inevitable. Twice on 21 October, he instructed the CPV commanders to abandon the original plan and "to prepare to engage the enemy in a few days without building a defensive line first." It is noteworthy, however, that Mao wanted to attack the South Korean Sixth, Seventh, and Eighth Divisions first and stressed that the first assault should be by surprise.[78] When he was told that the presence of Chinese forces in Korea was still unknown to the enemy, Mao urged the CPV to exploit this "secrecy" further. He instructed on 22 October that "all our troops should keep an appropriate distance from the enemy's forces in moving to the front so that the enemy will not discover our intentions too early; and to do so, we would even evacuate some areas and let the enemy move in." Mao pointed out that since "the enemy is in a hurry, it is important to exploit this opportunity."[79] Undoubtedly, Mao was applying a strategy familiar to him from the civil war, that of luring the enemy deep into one's own territory and then striking it with a "more powerful fist."

On the evening of 28 October 1950, the CPV Fortieth Army launched a surprise attack on the unprepared ROK Sixth and Eighth divisions. The fighting, which lasted all night, was not the victory the Chinese

76. Ibid., p. 561.
77. Deng Hua, Hong Xuezhi, and Xie Fang to Peng Dehuai, "On the Current Movement of the Enemy," 19 October 1950. Peng forwarded this telegram to Mao on the same day, see *ZYJZS*, p. 22.
78. Telegram, Mao to Peng Dehuai, "We Should Try to Win the First Victory in Korea," 21 October 1950, in *JGYLMWG* 1:575–76; Telegrams, Mao to Peng, 21 October 1950, ibid., pp. 577, and 578–79.
79. Telegram, Mao to Peng, "Instructions on Rapidly Encircling and Eliminating the ROK Sixth and Eighth Divisions," 22 October 1950, in *JGYLMWG* 1:582–83; telegram, Mao to Peng, "On the Combat Situation in Korea," 23 October 1950, ibid., pp. 588–89; telegram, Mao to Peng and Deng, "On the Military Actions of the Fortieth, Thirty-Ninth, and Thirty-Eighth Armies," 23 October 1950, ibid., pp. 594–95; telegram, Mao to Peng and Deng, "Instructions on Luring the Enemy into the Deep Mountain Areas," 24 October 1950, ibid., p. 599.

leaders had hoped for—only two South Korean battalions were destroyed. The Thirty-eighth Army, which was supposed to attack the ROK Seventh division, mistook South Koreans for Americans and did not start attacking until it was too late.[80] A new phase of the Korean War had begun. How would the United States respond?

The first encounter between the Chinese forces and the South Koreans did not make much of an impression on American officials. Administration officials still saw Soviet intervention as the primary threat to the UN move to unify Korea, but there were no indications of Soviet military activity. Instead, the Soviets were acting very cautiously even when their security interests were directly affected. One such occasion was the bombing in early October of a North Korean oil supply depot at Rashin (or Najin), only seventeen miles from the Soviet border. Kennan was furious. Stressing the Soviet Union's sensitivity to its border and disapproving such bombings, he pointedly argued that Rashin was "less than 100 miles from the entrance to the road-stead of Vladivostok, and that the Soviet authorities are pathologically sensitive even to any reconnaissance activities, let alone actual bombings in that vicinity." The bombings, in Kennan's view, made it "entirely plain [to the Soviets] . . . that the real reason [for these bombings] . . . was the desire to injure the Soviet strategic position in the Far East."[81] Yet the Soviets did not even verbally protest the bombings. Another event was the accidental bombing by U.S. F-80s of a Soviet airfield at the Dry River—on the coast one hundred miles from Soviet-Korean border—in October. The bombing, Ambassador Kirk pointed out, "took place within the most important and sensitive Soviet military area in [the] Far East." Again, the Soviet reaction was mild and, concerning Korea, conciliatory.[82] Nor did the Soviets actively oppose the crossing of the Thirty-eighth parallel. The only reaction was Soviet representative to the UN Vassili Kasaniev's statement to Hans Engen of the Norwegian

---

80. For the first engagement, see telegram, Peng Dehuai to the CMC, Deng Hua, and Hong Xuezhi, 22 October 1950, in *PJSWX*, p. 329; telegram, Peng to the CMC, 25 October 1950, ibid., pp. 330–33; telegram, Peng to the CMC and East Command, 30 October 1950, ibid., p. 333; Peng's address to the first CPV Party Committee meeting, 13 November 1950, ibid., pp. 335–37.

81. George F. Kennan to Acheson, 14 August 1950, in *FRUS: 1950*, 7:575.

82. Kirk to Acheson, 5 October 1950, in *FRUS: 1950*, 7:921; Kirk to Acheson, 10 October 1950, ibid., p. 917.

delegation that "MacArthur should stop at the 38th parallel, . . . and the North Koreans would lay down their arms."[83]

In mid-October, CIA observers predicted that the Soviets would not intervene even to prevent a UN occupation of North Korea. "Since the beginning of hostilities," the CIA noted, "the Soviet Union has sought in its official statement and its propaganda to give the impression that it is not involved in the Korean situation." Moscow would not consider its prospective losses in Korea worth direct military intervention unless it had seen a global war as in Soviet interests.[84] Neither did MacArthur believe that the Soviets would take military action to prevent his forces from unifying Korea. At the Wake Island meeting with Truman and other high officials on 15 October, he insisted that the chances of Soviet or Chinese intervention were "very little. . . . Had they interfered in the first or second month it might have been decisive." No one present disagreed with the general.[85]

What, then, about the Communist Chinese forces already in North Korea? U.S. officials believed the Chinese intentions were limited. In late October, Chinese troops actually fought with the South Koreans at Onjong, about forty miles south of the Yalu, and also engaged the U.S. forces at several points.[86] Although U.S. strategists were first puzzled because the Chinese intervention seemed to be "half way" between large scale and marginal involvement, they decided that the Chinese action had limited objectives. Walter B. Smith, the director of the CIA, explicitly asserted on 1 November 1950 that China's primary motivation was to "establish a limited 'cordon sanitaire' south of the Yalu River," in order to secure the Korean-Manchurian border and to guarantee a continued flow of electric power from the Suiho hydroelectric facility.[87]

Washington officials calculated that the Chinese lacked the military capability to take any full-scale action. A CIA estimate dated 9 November noted that the PRC had about thirty to forty thousand ground troops available in Korea to engage the UN forces, with a reserve of around 200,000 regular troops in Manchuria. The Chinese had only a small air force, which consisted of "200 combat aircraft in tactical units not tested in combat to date, . . . 40 TU-2 light bombers, 40 IL-10 ground-attack aircraft, and 120 LA-9 fighters, and may include 30–40

83. John C. Ross (of the U.S. mission to the UN) to Rusk, 6 October 1950, in *FRUS: 1950*, 7:897–99; Ross to Rusk, 7 October 1950, ibid., pp. 906–17.

84. CIA report, 15 October 1950, in *FRUS: 1950*, 7:953.

85. Minutes, Wake Island conference, 15 October 1950, in *FRUS: 1950*, 7:948–60.

86. Foot, *The Wrong War*, pp. 88–89; William W. Stueck, *The Road to Confrontation: American Policy toward China and Korea, 1947–1950* (Chapel Hill, 1981), p. 242.

87. Smith to Truman, 1 November 1950, in *FRUS: 1950*, 7:1025–26.

Soviet-type swept-wing jet fighters now stationed in Shanghai." The estimate concluded that "Chinese Communist military operations to date, including the nature of the forces employed, suggest an interim military operation with limited objectives."[88] Another CIA estimate, dated 24 November, even argued that China was probably trying to drive UN forces from Korea by intimidation and diplomacy. Should China's limited military means fail, the estimate anticipated, Beijing might then "conduct, on [an] increasing scale, unacknowledged operations to immobilize UN forces in Korea, to subject them to prolonged attrition and to maintain the semblance of a North Korean State in being."[89]

Many also believed that Chinese forces were in North Korea merely to achieve political gains. John Paton Davies of the PPS repeatedly stressed that Beijing's incursion would be "limited both in form and duration." He argued that the Chinese Communists only sought "to intimidate the UN hoping that a peace-maker will bring about a negotiated settlement providing for at least a buffer zone on their frontiers." Using bluff and bellicose propaganda, he concluded, the Chinese Communists intended to "persuade the UN to seek a solution of the Korean conflict by means other than military decision." Even though the Chinese could expand their intervention, Davies asserted, the UN forces should by no means call a halt, because it "would be interpreted by the Kremlin and Peiping as a precipitate retreat inviting bold exploitation."[90]

State Department officials believed that the United States could deter any full-scale Chinese intervention. John Leighton Stuart, then acting officer in charge of political affairs at the Office of Chinese Affairs, pointed out on 3 November that a large-scale Chinese action should not be inevitable if the United States or the UN would make it *"crystal clear"* that a Chinese intervention would only widen the war. Making that clear, Stuart argued, "may prevent the spread of hostilities; and if hostilities develop notwithstanding our every effort we shall most certainly stand in a stronger position for having made the effort."[91]

On 4 November, Paul H. Nitze discussed with General Herbert B. Loper, assistant for atomic energy, U.S. Army, "the question of possible U.S. use of atomic bombs to counter Chinese Communist military

---

88. NIE-2, CIA memorandum, 8 November 1950, in *FRUS: 1950*, 7:1101–5.

89. NIE-2/1, CIA memorandum, 24 November 1950, in *FRUS: 1950*, 7:1220–21.

90. Draft memorandum by Davies, "Chinese Communist Interests in Korea," 2 November 1950, in *FRUS: 1950*, 7:1078–84. momorandum by Davies, 17, November 1950, ibid., pp. 1178–81.

91. Memorandum by Stuart, 3 November 1950, in *FRUS: 1950*, 7:1029 [emphasis added].

action in Korea." For Nitze, threatening to use the bombs in Korea for tactical purposes against the enemy's troop concentrations and artillery support positions "might prove a *deterrent* against further Chinese participation." Nevertheless, he opposed the use of atomic weapons against China's cities on the grounds that such operations "would almost certainly bring the Soviet Union into the war, . . . [and] would help arouse the peoples of Asia against us."[92]

MacArthur believed that a decisive victory in North Korea would catch both Beijing and Moscow unprepared. Between October and November, he argued that neither China or Russia was ready to intervene in Korea, and that time for Moscow especially was running out. During the Wake Island meetings, he explained to Truman that the Soviets "have [an] Air Force in Siberia and [a] fairly good one. . . . They can put 1,000 planes in the air with some 200–300 more from the Fifth and Seventh Soviet fleets, [but they] have no ground troops available for North Korea. . . . It would take six weeks to get a division across and six weeks brings the winter." MacArthur did not worry much about the Chinese because "only 50/60,000 [Chinese troops] could be gotten across the Yalu River. They have no air force. . . . If the Chinese tried to get down to Pyongyang there would be the *greatest slaughter*." MacArthur, too, did not believe that Chinese ground forces and Soviet air cover could work together in Korea because "between untrained Air and Ground forces an air umbrella is impossible without a lot of joint training."[93] On November 24 he therefore asserted that a quick and decisive victory would be "the best—indeed the only—hope that Soviet and Chinese aggressive designs may be checked before these countries are committed."[94]

MacArthur also believed that despite the numerical superiority of the Chinese and North Koreans, their lines of communication and transportation were vulnerable to air strikes. Talking with William J. Sebald, acting U.S. political adviser in Japan, on 14 November, MacArthur insisted that his air assets could destroy the Yalu bridges and the built-up areas between the present UN lines and the border,

92. Memorandum by Nitze, 4 November 1950, in *FRUS: 1950*, 7:1041–2 [emphasis added]. For a more detailed account of the Truman administration's consideration of the atomic threat, see Roger Dingman, "Atomic Diplomacy during the Korean War," *International Security* 13 (Winter 1988/89): 51–65. Dingman found that in July 1950, the administration had approved the transfer of B-29 bombers to Guam. That action, however, was more directed at deterring the Chinese from attacking Taiwan than from intervening in Korea. In fact, the B-29s returned to continental United States before Chinese forces began crossing the Yalu.

93. Minutes, Wake Island conference, 15 October 1950, pp. 953–54 [emphasis added].

94. MacArthur to the JCS, 24 November 1950, in *FRUS: 1950*, 7:1231–33.

making it impossible for the Communist forces to live off the land.[95] Three days later, he repeated to U.S. Ambassador to South Korea John J. Muccio his assertion that U.S. air power would destroy the Yalu bridges and wreak such destruction "between our present position and the border" that "this area will be left desert." With this mortal vulnerability, the general believed, the Chinese would not dare to take large-scale action in Korea.[96]

MacArthur was quite confident. Equipped with large numbers of tanks and trucks, and under sufficient air cover, the UN forces could rapidly penetrate North Korea. They were also able to concentrate force to attack the enemy in two or even three points with local numerical superiority. MacArthur told Truman at Wake Island that he had considered "making up a tank and truck column and sending it up the road to take Pyongyang directly," and that he would land the Tenth Marines in North Korea to outflank the enemy. He was confident that quick and decisive victory could be attained easily.[97]

With the Joint Chiefs' approval, MacArthur started his operations on 24 October, ordering his field commanders "to drive forward with all speed and full utilization of their forces."[98] Even when the U.S. Eighth Army engaged Chinese forces in late October, MacArthur continued to press General Walton H. Walker to advance beyond Pyongyang. As soon as the Chinese disengaged in early November, MacArthur activated his "get-the-boys-home-by-Christmas" campaign. What he wanted, he explained to Sebald on 14 November, was to end the Korean War with "an all-out offensive designed to drive the Communist forces across the Yalu River."[99]

Washington policymakers actually gave MacArthur a green light. Acheson saw no need to check his move into North Korea. In a message to British prime minister Ernest Bevin in early November, Acheson listed ten possible Chinese goals in Korea from a mere show of force to territorial expansion. In his judgment, Chinese objectives seemed limited, and thus U.S. "purposes in Korea are unchanged."[100] Although they admitted that "the military objectives of the Chinese

95. Memorandum by William J. Sebald, "General MacArthur's Concept of the Korean Campaign," 14 November 1950, in *FRUS: 1950*, 7:1148–49.

96. John J. Muccio to the State Department, 7 November 1950, in *FRUS: 1950*, 7:1175–76.

97. Minutes, Wake Island conference, 15 October 1950, p. 949.

98. Cited in James, *The Years of MacArthur*, 3:498–99.

99. Memorandum by Sebald, 14 November 1950, pp. 1148–49. Also see James, *The Years of MacArthur*, 3:534.

100. Acheson to the U.S. embassy in Great Britain, 6 November 1950, in *FRUS: 1950*, 7:1050–53.

Communist intervention in Korea are not clear," the Joint Chiefs did not consider the Chinese Communists and the North Koreans capable of driving UN forces from Korea without Soviet assistance, which was unlikely."[101] Secretary of Defense George C. Marshall noted the administration's consensus on 21 November that MacArthur should launch his offensive, provided he stayed within the Korean territory. MacArthur's orders stated—a bit ambiguously—that he was not to send U.S./UN forces to the Yalu.[102]

President Truman had no objection to MacArthur's campaign as long as the war could be restricted to Korea. He was particularly concerned with domestic political pressure. With off-year elections coming, the Republicans had found that criticizing Truman's Korean War policies could win votes. Senator Robert Taft bluntly accused the administration of "strong Communist sympathy," and Senator Alexander Wiley thought there had been "a deal of Communist [c]oddling." Truman needed a victory to counter Republican charges of appeasement of the Chinese Communists.[103]

The Chinese forces in North Korea between late October and early November did not stop the UN advance to the Yalu River. The Truman administration did not believe the Soviets were prepared to intervene, considered Chinese military intervention limited, trusted the counterthreat to invade China to deter full-scale Chinese intervention, trusted that a decisive strategy would ensure success even if the Chinese did decide to engage fully, and could not afford the political setback of defeat. Unfortunately, MacArthur's "home-by-Christmas" campaign met large-scale Chinese counterstrikes that drove the UN forces out of North Korea altogether. How did that happen? And how did Washington react to the Chinese counteroffensive?

IV

As the UN forces continued to advance northward, the Chinese leaders became more determined to confront U.S. forces. "Only if we resist," the CCP press proclaimed in early November, "can American imperialists be *taught a lesson,* and can the issues of Korea, liberation, and the independence of other areas be solved on the basis of justice

101. Bradley to Marshall, 9 November 1950, in *FRUS: 1950,* 7:1117–19; Jessup to Acheson, "Points and Considerations with Secretary Marshall and the JCS," 20 November 1950, ibid., pp. 1193–97.
102. Minutes, State-Defense meeting, 21 November 1950, in *FRUS: 1950,* 7:1204–8.
103. See Alonzo L. Hamby, *Beyond the New Deal: Harry S. Truman and American Liberalism* (New York, 1973), pp. 418–22. Also see Foot, *The Wrong War,* p. 96.

and the will of the people." No one in Beijing, however, knew how good a lesson China could teach the United States—or how far the CPV should assist the North Koreans in regaining their lost territories.[104]

It is significant that the Chinese leaders were confident that their large-scale counter offensive would not lead to either a military stalemate or a general war with the United States. A CCP Politburo document dated 26 October pointed out that "the war can be limited to Korea, and our objective is by all means attainable." The Chinese leadership based its optimism on analysis of U.S. strategic problems. The Chinese considered the United States overextended at the global level, and therefore unable to concentrate on one point without neglecting others. Because of the relatively small number of its ground forces, the United States could not match Chinese efforts.[105] An analyst of U.S. affairs in the Ministry of Foreign Affairs believed that the United States maintained approximately 590,000 ground troops in Korea, and had already committed its eleven regular divisions, the Marine Corps, and four divisions of the National Guard. Even if Washington called for a national mobilization, it could muster no more than 1,200,000 to 1,300,000 additional soldiers. Even if they all deployed to the Far East, the analyst believed, the United States would still be unable to conduct general war in both Korea and China.[106]

The Chinese considered the U.S. supply lines too long to support the fighting in Korea. "The distance between Seattle . . . and Pusan, the nearest port in South Korea, is 4,649 miles," *Dongbei Ribao* [Northeast China Daily] asserted in late October, "it takes nineteen days for a fast naval warship to travel and one month for an ordinary transport vessel; plus loading and unloading, it takes altogether forty-five days for one complete transportation of munitions." The newspaper analysis further stated that "if one combat soldier needs seven to twelve tons of supplies, it will make it extremely difficult for the United States to supply its tens of thousands of soldiers in Korea." Beijing also believed that the UN troops were suffering from poor morale. "No invading forces could ever maintain high morale for long since the war

---

104. *Renmin Ribao*, 4 November 1950, p. 1 [emphasis added].

105. CCP Politburo, "Instructions on Public Propaganda of Current Situation," 26 October 1950, cited in Yao Xu, "The Wisdom of Deciding to Resist the United States and Assist Korea," p. 11, and in ZYJZS, pp. 13–14.

106. See Deng Chao, "The U.S. Strategic Weakness," *Shijie Zhishi*, October 1950, pp. 1–3. Obviously, Deng's figure included the forces of the ROK and of other countries. In fact, Beijing was aware that at that time the U.S./UN forces had 220,000 personnel in Korea, in six American divisions, two British brigades, one Turkish brigade, and nine ROK divisions. See ZYJZS, pp. 18–19. I could not find figures of comparable precision in American sources.

of aggression itself is unjust. . . . That is why the imperialists always try to launch a surprise attack to win the war as quickly as possible."[107] Peng Dehuai told other CPV commanders in late October, that "we should not be afraid of fighting such a war against the United States; it is the United States who should be afraid of fighting a war against us."[108]

The Chinese also believed that assistance could be extracted from the Soviets, despite their reluctance. As Zhou Enlai recalled in 1958, "We chose to confront the United States in Korea because Korea was where we could most easily acquire indirect Soviet assistance."[109] China also expected that Soviet atomic weapons would deter a U.S. atomic strike against China. Chinese news networks claimed in October that U.S. atomic weapons should not be feared and that the destructiveness of these bombs "only equals to two to three thousand tons of TNT; besides the United States is not the only country possessing such a weapon." A press article even asserted that "it is the United States who should be afraid of using atomic bombs against us, because its densely concentrated industries are more vulnerable to serious damage by Soviet nuclear retaliation." These assertions follow exactly the line of the CCP Central Committee's document of 26 October.[110]

Moreover, the Chinese leadership believed that it could control the political risks of a general war. In order to avoid the appearance of declaring war against the United States, Mao insisted on not publicizing Chinese intervention in Korea. "The Northeast Border Defense Army," he instructed in early October, "should be renamed the Chinese People's Volunteers, [with the objectives of] assisting the Korean people . . . in their struggle against foreign invaders."[111] On 17 Octo-

---

107. An Fei, "How to Understand the Korean War Situation," *Dongbei Ribao*, 20 October 1950, p. 3. Also see Peng Dehuai's address to the CPV high commanders, 14 October 1950, p. 322. Peng calculated that one U.S. supply shipment would take thirty-eight days, and that the U.S. soldiers were in low spirits because Wall Street was running out of dollars to pay them. Mao also regarded long U.S. supply lines as a strategic weakness; see Ye Yumen, *Heixue*, p. 53.

108. Peng Dehuai's speech, October [undated] 1950, in *Peng Dehuai Yuanshuai Fengbei Youngcun*, ed. Museum of Chinese People's Military Revolutions (Shanghai, 1985), pp. 418–19.

109. Zhou Enlai to the Korean War veterans, 1958, cited in Yao Xu, "The Wisdom of Deciding to Resist the United States and Assist Korea," p. 7.

110. Chen Zhong, "The United States Is a Paper Tiger," *Dongbei Ribao*, 20 July 1950, p. 3; Deng Chao, "The U.S. Strategic Weakness," p. 12; Huang Zhenming, "The Invincible Soviet Military," *Dongbei Ribao*, 7 November 1950, p. 5; "How to Perceive the Intentions of the United States," in *Shishi Shouce* (Beijing, 1950), pp. 29–37. Mao had reached the same conclusion. See Ye Yumen, *Heixue*, pp. 53–54. Also see the CCP Central Committee document, 26 October 1950, in ZYJZS, p. 14.

111. CMC instruction, "On Establishing the Chinese People's Volunteers," 8 October 1950, in JGYLMWG 1:543.

ber, Mao made it even clearer to other leaders that "our volunteers have already entered Korea. . . . But we should just do it and not talk about it in the newspapers or to the public for the next few months. We will only inform our high-ranking officials of our action [in Korea] and no others."[112] Late that month, Mao also telegraphed Peng Dehuai: "You should not release any news about our fighting in Korea to the public at this time; it is better to wait till the combat situation stabilizes."[113] In early November, although allowing Peng to talk to the public, Mao once again stressed that "we should only refer our troops as the volunteers—not the volunteer army—to the public; the name of Volunteer Army is only for inside use."[114] Moreover, the PRC leadership phrased its slogans for mobilizing public support very carefully. Liu Shaoqi, CCP vice-chairman, stressed to the Party's propaganda officials in late October that even though Britain, France, the Netherlands, Belgium, Canada, New Zealand, and Australia, among others, had joined the United States in Korea, "we would only proclaim to 'resist America.' " For him, "the phrasing of the slogan is of number one importance," because China did not want to offend world opinion or make more enemies.[115]

The Chinese "full-scale" offensive had in fact only limited objectives, the primary goal being to intimidate the enemy. But the Chinese leaders did desire to win the first massive counteroffensive and to inflict as many casualties as possible. Mao told Stalin on 13 November that winning the first battle "would turn the entire military situation in Korea in our favor."[116] The Chinese forces could ensure a victory only by catching MacArthur unprepared. To this end, Mao and Peng Dehuai decided to withdraw the CPV toward the Yalu in order to lure the enemy into territory that favored the Chinese, then counter attack. Such a strategy, according to Peng, would give the Chinese the

112. Telegram, Mao to Deng Zihui and Tan Zheng, 19 October 1950, in *JGYLMWG* 1:571.
113. Telegram, Mao to Peng Dehuai, 27 October 1950, in *JGYLMWG* 1:620.
114. Telegram, Mao to Peng and Gao Gang, 5 November 1950, in *JGYLMWG* 1:648.
115. Cited in Yao Xu "The Wisdom of Deciding to Resist the United States and Assist Korea," p. 14.
116. Telegram, Mao to Stalin, "The Military Situation Can be Turned to Our Favor," 13 November 1950, in *JGYLMWG* 1:658. (This telegram was in fact drafted by Zhou Enlai, but the portion I quoted was inserted by Mao.) For Mao's determination to win the first counteroffensive, see telegram, Mao to Peng and Deng Hua, "On the Movements of the ROK Sixth and Eighth Divisions," 27 October 1950, ibid., p. 619; telegram, Mao to Peng and Deng, "The Keys to Our First Campaign," 28 October 1950, ibid., p. 623; CMC instruction to the Ninth and the Nineteenth Group Armies, "The Combat Characteristics of the ROK Forces," 30 October 1950, ibid., pp. 630–31; telegram, Mao to Peng and Deng, "On the Military Planning of the Thirty-Eighth Army," 2 November 1950, ibid.; telegram, Mao to Peng and Deng, "Ordering the Thirty-Eighth Army to Attack One or Two Brigades of the ROK Seventh Division," 5 November 1950, ibid., pp. 640–41.

advantages of "(a) shorter supply lines, (b) more familiar battle field, (c) scattered enemy forces, and (d) prolonged enemy supply lines." With Mao's approval, Peng had all his troops retreat at a constant stand-off of thirty to fifty kilometers from the enemy. This "strategic retreat," Peng argued, would mislead MacArthur into thinking that "we are weak and frightened by U.S. air superiority," and thus into moving recklessly.[117] The strategy worked. Underestimating Chinese intentions and capabilities, MacArthur charged toward the Yalu. On 28 November, Mao instructed the CPV to "attack and eliminate the U.S. First, Second, and Twenty-fifth Divisions."[118] The Chinese offensive caught the UN forces by surprise and drove them south. By 6 December 1950 the CPV had retaken Pyongyang.[119]

Despite this victory, the Chinese did not intend to unify Korea for the North Koreans. As the Chinese forces approached the Thirty-eighth parallel, the Soviet ambassador to North Korea requested that the CPV be ordered across the parallel to take the entire peninsula. Peng Dehuai refused, halting his troops north of the line. "As far as I can see," he reported to Mao in late November, "we are still fighting a protracted and difficult war. Since the enemy has switched to the defensive, concentrated its forces along a narrow front, and reinforced its main units, the situation now favors their mobile and combined forces . . . so we should stop here and adjust ourselves to the new conditions."[120] Mao concurred and forwarded Peng's explanations to Stalin. As Mao later informed Peng, Stalin also agreed and offered to

117. For Mao's idea, see telegram, Mao to Peng and Deng, "On Preparing for Enemy's Counteroffensive," 4 November 1950, in *JGYLMWG* 1:645; telegram, Mao to Peng, "To Engage in the Area of Unjong Railway," 5 November 1950, ibid., p. 647; telegram, Mao to Peng, "On the Combat Task of the Ninth Group Army," 5 November 1950, ibid., p. 650; telegram, Mao to Peng, Deng, and Pok Yi-yu, "On the Military Planning to Encircle the First Division, U.S. Marine Corps," 12 November 1950, ibid., p. 657. For Peng's calculation, see Peng's address to the first CPV Party Committee meeting, 13 November 1950, p. 341; telegram, Peng to Song Shilun, Ninth Group Army commander, 6 November 1950, in *PJSWX*, pp. 343–44; Peng to the CMC, 8 November 1950, ibid., pp. 344–45; Peng to the CMC and East Command, 21 November 1950, ibid., pp. 345–46; and Peng's address to a joint CPV-NKPA [North Korean People's Army] high command meeting, 25 January 1951, ibid., p. 366.

118. Telegram, Mao to Peng, Deng Hua, Pok Yi-yu, and Hong Xuezhi, "To Concentrate All Our Four Armies to Attack the Three U.S. Divisions," 28 November 1950, in *JGYLMWG* 1:687.

119. Telegram, Peng to the CMC, 28 November 1950, in *PJSWX*, pp. 347–48; Peng to CPV commanders and the CMC, 1 December 1950, ibid., p. 349; Peng to Mao Zedong, 4 December 1950, ibid., pp. 349–50; and Peng to the CMC, 4 December 1950, ibid., pp. 343–55.

120. Telegram, Peng to Mao, 14 November 1950, cited in Yao Xu, "Peng Dehuai's Great Contribution to the War to Resist the United States and Assist Korea," *Tangshi Yanjiu Ziliao*, January 1982, p. 5.

send two thousand more trucks to the CPV.[121] Shortly thereafter, Stalin also dismissed the Soviet ambassador to Pyongyang and complimented Peng Dehuai, calling him "a real military strategist."[122]

It is interesting to note that in early December, Mao became optimistic when he received (probably North Korean) intelligence concerning the total withdrawal of the UN forces from Korea. Mao thought the CPV should cross the Thirty-eighth parallel and advance at least to the Thirty-seventh in order to compel Washington to leave Korea as quickly as possible. Mao telegraphed Peng on 4 December, that doing so might force the Americans to request a cease-fire, but they would not be sincere about settling the Korea problem unless the CPV seized Seoul and eliminated at least all the South Korean troops.[123] But Peng disagreed and insisted that the CPV stay in positions at least ten kilometers north of the parallel and postpone any offensives until the coming spring.[124]

Mao did not give up easily. On 21 December, he explained to Peng again that stopping would put the Chinese and the North Koreans at a political disadvantage. He instructed Peng to "simply concentrate on attacking the South Koreans" without going too far south and to stay ready to withdraw if necessary.[125] Although he still regarded crossing the Thirty-eighth parallel as "of no big political significance," Peng accepted Mao's instructions. But he insisted on not attacking Seoul, or at best on letting the North Koreans occupy it, should the enemy abandon it. On 31 December, the CPV launched their New Year's Eve offensive and, in a week, drove the UN forces back to the Thirty-seventh parallel, actually capturing Seoul.[126] Nevertheless, there was no indication of a UN withdrawal from Korea; instead, the military situation became a stalemate with both sides launching offensives and counteroffensives throughout the spring of 1951.[127] The war moved into its protracted phase.

Apparently Mao had miscalculated. He felt an urgent need to reconsider China's action. In his telegram to Stalin on 1 March 1951, Mao

121. Ibid.
122. Ibid., p. 6.
123. Telegram, Mao to Peng and Gao, "Our Forces Must Cross the Thirty-Eighth Parallel," 13 December 1950, in *JGYLMWG* 1:722–23.
124. Telegram, Peng to Mao, 19 December 1950, in *MJSWXNBB*, pp. 691–92, note 18.
125. Telegram, Mao to Peng, "On the Military Situation in Korea and Our Combat Planning," 21 December 1950, in *JGYLMWG* 1:731–32; telegram, Mao to Peng and Kim Il-sung, "Our Main Forces Will Withdraw for Rest after the Second Campaign," 26 December 1950, ibid., pp. 734–36.
126. Telegram, Peng to the CMC, 15 December 1950, in *PJSWX*, pp. 355–56; and Peng to Mao and Gao Gang, 28 December 1950, ibid., pp. 359–60.
127. Peng to the CMC and East Command, 4 January 1951, in *PJSWX*, pp. 360–61; and Peng's address to the joint CPV-KPA meeting, 25 June 1951, ibid., pp. 364–70.

admitted that "to fight for a quick ending is unrealistic and harmful. . . . Therefore, we should prepare for a protracted war although we may try to end it as soon as possible." He further explained that "the essence of this policy is not how much territory we can gain but how many U.S. troops we can eliminate in a few years. Only wiping out a few hundred thousand more American soldiers will compel the United States to get out."[128] In mid-June, Mao and the Central Military Commission once again stressed that "our policy is to wage a protracted war and conduct truce talks at the same time."[129] Following these instructions, the CPV command redeployed to maintain a "generally defensive posture only with small-scale offensive actions." Peng told the high commanders on 25 June 1951, that "due to the objective difficulties, we can not win the Korean War quickly, and we should therefore adopt the protracted-war strategy to wear the enemy down." The essential objective, the CPV commanders agreed, was to make everything feel so difficult for the enemy that it would have to retreat [*podi zhinan er tui*].[130]

Beijing's determination was further confirmed when Mao's famous 1938 article, "On Protracted War," was republished in 1951. The Chinese leaders had not forgotten how well the protracted-war strategy had worked against the Japanese. They understood that a final victory over—or denial of final victory to—an enemy with technical superiority and numerical inferiority depended not on taking enemy positions but on simply killing as many enemy soldiers as possible. How did the United States perceive China's intentions? How did it respond?

The sudden shift of the military balance in Korea alarmed Washington. U.S. officials quickly concluded that Moscow was behind the Chinese intervention, probably as part of the beginning of a larger-scale military action against the United States. In early December 1950, Clubb pointed out that the Chinese action was "largely meaningless, unless it is a component part of a global Communist plan—for a war by China alone against the UN could bear only bitter fruits." The Chinese Communists, he asserted, would thus invoke the Sino-Soviet alliance and tie down U.S. forces in Korea while "Communist blows" could be directed elsewhere throughout Asia. Clubb even believed that Soviet military actions had already begun. Noting the "energetic repair and construction of air fields in China, on a scale far in excess of

128. Mao Zedong to Stalin, 1 March 1951, in *JGYLMWG* 2:151–53; *Nie Rongzhen Memoirs*, pp. 741–42.

129. Mao's instructions are enclosed in Peng to the CMC, 1 July 1951, in *ZYJZS*, p. 162.

130. Peng's address to the CVP high commanders, "On the Protracted War Strategy and Our Guidelines of Future Combats," 25 June 1951, in *PJSWX*, pp. 403–5. For the minutes of the CPV high command meeting of 25–27 June 1951, see *ZYJZS*, pp. 162–65.

any conceivable needs," Clubb asserted that "the only logical inference to be drawn from such action is that preparations are being made for their use."[131] CIA analysts agreed that the Chinese and the Soviets knew that they were risking general war and may have even planned for it. Under these circumstances, the CIA predicted, "the Soviets would come openly to the military support of China, under the terms of [the] Sino-Soviet treaty, in the event of major US (UN) operations against China's territory."[132]

Believing that the Soviet Union would openly challenge the United States in Korea or elsewhere, U.S. officials saw the Chinese as merely the Soviet spearhead. They felt it imperative to do something vigorous to deter the Soviet Union and its allies from further action. One proposal was to retaliate against mainland China immediately and to compel the Chinese to withdraw from Korea by severely crippling Chinese warmaking capabilities. On 30 December, MacArthur recommended to the JCS that the United States "(a) blockade the coast of China; (b) destroy through naval gunfire and air bombardment China's industrial capability to wage war; (c) secure reinforcements for the Nationalist garrison on Formosa to strengthen our position in Korea; [and] (d) release existing restrictions upon the Formosa garrison for diversionary action, possibly leading to counter invasion against vulnerable areas of the Chinese mainland." The general stressed that these actions would "largely neutralize China's capability to wage aggressive war and thus save Asia from the engulfment otherwise facing it."[133]

Some military officers advocated using the atomic counterthreat against China. In early December, General Curtis LeMay expressed his willingness to send his bombers across the Pacific.[134] In response to the Joint Chiefs' inquiries concerning how such weapons might be used, MacArthur submitted in early 1951 "a list of retardation targets which he considered would require 26 [atomic] bombs." The field command calculated that one bomb would be needed on the enemy's invasion force and four on critical concentrations of the enemy air power.[135] Meanwhile, the Army's Plans and Operations division proposed to warn the Chinese that if they did not withdraw their forces from Korea at once, the UN forces would take appropriate military actions against China, including a "prompt use of the atomic

131. Clubb to Rusk, 1 December 1950, in *FRUS: 1950*, 7:1291–92.

132. Memorandum by the CIA, "Soviet Intentions in the Current Situation," 2 December 1950, in *FRUS: 1950*, 7:1308–9.

133. MacArthur to Bradley, 30 December 1950, in *FRUS: 1950*, 7:1630–33.

134. LeMay to Vandenberg, 2 December 1950; memorandum by LeMay 6 December 1950, cited in Dingman, "Atomic Diplomacy during the Korean War," p. 66 and note 80.

135. MacArthur to the JCS, 5 January 1951, cited in Foot, *The Wrong War*, pp. 114–15. Also see Gaddis, *The Long Peace*, p. 116.

bomb."[136] But at no point did Truman endorse these suggestions. At a press conference on 30 November, Truman only—perhaps accidentally—remarked that the use of the "atomic bomb in Korea is under active consideration." This was by no means an explicit threat to use the atomic bomb against China. There is no indication that Truman had intended to make such a threat. More important, the Truman administration never readied atomic weapons to be used against the Chinese in Korea, although atomic components were transferred to Okinawa.[137]

Acheson also asserted that neither retaliation nor atomic threats would be acceptable. He feared that either move would provoke a third world war—which the United States would probably have to fight alone. At an NSC meeting in mid-January of 1951 he pointed out that any large counterattacks would prove ineffective without the support of the allies, and that support was apparently lacking.[138] British prime minister Clement Attlee visited Washington in early December 1950 and convinced Acheson that Britain would not support expanding the conflict into China at the risk of undermining European security. More important, Britain "strongly opposed . . . the use of [atomic] bomb in China." The British prime minister had Truman acknowledge that "our *desire* not to use the bomb be stressed."[139]

State Department officials proposed a combination of limited military actions and political intimidation to counter further Chinese offensives without provoking a general war. On 7 December 1950 Clubb proposed that the UN forces be kept "in a relatively restricted beachhead with good port facilities which could be made into a 'Stalingrad' that the Chinese Communists would find very costly to reduce." At the same time, the UN should condemn the Beijing regime as the aggressor and "effectively check [its] drive for a UN seat" to cause the Chinese Communists to "suffer . . . political disadvantages."[140] Rusk fully concurred in Clubb's formula, adding that the United States should "enlist the energies of non-Communist Asia . . . to fully disclose the real character of Chinese Communist aggression." Late in

136. Recommendation by the Office of Plans and Operations, 28 November 1950, cited in Foot, *The Wrong War*, p. 116.

137. See Gaddis, *The Long Peace*, pp. 118 and 121. Also see Dingman, "Atomic Diplomacy during the Korean War," pp. 65–69. Dingman particularly noted that the majority of Pentagon strategists opposed the use of atomic weapons in Korea.

138. Minutes, NSC meeting, 19 January 1951, in *FRUS: 1951*, 7:93–94.

139. Minutes, Truman-Attlee talks, 7 December 1950, in *FRUS: 1950*, 7:1449–61; memorandum by R. Gordon Arneson, special assistant to Acheson, "Truman-Attlee Conversations of December 1950: Use of Atomic Weapons," 13 January 1953, enclosed in memorandum by Jessup, 7 December 1950, ibid., pp. 1462–65 [emphasis in original].

140. Clubb to Rusk, 7 December 1950, in *FRUS: 1950*, 7:1445–46.

that same month, Rusk further explained to Acheson that the only way to end the fighting was "to make it in the interest of the Chinese Communists to accept some stabilization by making it so costly for them that they could not afford not to accept." The secretary of state agreed with his aides. He directed the State Department to appeal for the UN to pass a resolution condemning the Beijing regime, and also suggested that further discussions should be undertaken "with the Military [on] how we move ahead" in the battlefield.[141]

The Joint Chiefs accepted the State Department's proposal in February 1951. An effective way of solving the Korean problem, the JCS concluded, was to stabilize military lines in order to achieve a cease-fire based on the Thirty-eighth parallel and to conduct a phased withdrawal of all foreign troops through negotiations.[142] This "solution" kept the United States at war in Korea for another two years.

V

Neither Washington nor Beijing expected to confront each other when the Korean War broke out. As the conflict developed, they began in a state of mutual deterrence and ended actually killing each other's soldiers. China entered the war to deter the United States from invading China. The United States entered the war to deter the Communists from expanding in Asia or elsewhere. The two countries then met in mutual military deterrence over North Korea. The United States tried to deter the Chinese from crossing the Yalu River and undertaking full-scale intervention, and the Chinese tried to deter the UN forces from crossing the Thirty-eighth parallel and occupying North Korea. Both sides failed.

The PRC leadership obviously exaggerated the U.S. threat. Having long suspected American hostility toward a Communist China, it quickly concluded that U.S. intervention in Korea and the interposition of the U.S. Seventh Fleet in the Taiwan Strait was part of a long-planned U.S. offensive. The Chinese leaders were therefore unable to understand that U.S. actions in Korea were generally defensive and reflected only limited aims. It is curious that Moscow never pressed Beijing to intervene in Korea. The Chinese took the initiative to defend their revolution and, sensitive to U.S. plans to split China from the Moscow-led socialist camp, to prove their internationalist—not

141. Rusk to Acheson, 21 December 1950, in *FRUS: 1950*, 7:1588–89; memorandum by Lucius D. Battle, 27 December 1950, ibid., pp. 1600–1604.
142. Bradley to Marshall, 6 February 1951, in *FRUS: 1951*, 7:156–68.

nationalist—communist identity. In the mid-1960s, Chen Yi, the minister of foreign affairs, noted that Stalin ceased to consider China a potential Yugoslavia only after the Chinese decided to intervene in Korea.[143]

Nor did Washington understand China's intentions in Korea. U.S. strategists could not see Beijing as other than subordinate to Moscow. Once they concluded that Moscow was not ready for a general war, they could not take Beijing seriously. They did not understand how China's security interests were actually affected by UN actions in Korea. Therefore, they could not understand why Beijing intervened when the United States announced it would not attack Manchuria or bomb the Chinese hydroelectric plants. It is also interesting to note that when U.S. officials assessed Beijing's intentions, they failed to consider that the Chinese Communist leaders were anxious to prove themselves. They did not realize that China's recent history of weakness in the face of foreign invasions had created a strong determination among the Chinese to stand up against Western powers, especially the United States. Washington also underestimated Beijing's intentions because it relied on military capability—in terms of weaponry, combat strength, and strategic resources—as an interpretive tool. The "experts" in Washington overlooked the fact that intentions sometimes have nothing to do with capabilities, indeed, that intentions may even be incompatible with capabilities. Furthermore, Washington did not realize that the Chinese understanding of military strength differs from its own. Military capability, in the Chinese view, involves not only combat strength but also *tianshi* ["timeliness"], *dili* ["topographical advantage"], and *renhe* ["domestic harmony"]. With all these conditions favoring them, even though they were inferior in weaponry, the Chinese leaders were optimistic about final victory. Washington officials seem to have never understood these differences.

The Chinese differed from the Americans particularly in how they calculated deterrence strategy. Washington strategists hardly understood that the Chinese leaders would regard a belligerent response to a crisis as the best deterrence against apparent long-term threats. U.S. officials never understood that China would rely on protracted war to deny a final victory to the enemy as a deterrent to discourage the United States from taking further actions in Korea and in other areas. Although Beijing tried to warn the UN forces not to cross the Thirty-eighth parallel, the Chinese leaders never wanted their signals to be explicit and consistent. When they decided to intervene, they de-

143. Chen Yi's news conference, 1964, cited in Yao Xu, "The Wisdom of Deciding to Resist the United States and Assist Korea," p. 10.

ployed secretly in order to lure the enemy into areas where the Chinese held superior tactical positions. U.S. strategists failed to understand Beijing's tactic of employing ambiguity, which in return weakened the deterrent force of China's actions.

Each misunderstood the other's intentions. Each mistook the other for an aggressor. Each failed to deter the other and ended up directly engaging the other in Korea. American strategists have long since realized that the United States entered "a wrong war," but the Beijing authorities have never admitted that China's involvement could have been avoided. Because of mutual misperception, the United States and China have been in a military stalemate in Korea ever since 1951.

[5]

The End of the Korean War,
1952–1953

On 27 July, 1953, only a few months after taking office, President Eisenhower signed an armistice agreement that ended the Korean war. He intended to resolve the war as quickly as possible and to avoid being caught in a similar situation in Asia in the future. To accomplish this, Eisenhower and his secretary of state, John Foster Dulles, changed the articulation and implementation of deterrence by *threatening* to widen the war even through the use of nuclear weapons within and outside Korea. How did the new administration adopt this policy? More important, did the U.S. nuclear threat really compel Beijing to accept a cessation of the Korean conflict?

I

A national intelligence estimate made just before Eisenhower's election reported that Sino-Soviet policy was still based on the "common hostility to a resurgent and non-communist Japan and to U.S. power in the Western Pacific."[1] Eisenhower's National Security Council accepted this assessment. Even if the Communists did accept an armistice in Korean, the NSC staff asserted in April 1953 that would not mean that they had abandoned their long-range intention to extend their own influence in the Far East. The NSC also insisted that there

1. NIE-58, "Relations between the Chinese Communist Regime and the USSR: Their Present Character and Probably Future Courses," 10 September 1952, in *FRUS: 1952–1954*, 14:99–101.

could be no peace in Korea as long as Communist expansion continued to threaten "Free world security in the area."[2]

The NSC found that the Soviet Union had a stake in the Korean War.
It argued that Moscow sought to control East Asia, Japan, and the offshore islands in the Western Pacific primarily through Communist
China. By typing down substantial U.S. forces and resources in Korea
without committing either its own forces or its prestige directly, the Soviet Union would strengthen its global position at the expense of the
United States and secure its eastern flank, allowing it to "concentrate
its offensive power in other areas." As long as the Soviets continued to
enjoy such advantages, the NSC concluded, "there will be less incentive from the USSR . . . to bring about a cessation of [the Korean]
hostilities."[3]

The Eisenhower administration also believed that the PRC would
not accept an armistice because it felt too powerful to need to make any
concessions. On 2 April, 1953, the National Security Council Planning
Board described the Chinese troops in Korea as having "good morale, . . . numerically superior in strength, with adequate logistic
support, and disposed in extremely well organized defensive positions
in depth." That added to the "growing air potential" of the Chinese
led the NSC to conclude that Beijing's ability to maintain troops in
Korea "unquestionably" reinforced its determination not to concede
on UN terms.[4]

A national intelligence estimate (NIE-80) supported this conviction.
The report cited a steady but substantial increase of Chinese ground
forces in Korea from July 1951 to March 1953, and a sizable reserve in
Manchuria and North China. The analysis assessed the combat effectiveness and morale of these troops as ranging from good to excellent,
and found that major reorganization, particularly in armor, heavy artillery, and anti-aircraft artillery units, had substantially increased the
firepower of the Chinese ground forces. The Chinese had also been
able, although at considerable cost, to transport sufficient supplies to
meet their combat requirements and to create stockpiles sufficient to
support about thirty-five days of offensive operations. In addition, the
combat strength of the Chinese Air Force was believed to have tripled
since mid-1951. The estimate noted that the Chinese Communists

2. National Security Council Staff Study, "Basic Objective toward Communist China,"
6 April 1953, in *FRUS: 1952–1954*, 14:179.

3. NSC 48, "Statement of Policy Proposed by the National Security Council on U.S.
Policies in the Far East," 6 April 1953, in *FRUS: 1952–1954*, 7:286–87.

4. NSC 147, "Analysis of Possible Courses of Action in Korea," 2 April 1953, in *FRUS:
1952–1954*, 15:842–43. In March 1953, the NSC Senior Staff was reorganized as the NSC
Planning Board. It was chaired by the special assistant to the president for national security affairs, then Robert Cutler.

already had 2,350 planes, including 1,000 jet fighters and 100 recently introduced IL-28 jet light bombers, in the North Korea-Manchuria area. Even by American standards, Chinese fighter units had reached "a fairly high standard of combat efficiency." Moreover, a highly organized, well-integrated defensive zone extended fifteen to twenty miles to the rear of present battle positions, rendering Chinese ground forces much less vulnerable to air attack. The intelligence estimate concluded that Chinese military capability made it unlikely that Beijing would "make concessions . . . to secure an armistice."[5]

Neither did Beijing have any domestic constraints that would compel it to make concessions in the truce talks. On 31 March, Julian F. Harrington, the U.S. consul general in Hong Kong, reported no increase in internal pressure upon the Communist regime. The antibureaucracy campaign had met no strong resistance. Preparations for elections showed that the establishment of a façade of democracy would not disturb the Chinese leadership. There appeared to be no drastic changes in agricultural programs or in the central planning process. Harrington saw no domestic difficulties that would make the Chinese leaders "alter their adamant stand" in the armistice negotiations.[6] Harrington's assertions echoed NIE-80, which pointed out that Communist China was stronger economically and politically than it had been in 1950 and 1951. Industrial and agricultural production had risen. Greater political and economic control had increased the resources at Communist China's disposal. The study found that the Beijing government had proved "certainly adequate to control any resentment which may develop.[7]

Washington also saw the continuing efficacy of the Sino-Soviet partnership. Although the Kremlin still dominated North Korean affairs, the Chinese Communists were playing an increasing role in wartime policymaking. Moscow was still furnishing a large share of the military equipment and supplies for Beijing's war effort. Even Stalin's death in March had not disturbed Sino-Soviet cooperation in Korea.[8]

Thus, administration officials did not believe that the Communists would accept UN terms, but the new president was under domestic pressure to end the conflict as soon as possible. With the slogan "Corruption, Communism, and Korea," the Eisenhower campaign had worked feverishly to create an impression that only "Ike" could bring

5. NIE-80, "Communist Capabilities and Probable Courses of Action in Korea through 1953," 3 April 1953, in *FRUS: 1952–1954*, 15:865–69.
6. Harrington to the Department of State, 31 March 1953, in *FRUS: 1952–1954*, 15:828–29.
7. NIE-80, 3 April, 1953, pp. 866 and 874.
8. Ibid., pp. 874–75.

an "honorable peace." The American public, impatient with the protracted war and the apparently fruitless negotiations, had been convinced.[9] Eisenhower understood that his claim would be tested immediately, and that the American public would probably not accept any excuses for failure.

Powerful conservative figures in the Senate—particularly Taft, Knowland, Joseph McCarthy, and William Jenner—explicitly rejected the idea that halting the Communists at the thirty-eighth parallel would constitute victory or honor. Instead, they called for the unification of Korea through an all-out offensive or by expanding the war to the Chinese mainland.[10] Claiming that "the United States cannot safely continue an indefinite military stalemate in Korea," Senator Ralph E. Flanders called Robert Cutler, the special assistant to the president for national security affairs, into his office on 19 March and asked him to tell the president that "the American people want to see the Korean war brought to a victorious end, even at a cost."[11]

But the new administration had promised to reduce American military costs. The "New Look" strategy developed during the campaign committed Eisenhower and his advisers to fiscal restraint. The new treasury secretary, George Humphrey, insisted that a "great equation" between restricted military expenditure and economic prosperity would result in enhanced national security. Under the "New Look" emphasis was to shift from maintaining high military manpower levels to relying on a broader industrial-technological base for emergencies, thereby justifying reductions in the defense budget. For Humphrey, a Republican administration committed to decreasing taxation had to "get Korea out of way."[12] Eisenhower was fully aware that if he allowed the war to go on, the United States would have to continue spending on a scale that would bankrupt the country.[13] But how could the administration resolve the Korean conflict without increasing the military budget?

Furthermore, the new administration knew that the allies would not support ending the war by escalating it. Britain had long opposed escalation. Prime Minister Winston Churchill had welcomed the election of Eisenhower, but had come to distrust Republican rightwingers and

9. On how Eisenhower used the Korean issue in the presidential campaign, see Ronald J. Caridi, *The Korean War and American Policies: The Republican Party as a Case Study* (Philadelphia, 1968), pp. 230–32.

10. Ibid., pp. 246–47.

11. Cutler to Charles E. Wilson, 21 March 1953, in *FRUS: 1952–1954*, 15:816–17.

12. Cited in Callum A. MacDonald, *Korea: The War before Vietnam* (New York, 1986), p. 179.

13. Dwight D. Eisenhower, *The White House Years: Mandate for Change, 1953–1956* (Garden City, N.Y., 1963), p. 180; Gaddis, *Strategies of Containment*, p. 164.

the Pentagon. Before Eisenhower's inauguration, Churchill announced his opposition to military escalation in Korea, which, in his view, would only pin down the United States and benefit Russia. In a talk with John Foster Dulles in March of 1953, British foreign minister Anthony Eden made it clear that London would not endorse any escalation of hostilities in Korea, and insisted that Britain be consulted in advance concerning any further military moves.[14] A NSC study in April 1953 noted that Britain was concerned that military escalation in Korea would risk general war with China, weaken the defense of Europe, and prompt a Chinese Communist attack on Hong Kong. This study also recognized that Canada, Australia, and New Zealand shared these British concerns, and that France worried about "Chinese Communist support or direct intervention in Indochina" as a possible result of the expansion of war in Korea. In the NSC's view, these nations would not back any military solution to the Korean conflict.[15]

Clearly, the Eisenhower administration was in a dilemma. The enemy would reject any armistice agreement on UN terms. The American public, especially the Republican conservatives who strongly supported a military solution, insisted on immediate and decisive action to achieve an "honorable" peace in Korea, a course of action fiscal restraint and reluctant allies would not accommodate.

Still open to options, Eisenhower and his advisers understood that the administration had to appear firm. To redeem his election pledge, Eisenhower traveled to Korea late in November of 1952. Upon his return, he announced that the United States would only seek an honorable peace in Korea by bringing the Communists to terms not "by words, however eloquent, but only by deeds executed under circumstances of our own choosing" that would, as well, deter the Communists from further aggression by making them "realize [that] it would be fateful folly to ignite other conflagrations like the Korean conflict elsewhere in the world."[16]

The Eisenhower administration's first deed was to "unleash" Chiang Kai-shek. In his 1958 State of the Union address, Eisenhower announced that the Seventh Fleet would no longer shield Communist China from nationalist attacks.[17] The conservatives in Washington

14. MacDonald, *Korea*, pp. 179–80, and 180–81.

15. NSC Staff Study, "Analysis of Possible Courses of Action in Korea," enclosed in NSC 147, 2 April 1953, pp. 848–49.

16. Eisenhower's speech at La Guardia Airport, 14 December 1952, *New York Times*, 15 December 1952, p. 6.

17. *Public Papers of the Presidents of the United States: Dwight D. Eisenhower, 1953–1961* (Washington, D.C., 1960–61), pp. 12–34 [hereafter *Public Papers*].

read this as an attempt to force a Communist retreat from Korea. Senator Knowland predicted that the Communists would no longer be able to "center their energies and their attacks upon our troops in Korea."[18] But such a course of action, in fact, was more symbolic than real. The KMT's capacity to attack the mainland was limited. Admiral Arthur W. Radford, the commander of the Seventh Fleet, had no "authority to cooperate with the Chinese [Nationalists]" in attacking the mainland.[19] On 3 April, the administration even decided to secure a commitment from Chiang that he would do nothing that the United States would consider contrary to its national interests and hold up shipments of combat aircraft until Chiang agreed.[20] "Unleashing Chiang" only appeared to pressure the Chinese Communists in the Taiwan Strait, it actually restored to the United States its freedom of action on Taiwan.

More important, administration officials considered pressing harder on the battlefield. General Mark Clark, the commander of the UN forces, had determined that a military victory sufficient to compel the CPV to accept UN terms would require "air atks [attacks] on critical tgts [targets] in Manchuria and China and an imposition of a naval blockade against China" to "inflict damage [on the enemy], strain enemy resources, and decrease enemy capabilities." In February 1953, the general asked the Joint Chiefs of Staff to authorize these actions.[21] Pentagon strategists seemed to have concurred in Clark's proposal. On 23 March 1953, the JCS listed the options for damaging Chinese Communist military capabilities. Following the JCS lead, the NSC Planning Board issued a proposal in early April to extend and intensify military action in Korea, including "air and naval operations directly against China and Manchuria and a coordinated offensive to seize a position generally at the waist of Korea."[22]

Washington also considered employing the nuclear threat to pressure the Chinese. Both the Joint Chiefs and the NSC Staff felt that the UN forces should consider the use of atomic weapons "on a sufficiently large scale to insure success." The NSC Planning Board explicitly stressed the "military, psychological and political implications" of using nuclear weapons in Korea. Such action would curtail the "Communist Chinese capability of continuing present hostilities . . . or of

18. *Congressional Record*, 6 February 1953, p. 917; *New York Times*, 13 February 1953, p. 4.
19. Memorandum by Dillon, 4 February 1953, in *FRUS: 1952–1954*, 14:142–43.
20. Memorandum of discussion, NSC meeting, 8 April 1953, in *FRUS: 1952–1954*, 14:180–183.
21. Clark to JCS, 29 September 1952, in *FRUS: 1952–1954*, 15:548–40; Clark to JCS, 9 February 1953, ibid., pp. 758–59.
22. NSC 147, 2 April 1953, pp. 838–57.

initiating aggression elsewhere, . . . maximize the deterrent effect of our atomic capabilities on the USSR," and eliminate "threats to our military position in Korea . . . more effectively, quickly and cheaply than by use of conventional weapons."[23] Clearly, American strategists regarded nuclear threats as an effective way—if not the only way—to press the Communists to accept an armistice.

Higher officials endorsed compelling the Chinese to end the war. On 21 March, Eisenhower directed the Pentagon to determine the cost of inflicting "maximum damage" on the Chinese forces and taking and holding the "waist line" of Korea.[24] The new president also discussed with his aides the utility of nuclear weapons in accomplishing these objectives. For him, "it would be worth the cost if, through the use of atomic weapons, we could (1) achieve a substantial victory over the Communist forces, and (2) get to the line at the waist of Korea"; besides, the use of nuclear weapons "might be cheaper and dollar-wise."[25] Secretary of State Dulles strongly supported imposing military pressure. He had long argued that the United States could not get much out of a Korean settlement "until we have shown—before all Asia—our clear superiority by giving the Chinese one hell of a licking."[26]

But how to convince the Chinese of an American "clear superiority"? Both Eisenhower and Duller appeared to have understood that the nuclear threat would have no credibility unless the enemy was convinced that such weapons *could* be used without restraint. One concern was targeting. As early as February, Eisenhower told a NSC meeting that he thought the Kaesong area in North Korea would be "a good target." In March, he repeatedly asked Pentagon strategists to find feasible targets in Korea. When the Joint Chiefs informed him in May that there were no such targets, Eisenhower "seemed not wholly satisfied." He then raised the question: "Could not such weapons be used with effect on tactical targets of the Chinese Communists?"[27] there is no evidence that the president received any satisfactory answer.

Eisenhower and Dulles also wanted to remove all political restraints on the use of nuclear weapons. Dulles felt it imperative "to break down the false distinction"[28] the Soviets made between nuclear weap-

23. Ibid., p. 845.

24. Cutler to Wilson, 21 March 1953, p. 815.

25. Minutes, NSC meetings, 13 May 1953, in *FRUS: 1952–1954*, 15:826; minutes, NSC meeting, 20 May 1953, ibid., p. 1067.

26. Cited in Emmett John Hughes, *The Ordeal of Power: A Political memoir of the Eisenhower Years* (New York, 1963), p. 105.

27. Minutes NSC meeting, 11 February 1953, in FRUS: 1952–1954, 15:170; Cutler to Wilson, 21 March 1953, p. 815; minutes NSC meeting 13 May 1953, p. 1014.

28. Minutes NSC meeting, 11 February 1953, pp. 769–70.

ons and all others. In March, both Eisenhower and Dulles were "in complete agreement that somehow or other the tabu which surrounds the use of atomic weapons would have to be destroyed." Dulles made it even clearer that "we should make every effort to dissipate the world opinion that we could not use an A-bomb."[29] Later that year, the president seemed to have believed that the taboo had been successfully broken when he told Anthony Eden that "the American public no longer distinguished between atomic and other weapons."[30] Eisenhower might have convinced the American public, but even though he had already directed the Department of State in May to "infiltrate these ideas into the minds of our allies," they never explicitly endorsed the use of nuclear weapons in Korea. He was, indeed, impeded by a lack of allies' support.[31]

Administration officials also worried about how to signal China that they were considering the use of nuclear weapons. "Prior to actual initiation of such military operations," a special policy estimate pointed out in April, "the Communists should become convinced that the strength and determination of the UN powers were sufficient to endanger their principal interest . . . [Only then] they would probably make the concessions necessary to reach an armistice."[32] Even before Eisenhower took office, the State Department had suggested having the CIA spread rumors that atomic weapons could be used in Korea, and if necessary, against China as well.[33] In New Delhi in late May 1953, Dulles informed Indian prime minister Nehru—assuming that he would, in turn, inform Beijing—that if an armistice did not emerge, "the United States would probably make a stronger rather than a lesser military exertion."[34] Meanwhile, when on 25 May 1953, the Chinese and North Korean negotiators rejected the U.S. proposal of no forced repatriation of POWs, Charles Bohlen, the U.S. ambassador in Moscow, warned the Soviet Foreign Minister V. M. Molotov of the "seriousness and importance" of the U.S. position. Bohlen made it clear that "a failure of the present armistice talks would lead to . . . a situation which the U.S. Government was most sincerely and earnestly

29. Minutes, special NSC meeting, 31 March 1953, in *FRUS: 1952–1954*, 15:826–27.
30. Cited in Foot, *The Wrong War*, p. 213.
31. Minutes, State Department–JSC meeting, 27 March 1953, in *FRUS: 1952–1954*, 15:817–18; NSC 147, 2 April 1953, p. 846; minutes, NSC meeting 20 May 1953, p. 1066.
32. SE-41, 8 April 1953, in *FRUS: 1952–1954*, 15:891.
33. Cited in Gaddis, *The Long Peace*, pp. 125–26.
34. Memorandum of conversation by Dulles, 21 May 1953, in *FRUS: 1952–1954*, 15:1068–69. Roger Dingman has a different interpretation. He finds that Dulles appealed for Soviet cooperation in persuading Beijing and Pyongyang to compromise on the POW issue rather than issuing an atomic threat. But I argue that Dulles might have had both purposes in mind. See Dingman, "Atomic Diplomacy during the Korean War," pp. 85–87.

attempting to avoid."[35] As an additional warning, missiles with atomic warheads were transferred to Okinawa in the early spring with the assumption that the Soviets and the Chinese would detect their deployment. Eisenhower further asserted in April that with "indications" that some nuclear arms were actually being placed under Pentagon control, "the desired effect could certainly be secured."[36]

Administration officials understood that pressuring the Communists demanded both militant rhetoric and cautious tactics. In the spring, it appeared that a rigid and demanding Syngman Rhee might disrupt U.S. strategy. Infuriated by the possibility of a cease-fire that would repudiate his goal of liberation, Rhee threatened repeatedly to fight on his own and even to withdraw ROK support for the UN forces. The danger, Ellis O. Briggs, the U.S. ambassador to Seoul, reported, was Rhee's "general unpredictability and tendency occasionally to act without adequate consideration of consequences." Even worse, in General Clark's view, was not knowing when and how Rhee carry out his threat.[37] Fearing that the United States would have to undertake military action to rescue Rhee from suicidal defeat, Eisenhower immediately warned him that any actions by the ROK that would nullify U.S. peace objectives "could not be supported by this or other governments supporting the defense of your country.[38] This warning, however, was not enough to calm Rhee down. A carrot was needed as well as a stick. In late spring, Eisenhower promised Rhee a mutual security pact guaranteeing a long-term U.S. commitment to South Korea's postwar security.[39] The U.S. intention was to prevent Rhee from messing things up.

35. Smith to Bohlen, 26 May 1953, in *FRUS: 1952–1954*, 15:1103–04; Bohlen to the State Department, 28 May 1953, ibid., pp. 1108–11.

36. For the deployment of atomic weapons on Okinawa, see Sherman Adams, *First Hand Report: The Inside Story of the Eisenhower Administration* (New York, 1961), p. 55. Dingman, however, finds no evidence for such a deployment. He argues that archival sources only suggest that Eisenhower decided to authorize transfer of completed atomic weapons to military custody for oversea deployment in June 1953, and finds no indication that Okinawa was one such deployment site ("Atomic Diplomacy during the Korean War,"pp. 84 and 87). Rosenberg, too, finds that Eisenhower authorized the transfer of "a sizable number of complete atomic weapons to the military for deployment to specified bases afloat and ashore" (David Alan Rosenberg, "The Origins of Overkill: Nuclear Weapons and American Strategy, 1945–1960," *International Security*, 7 (Spring 1983): 27).

37. Briggs to the State Department, 14 April 1953, in *FRUS: 1952–1954*, 15:906–07; Briggs to the State Department, 26 April 1953, ibid., pp. 938–39; Clark to Collins, 26 April 1953, ibid., p. 940.

38. Eisenhower to Rhee, 23 April 1953, in *FRUS: 1952–1954*, 15:930.

39. Clark to the JCS, 13 May 1953, in *FRUS: 1952–1954*, 15:1010–12. Clark reported that Rhee "strongly desired a mutual security pact." Also see minutes, State Department–JCS meeting, 15 May 1953, ibid., pp. 1025–26; Smith to Briggs, 15 May 1953, ibid., pp. 1029–32. In Briggs' view, it was "questionable" whether Rhee would stop opposing the armistice even with such a mutual security pact (ibid., p. 1029 and note 2).

The United States had made its threats. Washington was now awaiting a response from its opponents. On 4 June, the Chinese and the North Koreans accepted the UN proposal of 25 May with a few minor changes, which paved the way toward an armistice. For Dulles, "It was the knowledge of the [U.S.] willingness to use force that had brought about an end to hostilities." Years later, when asked why the Chinese had accepted the armistice, Eisenhower replied succinctly: "Danger of an atomic war."[40] Were they correct?

II

There is not much in literature about how Beijing actually managed the end of the Korean War.[41] Now that more Chinese materials are available, it is possible to explore what Beijing's objectives were, what the Chinese identified as Eisenhower's intentions, and how they decided to respond.

The Chinese leadership had had a consistent, twofold objective in mind since late December 1950, when their forces were approaching the Thirty-eighth parallel and driving the UN troops out of North Korea. First, Korea's physical status quo must be restored, meaning that there should be no U.S. or ROK troops north of the parallel. As Mao explained in his instructions to Peng Dehuai, the Chinese would continue to fight until this objective was accomplished. Second, Korea's political status quo must also be restored. Mao insisted that a final settlement of the war would have to be "to let the Korean people elect their own government under United Nations supervision with as much Sino-Soviet participation as possible." To achieve these objectives, the Chinese forces would "prepare to fight for at least one or a few years."[42]

Peng Dehuai fully agreed. In a telegram to Mao on 16 January 1951, he asserted that "the most fundamental principle should be to have all the foreign troops withdraw from Korea within a limited time period; a second goal is to restore the status quo prior to 25 June 1950, with a demarcation at the Thirty-eighth parallel." In his view, "other issues than these two (such as the repatriation of POWs) are only of minor significance and merely concern technical questions." Peng further explained that "it is reasonable [you li] for us to request the withdrawal of all foreign troops from Korea; it is appropriate [you jie] to restore the

40. Cited in Gaddis, *The Long Peace*, p. 128.
41. A very recent study of Chinese responses is Rosemary Foot, "Nuclear Coercion and the Ending of the Korean Conflict," *International Security* 13 (Winter 1988/89): 99–112.
42. Mao's argument is enclosed in CMC to Peng, 4 December 1950, cited in ZYJZS, pp. 76–77.

demarcation at the Thirty-eighth parallel; and it serves both the Chinese and the Korean interests [you li] to end the war as soon as possible.[43] On 3 June 1951, Kim Il-sung arrived in Beijing to discuss the Korean settlement with Mao and Zhou Enlai. The Chinese leaders succeeded in persuading Kim to accept "the restoring of the Thirty-eighth parallel and negotiating on gradual withdrawal of all foreign troops and settling the future of Korea by peaceful means."[44] In short, the Chinese leaders aimed at not only restoring the status quo prior to the outbreak of the war but more importantly, compelling the U.S. military to withdraw from Korea.

But what could the Chinese People's Volunteers do to attain these objectives? For Peng Dehuai, China could not expect total victory, but it could compel its opponents to accept China's terms by denying victory to them. The most effective way to do this, as he explained in a CPV high command meeting on 25 June, 1951, was to wage protracted war. He had several reasons for his argument. First, the U.S. strategic front was too long to allow it to concentrate its efforts in Korea for long. He noted a statement made by Warren R. Austin, U.S. representative in the UN, on 1 June that with its main forces tied down in Korea and Western Europe, the United States "can no longer reinforce the UN collective security forces." Second, Washington could not afford a war of attrition in Korea. Peng mentioned Senator Robert Taft's remarks that America would go bankrupt if its military budget exceeded $70 billion, and that U.S. newspapers had reported on 8 June that U.S. military expenditures had already reached $60 billion a year, excluding $15–20 billion for the Korean War. Peng believed that the U.S. government was already "on the edge of economic crisis." Third, he saw an increase of American domestic opposition to continuing the war. "The peace movement in America," he told the CPV commanders, "has recently become better organized; the states in the East coast will hold five hundred mass protest rallies and New York City alone will have one hundred on 15–20 June." Washington's war effort had never been popular in America. With all these difficulties, Peng concluded, the U.S. government could not afford a war of attrition in Korea. In a telegram to Mao in mid-July, Peng explicitly expressed his confidence that a protracted war strategy would "*compel* the enemy to yield to peace while facing difficulties [*zhi nan er tui*]."[45]

43. Telegram, Peng to Mao (extracts), 16 July 1951, in *PJSWX*, pp. 413–14.
44. *Chai Chengwen Memoirs*, p. 125.
45. Peng's address to the CPV high commanders' meeting, 25 June, 1951, in *PJSWX*, pp. 404–10. There is no indication of Peng's sources for the anti-war demonstrations in the United States. No such events are reported in U.S. newspapers of that period either. Telegram, Peng to Mao, 16 July 1951, ibid., p. 414 [emphasis added].

Mao agreed completely that a protracted war in Korea would eventually bring the United States to terms. As early as 1 March 1951, he asserted that "the Korean problem can only be solved if we are prepared to strike for protracted war there, and . . . eliminate some hundred thousand American soldiers in the next few years."[46] He pointed out in August 1952 that he did not expect a "Thirty Years war or Hundred Year War" because the United States could not wage such a long war. His reasons were:

First, it costs them lives. In their struggles, more than thirty thousand of their soldiers have been killed and ten thousand have been captured. Besides, they have a much smaller population than we do.

Second, it costs money. They have so far spent more than tens of billion of U.S. dollars each year. . . .

Third, they have insurmountable contradictions both in the international and domestic arenas.

Fourth, they also have a strategic problem. The strategic focus of the United States is still on Europe.

They dispatched forces to invade Korea without anticipating that we would dispatch forces to aid Korea.[47]

In short, Mao predicted that "as far as the U.S. government is concerned, the general tendency is that the United States will be in trouble if peace does not come soon." China "must stand firm to the end . . . [and] the talks must go on, and the fighting must continue." The logic of Mao's calculation was simple: only when the enemy was hurt and hurt badly would it accept peace.

In June 1951 Mao officially instructed Peng to follow a protracted-war strategy. For this purpose, he emphasized "building an active defense front along the thirty-eighth parallel, and preparing to negotiate an armistice." Peng Dehuai described the plan as "painting a picture with two brushes at the same time [*shuangguan qixia*]." He intended to combine war with diplomacy.[48] To implement Mao's policy line, the CPV high commanders decided on 27 June that unless the UN forces mass to the front of the CPV or attempt any flanking movements, the CPV will remain on or just north of Thirty-eighth parallel. To secure this position, the CPV would build at least three penetration defense lines.

46. Telegram, Mao to Stalin (a copy was sent to Peng), 1 March 1951, cited in *JGYLMWG* 2:153.

47. Mao's speech at the thirty-eighth meeting of the Standing Committee of the First National Committee of the CPPCC, "Unite and Clearly Draw the Line between the Enemy and Ourselves," 4 August 1952, in *SWM* 5:80.

48. Mao's instructions are enclosed in Peng to the CMC, 1 July 1951, cited in *ZYJZS*, p. 162.

"If tactically we need to take the offensive," the CPV Command ordered, "we should not go too far [into the South] and should always stop at the Wanhan and Shaokiang rivers."[49] Clearly, the Chinese leaders sought to have the CPV military operations focused on defending the Thirty-eighth parallel rather than on seizing South Korean territory.

The People's Republic might want to see Korea united under a government friendly to China, but the Chinese leaders knew that expanding the conflict once again into South Korea would be unrealistic. One important obstacle was reluctant Soviet military assistance. Most Soviet munitions arriving in Korea were either too old or too poor in quality to be of any use. In the early summer of 1951, Mao had to send Xu Xiangqian, the chief of staff, to Moscow to appeal for urgently needed munitions as well as military technology. But Xu's meetings with the Soviets lasted four months and produced no substantial results. Mao then sent Gao Gang together with North Korean leader Kim Il-sung to Moscow to reinforce Xu. In a talk with them, Party Secretary Nikolai A. Bulganin insisted that the agreed-upon provision of munitions for sixteen infantry divisions on an annual basis had to be reduced to a ten-division level. Neither Gao nor Kim could do anything about it. When Xu returned late that year, he explained to Mao that Soviets feared a world war with the United States and that China would become another Yugoslavia.[50] Xu's analysis was confirmed when another military mission to Moscow, in April of 1952, turned out to be even more disappointing. That mission, led by Xiao Jingguang, the commander of the People's Navy, was intended to buy Soviet naval vessels and aircraft, but the Soviets refused to lend the necessary funds and demanded hard currency, which Beijing did not have. Xiao reported that even if the Soviets continued to supply munitions, they had no intention of letting China have any new weapons or access to new technology.[51] Thus, when Soviet military assistance in Korea dwindled, the Chinese could hardly seek a more ambitious war even if they had wanted to.

Domestic problems in China also mandated caution in Korea. The Beijing authorities were hardly able to finance the war on their own even on a limited scale. When China intervened in Korea, the new regime had accomplished little in its reconstruction programs, which were badly needed after the long civil war. The Chinese leaders had to

49. Minutes of the CPV high command meeting, 25–27 June 1951, in ZYJZS, pp. 162–63. Also see Hong Xuezhi, *Kangmei Yuanchao Zhanzheng Huiyi* (Beijing, 1990), pp. 192–93. General Hong was deputy commander of the CPV and commander of the CPV Logistic Command.

50. Xu Xiangqian, *Lishi De Huigu*, vol. 2 (Beijing, 1987), pp. 797–805; *Nie Rongzhen Memoirs*, pp. 757–58.

51. DDZGHJ, pp. 70–71.

create a wartime economy in order to collect—sometimes by force—the necessary revenue and materiel, such as medicine, clothing, and food. In late 1951, they called for "increasing production and strictly producing economy," but serious problems still existed. Mao noted in August 1952 that "the prices of commodities cannot be stabilized yet, and . . . revenues and expenditures have not yet been balanced."[52] Chen Yun, vice-premier and then in charge of sta⁺e economy, even predicted that "we will, one day, be unable to provide what we need in Korea."[53] In addition, the domestic political situation was no better. Shortly after the Chinese forces entered the war, Beijing started a nation-wide campaign of "love-the-country commitment." Patriotism ("to defend China") and internationalism ("to aid the Korean people") were virtually compulsory; still, the CCP leaders worried that they would not be able to sustain such a patriotic fever through the end of the war, given that KMT remnants were not yet eliminated, the future of Tibet was not settled, and pro-American elements within and outside the Party were not totally suppressed. The "Three-Anti's" (opposing corruption, waste, and obstructionist bureaucracy) and "Five-Anti's" (opposing bribery, tax evasion, theft of state property, cheating on government contracts, and stealing state economic information) campaigns launched by the CCP in December 1951 clearly reflected CCP concerns about economic problems and internal disorder.[54] Undoubtedly, the Beijing authorities had to take into account these domestic difficulties in their wartime decision making.

The Chinese leaders never regarded the military situation in Korea stable, and they were cautious about unexpected developments. They strongly believed that the new U.S. administration would launch a large-scale offensive in Korea in late 1952 in order to end the war on favorable terms. On 16 December Mao pointedly argued that "now that the armistice negotiations have come to a halt, and the difficulties that American forces are facing in Korea have not reached the extent to which the United States would be compelled to cease fighting, the Korean combat situation will be intensified in coming period (assuming one year). Eisenhower is probably preparing a larger military action in Korea after he becomes the U.S. president." What, then, would Eisenhower be most likely to do? Mao argued that "the possibility of amphibious operations on both sides of our rear is much bigger than an

52. Mao, "Unite and Clearly Draw the Line between the Enemy and Ourselves," 4 August 1952, pp. 78–81.
53. "Footnote to the *Selected Works of Chen Yun: 1949–1956,*"*Wenzian Yu Yianjiu,* February 1982, p. 11.
54. CCP Central Committee document (drafted by Mao), 8 December 1951, in *JGYLMWG* 2:548–49.

enemy attack on our front line of an in-depth defense."[55] Anticipating that the enemy might undertake such operations "in the early spring" of 1953," he called Deng Hua, then acting commander-in-general of the CPV, back to Beijing. Mao wanted to instruct Deng "in person" on how the CPV could get fully prepared.[56]

The Chinese leaders believed that their anticipation of U.S. amphibious operations was not pure imagination. They had been closely watching out for possible changes in U.S. policy. As early as the summer of 1952, Zhou Enlai—possibly instructed by Mao—directed the Ministry of Foreign Affairs to follow closely each public speech of Eisenhower, the Republican nominee. It seemed clear that Eisenhower would be more aggressive in Korea. Beijing noted that Eisenhower had promised on 11 July that he would lead a crusade against World Communism; he announced on 24 August that he would build a stronger military force to contain the Communists, and that his administration would be prepared to "roll back" Communist expansion.[57] Eisenhower's promise of an "honorable" peace in Korea through "deeds" not "words" also greatly impressed the Chinese. The Chinese leaders understood that "the peace honorable to the U.S. imperialists will never be honorable to the Chinese and the Korean people." To achieve such an "honorable" peace, the Chinese believed, Eisenhower would definitely "intensify the [Korean] combat situation." Since Eisenhower had won the election primarily because of his Korean promise, the Chinese press further pointed out, the new U.S. president would inevitably treat the Korean problem as his first priority.[58]

---

55. Mao to the Central Military Commission, "An Analysis of the Korean Situation and Our Policies," 16 December 1952, cited in ZYJZS, p. 230.

56. Yang Dezhi, *Wei Le Heping* (Beijing, 1987), pp. 177–78 [hereafter cited as *Yang Dezhi Memoirs*]. General Yang was deputy commander of the CPV for combat operations from 1952 to 1954. Also see in ZYJZS, p. 257.

57. Wang Bingnan, then the director of the administrative office in the Ministry of Foreign Affairs, remembered Zhou's instructions to watch Eisenhower's public speeches on Korea when I interviewed him in October 1988 in Beijing. For Chinese collections of Eisenhower's speeches, see *Renmin Ribao*, the editorial "Eisenhower Is Cheating the American People," 11 November 1952, which was reprinted in the *Xinhua Yuebao*, December 1952, pp. 104–5. Checking the American sources, I find that Eisenhower made his promise to lead a "Republican crusade" in his speech accepting the GOP nomination for the presidency at Chicago on 12 July 1952. But the "crusade" Eisenhower promised was against corruption in government rather than against communism. See The *Washington Post*, 12 July 1952, p. 1. Also, his promise to roll "Communist influence back to the borders of Russia" was supposedly made in a speech on foreign policy before the American Legion in Madison Square Garden, on 25 August 1952, but Eisenhower did not promise to roll back the Communists—these were the words of the news correspondent. See the *New York Times*, 25 August 1952, p. 1. The complete text of Eisenhower's speech is on page 12.

58. See *Yang Dezhi Memoirs*, pp. 173–175. Also see the *Renmin Ribao* editorial, "Eisenhower Is Cheating the American People," reprinted in the *Xinhua Yuebao*, December 1952, p. 105.

As to how Eisenhower would execute his "deeds," the Beijing authorities, particularly the military commanders, predicted that the new president would probably conduct amphibious operations. The United States, they calculated, had four alternatives for intensifying the fighting: a large-scale frontal offensive, intensive strategic bombing in North Korea and even northern China plus a naval blockade of China's coastline, the use of atomic weapons, and amphibious landings on both sides of the Chinese rear in North Korea. Chinese military officers considered a ground offensive and strategic bombing unlikely because such measures had already been tried, and the use of nuclear weapons impossible, because of the pressure of world opinion and the threat of Soviet nuclear retaliation. At no point, as a former CPV officer recalls, did Eisenhower and his staff make it clear that nuclear weapons would be used in Korea.[59] Therefore, amphibious operations seemed to be the only feasible option left for the United States. The Chinese generals argued that "both Mark Clark and Van Fleet have been greatly interested in this kind of operation." It is interesting that deputy commander of the CPV Yang Dezhi even "carefully studied records of Eisenhower's personal experience," and told other commanders that "we shall never forget that Eisenhower was the person who commanded the Normandy operation during the Second World War."[60]

Chinese intelligence also indicated that the UN forces were prepared for amphibious operations. The Central Military Commission warned CPV headquarters on 2 December that Eisenhower's visit [to South Korea], with his top military advisors, including the new secretary of defense, the chairman of the Joint Chiefs of Staff, and the commander of the U.S. Pacific Fleet, can be a prelude to a large-scale offensive."[61] One intelligence study indicated that the enemy's maneuvers for amphibious operations had intensified at the end of 1952. The enemy had dispatched more special agents to North Korea to collect weather and hydrographic data along both the eastern and western coasts of North Korea. Moreover, the ROK forces had been recently reinforced with two newly created divisions, six regiments, and twenty-eight artillery

---

59. Xue Qi, "An Important Strategic Decision by the CPV," *Dangshi Yanjiu* [Studies of the CCP History], May 1985, pp. 60–61. Concerning the atomic threat, Yao Xu, then in charge of intelligence of the CPV, confirmed in my interview with him on 9 October 1988 that the CPV command did not think that the United States would use atomic weapons in Korea or Manchuria. Yao recalled that the CPV headquarters neither had any information that atomic weapons had been deployed in the Far East, nor received any warning from the United States about the possibility such weapons might be used.

60. Que Qi, "An Important Strategic Decision," p. 61; *Yang Dezhi Memoirs*, p. 174.

61. *Yang Dezhi Memoirs*, p. 173.

battalions added to its present forces at the front.[62] Another intelligence report even suggested that the enemy would launch the anticipated offensive no later than February 1953.[63]

To deter the possible enemy offensive Beijing authorities took several large-scale defensive measures. Mao pointed out on 12 December: "If we can prohibit the enemy from executing its landing operations by holding fast to the western and eastern coasts of North Korea, and at the same time, take tactical offensives in the front line to decimate more enemy troops, the Korean War situation will . . . turn to our favor." He also instructed Deng Hua in Beijing that the entire defensive campaign should be based on the assumption that "the enemy will land at our rear, at the western coast, and in the area between the Chongchon and the Han rivers." He also insisted that military preparations "should start as soon as possible."[64]

On 20 December, the CCP Central Committee issued a formal order— drafted by Mao himself—to the CPV commanders, entitled "Instructions on Preparing All Possible Conditions to Smash the Enemy's Amphibious Operations and Increase the Magnitude of Victory in Korea." The order anticipated enemy landings "along the western coast between the Han and Yalu rivers." It directed the CPV to strengthen the in-depth defense along the western coast. To this end, Deng Hua was ordered to establish a special command to counter amphibious landings. All the logistic units responsible for the transportation of supplies, communication lines, and storage of munitions and other materials were urged to provide their best service to the combat troops committed to this anti-amphibious campaign. The document also stated that April 1953 was the deadline for completing all the required preparations. It further pointed out that "the amphibious operations are . . . probably the last action the enemy will take in Korea. As long as we can successfully smash it, the enemy's final defeat will be assured." The order pointedly stressed that "the key to our success is how well we prepare," implying that the better the CPV prepared, the more likely the enemy would be deterred from even attempting such an attack.[65]

The CPV leaders immediately met for four days (from 17 to 21 December) and drew up the "Military Plan for Smashing the Enemy's

---

62. *ZYJZS*, pp. 255–56.

63. Ibid., p. 256. Also see *KMYCZZ*, p. 276.

64. Mao's analysis of the Korean situation, 16 December 1950, In *ZYJZS*, pp. 256–57; minutes of the Mao–Deng Hua talks, mid-December 1952, ibid., p. 276.

65. CCP Central Committee to the CPV Party Committee, "Preparing All Possible Conditions to Smash the Enemy's Amphibious Operations and Increase the Magnitude of Victory in Korea," in *JGYLMWG* 3:656–58.

Amphibious Offensive."[66] The CPV plan was composed of four main parts. The first was redeployment of forces to strengthen the defense of both eastern and western coasts. The CPV command transferred more experienced forces—those who had previously fought on the main front—to the two flanks. The Thirty-eighth and the Fortieth armies would move to the western coast, and the Fifteenth and Twelfth armies to the eastern coast. Altogether seven CPV infantry armies and one North Korean corps guarded the western coast with fourteen artillery regiments plus nine battalions, two artillery regiments plus three battalions, five anti-aircraft artillery battalions, and one tank regiment in support. The second move was the organization of the reserves. The First, Sixteenth, and Twenty-first armies, the Thirty-third Division, and the First Tank Division stationed in North Korea formed the first echelon of reserves, and the Fifty-fourth Army, which had just entered Manchuria, formed the second. In addition, fourteen divisions of the Air Force and one Navy brigade were attached to assist this campaign. Third, to strengthen the CPV rear services, the Fifth, Sixth, Seventh, Ninth, and Tenth divisions of the Railway Engineering Corps with five thousand workers were immediately sent into North Korea, mainly to secure the three main railroads in North Korea. Fourth, the CPV directed all the forces in Korea to extend and enlarge their defensive fortifications and to practice defending against amphibious assault.[67] The results of these preparations were encouraging: at the end of April, the CPV reported to Beijing that "all the arranged preparations have been satisfactorily accomplished."[68]

Beijing leaders became more certain that Eisenhower would mount an immediate offensive in Korea during these months. Their concern was in particular aroused by the new president's 2 February announcement that he was "unleashing Chiang" and his call the next day for an intensified economic blockade against China. The CCP leaders believed that allowing the Chinese Nationalists to attack the south and east was part of Eisenhower's military offensive scheme.[69] Mao pointedly told the CPPCC (Chinese People's Political Consultative Conference) audience on 7 February, that

> We desire peace, but as long as U.S. imperialism does not discard its barbaric and unreasonable demands, and its plots to expand its aggression, the resolution of the Chinese people can only be to continue to fight together with the Korean people to the end. This is not because we like war,

66. Order of the CPV headquarters, 23 December 1952, cited in *ZYJZS*, pp. 259–60.
67. Ibid., p. 234. Also see *Yang Dezhi Memoirs*, p. 180, and *Du Ping Memoirs*, pp. 559–61.
68. *ZYJZS*, p. 263.
69. *KMYCZZ*, pp. 278–79.

we would like to stop the war immediately and wait to resolve the remaining problems in the future; but the U.S. imperialism does not want to do things this way.

Mao then warned, "If that is the case, that's all right; we will continue to fight. No matter how many years U.S. imperialism is willing to fight, we are *prepared* to fight with them for as many years, right up to the time when U.S. imperialism is willing to stop."[70] His speech was published in the *Renmin Ribao* the next day. Mao obviously expected Eisenhower to take his warning seriously.

The U.S. amphibious assaults, however, never took place. Quite to the contrary, the CPV headquarters received a proposal from General Clark on 22 February that both sides should exchange sick and wounded prisoners of war, pending any agreement on an armistice. In assessing the motives behind Clark's offer, Mao asserted that "recent [enemy] actions are of such an obviously provocative and threatening nature that we can't but heighten our vigilance and prepare for the worst, but it is also likely that our opponents' offer is intended to compel us to discuss . . . a cease-fire. This suggests that our opponents are getting desperate." He then pointed out: "Since taking office, Eisenhower has taken several actions in Asia which indicate that he is trying to shake off the yoke created by Truman in order to regain the initiative. [Clark's] suggestion to exchange sick captives may aim at probing our intention [before they] make a concession at Panmunjom." Mao decided to accept Clark's offer. Zhou Enlai announced China's acceptance on 28 March and also suggested that the truce talks be reopened at Panmunjom. Two days later, Zhou announced over Radio Peking that China was willing to have all POWs refusing repatriation be turned over to a neutral state "to ensure a just solution to the question of their repatriation."[71]

This action did not mean that the Chinese leaders now believed that Washington would be willing to talk about ending the war on China's terms, but it did reflect the expectation that their moderate response with some apparent concessions would have a favorable impact on world opinion. In his instruction to the CPV in April, Mao stated that "[diplomatically] we will try to reopen the truce talks and also prepare for protracted negotiations; but militarily our forces should only prepare for protracted fighting." He explicitly urged that "[the CPV]

70. "Chairman Mao's Speech to the CPPCC," *Renmin Ribao*, 8 February 1953, p. 1 [emphasis added].
71. Mao to Ding Guoyu, head of the Chinese delegation at Panmunjom, 23 March 1953, in *JGYLMWG* 3:148–49; Zhou Enlai's public statement, 30 March 1953, cited in *KMYCZZ*, p. 287.

should always keep highly alert and do what has been already planned [to counter possible amphibious attacks]." Yang Dezhi notes in his memoir that "Chairman Mao still wanted us to prepare for possible U.S. amphibious operations."[72]

By the late spring of 1953, there was still no sign of the expected attack. The Beijing authorities started to wonder why. Reassessing the situation, they came up with three explanations. First, the United States confronted great difficulties reaching agreement internally and with its allies on how to end the conflict. The Chinese leaders particularly noted that Britain and France were afraid that any large-scale offensive might provoke a worldwide war. Second, the Eisenhower administration, due to U.S. military and strategic problems, might need more time to prepare if another large-scale amphibious offensive was to come. The Chinese leaders believed that Eisenhower was playing to world opinion by agreeing to reopen the talks and at the same time, intensifying military preparations. Thus U.S. willingness to resume truce talks, in the eyes of the Chinese, was a smoke screen intended to win more time for military preparations. Third, even if Washington was willing to resume the armistice talks, the United States might still expect to obtain more favorable terms by intensifying the military situation on the battlefield. The Chinese leaders concluded that the enemy would never willingly come to terms unless it faced military costs it could not afford. To compel the enemy to accept peace, they believed, a policy of tit-for-tat [*zhenfeng xiangdui*] should be adopted.[73]

Beijing's tit-for-tat policy was to undertake tactical offensive actions in the front line. It is interesting to note that the idea of striking out very much appealed to CPV field commanders, whose patience seemed to have run out. On 31 March, Wang Jianan, the commander of the Ninth Group Army, suggested to the CPV headquarters that an all-out tactical offensive targeting ten points of the enemy's defensive line should be launched in early May "to give the enemy a fatal blow." The commanders at the headquarters concurred and immediately requested from Beijing approval. On 3 April, the Central Military Commission under Peng Dehuai quickly endorsed the request. Confirming that "this suggested action will certainly be favorable to our position in the truce talks," the CMC, however, instructed that "the offensive actions should be based on a full preparation, and should start in middle

72. Mao's instructions are enclosed in Deng Hua to each CPV Group Army Command, 20 April 1953, in ZYJZS, p. 269; *Yang Dezhi Memoirs*, p. 194.

73. Mao–Du Ping talks, march 1953, in *Du Ping Memoirs*, pp. 574–78. Also see a letter from the Chinese delegation at Panmunjom to Mao and Zhou Enlai, 19 February 1953, in *Chai Chengwen Memoirs*, pp. 255–56.

or late may." Mao also agreed to let the CPV prepare for this offensive, but he cautioned Peng Dehuai on April: "If a cease-fire agreement is reached soon or the truce negotiations requires us to take no more offensive actions, we shall reconsider [the military] action and make a final decision sometime in May."[74]

The CPV headquarters immediately informed all the lower-level commanders of CMC's approval of the tactical offensive. CPV headquarters held a planning meeting between 30 April and 4 May, with all the army group commanders participating. The day after the meeting ended, the CPV Command issued "Complementary Instructions on Preparing for the Summer Counteroffensive." The order explicitly stated that the main objective of this counteroffensive was "to reinforce our diplomatic efforts at Panmunjom with military actions in the battlefield," and that a second purpose was "to stretch out our defense line southward as much as possible so that we will be in a more favorable strategic position after the war is over." Militarily, the CPV order pointed out, this offensive sought "to eliminate and hurt as much as possible the enemy's combat effectiveness." To do so, the order instructed CPV ground forces to target the ROK forces in the east and the UN troops in the west. Concerned about the enemy reaction, the order directed that the whole campaign would be divided into three phases: each phase would include ten days of actual fighting and five days of pausing to await the enemy's reaction. In this way, "we will always firmly hold the power of initiative and the right of escalation." The CPV headquarters then set the end of May as the deadline for completing all the preparations, "so that the troops in the front will take the action in early June and complete the campaign by early July."[75] General Yang, the main organizer of the campaign, recalls that "[we] just wanted to impress the enemy with the 'iron' facts that we were capable and not afraid of fighting the war [through to the end]."[76]

In mid-May, Xie Fang, former CPV chief of staff, returned to the headquarters from Panmunjom. He brought back a disturbing news that the armistice negotiations had once again stalemated because a "rigid U.S. insistence on its counterinitiative on the POW issue."Upset by this new change, the top four CVP commanders, Deng, Yang, Xie, and Li Zhimin [CPV political commissar), all felt that since one could only negotiate from strength, they should start the first phase of the

---

74. The text of the CPV headquarter's report of April 1953 and the telegram from the Central Military Commission on 3 April are cited in full in *Yang Dezhi Memoirs*, pp. 197–99. For the CMC telegram, dated 3 April, see *PJSWX*, p. 414; Mao to Peng Dehuai, 23 April 1953, in *JGYLMWG* 4:201.

75. CPV headquarters on the summer offensives, 5 May 1953, in *ZYJZS*, pp. 270–72; *Yang Dezhi Memoirs*, pp. 199–202.

76. *Yang Dezhi Memoirs*, p. 202.

planned counteroffensive right away. In order to show the unanimity of their opinions, all of them signed an order on 11 May directing the CPV to complete all the preparations by 30 May and start attacking on 1 June.[77] Lower-level commanders in fact hailed this decision. The acting commander of the Twentieth Group Army, Zheng Weishan, telephoned Yang Dezhi the next morning, congratulating him: "This is a great decision. If you did not decide to do so now, I would start attacking by myself."[78] Without even obtaining Beijing's approval, the Twentieth Group Army began the offensive on May 13—much ahead of the original schedule. When the Beijing authorities found out about it, they were concerned that such a move might be too premature both militarily and politically. On 16 May, the Central Military Commission sent a telegram to the CPV headquarters, insisting that the actions already taken should be kept on a small scale so as to "avoid unfavorable effects upon world opinions." The CMC also instructed that any all-out offensive should strictly follow the original schedule, and that all the commanders should take "operational difficulties into more careful consideration."[79]

It seems that the CPV tactical offensives had a big impact on the truce talks. On 25 May, the U.S. negotiators offered a significant concession on the POW repatriation issue and agreed to sign the long-expected armistice agreement on 8 June. The South Korean leader, Rhee, however, bluntly rejected the armistice and claimed that his forces would continue fighting toward the Yalu. Rhee's representatives at Panmunjom walked out of the negotiations. South Korean authorities also organized several mass rallies in Seoul to support the ROK decision to fight on alone.[80] When the news reached the CPV headquarters, the commanders were furious. "If a disease changes ten thousand times," General Yang pointed out, "so should the medical treatment." To compel Rhee to accept peace, the CPV commanders held that they should now concentrate on the ROK forces. On 1 June, they made a major change to the original plan: instead of attacking the UN forces, the primary target of the next offensive would only be the South Koreans. "We mean to kill the chicken to scare the monkey," Deng Hua commented, "whoever makes trouble, we are surely to punish him."[81] With Beijing's final approval, an all-out offensive against the South Koreans troops began with a surprise attack on 10

77. Ibid., pp. 205–6. Also see *KMYCZZ*, p. 293.
78. *Yang Dezhi Memoirs*, p. 206.
79. A telegram from the Central Military Commission to the CPV commanders, 16 May 1953, cited in *ZYJZS*, pp. 274–75.
80. Ibid., p. 277; *Yang Dezhi Memoirs*, p. 209.
81. *Yang Dezhi Memoirs*, 209–10. Also see *KMYCZZ*, p. 298

June. The CPV smashed Rhee's troops at several points along the front. This offensive did not cease until Peng Dehuai's cease-fire order arrived at the CPV headquarters on 15 June, directing that "the agreement on the settlement of a military dividing line had been reached, and we should cease fighting on 16 June." This offensive action, the Chinese recorded, had eliminated 41,000 South Korean soldiers at a cost of 19,354 CPV casualties. Rendering the ROK Fifth and Eighth divisions combat ineffective, the Chinese troops advanced ten to twelve kilometers south of the Pukhan River. More important, the CPV commanders believed that this military victory played a significant role in finally bringing the enemy to terms.[82]

Fighting in Korea practically ceased on 16 June, and Peng Dehuai was already on the way to Panmunjom to sign the armistice agreement. But an unexpected incident held Peng in Pyongyang. The South Koreans forcibly sent 27,000 North Korean POWs to the front on 17 and 18 June. After talking with Kim Il-sung in Pyongyang, Peng decided not to go to Panmunjom because of Rhee's "unfaithful act." At 10:00 p.m., on 20 June, he telegraphed Mao, suggesting to "put off the [truce] signing till after [we] eliminate fifteen thousand more South Koreans in order to intensify the contradictions among the enemies." Mao immediately agreed. He pointed out: "Now that the dissension and wrangling within the imperialist camp are getting worse, we must take a major action to impose greater pressure on the enemy to make sure that the enemy won't dare let this type of incident happen again. [By doing so], we will retain the initiative." Mao stressed that it was "quite necessary to eliminate ten thousand more South Koreans before signing the truce agreement."[83]

After two weeks of secret preparation—including gathering troops through underground tunnels and luring the enemy's attention toward other parts of the front—the CPV launched another surprise attack on 13 July in the Kimsong area where the ROK forces were centered. After only twenty-four hours of combat, the CPV had wiped out the ROk Capital Division and devastated the Sixth, Eighth, and Third Divisions. On 16 July, Generals Clark and Taylor had to fly to the front to organize counteroffensives, which quickly resulted in a stalemate. The rainy season arrived, which made the fighting very difficult for both sides.[84]

82. Peng's telegram of 15 June 1953 is cited in *KMYCZZ*, p. 304. For the organization of this campaign, see ibid., pp. 298–304.

83. Both the texts of Peng's telegram to Mao on 20 June, and Mao's reply of 21 June are cited in *Yang Dezhi Memoirs*, pp. 218–19, and *ZYJZS*, pp. 282–83. Also see *Du Ping Memoirs*, pp. 594–95.

84. For the Chinese tactical offensives in early July 1953, see *ZYJZS*, pp. 284–92.

The Chinese, however, noted that General William K. Harrison, Jr., the new U.S. negotiator at Panmunjom, had twice stated that the United States would not let Rhee disrupt the armistice again. UN Commander-in-Chief Clark also wrote to Kim Il-sung and Peng Dehuai pledging that his forces would comply with the truce agreement. Probably afraid of provoking the United States too much, Mao, on 23 July, ordered the CPV to stop fighting and evacuate from the newly occupied areas south of the Thirty-eighth parallel. He then directed Peng to sign the armistice. the UN Command welcomed the Chinese initiative and agreed to cease firing. In response, the CPV Command issued its final cease-fire order on 26 July 1953.[85] The armistice was signed the next day.

III

With the armistice agreement finally signed, the Korean conflict came to an end. The truce was hailed as a victory in China, but in the United States there followed no sense of euphoria. Instead, there was merely gratification that an unpopular war was over. In announcing the cessation of the Korean War, Eisenhower stated that "we have won an armistice in a single battleground—not peace in the world." This sense of insecurity and uncertainty about peace on the peninsula was further conveyed when the president proclaimed, "We may not now relax our guard nor cease our quest."[86]

Washington officials in fact were worried about renewed hostilities in Korea. In mid-June, even before the armistice was signed, the NSC Staff had asserted that "an armistice in Korea would signify merely that the Communists have found it unprofitable to continue the war there, but the danger of renewed aggression would be unrelieved." For them, the cessation of fighting in Korea "would not in itself constitute sufficient evidence that Communist China has abandoned its basic objectives nor . . . its willingness to seek these objectives by . . . force."[87] This assertion led to a new consensus in the Eisenhower administration that the United States would have to undertake vigorous measures to deter violations of the Korean armistice as well as to prevent Communist China from taking aggressive actions in other parts of

85. Ibid., p. 293. For the planning details, see *Yang Dezhi Memoirs*, pp. 219–24.
86. "Radio and Television Address to the American People Announcing the Signing of the Korean Armistice," 26 July 1953, in *Public Papers*, pp. 520–22.
87. NSC Staff Study, "United States Tactics Immediately Following an Armistice in Korea," enclosed in NSC 154, 15 June 1953, in *FRUS: 1952–1954*, 15:1174–76.

Asia.[88] The administration certainly had no desire to continue stationing a large contingent of troops along the armistice line. Some other
means of deterrence was needed.

The first action the administration took was to confirm publicly the
long-term commitment of the United States to South Korea. On the
day after the cease-fire was announced, Eisenhower fulfilled one of his
pledges to Rhee by sending a special message to Congress, asking au-
thorization to allocate up to $200 million for the ROK's economic re-
habilitation and military defense. Without any difficulty, the Congress
approved this "necessary legislation" on 6 August.[89] Two days later,
Eisenhower fulfilled another pledge by announcing the signing of a
U.S.–ROK mutual defense treaty. Just as Dulles had promised Rhee at
the end of the war, this treaty sought to make it clear that "If in violation of the armistice the Republic of Korea is subjected to unpro-
voked attack, you may of course count upon our immediate and
automatic military reaction." The secretary of state further explained
that such a renewed attack would not only mean an attack upon the
Republic of Korea "but an attack upon the United Nations Command
and U.S. forces within that Command."[90]

Administration officials also considered that the United States and
its allies should demonstrate their resolve to defend the Korean armistice in a manner that could not be misunderstood. They had earlier
worked on proclaiming a "Greater Sanctions" statement to the effect
that the United States and its allies would collectively defend the armistice line. Washington persuaded sixteen UN members who had
contributed armed forces to the Korean War to sign such a statement
on 27 July 1953, the day of the armistice. It contained a clear description of the consequences of a violation of the armistice:

> We affirm, in the interests of world peace, that if there is a renewal of the
> armed attack, challenging again the principles of the United Nations, we
> should again be united and prompt to resist. The consequences of such a
> breach of the armistice would be so grave that, in all probability, it would
> not be possible to confine hostilities within the frontier of Korea.[91]

The "Greater Sanctions" statement, the NSC staff explained, had a
twofold significance: (1) it demonstrated that "the free world's resistance to communist expansion had not weakened even after the

88. This consensus is reflected in NSC 154, 15 June 1953, pp. 1170–73.
89. "Special Message to the Congress Concerning Increased Aid to the Republic of
Korea," in *Public Papers*, pp. 522–24.
90. Dulles to Rhee, 24 July 1953, in *FRUS: 1952–1954*, 15:1430–32.
91. This statement is contained in NSC 154, 15 June 1953, pp. 1173–74.

armistice"; and (2) it confirmed "the necessity of maintaining pressures . . . designed to weaken . . . [the Chinese Communists'] ability
to break out in renewed aggression."[92]

Meanwhile, there were vehement discussions within the administration about extending the U.S. nuclear umbrella to Korea. The National
Security Council Staff worked out an agreement in the NSC on this
matter by October 1953. Robert Cutler, then in charge of the NSC Staff,
noted that "if the Communists broke the armistice and renewed hostilities, it was agreed that we would use atomic bombs to meet the
situation."[93] the Joint Chiefs also pointed out in November that the
best course of action in the event of renewed Communist aggression in
Korea would be to employ "atomic weapons, [and] conduct large-scale
air operations against targets in China, Manchuria, and Korea." Admiral Arthur Radford, the new JCS Chairman, thought such operations should be directed against targets "from Shanghai all the way
north." Eisenhower clearly concurred. At a 3 December NSC meeting,
the president stated that this approach "fitted exactly into his thinking,
and he could see no other way of treating a renewed Communist attack." He further explained that "if the Chinese Communists attacked
us again we should certainly respond by hitting them hard and whatever it would hurt most, involving Peiping itself." This counterattack,
in his view, "would mean [an] all-out war against Communist
China."[94]

Eisenhower and his military advisers discussed massive retaliation
as a deterrent against renewed hostilities in Korea. But how could the
United States convince the Communists of this counterthreat? The
Joint Chiefs of Staff proposed in October that the UN Command should
"*inform* the Communists that the UNC, if endangered by Communist
operations against ROK forces, would undertake counteraction against
the Communists, and that if the Communists attacked UNC forces, the
counteraction would not necessarily be confined to Korea." Both
Eisenhower and Dulles stressed the importance of warning the Chinese and North Koreans explicitly. The president pointedly argued at
a 29 October NSC meeting that "in short, . . . the Communists *must be
made to understand clearly* that any attack on the UN forces would mean
general war." To this end, Dulles prepared a study on the subject to be

92. Ibid., pp. 1175–76.
93. Minutes, NSC meeting, 29 October 1953, in *FRUS: 1952–1954*, 15:1571; Eisenhower's meeting with legislative leaders, 5 January 1954, cited in Gaddis, *The Long Peace*, p.
127. Also see minutes, NSC meeting, 8 January 1954, in *FRUS: 1952–1954*, 15:1709.
94. JCS to Wilson, 27 November 1953, in *FRUS: 1952–1954*, 15:1626–28; minutes, NSC
meeting, 3 December 1953, ibid., pp. 1836–38.

circulated to the members of the National Security Council for further consideration.[95]

While considering how to warn the Chinese Communists, U.S. strategists proceeded with contingency planning. As a "concept of operations"for counterattack, the Joint Chiefs recommended in early December an initial "massive atomic air strike which would defeat the Chinese Communists in Korea and make them incapable of aggression there or elsewhere in the Far East for a very considerable time." They asserted that U.S. ground forces should "largely be limited to the actual theater of war in Korea and not spread out to Manchuria or china proper."[96] Administration officials were also concerned about targeting. Eisenhower thought that the airfields in Northeast China should be destroyed so that "in any future war there was to be no sanctuary for Communist aircraft in Manchuria." The Joint Chiefs argued in December that U.S. air strikes should be conducted "against military targets in Korea, . . . in Manchuria and China which are being used by the Communists in direct support of their operations in Korea, or which threaten the security of U.S./UN forces in the Korean area." In early March 1954, administration officials generally agreed to bomb military targets in "the general vicinity of Korea (i.e., the area bound by and including Kirin-Mukden-Tientsin-Tsingtao)" or "anywhere in China or Manchuria" (except Port Arthur and Dairen). They also stressed that "targets would include military concentrations, airfields, naval bases, military installations, and transportation system, etc., even if these targets were adjacent to or within urban concentrations."[97]

American officials were also concerned about command, control, and communication in the event of nuclear bombing. At the NSC meeting on 8 January 1954, the military proposed to "convey authority to the U.S. commander [in Korea] to use atomic weapons without reference back to Washington." Admiral Radford asserted that it would take twenty-four hours for the USC to initiate an atomic strike if a final decision had to be made in Washington. But Eisenhower insisted that any decision to use atomic weapons "would have to be referred to Washington," and that the USC "would in the first instance attack [Communist] targets merely with conventional armaments." The pres-

95. The JSC view is enclosed in Bowie to Dulles, 28 October 1953, in *FRUS: 1952–1954*, 15:1568 [emphasis added]; minutes, NSC meeting, 29 October 1953, p. 1578 [emphasis added].

96. Radford's proposal, enclosed in minutes, NSC meeting, 3 December 1953, p. 1637.

97. Ibid., p. 1641; JCS to Wilson, 18 December 1953, in *FRUS: 1952–1954*, 15:1674; JCS and the State Department to the NSC, 27 January 1954, ibid., pp. 1700–1701; SNIE 100-2-54, "Probable Reactions of Communist China, the USSR, and the Free World to Certain U.S. Courses in Korea," 5 March 1954, ibid., pp. 1758–62.

ident, however, directed that "the commander in the field was to be told to be ready as promptly as possible to use atomic weapons when the decision had to be made." Radford assured Eisenhower that "all advance preparations would be made."[98]

The Eisenhower administration, indeed, incorporated the defense of the Korean armistice into its long-term strategy of nuclear deterrence at the global level. In June, Washington did decide to transfer completed nuclear weapons to military custody for overseas deployment. Pentagon strategists asked for 3,896 nuclear "hardware" kits, slightly less than a quarter of the American stockpile, for deployment outside the continental United States. Evidence shows that Guam was one of the intended deployment sites; however, there is no indication of whether or not nuclear components were actually deployed on Guam and if so, how many of them.[99]

The administration clearly believed in the efficacy of the extended nuclear threat to defend the Korean armistice. An intelligence estimate pointed out in March 1954 that the Soviet Union and Communist China were deterred from attacking Japan, Taiwan, the Philippines, and South Korea because they understood that aggressive actions there "would almost certainly bring U.S. action against the Chinese mainland, possibly including attacks with nuclear weapons." The estimate then concluded that "the Communists will probably not initiate new local aggression in Asia with identifiable Soviet, Chinese Communist, or North Korean forces."[100] Does this sound self-congratulatory? To see whether such smugness was justified one needs to look at Beijing's responses and its postwar policy toward Korea.

IV

In China, instead of dissatisfaction, a wide-spread victory celebration followed the announcement of the Korean armistice. Speaking at the twenty-fourth session of the Central People's Government Council on 12 September 1953, Mao claimed a significant victory. In his report to the council on the same day, Peng Dehuai also asserted that "the

98. Minutes, NSC meeting, 8 January 1954, pp. 1905-7.
99. Secretary of defense to the executive secretary of the NSC, 8 June 1953, cited in Dingman, "Atomic Diplomacy during the Korean War," p. 87; see also note 195. Rosenberg, too, does not indicate whether the deployment of atomic weapons on Guam had been completed. He notes that only by 1961 had ninety percent of the stockpiles been transferred to military control (Rosenberg, "The Origins of Overkill," pp. 27-28).
100. NIE 10-2-54, "Communist Courses of Action in Asia through Mid-1955," 15 March 1954, in FRUS: 1952-1954, 2:389-95. Also see Gaddis, The Long Peace, p. 125.

great victory . . . would have a grave and profound impact upon the situation in the Far East as well as in the world."[101]

The Chinese leaders were happy about the outcome of their intervention in Korea. They thought that China had achieved its objectives, since "we fought our way back to the Thirty-eighth parallel and held firmly." Mao regarded this as critical because "if the front lines had remained at the Yalu and Tammen rivers, then the people at places such as Shenyang, Anshan, and Fushun would not be able to feel secure while carrying out domestic reconstruction." Moreover, the Chinese soldiers had fought the United States and would no longer fear American military power. Mao explained: "This time we have really felt out the U.S. armed forces. If you do not come into contact with [them], you might be afraid of them. We fought with them for thirty-three months, and we have become thoroughly acquainted with them. U.S. imperialism is not such an awesome thing, it is just what is and that's all."

Believing in Sun Tze's principle of knowing as much as possible about the enemy to secure success, Mao apparently gained confidence from the fact that China had met the United States in combat. Mao believed that an imperialist invasion of China and a third world war had been postponed. Furthermore, he asserted that "the imperialist aggressors ought to realize [now] that the Chinese people have become organized and had better not be provoked. If the Chinese people are provoked, they will not be easy to deal with." The implication is clear: by fighting Americans in Korea, China had demonstrated its strength and resolve, and thus had reinforced its long-term deterrent against possible U.S. military action against China in the future.[102]

There is no indication that the Chinese leaders ever intended to resume military action in Korea. Quite to the contrary, they consistently advocated maintaining the armistice. As soon as the truce was signed, domestic rehabilitation became the first order of business. In August 1953 Mao called for "ten years [of peace] to build our industry and to create a firm and powerful foundation [of national defense]."[103] The CCP Central Committee directed "an immediate shift of attention to [domestic] reconstruction, planning, and the preparations of cadres, thereby welcoming the coming of a large-scale economic build-up."

101. Mao's address to the twenty-fourth session of the Central People's Government Council, 12 September 1953, in *SWM* 5:101–06; Peng's report to the twenty-fourth session of the Central People's Government Council, 12 September 1953, in *PJSWX*, pp. 440–61.

102. Mao's address to the twenty-fourth session of the Central People's Government Council, 12 September 1953, pp. 101–6.

103. Mao, "Unite and Clearly Draw the Line between the Enemy and Ourselves," 4 August 1952, pp. 66–69.

Zhou Enlai, Li Fuchun, vice-premier in charge of industries; and Chen Yun, the vice-premier responsible for finance and revenues, were assigned by the CCP Politburo to design and implement the First Five-year Plan. The first priority, the three leaders indicated, was to balance China's national revenue in order to spare more funds for rehabilitating agriculture and heavy industry.[104] With this shift, there would undoubtedly be no extra funding for any belligerent policy in Korea.

The Chinese leaders worried that the United States or the South Koreans might violate the Korean armistice, and decided that the CPV should remain in North Korea to defend the armistice line. On 15 June, Peng Dehuai had already stressed to the CPV headquarters that "from now on we will no longer initiate offensive actions, but we shall be at a high state of readiness should the enemy attack. We will certainly not tolerate the slightest relaxation on our part." After signing the armistice and on the way back to Beijing, Peng again urged Yang Dezhi to "make it clear to everyone that now that the truce is signed, we must strictly observe it. Whether the other side will observe it or not, we will wait and see. However, we must not only welcome their observance but also prepare for their violation."[105] Mao also warned the CPV headquarters on 25 July to remain vigilant against complacency, and to ensure strict compliance on the part of the Chinese forces with, and guard against possible enemy violations of the provisions of the armistice. In another telegram to the CPV commanders on 12 September, Mao further pointed out that "the bellicose elements in the United States and the Syngman Rhee faction in Southern Korea [will] carry out all sorts of plots and conspiracies . . . to undermine the armistice." He explicitly instructed the CPV commanders to "double their vigilance and continue to strive to raise their military and political standards [for fighting] . . . in order to prevent any acts of aggression or provocation by the enemy."[106] Late in 1953, the Central Military Commission formally directed that the CPV should strictly observe the armistice agreement but with high vigilance, and at the same time, to assist the North Koreans as much as they could in rehabilitating their own domestic economy and political rule.[107]

The Chinese leaders had what they considered a realistic fear that hostilities in Korea could resume. "The U.S.-led imperialist clique," Peng Dehuai pointedly told the Central People's Government Council

104. "Footnote to the *Selected Works of Chen Yun: 1947–1956,*" *Wenxian Yu Yanjiu,* pp. 12–13.

105. Telegram, Peng to Deng Hua and Li Kenong, 15 June 1953, in *PJSWX,* pp. 414–15; *Yang Dezhi Memoirs,* p. 231.

106. Mao's instructions to the CPV headquarters, 25 July 1953, in *JGYLMWG* 4:285.

107. *Yang Dezhi Memoirs,* p. 241.

on 12 September 1953, "is actually destabilizing the Korean armistice in a planned manner, and is blocking and destroying the opening of a political conference on a Korean settlement." In this respect, he found several "serious deeds reflecting U.S. intentions to repudiate the armistice": Dulles had signed a mutual security treaty with Rhee on 8 August, "providing the U.S. troops with the right to stay in Korea indefinitely." The United States had "forced fifteen other nations to proclaim the so-called Greater Sanctions Statement, warning that the resumption of military conflict in Korea will not be confined within Korea," and Dulles, speaking to American veterans on 2 September, had "repeated this threat." Finally, Washington had "deliberately excluded India and other neutral countries from the political conference on the Korean settlement, seeking to turn this conference into another Panmunjom negotiation." Moreover, Peng mentioned that "the U.S. Navy is still occupying our territory Taiwan, American warlike elements continue to deny our legitimate rights in the UN, and the U.S. government continues to impose an economic blockade on our country, impairing the resumption of normal East-West trade relations." (It is, however, interesting that nowhere did Peng or other leaders mention the U.S. nuclear threat.) On the basis of these observations, Peng believed that "the U.S. imperialist clique will not easily accept their defeat in Korea, and will never abandon its aggressive ambition, and all kinds of conspiratorial challenges to the Korean peace will take place at any time." Facing this perceived threat, he announced on behalf of the People's Republic: "We must seriously warn the U.S. warlike elements that if you and your running-dog Rhee should dare to break the Korean armistice and resume the invasion, you will surely be counterattacked and end up with a broken head and bleeding body."[108]

The Beijing authorities emphasized that an eventual solution to the Korean problem would be diplomatic and political. Mao asserted in September 1953 that "the signing of the Korean Armistice Agreement is but the first step toward the peaceful resolution of the Korean problem. The peaceful resolution of the problem, leading to the withdrawal of all foreign troops from Korea and the spirit of having the Korean people handle their own affairs, is something that is left to the discussions and settlement of a higher level political assemblage."[109] The Chinese leaders were eager to settle the Korean problem at such a high-level political conference where they could impress world opin-

108. Peng's report to the twenty-fourth session of the Central People's Government Council, 12 September 1953, pp. 458–60.

109. Telegram, Mao to the Chinese People's Volunteers, 12 September 1953, in Michael Y. M. Kau and John K. Leung, eds., *The Writings of Mao Zedong, 1949–1976*, vol. 1, *September 1949–October 1955* (Armonk, N.Y., 1986), pp. 392–94.

ion with China's sincerity and maturity in dealing with international conflicts. On 26 October, Beijing agreed to talk about preliminary arrangements for the conference at Panmunjom, and strongly supported the Soviet suggestion to convene such a multilateral conference on 28 February 1954. After this planned conference actually opened at Geneva on 26 April, Zhou Enlai in his first speech stressed a total withdrawal of foreign troops from the Korean peninsula as "the premise" to Korea's self-determination. Even when the conference was about to break down, Zhou insisted that "all participating countries should agree to further work for a peaceful solution to the Korean problem, and be open to further negotiations regardless."[110] The Geneva conference, however, ended without any positive resolution. The Chinese continued to station a large number of troops in North Korea. Not until mid-March of 1958 did China's fifteen regular divisions begin a phased withdrawal. Nevertheless, there is no evidence that the Peoples' Republic had ever planned to settle the Korean issue by resuming military hostilities.

V

The end of the Korean War reflects a mixture of mutual compellence and deterrence, with each side trying to compel the other to accept peace on its terms and to deter the other from violating the armistice.

The Eisenhower administration repeated the mistakes of the Truman administration in judging China's intentions. Washington once again exaggerated the Soviet role in the Korean War, for once the Chinese forces intervened, the Kremlin remained very passive, showing actual reluctance to support the Chinese. Apparently, Beijing's efforts to promote Sino-Soviet cooperation in Korea misled American officials. Washington overestimated China's strength and China's determination to end the war on its own terms. American officials, in fact, never clearly understood Beijing's real objectives, which were actually no more than restoring the status quo prior to the outbreak of the conflict and reducing the perceived U.S. military threat in that region.

The new administration itself never had a clear objective either, except a vaguely expressed desire for an "honorable end" to the conflict. The Chinese mistook the appeals for total victory by a conservative bloc of Republicans for the stated policy goals of a moderate Republican administration. Believing that the United States would be invariably hostile and would certainly take more aggressive action in Korea provoked the Chinese to intensify their military activities.

110. *DDZGWJ*, pp. 50–54.

The nuclear threat never functioned properly as a deterrent factor. "Massive retaliation" was not really applicable to achieving an "honorable peace" in Korea. U.S. officials expected that nuclear threats against North Korea and Manchuria would compel the Chinese to accept the UN peace terms, but the Chinese regarded the use of atomic weapons as "impossible" in the face of the counterthreat of Soviet nuclear retaliation and the moral pressure of world opinion. In fact, Washington had never clearly warned the Chinese that the United States could and would use nuclear weapons against them. The Chinese never knew that the United States possessed tactical nuclear weapons, and they never detected the deployment of these weapons in the Far East.[111] The Eisenhower administration simply took it for granted that the PRC had understood its signals.

Moreover, the Eisenhower administration believed that Communist China, backed by the Soviet Union, intended to resume hostilities in Korea at the earliest practical opportunity. In fact, the Beijing authorities sought to have all foreign troops withdrawn from Korea and never intended to assist the North Koreans in liberating the whole of the peninsula. By deterring a Chinese threat that did not exist with the forward deployment of ground forces and a long-term commitment to South Korea, Washington projected an image of implacable hostility to the People's Republic.

The Chinese congratulated themselves for what they had accomplished in Korea. It seemed to them that their use of controlled military action had worked very well to block the enemy's ambitions in Korea and to bring him to terms. "Had they not made peace," Mao concluded, "their entire front would have been broken, and Seoul would have fallen into the hands of the Korean people."[112] More important, Beijing officials believed their short-term belligerency had served their long-term deterrence purposes, since "we dealt the U.S. imperialists a severe blow and frightened them quite badly."[113] Consequently, the Chinese leadership became—rather dangerously—overoptimistic when confronting the United States.

The Chinese leaders never asked themselves how accurately they had perceived U.S. intentions in Korea. Beijing evidently regarded Eisenhower's "honorable end" as a reflection of continued U.S. ag-

111. At no point during the spring of 1953 did the CCP news networks mention a possible atomic attack by the United States. When I interviewed Yao Xu, I asked whether the CPV headquarters had known about U.S. tactical atomic weapons. His answer—they had not.

112. Mao's address to the twenty-fourth session of the Central People's Government Council, 12 September 1953, p. 101.

113. Mao's speech at the National Conference on Financial and Economic Work, 12 August 1953, in *SWM*, 5:96.

gressiveness. Subsequently, the Chinese leaders saw both Eisenhower's visit to South Korea and his "unleashing Chiang" announcement as evidence of the preparations for a larger-scale offensive. But both the visit and the announcement were intended chiefly for domestic consumption. Even more interesting, Chinese military officers anticipated another U.S. amphibious operation because they knew that General Van Fleet preferred such operations and that Eisenhower had commanded the Normandy invasion. Thus, taking American hostility for granted, Chinese leaders mistook Washington's threats intended to deter violations of the armistice for evidence that the United States intended to exacerbate hostilities in Korea.

When the war finally came to an end, neither side felt secure. Mutual misperception reinforced mutual distrust. Vigilant and skeptical, both states immediately shifted their attention to Indochina.

[6]

Confrontation in Indochina,
1953–1954

In the spring of 1954, the Eisenhower administration perceived an emerging crisis in Indochina. The Communist Viet Minh, with Beijing's support, was preparing an all-out offensive against the French at Dien Bien Phu, and the French seemed unable to save themselves. Washington officials unanimously believed that the fall of Indochina to the Viet Minh would immediately threaten U.S. interests in that region and harm U.S. security over the long term in both East and Southeast Asia. How did this perception evolve? What did the United States do to counter the potential danger? And why did the Chinese Communists support the Viet Minh? How did Beijing authorities view and respond to U.S. policy toward Indochina?

I

Washington's preoccupation with Indochina had evolved over several years, during which American officials had been primarily concerned about how important denying that territory to the Vietnamese Communists would be to the United States and how seriously Communist China's intentions regarding Indochina threatened U.S. interests in that area.

Before 1950, the Truman administration had considered defending Indochina more important than defending either Taiwan or South Korea.[1] The reason for this was Indochina's presumed military and

1. For this point, see Gaddis, *The Long Peace*, pp. 89–92.

strategic value. The Joint Chiefs of Staff noted in April 1950 that denying Indochina to communism was critically significant to "the integrity of the offshore island chain from Japan to Indonesia." In their view, losing Indochina would mean that Japan, India, and Australia, the "three non-communist base areas," would be "isolated from one another."[2] Of related concern was the importance to these three regions of the food and strategic raw materials produced in Indochina. The National Security Council pointed out in late 1949 that both Japan and India imported substantial quantities of food and cotton from Southeast Asia.[3] But "Communist control of this area," a Joint Chiefs analysis confirmed in April 1950, "would alleviate considerably the food problem of China and would make available to the USSR important strategic materials."[4]

The Eisenhower administration accepted this reasoning completely. "The loss of Indochina," the National Security Council averred in August 1953, "would make more difficult and more expensive the defense of Japan, Formosa and the Philippines, and complicate the creation of a viable Japanese economy."[5] In January 1954, the NSC stated even more explicitly:

Communist control of all of Southeast Asia and Indochina would threaten the U.S. position in the Pacific offshore island chain and would seriously jeopardize fundamental U.S. security interests in the Far East. The loss of Southeast Asia would have serious consequences for many nations of the free world and conversely would add significant resources to the Soviet bloc. Southeast Asia, especially Malaya and Indonesia, is the principal world source of natural rubber and tin, and a producer of petroleum and other strategically important commodities. The rice exports of Burma, Indochina and Thailand are critically important to Malaya, Ceylon and Hong Kong, and are of considerable significance to Japan and India, all

2. JCS to Johnson, enclosed in Johnson to Acheson, 14 April 1950, in *FRUS: 1950*, 6:780–81.
3. NSC 48/1, "The Position of the United States with Respect to Asia," 23 December 1949, in *United States–Vietnam Relations*, 7:258–59. For more analysis of NSC 48/1 and 48/2, see Andrew J. Rotter, *The Path to Vietnam: Origins of the American Commitment to Southeast Asia* (Ithaca, N.Y., 1987), pp. 120–24, and p. 165. Rotter argues that in order to check Communist aggression, "direct or indirect," NSC 48/1 urged the countries of Southeast Asia to increase their production of agricultural goods and especially raw materials in order to supply the United States, provide a "market for the processed goods of industrialized states," and once again offer Western Europe "a rich source of revenue for investments and other invisible earnings" (*The Path to Vietnam*, pp. 121–22).
4. JCS to Johnson, enclosed in Johnson to Acheson, 14 April 1950, p. 781.
5. Cited in Russell D. Buhite, *Soviet-American Relations in Asia, 1945–1954* (Norman, Okla., 1981), pp. 206–7.

important areas of free Asia. Furthermore, the area has an important potential as a market for the industrialized countries of the free world.[6]

Perhaps more important, American strategists also perceived Indochina's importance in terms of the psychological consequences for other non-communist countries should Indochina fall to the Viet Minh. As early as the spring of 1950, the Truman administration had demonstrated its concern about the possible psychological impact Communist control of Indochina would have upon countries in Southeast and South Asia.[7] Available documents leave no doubt that the Eisenhower administration, too, was convinced that if Indochina fell to the Viet Minh, other countries vital to American interests in that part of the world would follow suit. At a joint State-Defense-JCS meeting on 28 June 1953, General Omar N. Bradley warned that the fall of Indochina "would be very bad, . . . [because] it would lead to the loss of all Southeast Asia." Secretary of State Dulles added that "if Southeast Asia was lost, this would lead to the loss of Japan." He explained that "the situation of the Japanese is hard enough with China being commie. You would not lose Japan immediately, but from there on out the Japs would be thinking on how to get on the other side."[8]

The new administration clearly believed that the Viet Minh invasion of Laos in the spring of 1953 was part of a scheme to exert continuous psychological pressure on the non-communist countries in that area. In June the CIA explicitly called it "part of a long-range Communist design to . . . gain control of all southeast Asia." The estimate explained that the Viet Minh's strategy involved "gradually extending their base areas in lightly defended regions of Laos, Cambodia, and central Vietnam; . . . to sap the morale of the Vietnamese and the French and finally to alter the balance of power."[9] Eisenhower expressed "great disappointment over the development in Laos." In his words, "The real point was [that] if Laos were lost we were likely to lose the rest of Southeast Asia and Indochina." Even worse in the president's view was the prospect that "the gateway to India, Burma and Thailand would be open."[10]

6. NSC 5405, "United States Objectives and Courses of Action with Respect to Southeast Asia," 16 January 1950, in *FRUS: 1952–1954*, 12:367–68.
7. On the Truman administration's concern about the psychological impact of the fall of Indochina, see Gaddis, *The Long Peace*, pp. 91–92. Also see Rotter, *The Path to Vietnam*, pp. 119–21.
8. Minutes, State-Defense-JCS meeting, 28 June, 1953, in *FRUS: 1952–1954*, 13:361–62.
9. NIE-91, "Probable Developments in Indochina through Mid-1954," 4 June 1953, in *FRUS: 1952–1954*, 13:593–95.
10. Minutes, NSC meeting, 28 April 1953, in *FRUS: 1952–1954*, 13:516–19. Eisenhower, however, did not publicly use the term "falling domino" to refer to Indochina

At a White House meeting in May 1953, Eisenhower pointedly observed that "the situation in Laos . . . in many respects poses a more serious threat than Korea."[11]

By early 1954 this fear over psychological consequences had grown. In March, Charles C. Stelle of the Policy Planning Staff vividly anticipated the consequences of the fall of Indochina. First, with its sizable Chinese minority, "Thailand would shortly accommodate itself to international communism unless there was direct U.S. military intervention." Second, a "Communist victory in Indochina and Communist pressure on Thailand would undoubtedly move the Burmese from their present position of fearful neutralism to one of active cooperation with the Communists." Third, the Chinese half of the Malayan population "would move off of the fence onto the Chinese Communist side"; the Malayans would lose faith in the British and would consider alternatives. Fourth, "Communist success on the mainland would undoubtedly increase the already considerable strength of the Communist position in Indonesia and that country, too, would be expected to move into the Communist orbit." And last, the expansion of Communist influence in all these countries "would spread doubt and fear among other threatened non-communist countries and create the feeling that Communism was the 'wave of the future' and that the United States and the Free World were unable to halt its advance." Consequently, "countries in the Far East, South Asia, and elsewhere in the world would be encouraged to adopt policies of accommodation to communist pressures and objectives."[12] The NSC added:

The loss of the struggle in Indochina, in addition to its impact in Southeast Asia and in South Asia would therefore have the most serious repercussions on U.S. and free world interests in Europe and elsewhere. . . . [Because] in the event all of Southeast Asia falls under communism, an alignment with communism of India, and in the longer term, of the Middle East (with the probable exceptions of at least Pakistan and Turkey) could follow progressively. Such widespread alignment would seriously endanger the stability and security of Europe.[13]

---

until 7 April 1954 at a press conference; see *Public papers*, p. 383. Also see Melanie Billings-Yun, *Decision against War: Eisenhower and Dien Bien Phu, 1954* (New York, 1988), p. 119.

11. Minutes, White House meeting, 7 May 1953, in *FRUS: 1952–1954*, 13:351–52.

12. Memorandum by Charles C. Stelle of PPS, "Importance of Southeast Asia," 23 March 1954, in *FRUS: 1952–1954*, 13:1146–47.

13. NSC 5405, 16 January 1950, pp. 366–68.

The President's Special Committee on Indochina therefore considered Indochina "the keystone of the arch" of Southeast Asia and other regions as well.[14]

Concern over Communist China's intentions was another important element of Washington's Indochina policy. The Truman administration had believed that the Soviet Union and Communist China supported the Viet Minh. Aware that Beijing was extending its influence through military aid to the Vietnamese Communists, administration officials had asserted that the Chinese Communists might intervene in either of two circumstances: (1) if the French were to defeat the Viet Minh; or (2) if the United States were to intervene on behalf of the French and the Associated States.[15] In August 1952, a national intelligence estimate found that Beijing was playing a "waiting game" in Indochina. As long as the area remained stalemated, the study predicted, "the Chinese Communists will not invade." It indicated that China's logistic support to the Viet Minh had fluctuated considerably: "During the last quarter of 1951 the Viet Minh . . . have received about 2,000 tons of supplies. Deliveries probably fell considerably below this level in the first quarter of 1952; . . . Chinese Communist support . . . appears still to be limited to logistic, technical, and advisory assistance." Moreover, the Chinese Communists were not ready for any large-scale action in Indochina. The study pointed out that "development of the air facilities in South China, particularly these along the Nanning rail line, would require three to six months for preparation for sustained combat operations; those on Hainan Island would require two to six weeks to develop for such operations" and there was "no indication that the Chinese Communists have begun the necessary preparation of airfield or other facilities in South China." The estimate thus concluded that "the Chinese Communists probably have the capability successfully to invade Indochina, but present evidence does not indicate that such an invasion is imminent."[16]

When Eisenhower took office, there immediately followed a debate on whether the Korean armistice would increase the possibility of Chinese intervention in Indochina. Livingston J. Merchant, assistant secretary of state for European affairs, wrote to Assistant Secretary of State for Far Eastern Affairs Walter Robertson in May 1953, expressing his fear that unless Korea and Indochina were linked, Communist

14. Report by the President's Special Committee on Indochina, 2 March 1954, enclosed in Smith to Eisenhower, 11 March 1954, in *FRUS: 1952–1954*, 13:1106–11.

15. George and Smoke, *Deterrence in American Foreign Policy*, pp. 243–44. Also see Buhite, *Soviet-American Relations in Asia*, pp. 205–6, and Gaddis, *The Long Peace*, pp. 90–91.

16. NIE-35/2, "Probable Developments in Indochina through Mid-1953," 29 August 1952, in *FRUS: 1952–1954*, 13:243–48.

China "could be freed to intervene with 'volunteers' in the Indochinese theater and in a few weeks achieve a fait accompli with de facto Red occupation of Indochina except possibly for French pockets at Hanoi, Haiphong and Saigon."[17] Robertson agreed that "an overt aggression by the Chinese Communists *after* an armistice in Korea [is] presumably made possible by such an armistice." He believed that Indochina presented a good opportunity for Communist Chinese expansion, because it "costs the Russians and Chinese very little while it is bleeding France and is a heavy burden for the United States."[18]

The national intelligence analysts, however, insisted that the Chinese Communists were not planning to intervene in Indochina. An intelligence study prepared in June 1953, argued that the Chinese would not take military action in Indochina through mid-1954, for three reasons. First, the Chinese could not conduct "sustained air operations in Indochina because of a lack of improved airfields in South China and stockpiles of supplies." Second, the Beijing authorities saw no reason to change their present strategy in Indochina in which they enjoyed "small cost but immediate advantage by exerting military and psychological pressures on the peoples and Governments of Laos, Cambodia and Thailand." Third and most important, the Chinese leadership was aware of the prospect of U.S. military retaliation if they intervened in Indochina.[19]

Top officials agreed that immediate Chinese intervention in Indochina was unlikely. Although he acknowledged the "possibility that the Viet Minh forces might be strengthened either by Chinese volunteers or by aviation based on China," Dulles told French foreign minister Georges Bidault in July of 1953, "an overt Chinese Communist aggression against Indochina . . . [was] highly improbable."[20] Worried about French reluctance to take the initiative in Indochina, the new secretary of state noted that "the French have always given as an excuse for not undertaking offensive action the possibility that offensive action might result in Chinese Communist intervention." Dulles thus proposed in September that the administration should take "a very serious view of any Chinese Communist intervention, [and] should go far towards eliminating this French excuse."[21] Admiral Arthur W. Radford, the new chairman of the Joint Chiefs of Staff, also thought that the Chinese were unlikely to come into Indochina as they

17. Merchant to Robertson, 5 May 1953, in *FRUS: 1952–1954*, 13:540–41.
18. Robertson to Merchant, 8 May 1953, in *FRUS: 1952–1954*, 13:556–57 [emphasis in original].
19. NIE-91, 4 June 1953, pp. 592–602.
20. Minutes, Dulles-Bidault meeting, 12 July 1953, in *FRUS: 1952–1954*, 13:662.
21. Minutes, State-JCS meeting, 4 September 1953, in *FRUS: 1952–1954*, 13:754.

had in Korea since, as he explained it, "they would find such intervention extremely difficult as long as we control the sea, since the land transportation system and the terrain would make the land approach very difficult for large-scale intervention."[22] Without much difficulty, the NSC reached a unanimous agreement in January 1954 that an "overt Chinese Communist attack on any part of Southeast Asia is less probable than continued Communist efforts to achieve domination through armed rebellion or subversion."[23]

Nevertheless, the consensus that Chinese intervention was unlikely became vulnerable as French resistance deteriorated in early 1954. The central question became whether the Chinese would intervene if the United States came in to save the French. A special intelligence assessment argued that they would not because Beijing would consider "the political advantage to be gained by portraying the U.S. as an 'aggressor'" greater than "the military advantage of moving large Chinese Communist forces into Indochina." The authors of this assessment reasoned that the Chinese might prefer to "take a number of steps which, without a serious risk of expanding the war to China, might *deter* a U.S. military commitment or seriously impair its effectiveness." Short of open armed intervention, the Chinese could increase aid to the Viet Minh, assist the Viet Minh's covert operations, build up military forces in South China, seek by diplomatic and propaganda means in the UN to forestall U.S. action, and negotiate a defense pact with the Viet Minh.[24]

But as the Viet Minh began preparing an all-out attack on the French forces at Dien Bien Phu, there emerged in Washington a sharp division of opinion regarding Chinese intervention. At an NSC meeting on 6 April, Allen Dulles, director of the Central Intelligence Agency, noted a "split of opinions in the Intelligence Advisory Committee regarding Chinese Communist overt intervention" in response to possible U.S. armed action in Indochina. He and an unnamed deputy director for intelligence of the Joint Chiefs believed that "the chances are better than even that the Chinese Communists would not openly intervene in Indochina, even if they believed that failure to intervene could mean the defeat at that time of the Viet Minh field forces in Indochina." But the intelligence analysts of the cabinet departments all argued that "the chances are better than even that the Communists would accept

22. Minutes NSC meeting, 9 September 1953, in *FRUS: 1952–1954*, 13:780–86.

23. NSC 5405, 16 January 1954, p. 971.

24. SE-53, "Probable Communist Reactions to Certain Possible U.S. Courses of Action in Indochina through 1954," 18 December 1953, in *FRUS: 1952–1954*, 13:924–31 [emphasis added].

the risk involved . . . and would intervene openly and in force to save the Communist position in Indochina." Nevertheless, it was not difficult for these groups to reconcile their differences. As Allen Dulles reported to the NSC, "All the members of the [Intelligence Advisory] Committee recognized that if the United States intervened in such force as to contrive the defeat of the Vietminh, there would be very great danger of overt Chinese Communist intervention. The only issue, therefore, was one of degree."[25]

Communist China was militarily capable of intervening. Allen Dulles reported to the NSC "five Chinese Communist divisions deployed along the border of Indochina; within some 300 miles of the borders there were in addition seven Chinese armies, numbering in all about 200,000 men, which could be sent into Indochina along the four available roads."[26] Administration officials also noted that Beijing had already signaled that it would counter U.S. armed intervention in Indochina. W. Park Armstrong Jr., the special assistant for intelligence in the State Department, told Secretary of State Dulles in that same month that the Communist Chinese propaganda campaign since February had become "more explicit as to the 'threat' to Communist China" and continued to stress that "the US will be foiled by irresistible forces seeking world peace and easement of tension."[27] Based on his observations of the Soviet and the Chinese attitude, Dulles felt that "open US intervention in Indochina would be more likely to be followed by open Chinese intervention, with the strong possibility that general war would result."[28]

Eisenhower was also convinced that the Chinese might intervene in Indochina as they had in Korea if U.S. ground forces became involved. In an NSC meeting in February, he strongly maintained that open U.S. intervention in Indochina could "provoke" China. With the Korean War still very fresh in his memory, he also worried about how the American public would react.[29] In April, Eisenhower again expressed his conviction that "if the U.S. were to intervene in Indochina alone, it would mean a general war with China and perhaps with the USSR, which the U.S. would have to prosecute separated from its allies." The president even predicted that unilateral intervention against the Viet

25. Minutes, NSC meeting, 6 April 1954, in *FRUS: 1952–1954*, 13:1251 and note 3.
26. Ibid., pp. 1252–53.
27. Armstrong to Dulles, "Chinese Communist Commentary on Indochina," 7 April 1954, in *FRUS: 1952–1954*, 13:1288–89.
28. Minutes, NSC meeting, 29 April 1954, in *FRUS: 1952–1954*, 13:1433; minutes, NSC meeting, 6 May 1954, ibid., pp. 1485–86.
29. Minutes, NSC meeting, 17 February 1954, in *FRUS: 1952–1954*, 13:1054–55.

Minh in Indochina would prompt the Chinese to move against Korea.[30]

This new, almost unanimous consensus regarding possible Chinese armed intervention remained strong through the summer of 1954. A State Department memorandum recorded in May that "all U.S. estimates agree on at least 50 percent chance of Chinese Communist reaction to U.S. intervention."[31] A Special National Intelligence study in June reconfirmed that "available evidence gives no unmistakable indication of what the Chinese Communist decision would be. On balance, we believe that the chances are somewhat better than even that the Chinese Communists . . . would intervene militarily to prevent destruction of the Viet Minh, including open use of Chinese Communist forces in Indochina."[32] How, then, did the Eisenhower administration decide to act in Indochina?

II

The situation was difficult: Indochina was undoubtedly vital to U.S. security interests in both East and Southeast Asia and, without a vigorous U.S. commitment to its defense, it seemed destined to fall to Communist control. Yet, any U.S. action to deny Indochina to the Communists might provoke Chinese intervention. The central question then was how the United States could *deter* the Chinese from intervening militarily to save the Viet Minh, *prevent* Indochina from falling to communism, and *contain* Communist expansion in Southeast Asia in the long run.

The Truman administration had been pessimistic, particularly after China's intervention in Korea, that the United States could afford to send military forces into Indochina to help the French stop the Viet Minh. In November 1950, the Joint Chiefs of Staff openly warned that any U.S. commitment should stop "short of the actual employment of United States military forces."[33] In June 1952, Secretary of State Acheson recognized that the United States "would have to do some-

30. Minutes, NSC meeting, 29 April 1954, pp. 1440–41. Also see Billings-Yun, *Decision against War*, pp. 50–51. Eisenhower "heatedly" argued with Harold Stassen about the possibility that U.S. intervention might provoke Chinese and perhaps Russian retaliation (p. 151).

31. State Department memorandum, 11 May 1954, in *FRUS: 1952–1954*, 13:1533.

32. SNIE 10-4-54, "Communist Reactions to Certain U.S. Courses of Action with Respect to Indochina," 15 June 1954, in *FRUS: 1952–1954*, 13:1702–3.

33. JCS to Marshall, 28 November 1950, enclosed in NSC 64/1, "The Position of the United States with Respect to Indochina," 29 December 1950, in *FRUS: 1950*, 6:946. For the Truman administration's policy on Indochina, see Gaddis, *The Long Peace*, pp. 92–94.

thing" about Indochina, and that warning the Chinese not to enter Indochina was "highly desirable." But he refrained from issuing such a warning. He explained to British foreign secretary Anthony Eden that "it will be essential to have a general understanding as to the action we might take if the warning were to go unheeded. . . . To issue a warning and take no effective action would be calamitous." To be caught bluffing, Acheson felt, "would make us look silly and would weaken the effect of any other warning."[34]

Nevertheless, the Eisenhower administration was convinced that the United States should and could react more vigorously to the Indochinese problem. One way was to demonstrate United States willingness to employ air and naval forces on behalf of the French in Indochina. At the administration's first State-Defense-JCS meeting in January 1953, Harold E. Stassen, director for the Mutual Security Program, asserted that the key to preventing an overt Chinese move into Indochina was the deterrent of "retaliation by our air." Even if the French should weaken the Viet Minh's position through further counteroffensives, Stassen explained, the Chinese "might move in some way unless they thought we were prepared to hold at least a beachhead" from which to retaliate.[35] In March, Dulles wanted to discuss with the French "the policies which we should adopt in order to discourage further Chinese Communist aggression." He hoped that the United States and the French could agree that a "speedy defeat of Viet Minh forces in Indochina would *deter* rather than provoke Chinese Communist aggression in Tonkin since it would be a clear indication of our joint determination to meet force with effective force."[36] At the same time, in a meeting with Eisenhower, Secretary of Defense Charles E. Wilson, and Secretary of the Treasury George M. Humphrey, Dulles argued the need for "deterrence against the Chinese Communists, so they would not send their forces into Vietnam as they had done in Korea.[37]

On two occasions in 1953, the administration openly warned the Chinese not to intervene in Indochina. In early April, when the French expressed concern that a Korean armistice would make more probable the transfer of Chinese military forces from Korea to Indochina, State Department officials felt it imperative to clarify U.S.

---

34. Memorandum of conversation with Eden on the Indochinese problem, 26 June 1952, *United States–Vietnam Relations*, 1:391. Also see George and Smoke, *Deterrence in American Foreign Policy*, p. 245 and note 15.

35. Minutes, State-DMS-JCS meeting, 28 January, 1953, in *FRUS: 1952–1954*, 13:362–63.

36. Dulles to the U.S. embassy in France, 19 March 1953, in *FRUS: 1952–1954*, 13:416–17 [emphasis added].

37. Memorandum by Dulles, 24 March 1953, in *FRUS: 1952–1954*, 13:429–30.

determination to counter such a transfer.[38] The outcome was a warning message in Eisenhower's "Chance for Peace" speech on 16 April. Stressing the "interdependence" of the Korean and Indochinese conflicts, the president emphasized that the Korean armistice "should mean . . . an end to the direct and indirect attacks upon the security of Indochina and Malaya. For any armistice in Korea that merely released aggressive armies to attack elsewhere would be a fraud."[39] Another clarification of the U.S. commitment came when General Henri Navarre, the newly appointed French commander in Indochina, planned an all-out offensive to be launched that summer. Concerned that the Chinese might openly intervene if that offensive succeeded, both French and American strategists felt an urgent need to issue an explicit deterrent threat against Chinese entry into the war. Dulles thus delivered a forceful warning on 2 September, when he spoke before the American Legion at St. Louis. Pointing out that "as in Korea, Red China might send its own army into Indochina," he declared that such a move could have grave consequences in China itself.[40]

It was not at all clear what Eisenhower and Dulles would do. Administration officials understood that they needed a plan to back up their rhetoric. Robert Cutler, special assistant to the president for national security, stressed this at a 6 May NSC meeting, and urged the Pentagon to plan military responses to any "basic change" in Indochina.[41] The Joint Strategic Survey Committee warned in June that the United States was not able to prevent the Chinese from overrunning Indochina. The United States would have to rely on the indigenous ground forces with U.S. air and naval assistance and retaliate against China somewhere else. To this end, the United States should "obtain significant force contributions from Australia, New Zealand, the United Kingdom, France, and the National Government of the Republic of China (NGRC): [and] call for the immediate formation of an Asiatic League which could include the NGRC and would provide forces to combat Communists in the Far East."[42]

Dulles agreed that it was "reasonable to make plans in Indochina . . . [so that] the Communists *know* that it is possible that such

38. Allison to Dulles, "Status of Indochina Problem," 3 April 1953, in *FRUS: 1952–1954*, 13:455–57.

39. Eisenhower's "Chance for Peace" speech, 16 April 1953, in *FRUS: 1952–1954*, 13:472. Also see the accompanying editorial note.

40. Dulles's statement before the American Legion in St. Louis, 21 September 1953, in *FRUS: 1952–1954*, 13:747.

41. Minutes, NSC meeting, 6 May 1953, in *FRUS: 1952–1954*, 13:546–49.

42. JCS 1992/227, "Possible Military Courses of Action in Indochina," 22 June 1953, in *FRUS: 1952–1954*, 13:615–16.

[Chinese] operations would lead to a rather general war in the Pacific area and that sea and air forces from the United States might be brought to bear in areas other than Indochina."[43] To this end, in July 1953 Dulles instructed Douglas MacArthur II, the counselor to the State Department, to inform French premier Joseph Laniel that "United States action with respect to Seventh Fleet and strengthening of Formosa had been designed to create a deterrent threat along the Chinese mainland coast so as to lessen chance[s] of introduction of Chinese 'volunteers' into Indochina." The secretary of state also wanted to remind the French that the United States had attempted in the Korean truce talks "to create conditions which would make it likely that the Chinese would withdraw strength from Korea immediately following the armistice for possible use against Indochina."[44] To deter Chinese Communist armed intervention, the NSC reported in January 1954, "the U.S. Government has engaged in consultations with France and the United Kingdom on the desirability of issuing to Communist China a joint warning as to the consequences to Communist China of aggression in Southeast Asia." The administration had also participated with France, the UK, Australia, and New Zealand in military talks "on measures which might be taken in the event of overt Chinese Communist aggression against Indochina."[45] The main objective of United States deterrence, as Dulles explained it in September 1953, was to assure that the Communist Chinese would find it unpleasant to contemplate American counterthreats, while at the same time "encourag[ing] the French to make new effort in Indochina."[46]

During early 1954, China did not send any troops into Indochina, but a collapse of French resistance to the Viet Minh appeared to be imminent. At a cabinet meeting on 29 March, Dulles pointed out that "we must help Fr[ance] win in Indochina—if not, Reds would win that part of world and cut our defense line in half." The United States might have to take "fairly strong action" in that area.[47] Pentagon strategists also felt a real sense of urgency. Radford emphasized on 26 March that "the U.S. must be prepared to act promptly and in force" in the event of a last-minute call from the French for help.[48] Other

43. Minutes, Dulles-Bidault meeting, 12 July 1953, pp. 662–63 [emphasis added].
44. MacArthur II and Dillon to State Department, 31 July 1953, in FRUS: 1952–1954, 13:706–9.
45. NSC 5405, 16 January 1954, p. 368.
46. Minutes, NSC meeting, 9 September 1953, pp. 780–89.
47. Hagerty Diary, 26 March 1954, in FRUS: 1952–1954, 13:1173. Also see Gaddis, The Long Peace, p. 129.
48. Memorandum, JCS meeting in FRUS: 1952–1954, 13:1172.

administration officials now agreed that the United States "could intervene and drive right up to the borders of Communist China" to save the French at Dien Bien Phu.[49]

But openly sending American soldiers into Indochina might well provoke the Chinese. At a NSC meeting on 25 March, Secretary of Defense Wilson raised the possibility that the Chinese would at least send in aircraft if U.S. forces became involved.[50] On 29 March, the NSC Planning Board stressed that the United States should take into account "the risk of large-scale Chinese Communist intervention" in considering "direct U.S. military participation in the French military effort."[51] In the following month, Eisenhower explicitly argued at a NSC meeting that "it was well to remember that there were a million Chinese soldiers across the borders ready to pounce on South Korea if its defense was weakened."[52]

At this moment, the issue was as much about how to compel the Viet Minh to retreat from Dien Bien Phu as about how to deter Chinese military intervention. The President's Special Committee on Indochina maintained in early March that "the Communists in Indochina, Southeast Asia, China and Moscow *must be made aware* that the United States, France and the free governments of the Far East are united, steadfast, and capable of accomplishing their aims" to contain Communist expansion.[53] On 24 March, Dulles told the president that it was necessary to make a "Monroe address" signaling that "the freedom of the Southeast Asia area was important from the standpoint of our peace, security and happiness, and that we would not look upon the loss to Communists of that area with indifference."[54] Five days later, in his speech "The Threat of a Red Asia" before the Overseas Press Club of America, in New York, the secretary of state announced: "Under the conditions of today, the imposition on Southeast Asia of the political system of Communist Russia and its Chinese Communist ally, by whatever means, would be a grave threat to the whole free community. The United States feels that that possibility should not be passively accepted but should be met by united action. This might invoke

49. Minutes, NSC meeting, 6 April 1954, pp. 1250–65.
50. Minutes, NSC meeting, 25 March 1954, in *FRUS: 1952–1954*, 13:1165.
51. NSC Planning Board, Special Annex on Indochina, enclosed in Lay to the NSC, 29 March 1954, in *FRUS: 1952–1954*, 13:1183.
52. Minutes, NSC meeting, 29 April 1954, pp. 1440–41.
53. Report by the President's Special Committee on Indochina, 2 March 1954, enclosed in Smith to Eisenhower, 11 March 1954, pp. 1106–15 [emphasis added].
54. Dulles, memorandum of conversation with the president, 24 March 1954, in *FRUS: 1952–1954*, 13:1150.

risks. But these risks are far less than those that will face us a few years from now if we dare not be resolute today."[55]

What counteraction the United States would and could take, however, was still unclear. In late March, Dulles advocated "slow[ing] up the Chinese Communists in Southeast Asia by harassing tactics from Formosa and along the seacoast which would be more readily within our natural facilities than actually fighting in Indochina."[56] Eisenhower, however, asserted that the United States might just "keep up pressure for collective security and show [the] determination of [the] free world to oppose chipping away of any part of the free world." The president also stated that he would not mind if the French made use of "the idea of U.S. intervention as a means of influencing the Communists."[57] To Eisenhower, Indochina had become a dilemma. He explained in late April that "there was no end to the fighting in sight, yet the alternative of losing Indochina could be worse." He made it plain to his cabinet that "he hated to see all action bogged down on one detail [of the commitment of U.S. ground forces]," and that it was "a matter of finding the *cheapest* way out of the dilemma." He urged his advisors to find "our best bet" in resolving the crisis.[58]

One effective method, in Eisenhower's view, might be the nuclear threat. In late April, he suggested to Cutler that the loan of a "new weapon" be discussed with the French.[59] The NSC Planning Board assessed the military feasibility of the using of a "new weapon" in Vietnam. It concluded that "U.S. use of 'new weapons' in Vietnam would tend to *deter* Chinese aggression in retaliation, and that failure to use the 'new weapon' in Vietnam would tend to increase chances of Chinese aggression in retaliation (i.e. the Chinese would feel the U.S. was afraid to use its one massive superiority)."[60] The Joint Chiefs of Staff agreed in May that "atomic weapons will be used whenever it is to our military advantage."[61]

55. An extract of Dulles's speech is in the editorial note, in *FRUS: 1952–1954*, 13:1181–82. For the full text, see U.S. Department of State, *Department of State Bulletin*, 12 April 1954, pp. 539–42.

56. Dulles, memorandum of conversation with the president, 24 March 1954, p. 1150.

57. Hagerty Diary, 26 April 1954, p. 1441; minutes, NSC meeting, 6, May 1954, p. 1488.

58. Eisenhower's statement, 26 April 1954, enclosed in the assistant staff secretary to Eisenhower, undated, in *FRUS: 1952–1954*, 13:1447–48. [emphasis added].

59. Cutler to Smith, 30 April 1954, in *FRUS: 1952–1954*, 13:1447–48. Also see Gaddis, *The Long Peace*, p. 131.

60. NSC Planning Board discussions, 29 April 1954, enclosed in Cutler to Smith, 30 April 1954, pp. 1445–47 [emphasis added].

61. JCS to Wilson, 20 May 1954, in *FRUS: 1952–1954*, 13:1591. For the military opinion of the use of atomic weapons in Indochina, see Betts, *Nuclear Blackmail and Nuclear Balance*, pp. 48–51.

Nevertheless, administration officials were primarily concerned with forming a collective effort committed to the defense of Indochina and the rest of Southeast Asia. They assumed that a coalition composed of the United States, the United Kingdom, Australia, New Zealand, Thailand, the Philippines, and the Associated States in Indochina, accompanied by stern warnings, might deter Chinese intervention as well as bolster the French will to resist. "The important thing," Eisenhower asserted in April, "was to get a regional grouping together . . . as rapidly as possible."[62] Since "the only ray of hope would be Communist fear of United States intervention in Indochina or of a general war," Dulles explained to the NSC in May, a united front was necessary to ensure that the Chinese "realize that the United States is not permitting the British a veto on our actions in that area."[63]

Dulles worked feverishly to promote the proposed collective intervention in Indochina. He had difficulty persuading the French, who feared that internationalizing the war might end their control over the Associated States in Indochina. The British flatly refused. They had no interest in intervening in an unwinnable war. Both Prime Minister Churchill and Foreign Secretary Eden expressed their fear that outside intervention would provoke war with the Chinese, who would then retaliate against Hong Kong.[64] Disappointed with the French and the British, the Eisenhower administration delayed military action, pending developments at the Geneva Conference, at which the United States, Britain, France, the USSR, and the PRC were to discuss political settlement in both Korea and Indochina. Not unexpectedly, the hopelessly outnumbered French garrison at Dien Bien Phu surrendered on 7 May, the day before the Indochina phase of the conference was to begin.[65]

Dulles did not give up, but rather considered Geneva another occasion to demonstrate United States determination to deny Indochina to the Viet Minh. During the discussion of the Korean problem, Dulles remained aloof. He had left Geneva before the phase concerning the Indochina problem began, to indicate American distance from the conference. Dulles insisted in May that the United States should participate in the conference only as an "interested nation," not as a

62. Cutler to Smith, 30 April 1954, p. 1448.
63. Minutes, NSC meeting, 20 May 1954, in *FRUS: 1952–1954*, 13:1586–88.
64. Memorandum for record by the president, 27 April 1954, in *FRUS: 1952–1954*, 13:1422–23; minutes, NSC meeting, 29 April 1954, pp. 1434–35; memorandum of a White House meeting, 5 May 1954, in *FRUS: 1952–1954*, 13:1466–67; minutes, NSC meeting, 6 May 1954, pp. 1481–84.
65. George C. Herring and Richard H. Immerman, "Eisenhower, Dulles, and Dienbienphu: 'The Day We Didn't Go to War' Revisited," *Journal of American History* 41 (September 1984): 358–62.

"belligerent or a principal in the negotiation," and thus should not endorse an agreement in any way impairing the territorial integrity of the Associated States of Indochina.[66] Later he explained that he had tried to create an "impression in the minds of the French and those in Geneva" that the United States was still preparing a collective action in Indochina and also hoped that "the French might ultimately agree to internationalize the conflict"; however, Dulles worried that "the Communist negotiator at Geneva would continue to dangle false hopes before the French so that the latter would be unable to reach any firm decision until the situation in Indochina had deteriorated to a point where it was beyond salvation by any means."[67]

Despite the events at Geneva, Washington continued to develop an elaborate contingency scenario for Indochina. JCS Chairman Admiral Radford traveled to London and Paris in late April, where he talked with Churchill, the British chiefs of staff, and French military officers about coordinating military action in Indochina.[68] In the same month, Dulles also went to London and Paris to talk about "the lines of our plans." Dulles succeeded in having an Anglo-American communiqué, also agreed upon by the French, calling for "a meeting of the 10 nations for April 20 to discuss 'united action.' "[69] In late May, Washington hosted a military staff meeting with participants from Britain, France, Australia, and New Zealand. Dulles maintained that all these talks, regardless of their real outcomes, would have some impact at Geneva, serving as a "window dressing with the Russians who had no way of knowing what was going on."[70] In May, Eisenhower instructed the State Department to draft a congressional resolution that would enable him "to use the armed forces of the United States to support the free governments that we recognize in that area; . . . which would indicate that the United States was acting in concert with its friends and allies in the area."[71]

Meanwhile, administration officials were working on contingency plans for "United Action." In May, the Joint Chiefs urged the Department of defense to consider "the size and composition of U.S. force

66. Dulles to Smith, 12 May 1954, in *United States–Vietnam Relations*, 4:457–59.
67. Minutes, NSC meeting, 20 May 1954, pp. 1586–90.
68. Minutes, NSC meeting, 29 April 1954, pp. 1434–38.
69. Record of Dulles's briefing for members of Congress, 5 May 1954, in *FRUS: 1952–1954*, 13:1473–74. There is no indication which ten nations agreed to attend the meeting. Dulles did mention, however, that the meeting did not take place because of Eden's rejection, and that it was "quite embarrassing to us" (p. 1473).
70. Cutler memorandum, 28 May 1954, in *FRUS: 1952–1954*, 12:526; report of the Five-Power Military Conference of 3–11 June 1954, ibid., pp. 555–63.
71. Memorandum of conversation by MacArthur II, 11 May 1954, in *FRUS: 1952–1954*, 13:1526–28.

contributions to be made and the command structure to be established." They argued that "although the Allied Commander in Chief in Indochina should be French, there must be a U.S. Deputy with sufficient staff assistance to provide liaison with the French and coordinate U.S. activities with over-all operations." The JCS proposed to formulate "a Military Representatives Committee with membership from those nations contributing the principal forces of the coalition."[72] Furthermore, as required by Eisenhower, the NSC Planning Board in June designed a comprehensive outline directing different agencies of the administration to prepare detailed studies on such issues as economic warfare, intelligence on enemy capabilities, military planning and mobilization, juridical relations in the French Union, relations with the United Nations, and generating domestic support, in the event of "United Action" in Indochina.[73]

Developments at Geneva in June and July, however, surprised Washington. British foreign minister Eden pushed strongly for a cease-fire in Indochina, the partition of Vietnam, and the neutralization of Laos and Cambodia. In addition, Pierre Mendes-France had replaced Laniel as French premier, and he proclaimed that he would resign if a settlement based on Eden's proposal was not reached at Geneva by 21 July. It is interesting to note that Eisenhower and Dulles considered these dramatic changes as a chance to achieve a second-best solution to the Indochinese problem, if not the denial of the whole of Indochina to the Vietnamese Communists. They then abandoned their hope for a collapse at Geneva.[74] Regardless of U.S. pressure, the Soviet, Chinese, and the Viet Minh delegates accepted the Eden proposal, which for them was also a compromise. An agreement generally based on the British proposal was finally completed at Geneva just hours before Mendes-France's deadline.[75]

The Eisenhower administration did not feel relieved. How could the United States prevent the Viet Minh from reinitiating military conflict in Indochina? At a NSC meeting in August, Dulles argued that "the deterrent nuclear power of the United States" should be "the principal factor." Eisenhower disagreed on the ground that retaliation is no deterrent "unless we can identify the aggressor. . . . In many cases ag-

72. JCS to Wilson, 20 May 1954, p. 1591.

73. NSC 5421, "Studies with Respect to Possible United States Action Regarding Indochina," 1 June 1954, in *FRUS: 1952–1954*, 13:1651–52.

74. Dillon to the Department of State, 9 July 1954, in *FRUS: 1952–1954*, 13:1812; memorandum of conversation of Dulles, Eden, and Mendes-France, 13 July 1954, ibid., pp. 819–28; minutes, NSC meeting, 15 July 1954, ibid., pp. 1835–40.

75. See Herring and Immerman, "Eisenhower, Dulles, and Dienbienphu," pp. 360–62.

gression consists of subversion or civil war in a country rather than an overt attack. . . . In such cases it is difficult for us to know whom to retaliate against."[76] Dulles then held that at least a collective security arrangement had to be made "in advance of [local] aggression, not after it is under way." He believed that the United States had obtained at Geneva an "opportunity to prevent the loss in Northern Vietnam from leading to the extension of Communism throughout Southeast Asia and the Southwest Pacific." To deter communist aggression in the long run, Dulles asserted, a collective security treaty in Southeast Asia should be the first priority once the crisis in Indochina was resolved.[77] Eisenhower concurred. On 21 July, he announced that "the United States is actively pursuing discussions with other free nations with a view to the rapid organization of a collective defense in Southeast Asia in order to *prevent* further direct or indirect communist aggression in that general area."[78]

The United States did not plan to commit ground forces in Southeast Asia as it had in Europe. In early August, Dulles told the NSC that negotiations on the Southeast Asia Treaty Organization (SEATO) were based on "the assumption that there would be no build-up of U.S. military power in Southeast Asia sufficient to stop an aggressor." Eisenhower also stressed that the United States had to depend on "the indigenous victims of aggression for some of the fighting." Only if the local states "fight hard and need help, [can we] send in the Marines and the Air Force."[79] Washington was generally satisfied with the SEATO negotiations at Manila in September: a line was drawn across Southeast Asia; member states would retaliate if the Communists crossed the line; and they would deal with aggression in "the most feasible and effective way" if the pact failed to deter.[80] Although the United States would not station ground troops in Indochina and the member states agreed only to "meet common danger" in accordance with their "own constitutional processes and to consult," from Dulles's standpoint, SEATO would serve as a long-term deterrent to Communist expansion in the region.[81]

76. Minutes, NSC meeting, 5 August 1954, in *FRUS: 1952–1954*, 2:708–9.

77. Dulles news conferences, 23 July 1954, John Foster Dulles Papers, Box 79, Seeley Mudd Library, Princeton University.

78. Eisenhower's statement is enclosed in an editorial note in *FRUS: 1952–1954*, 13:1864–65 [emphasis added].

79. Minutes, NSC meeting, 5 August 1954, pp. 708–9; Dulles memorandum, 17 August 1954, in *FRUS: 1952–1954*, 13:1953.

80. Minutes, NSC meeting, 12 August 1954, in *FRUS: 1952–1954*, 12:729; memorandum of conversation, 17 August 1954, ibid., p. 735; minutes, NSC meeting, 12 September 1954, ibid., p. 903.

81. Minutes, NSC meeting, 12 September 1954, pp. 903–8.

Clearly, Washington's understanding of Beijing's intentions in Indochina shaped U.S. policy. What, then, about the Chinese involvement in Indochina during this period?

III

What were Beijing's policy objectives toward Indochina prior to the
Geneva settlement? How did it implement them? Did the outcomes
parallel its policy expectations? So far, little attention has been given to
these questions either by Chinese scholars or in the Western literature.
Materials recently made available, though still insufficient and scattered, encourage further study.

From the beginning of the Vietnamese Communist movement the
Chinese leaders were determined to offer moral and material support.
That determination was based on the sense that, since they shared the
common objective of eliminating imperialist and foreign influence in
Asia, Chinese revolutionaries were obliged to support their Vietnamese "comrades-in-arms." Shortly before the founding of the People's
Republic of China in October 1949, Liu Shaoqi, the second-ranking
CCP leader, proclaimed that the Chinese people would fulfill their
"proletarian internationalist duty to support the entirely righteous
war of national liberation to a complete victory."[82] As early as the
spring of 1947, long-wave radio communications had been established
between CCP headquarters in Shanxi and the Indochinese Communist
Party led by Ho Chi Minh. Through this connection, Zhou Enlai maintained frequent contact with Ho, particularly in the matters of "shar-
ing information and discussing important issues."[83]

This sense of responsibility on the part of the CCP increased after
the success of the Communist revolution in China. In late 1949, Ho Chi
Minh established the Viet Minh (the Vietnamese National Liberation
Front) for the purpose of ending French control in Indochina. In early
January 1950, Ho sent his foreign minister Huang Minh Chian to
Beijing, to establish formal relations. When Mao Zedong was informed
of the Vietnamese request in Moscow, he immediately instructed Liu
Shaoqi on 17 January to recognize the Viet Minh government "at
once."[84] At the same time, Mao himself drafted an official reply to Ho
Chi Minh, in which he stressed that "the establishment of our

82. Liu Shaoqi, *On Internationalism and Nationalism* (Peking, 1949), p. 14.
83. Zhang Yisheng, "The Revolutionary Friendship between Premier Zhou and
Chairman Ho," *Yindu Zhina Yanjiu*, March 1981, p. 14.
84. Telegram, Mao Zedong to Liu Shaoqi, "On Our Reply to the Viet Minh Government," 17 January 1950, in *JGYLMWG* 1:238–39.

The China-Vietnam border

diplomatic relationship . . . will serve the purpose of strengthening the friendship and cooperation of our two nations in our common course." Beijing established diplomatic relations with the Viet Minh on 19 January 1950, thus becoming the first country to do so. Moreover, in order to find more supporters for the Viet Minh, Mao appealed to Moscow and Eastern European Communist countries to grant diplomatic recognition.[85]

The Vietnamese Communists—and particularly Ho Chi Minh—had tried vigorously to secure a CCP–Viet Minh connection. As early as November 1949, Ho sent a personal representative to Beijing with a letter addressed to Zhou Enlai. That letter was written in Chinese and disguised as business correspondence. As Ho put it, "In order to seize the opportunity of defeating the opponent we are desperate for your help."[86] After obtaining formal recognition from China, Ho decided to go to Beijing for further talks in mid-January 1950. During his secret visit, Ho talked a great deal with both Liu Shaoqi and Zhou, primarily about what the Chinese could do to advance his cause. Liu and Zhou clearly understood what Ho wanted from China, but they would not commit themselves without Mao's endorsement. They suggested that Ho go to Moscow and talk directly with Mao and Stalin about these matters. The Vietnamese leader immediately contacted the Soviet Ambassador to Beijing, requesting that arrangements be made for his visit. With Moscow's approval late that month, Ho Chi Minh went to Moscow together with Zhou, who had been ordered there by Mao to negotiate the details of Sino-Soviet alliance.[87]

In Moscow, Ho Chi Minh met Mao and Stalin several times to discuss how the Soviet Union and the People's Republic of China could assist the Vietnamese revolution. As General Wu Xiuquan—one of the interpreters during these meeting—recalls, Stalin showed considerable understanding of Ho's problems, but rejected Ho's requests for Soviet military assistance. At a banquet on 26 February, Ho once again requested an alliance between the Soviet Union and the Viet Minh. Stalin had to remind Ho that his visit in Moscow was still being kept secret. Ho quickly responded: "That is easy. You can simply have me flying in the air for a while, then organize a welcoming reception at

85. Mao Zedong's reply to the Viet Minh Government, 19 January 1950, *Renmin Ribao*, 19 January 1950, p. 1; telegram, Mao and Zhou Enlai to Liu Shaoqi, 1 February 1950, in *JGYLMWG* 1:254. They told Liu that the Soviet Union had agreed to recognize the Viet Minh, and that Mao had already sent his request to the embassies of Eastern European countries to Moscow. Mao expressed his gladness that "the Viet Minh will join the big democratic anti-imperialist family."
86. Ho's letter is cited in Huang Zhen, *Hu Zhiming Yu Zhongguo* (Beijing, 1987), pp. 123–24.
87. Ibid., pp. 24–25.

the airport and release news of my visit to the public. After that we can work on a Soviet-Vietnamese alliance treaty." Stalin rejected Ho's idea but smiled at him, saying that "only you Orientals could have this kind of imagination."[88] At another meeting, Stalin explicitly explained to Ho that he was very much concerned about the Vietnamese struggle, but he preferred that "the Chinese comrades take over the principal responsibility of supporting and supplying the Vietnamese people." Mao could hardly say anything, but agreed to give some thought to how that could be appropriately accomplished when he returned to Beijing.[89] In order to secure Mao's promise, Ho Chi Minh addressed a memorandum to Zhou Enlai right away, outlining the main points of the Stalin-Mao-Ho talks and asking Zhou to verify them. He also reminded Zhou that he would wait for him in Beijing to discuss detailed arrangements for Chinese military assistance.[90]

From the beginning of 1950, Viet Minh authorities regarded the PRC as the only source of external support and assistance for their struggle. Previously, the Viet Minh had concentrated on obtaining Thailand's sympathy and support for its national liberation movement, but in January 1950, Ho Chi Minh told Hoang Van Hoan, the Viet Minh official in charge of external affairs and later the first Viet Minh Ambassador to Beijing, that "our attention and efforts regarding external affairs should now shift from Thailand to China." Now that the principal Chinese leaders had promised to do their best, Ho instructed Hoang that "we shall not allow the best opportunity to go out of our hands."[91] At the Second National Convention of the Indochinese Communist Party in February 1951, Ho Chi Minh invited a CCP delegation, and openly confirmed the importance of Chinese support and assistance in the Vietnamese struggle for final victory over the French colonialists. Ho pointedly stated:

Because of the geographic, historic, economic, and cultural connections between Vietnam and China, the Chinese revolution has tremendous impact upon the Vietnamese revolution. Our revolution therefore shall follow—as we have already learned—the course of the Chinese revolution. By relying on the Chinese revolutionary lessons, and relying on Mao Zedong Thought, we have further understood the thoughts of Marx, Engels,

88. *Wu Xiuquan Memoirs*, p. 13.

89. Hoang Van Hoan, *Canghai Yisu: Hoang Van Hoan Geming Huiyilu* (Beijing, 1987), p. 259 [hereafter *Hoang's Revolutionary Reminiscences*].

90. Huang, *Hu Zhiming Yu Zhongguo*, p. 125.

91. *Hoang's Revolutionary Reminiscences*, p. 254. There is no indication why the Viet Minh had previously sought Thailand's support.

Lenin, and Stalin so that we have won a great deal of victories in the past year. *This shall we never forget.*[92]

Beijing authorities understood Indochina's strategic importance to the security of China's southern border. The CCP considered its external threat as concentrated on three fronts. They consistently viewed Korea, Taiwan, and Indochina as the three most likely places where the United States might initiate military hostilities. Chinese leaders had not forgotten that the French had invaded China's southern provinces directly from Indochina in the late nineteenth century. They believed that a French occupation of that entire region, with possible U.S. intervention on behalf of the French, would turn Indochina into an U.S. military base and threaten China in the long run if not immediately.[93]

Available evidence suggests that after the founding of the People's Republic, Beijing's immediate concern was with the scattered KMT elements, retreating toward Indochina and other Southeast Asian countries. In a telegram from Moscow to Liu Shaoqi on 29 December 1949, Mao Zedong directed that the PLA should take appropriate measures "to prevent the KMT troops in Guangxi and Yunnan [provinces] from entering Vietnam and Burma." He instructed the PLA not just to "pursue the enemy from behind," since, in his view, this "would drive the enemy into Indochina, and then the consequence would be big trouble."[94] Although it is not clear what Mao meant by "big trouble," there is reason to assume that he worried that the KMT remnants in Indochina, if assisted by the French or the United States, would make a foreign invasion from there more likely.

The outbreak of fighting in Korea reinforced Beijing's fears of invasion from Indochina. When Truman announced his decision to send the U.S. Seventh Fleet into the Taiwan Strait, to increase American aid to Southeast Asia, and to intervene in Korea, the CCP leaders felt threatened from all three directions. On 28 June, Zhou Enlai openly condemned the U.S. announcement, pointing out that U.S. policy toward Vietnam and the Philippines was part of "a premeditated move by the United States to invade Taiwan [and] Korea."[95] On the same day, Mao also told the eighth meeting of the Central People's Government Council that "present U.S. interference in Korea, the Philippines,

92. Cited in Huang, *Hu Zhiming Yu Zhongguo*, pp. 133–34 [emphasis added].
93. "The United States Conspired to Enlarge the War in Indochina," *Shijie Zhishi*, September 1953, pp. 4–6.
94. Telegram, Mao Zedong to Liu Shaoqi, "We Should Halt the KMT Remnants and Now Allow Them to Enter Vietnam and Burma," 29 December 1949, *JGYLMWG* 1:198.
95. Premier Zhou Enlai's proclamation, *Renmin Ribao*, 28 June 1950, p. 1.

and Viet Nam . . . proves that Truman's previously proclaimed 'non-interference' policy in Asia is a fraud." He insisted that "the peoples of our country and the whole world must be united and fully prepared in order to defeat imperialist provocation in any form."[96]

As the United States increased its military involvement in Korea, the Chinese leaders considered the threat from Indochina less immediate. But they were determined to help the Vietnamese Communists gain control of Indochina if only to secure a buffer zone for China's southern border. Both Zhou and Liu Shaoqi made it very clear to Ho Chi Minh in early 1950 that the Vietnamese struggle against the French was part of the Chinese struggle against imperialism in Asia, because if Vietnam were reoccupied by the imperialists, China's southern border would be exposed to direct threat.[97] Mao also emphasized to Ho the importance of "the eternal unity of the peoples of the two countries, China and Vietnam, and their common effort in the cause of peace in Asia."[98]

But what could the People's Republic do against the imperialists in Indochina? One step was to furnish the Viet Minh with as much material aid as possible. Hoang Van Hoan, then the Viet Minh ambassador to Beijing, remembered that the top Chinese leaders "expressed their determination without any hesitation that China would provide the Vietnamese people all the necessary material assistance, and would be prepared to send troops to fight together with the Vietnamese people when necessary."[99] Hoang did not mention who said this or when, but if true, it seems that Beijing had offered the Vietnamese a blank check.

Other sources suggest that Beijing did not support the Viet Minh unconditionally. In early March 1950, Ho Chi Minh handed Zhou Enlai in Beijing a long list of material needs that he wanted China to fill. After a few discussions, the Chinese leaders agreed to supply these materials but on the condition that there should be no transportation problem along the Sino-Vietnamese border. Since the French controlled the main transportation lines in the border area, a large shipment of Chinese materials to the Viet Minh was practically impossible. The Chinese leaders implied that there was nothing they could do if the Viet Minh did not control these transportation lines. Anxious to

96. Mao Zedong's address to the eighth session of the Central People's Government Council, 28 June 1950, *Renmin Ribao*, 29 June 1950, p. 1.
97. Huang, *Hu Zhiming Yu Zhongguo*, p. 126.
98. Telegram, Mao Zedong to Ho Chi Minh, *Renmin Ribao*, 20 May 1950, p. 1. Also see *Xinhua Yuebao*, 16 June 1950, p. 290.
99. *Hoang's Revolutionary Reminiscences*, p. 263.

obtain Chinese material assistance, the Vietnamese leaders decided to take control of the border transportation at any cost.[100]

Also, the Chinese leaders were only willing to dispatch military advisers—not armed forces—to Vietnam. In the early spring of 1950, General Chen Geng, commander of the Third Group Army stationed in Guangxi, had a secret meeting with Ho Chi Minh in Nanning, the provincial capital. Persuaded by Ho, Chen moved his troops closer to the Sino-Vietnamese border. General Chen also directed his soldiers to take with them all the munitions captured from the KMT and "to take good care of these weapons." He explained to his subordinates that "we need these weapons to carry out our internationalist duty.[101] But none of Chen's troops entered Vietnam. In April 1950, the Viet Minh formally requested that Beijing dispatch high-ranking military advisers to help build Viet Minh's military command and middle-ranking officers to direct the Vietnamese troops at regimental and battalion levels. The Chinese leaders responded that they were willing to send a military advisory group to Vietnam, but that they would not allow Chinese officers to command the Vietnamese forces directly. In July, seventy-nine high-ranking army officers, most from the Fourth Field Army, gathered in Beijing and went to Vietnam after one month of training. General Wei Guoqing, head of the advisory group, worked in Viet Minh's military headquarters; his aides Mei Jiasheng, Deng Yifan, and Ma Yifu advised Viet Minh's General Staff, Political Affairs Department, and Logistics Department respectively. A number of Chinese officers served as military advisers in the 304th, 308th, and 314th divisions, the Viet Minh's best.[102] There is no indication that Chinese regulars were in Vietnam during this period.

Meanwhile, Beijing authorities sent Chen Geng to Vietnam as China's representative "to supervise material assistance and help the Vietnamese comrades direct the [Sino-Vietnamese] border campaign." Chen left for Vietnam in early July.[103] On the way to Viet Minh's headquarters, Chen was enthusiastic about his mission. Noticing North Korea's military successes, he wrote in his diary on 8 July: "The U.S. troops are pitiful. Now I am getting more confident about the military struggle in Vietnam. We shall coordinate the [North] Korean action by

100. Huang, *Hu Zhiming Yu Xhongguo*, p. 126.
101. Xu Peilan and Zheng Pengfei, *Chen Geng Jiangjun Zhuan* (Beijing, 1988), pp. 573–74.
102. Li Ke, "The Chinese Military Advisory Group in the Struggle to Resist France and Aid Vietnam," *Junshi Lishi*, March 1989, p. 27. Also see *DDZGJSGZ* 1:518–20.
103. *DDZGJSGZ* 1:523. Also see Chen Geng, *Chen Geng Riji (Xu)* (Beijing, 1982), p. 6. When the Korean War broke out, Chen Geng was first assigned to command the Northeast Border Army. In July, he was reassigned to assist the Viet Minh and arrived in Vietnam early that month.

launching a large-scale offensive [in Vietnam] to strike a two-pincer blow. The Asian peoples are bound to final victory in Asia." To this end, he proposed to concentrate all the Viet Minh forces on the French garrison in Cao Bang. In his view, a complete success of this attack "will be so decisive that it would turn the military situation in North Vietnam [to our favor]." Mao, however, disapproved Chen's proposal. In his telegram to Chen on 26 July, Mao pointed out, "Now it is not an appropriate time for the Viet Minh to take any large-scale offensives, and I suggest that you cancel the operation plan for attacking Cao Bang." With no explanation of why he though the attack was inappropriate, Mao urged Chen to be cautious, because "his presence [in Vietnam] should be . . . secret."[104]

The intensification of the Korean War made Beijing authorities even more cautious about supporting the Viet Minh. In September 1950, Mao twice warned General Deng Zihui, military commander of Guangxi Military Region, that "our troops should not go across the Sino-Vietnamese border by any means or on any occasions, and it would be better to keep a distance from the border even if in pursuit of KMT remnants." He also wanted Deng to see to it that his order was strictly observed "otherwise we would be in big trouble."[105] Clearly, by "big trouble," Mao this time meant that the United States might increase its military involvement in Indochina if the Chinese troops entered Vietnam. The Chinese leaders did not want to provoke the United States into taking action in that region, because they were already considering entering the Korean War. To fight a two-front war, in their view, was not in China's best interest.

As the Chinese troops became actively engaged in Korea in late 1950, Mao remained worried about the Sino-Vietnamese border security. In a telegram to the Guangxi Military Command on 29 January, 1951, he directed construction of an in-depth defense in Southern China. An enemy attack on China from Vietnam, he explained, could be allowed to penetrate deep into the interior, even to Nanning, before Chinese forces counterattack.[106] Meanwhile, the Chinese leaders wanted to keep the Viet Minh in a defensive position against the French. When General Wei Guoqing reported that the Viet Minh were getting impatient, Mao immediately responded: "You must persuade

104. Chen Geng, *Chen Geng Riji*, pp. 7, 9, and 13; Mao's instructions to Chen Geng, 26 July 1950, in *DDZGJSGZ* 1:523.
105. Telegram, Mao Zedong to Deng Zihui, "The Central Military Commission Agrees on the Military Employment of Guangdong and Guangxi," 16 September 1950, in *JGYLMWG* 1:519–20; telegram, Mao to Deng Zihui, "Our Troops Must Not Cross Our Border," 16 September 1950, ibid., p. 521.
106. Mao Zedong to the Guangxi Military Command, 29 January 1951, in *JGYLMWG* 2:85–86.

the Vietnamese comrades to be patient and let them know that they should not take any large-scale actions unless the military situation in Vietnam becomes favorable to us."[107]

When the Korean conflict ended in the summer of 1953, the Viet Minh seemed to be winning against the French. With China's assistance, the Viet Minh had inflicted severe defeats on the French in the border area. The Vietnamese Communists controlled the Cao Bang–Dong Khe–That Ke triangle and had consolidated several transportation lines between the rear bases in China and the front. Now they were confident that they could fight their own war. Ho Chi Minh proclaimed in late 1953, that "the united strength of the peoples of Viet Nam, Pathet Laos, and Khmer will suffice to wipe out the French colonialists and U.S. interventionists."[108] Ho's implication was clear: Beijing could no longer restrain the Viet Minh from taking the offensive.

Indeed, Beijing would have supported the Viet Minh effort to drive the French out at this point, if this could be done without bringing in the United States. But, with the costly experience of Korea and the urgency of economic construction at home—the First Five-Year Plan had just been inaugurated—Chinese leaders felt that they should not increase their assistance to the Viet Minh, as long as the Vietnamese were able to continue fighting on their own. But what should China do if the United States directly intervened to save or replace the French in Indochina?

IV

After the Korean armistice was signed, U.S. assistance to the French in Indochina grew rapidly. Beijing perceived an immediate threat that the United States might help the French force the Viet Minh into total retreat. A *Shijie Zhishi* commentary noted in September 1953 that Eisenhower had openly expressed his intention to intervene on behalf of the French, and that Congress had allocated $400 million in military aid to France for use in Indochina. The *Shijie Zhishi* also cited a *Wall Street Journal* report that Dulles had been secretly meeting with French officers on how to cooperate in implementing the Navarre Plan, a proposed "all-out offensive seeking to wipe out the Viet Minh within eighteen months."[109] In March 1954 another *Shijie Zhishi* article

---

107. Mao Zedong to Wei Guoqing, 29 January 1951, in *JGYLMWG* 2:90.
108. Cited in Kalicki, *The Pattern of Sino-American Crises*, p. 88.
109. "The United States Conspired to Enlarge the War in Indochina," pp. 4–6.

pointed out that Washington had been directly involved in the Indochinese war: Eisenhower had sent five hundred air force technicians to Indochina; the commander of the U.S. Pacific Air Force had announced in Tokyo on 15 February that B-26 bombers were being sent to Indochina; and Harold E. Stassen, director of the Mutual Security Program, had stated on his return from Indochina that the United States would provide another $100 million in military aid to the French forces.[110] The Chinese leaders concluded that the United States intended to assist the French to regain Indochina.

They also saw increased U.S. involvement as part of a long-term plan to bring Southeast Asia into the U.S. military sphere of influence. The Chinese press repeatedly stressed that the United States, after taking over Indochina from the French, would start to train the "local rebels" in order eventually to realize the objective of "turning Asians against Asians." The press noted that Washington had already sent a thousand military advisers to Thailand, increased military aid to the KMT remnants in Burma, and, with Britain and France, had held military maneuvers along the coasts of Indochina and in the South China Sea. Furthermore, Dulles was "openly" devoted to forming a "NATO in Asia" in order to "legalize the U.S. interference and intervention." The Chinese concluded that military activity in Indochina foreshadowed an invasion of China.[111]

Still, Beijing did not believe that the United States would commit ground forces to Indochina. The Chinese leaders calculated that the United Stated faced tremendous strategic obstacles to intervening again in Asia. An analysis in *Shijie Zhishi* asserted that Washington had learned "bloody lessons" in Korea, and that another "Korea" would bankrupt the American government. Besides, the United States had to maintain military strength in Korea and Taiwan and could not spare many troops for Indochina. The distance between the United States and Indochina was much longer, and supplies would be even more difficult to ship than to Korea.[112] The Chinese also believed that the French and the British, as old imperialists, had conflicts of interests with the United States. France was already in a dilemma: as a fading power, it could not control Indochina, but it was hardly ready to turn

110. Huang De, "Who is Blocking a Peaceful Solution to the Indochinese Problem?" *Shijie Zhishi*, March 1954, pp. 14–15.

111. "The United States Conspired to Enlarge the War in Indochina," p. 5; "Oppose U.S. Direct Intervention in Indochina," *Shijie Zhishi*, February 1954, pp. 5–7; Lin Meiqing, "The United States Has Always Intended to Form a Pacific Invading Bloc," ibid., August 1954, pp. 10–12.

112. Zheng Wan, "On the United States's New Diplomatic Models," *Shijie Zhishi*, November 1953, pp. 11–13.

its former colony over to the Americans.[113] The British were not at ease with the expansion of U.S. influence in Asia either, and probably would not join a U.S. military action. Without its principal allies, the Chinese concluded, the United States could not go too far in Indochina in the near future.[114]

Clearly, the PRC leadership did not feel any urgent need to intervene in Indochina. They held that since the United States could not afford to fight another Korean-style war, open U.S. intervention would be *deterred* if China could make the United States understand that overt military action in Indochina would bring the Chinese in on the side of the Viet Minh. Radio Peking did broadcast a warning in January 1954 that China remained resolute in its support of the Vietnamese people in their war "to annihilate the French colonialists, the American interventionists, and the Vietnamese traitors."[115] That, however, was the hardest warning the Beijing government made, and it did not indicate how China might react to U.S. armed intervention. There is no evidence that China transferred combat troops from Korea to the Sino-Vietnamese border, nor are there any indications that the Central Military Commission had ever prepared contingency plans for supporting the Viet Minh.

Beijing authorities understood that uninterrupted support of the Viet Minh would strengthen the Chinese military counterthreat in that region. In late 1953, Liu Shaoqi explicitly told the heads of Chinese advisory groups in Vietnam that (1) China "will continue to provide military assistance to the Vietnamese people but without directly involving our own forces even though we all should watch closely the United States"; (2) the key to final victory "mainly lies in the Vietnamese people themselves, but we will firmly support them as much as we can through to the end"; and (3) "it is important that we should assist the Vietnamese comrades in strengthening their political rule and economic construction." Liu stressed that "only when the Vietnamese people become stronger and our attitude to support them much firmer would the imperialists dare not to take a risk."[116]

Following these guidelines, Chinese aid to the Viet Minh continued throughout 1954. By the end of that year, China had provided the Viet

113. Qiu Nan, "Where Is France Heading?" *Shijie Zhishi*, May 1954, pp. 17–19.

114. Editorial, "The Anglo-American Strategic Contradictions," *Shijie Jishi*, April 1954, pp. 20–22.

115. Slogan for the 1954 Vietnamese-Soviet-Chinese Friendship Month, *Radio Peking*, 9 January 1954, cited in Kalicki, *The Pattern of Sino-American Crises*, p. 91.

116. Liu Shaoqi to Wei Guoqing, "Three-Point Instruction on Our Present Policy toward Vietnam," September, 1953, in *Liu Shaoqi Daxing Chaizhao Ji*, ed. Museum of Chinese People's Military Revolutions (Beijing, 1986), p. 78.

Minh more than 116,000 light infantry weapons, 420 heavy artillery guns, and large quantities of munitions. These weapons had equipped five of Viet Minh's infantry divisions, one heavy artillery division plus one regiment, one regiment of engineers, one anti-aircraft regiment, and one security regiment to guard rear-echelon installations such as supply depots. The Chinese military advisers had also trained more than 15,000 middle- and junior-grade Vietnamese officers in border-area training centers.[117]

It is important to note that Beijing encouraged the Viet Minh to take the offensive in North Vietnam. In late August 1953, Mao discussed with Peng Dehuai, then vice-chairman of the Central Military Commission, how the Viet Minh could secure and enlarge its base contiguous to South China. Both agreed that the Vietnamese Communists should first expand their activities where the French defense was weak and then advance from the Cao Bang area to attack Hanoi at an opportune moment. A complete victory in this campaign, Mao and Peng stressed in their telegram to Wei Guoqing on 29 August, "will surely doom the imperialist plan to retain control in Vietnam, Cambodia, and Laos." The Viet Minh rejected Beijing's suggestion on the ground that such an action might provoke U.S. intervention. The Chinese then tried to convince the Vietnamese that a quick and decisive move to Cambodia would put the Viet Minh in a better position to counter the French or the U.S. The head of the Chinese Military Advisory Group, Wei Guoqing, succeeded in getting Ho Chi Minh's endorsement. In late October, the Viet Minh headquarters dispatched five infantry regiments to lead the northward movement. Their first action was to attack Lai Chau in mid-November.[118]

To block the Viet Minh advance and defend Lai Chau, the French dropped six airborne battalions at Dien Bien Phu late that same month. To Wei Guoqing, who was with the Viet Minh force, this was a good opportunity to annihilate a large number of French soldiers. He proposed taking Dien Bien Phu. Mao and Peng concurred. Believing that "such an attack has not only military but also political significance, and [that] its success will have a great impact upon the international situation," they urged Wei to "get the [Viet Minh] headquarters to take a decisive action." Ho Chi Minh held a meeting of his politburo on 6 December to discuss the Chinese proposal, and they agreed to act as the Chinese suggested. After three months of

117. *DDZGJSGZ* 1:520–21. Also see Li Ke, "The Chinese Military Advisory Group," p. 29.
118. Li Ke, "The Chinese Military Advisory Group," p. 28.

preparation, the Vietnamese attacked Dien Bien Phu on 13 March, 1954. By the end of that month, the French were desperate.[119]

The United States increased its military assistance to the French in Indochina. Two U.S. aircraft carriers approached Vietnamese waters. Washington announced its decision to deploy U.S. Air Force units including B-28s in Indochina, and, more striking, JCS Chairman Radford proposed using atomic weapons to prevent the fall of Dien Bien Phu. The Viet Minh leaders began to worry, but Beijing dismissed the U.S. reaction as a bluff. Wei Guoqing explained to the Vietnamese that retreating under U.S. military pressure would be a grave political and military setback for the Viet Minh.[120] Mao Zedong also believed that the Viet Minh should continue assaulting Dien Bien Phu despite U.S. military threats. On 3 April, he wrote to Wei that "[the Viet Minh] should seize Dien Bien Phu without any hesitation. If [Viet Minh] reinforcements can quickly move to the front, an all-out offensive should begin ahead of schedule."[121] In order to boost the confidence of the Vietnamese leaders, Mao promised complete logistical support.[122]

Meanwhile, Beijing decided to enhance the Viet Minh's combat effectiveness in case the United States did intervene. In early April 1954, Mao instructed Defense Minister Peng Dehuai to "help the Viet Minh build four more heavy artillery and two more engineering regiments" to be combat ready in six months. To meet this deadline, Mao authorized the transfer of the field pieces from the PLA artillery in Guangxi. He also directed the selection and assignment of the best artillery personnel from the CPV as advisers and instructors to the Viet Minh. Although he thought it better to train these troops in Vietnam, Mao doubted that there was enough time to construct new training centers in Vietnam and authorized the use of the existing centers in Guangxi. He stressed: "Even if the peace talks in Geneva end in a cease-fire, [we] shall not change this plan for assisting [the Viet Minh] in building a new artillery force."[123] Two weeks later, Mao wrote to the General Staff Department directing that "since it is likely that an armistice concerning Vietnam may be achieved soon, now it is not appropriate to continue training new [Viet Minh] artillery troops on our territory, and you should arrange to move the troops and equipments into Vietnam as soon as possible."[124] Despite his anxiety to strengthen the Viet

119. *DDZGJSGZ* 1:529–30.
120. Ibid., p. 533.
121. Mao to Peng Dehuai, 3 April 1954, in *JGYLMWG* 4:474.
122. *DDZGJSGZ* 1:533–34.
123. Mao to Peng Dehuai, 3 April 1954, pp. 474–75.
124. Mao to Huang Kecheng and Su Yu, deputy chiefs of staff, 17 April 1954, in *JGYLMWG* 4:480.

Minh's military capability, Mao was cautious about increasing Chinese military involvement in Vietnam. He was in a difficult position. He wanted China's commitment to the Vietnamese Communists to deter U.S. armed intervention, not provoke it.

It is interesting that Beijing authorities seemed to have stressed the role of diplomacy—and not open belligerence—in preventing the United States from openly undertaking military action. In particular, they sought to split the Western bloc. Zhou Enlai was the main advocate of this approach. "The capitalist world is not a monolith," Zhou had earlier stated at a meeting of all the Chinese ambassadors to be sent out to foreign countries, "we must treat each individual country differently. Particularly at the time when the imperialists are preparing for war, it is possible that many nations would stand neutral, and that some would even side with us against imperialist war efforts. . . . After all, war or no war depends not only on the increase of our peaceful camp's strength but also on the disunity within the enemy's camp."[125] In September 1953, Zhou pointed out again that the success of the Korean War "provides a good opportunity for further promoting the internal conflicts within the capitalist camp."[126]

It is obvious that the Chinese leaders would seize every chance to promote disagreement between the United States and its allies over Indochina. In mid-February 1954, Soviet foreign minister Molotov informed Beijing that the foreign ministers of the USSR, the United States, Britain, and France had agreed to put Indochina on the agenda of the forthcoming Geneva Conference for a Korean settlement. It is interesting that, in his telegram to Zhou, Molotov clearly states that the Chinese should discuss with the Vietnamese particularly "how to use the conference to obtain a peaceful solution in Indochina."[127]

The Chinese leaders certainly wanted to make full use of the Geneva Conference to inhibit any escalation of hostilities in Indochina. In early March, the CCP Politburo held a special meeting to discuss China's policy lines regarding the conference. The outcome was a CCP document titled "Our Estimation on the Geneva Conference and Preliminary Instructions on Our Preparation." This document explicitly pointed out that "the United States, France and Britain disagree with each other particularly on the Indochina issue, and they have great

125. Zhou Enlai, "Our Principles and Diplomacy," 30 April 1952, in *SWZ*, pp. 88–89. It is interesting that Zhou's thinking was quite similar to that of the American "wedge strategy," which sought to drive a wedge between Beijing and Moscow. For both the Truman and the Eisenhower administrations' thinking on the "wedge strategy," see Gaddis, *The Long Peace*, pp. 147–95, and Mayers, *Cracking the Monolith*.

126. Zhou Enlai, "General Policy Lines in a Transitional Period," 8 September 1953, in *SWZ*, p. 107.

127. Huang, *Hu Zhiming Yu Zhongguo*, p. 139.

difficulty in reconciling their views"; the internal conflicts of the Western bloc could be further "exploited to our advantage." The instructions then directed that "our delegation at Geneva should take all the possible initiatives and seize all the chances to contact the British, the French, and other neutrals" to "make our positions for a settlement and preference for peace known and understood by them." The Politburo pointed out that the Chinese delegation should try all means to generate positive outcomes. To this end, "we should concentrate on the issues that contain no big differences of opinion and try to accomplish at least tentative agreement on them. We shall not allow the conference to drag to the end without any result."[128]

The Chinese leaders, however, understood that the attitude of the Viet Minh would be the key to any Indochina settlement. So the leaders decided to invite Ho Chi Minh to Beijing to discuss "how the two countries can cooperate at Geneva."[129] Ho traveled to Beijing in late March. Probably because the two disagreed, Ho and Zhou Enlai went to Moscow for further discussions. Although the details of these meetings are still unknown, it seems that they did decide to seek a ceasefire in Indochina. On 19 April, the People's Republic formally named Zhou Enlai as the head of the Chinese delegation, and the next day, Zhou left via Moscow for Geneva with a large entourage.[130]

No one in Beijing knew what would be accomplished at the negotiating table, but the Chinese leaders clearly understood that military victory would strengthen their negotiating position. In March, China warned the Viet Minh that they should not relax their efforts in combat, and that "we should make it clear that peace would come only after hard struggles."[131] Ho Chi Minh agreed and pointed out in a Viet Minh headquarters meeting on 19 April: "this [Dien Bien Phu] campaign will surely prove to be historically important in our struggle for a final peace in Indochina."[132] The Viet Minh's offensive ended on 7 May, with 16,000 French casualties. The French were forced into a total defensive position in Vietnam. This success greatly encouraged the Chinese delegates at Geneva. They believed that France would no longer hesitate to accept a peaceful solution to the Indochinese problem and that Britain would certainly grant its support. Without the

128. *DDZGWJ*, pp. 64–65.
129. Huang, *Hu Zhiming Yu Zhongguo*, p. 139.
130. *DDZGWJ*, p. 65.
131. Huang, *Hu Zhiming Yu Zhongguo*, p. 139.
132. Ho's instructions, 19 April 1954, cited in Huang, *Hu Zhiming Yu Zhongguo*, pp. 135–36.

British and the French cooperation, the United States would have to accept peace terms in Indochina.[133]

Chinese anticipations were realized at Geneva by mid-June. The new Mendes-France government of France proclaimed that it would agree to peace in Indochina on the conditions of a temporary partition of Vietnam, and the self-determination and neutralization of Laos and Cambodia under the supervision of an international control commission. British foreign minister Eden had actually initiated these proposals. The Chinese undoubtedly like the proposed settlement, but they seemed to think that the Vietnamese might not. On 3 July Zhou Enlai flew back to China and met Ho Chi Minh at Liuzhou, Guangxi province. He explained to Ho that the Viet Minh could now continue to fight or accept peace, and fight later. It would be wise, Zhou stressed, to halt and consolidate now. "We should do our best to support the Mendes Government," he said to Ho, "so that we can prevent the warlike elements in France from overthrowing the moderates. This would be certainly beneficial to both of us." Ho seems to have had no objection to the proposed settlement, except he expected the proposed partition to be placed at the seventeenth parallel.[134]

On the way back to Geneva, Zhou stopped at Moscow. The Kremlin leaders pointed out that "the United States is trying to destroy any Geneva settlement. . . . If we rejected Mendes's proposal, the United States will seize the chance to replace Mendes with a more belligerent government. That would make the settlement of the Indochinese conflict more difficult."[135] Probably afraid of upsetting both Beijing and Moscow, Ho Chi Minh gave up his request for a partition at the Seventeenth parallel. The Chinese, the Vietnamese, and the Soviet delegations proclaimed their acceptance of the Mendes proposal. That paved the way for the signing of the Geneva Accords on Indochina on 21 July, which effected an immediate cease-fire, partitioned Vietnam, and gave neutral status to Laos and Cambodia. The settlement of these issues satisfied the Chinese. A friendly government controlled most of Vietnam, and "no foreign forces or military bases" would be placed in Laos or Cambodia.[136]

No less significant was the fact that, in late June of 1954, Zhou Enlai visited Burma and India on the way back to China, obtaining from both countries the promise of "mutual respect of territorial sovereignty, no intervention against each other, no interference in each

133. Wang Bingnan, *Zhongmei Huitan Jiunian Huigu* (Beijing, 1985), p. 4.
134. Ibid., p. 5. Also see Huang, *Hu Zhiming Yu Zhongguo*, pp. 139–41.
135. *DDZGWJ*, pp. 66–67.
136. *Wang Bingnan Memoirs*, p. 6.

other's internal affairs, mutual equality and benefit, and peaceful co-existence." Zhou was pleased that these "neutral" countries, as he had expected, agreed to stand aside in the event of an imperialist war against China.[137] In the same month, Mao instructed the Chinese Military Advisory Group in Vietnam to prevent the Viet Minh from taking any large-scale offensives. In his telegram to Wei Guoqing, Mao explained: "It is appropriate to deploy more troops in the Delta area to deter renewed French offensives, but [the Viet Minh] should not take any offensive actions in July. When to resume large-scale assaults will depend on the outcome of the Geneva Conference."[138] With the cease-fire in Indochina, Beijing began to withdraw its advisers in 1955.[139]

Nevertheless, Chinese authorities only felt a temporary relief. "Now that the Korean War is ended and Indochina is restored to peace," Zhou Enlai told the Central People's Government Council on 11 August 1955, "the result at Geneva proves a victory for the peace-loving forces but a defeat for the warlike powers." Zhou warned that "the aggressive U.S. bloc will not so easily accept these defeats. . . . [They have] always been hostile to the People's Republic of China. They have threatened and will continue to threaten China with armed intervention and war from the three fronts of Taiwan, Korea, and Indochina.[140] Shortly after, the Chinese leaders found tensions increasing in the Taiwan Strait.

V

In the first Indochinese crisis it seemed as though the Viet Minh and the French were actually proxies for China and the United States, each of whom still saw the other as a threat to its own security. Each therefore sought to prevent the potential threat from turning into an actual one.

The war in Korea undoubtedly caused each to see the other as invariably hostile. Neither Washington nor Beijing could "shake off" the sense of insecurity and open mutual hostility that developed from Korea. Worried that the Chinese might shift their focus from Korea to Indochina, the Eisenhower administration repeatedly warned Beijing

---

137. *DDZGWJ*, pp. 80–81.
138. Mao to Wei Guoqing and Zhou Enlai, 26 June 1954, in *JGYLMWG* 4:509.
139. *DDZGJSGZ* 1:536.
140. Zhou Enlai's report on diplomacy at the thirty-third session of the Central People's Government Council, 11 August 1954, in *Yindu Zhina Wenti Wenjian Huibian, 1955–57*, ed. Editorial Division of *Shijie Zhishi* (Beijing, 1959), pp. 107–13.

not to intervene. The Chinese, who had thought that the United States would not easily swallow its setbacks at Korea, evidently interpreted Washington's warnings as evidence of actual aggressive intent directed toward Indochina. The Chinese leadership believed that the long-anticipated U.S. invasion might actually occur this time. Having long believed in showing no weakness in the face of threats, Beijing explicitly projected itself as a firm supporter of the Viet Minh, ready to confront the United States at any cost. This image further reinforced the U.S. fear of Chinese armed intervention in Indochina. Neither side was able to analyze the crisis in Indochina without assuming the other's hostile intentions; and as a result, each side exaggerated those intentions.

Both Washington and Beijing considered Indochina strategically important, but neither understood how the other valued the region. U.S. officials considered prestige important as far as national interests were concerned, but tended to take U.S. prestige for granted and never questioned the "domino" theory, which predicted that all Southeast Asia would fall to communism if the Viet Minh gained control of Indochina. The opposite happened. Vietnamese Communists finally controlled the whole of Indochina, the rest of Southeast Asia stood firm against communism. Subsequently, Vietnam lost control of Cambodia; and Beijing and Hanoi have split. Obsessed with Communist China and the Soviet Union, Washington overlooked Ho Chi Minh. Moscow did little to "direct" the Viet Minh, and the Chinese never intended to spread communism all over Southeast Asia by supporting the Viet Minh. Beijing at most sought security from U.S. aggression behind a friendly buffer state. Clearly, Ho Chi Minh was loyal to Vietnam, not to Beijing or Moscow. Washington exaggerated Indochina's importance to U.S. interests as well as to the Communists—and it never clarified *which* communists.

The Chinese could not see any sense in the "domino theory." They could hardly credit the idea that the United States increased its commitment to Indochina and Southeast Asia just to defend its prestige. Not adequately understanding U.S. strategic thinking, Beijing believed that Washington, driven by its imperialist nature and by hostility toward the new China, sought a beachhead in Indochina from which to dominate Southeast Asia and to invade China whenever the opportunity presented itself. Acting on this perception, Beijing supported the Viet Minh to deter the United States. The Chinese military assistance encouraged the Vietnamese Communists to pursue large-scale offensives against the French, which triggered the first Indochinese crisis.

Alexander George and Richard Smoke maintain that the situation in Indochina was nondeterrable, and thus that Washington should not have applied deterrence in the first place.[141] Perhaps, but the relationship of mutual deterrence between Washington and Beijing did exist: the former aimed to deter the latter from spreading communism to Southeast Asia, whereas the latter tried to inhibit the former from intervening to carry out an imperialist conspiracy to invade the new China. It is interesting to note that the lesson of Korea worked: the fear of another Korea, which neither country could afford, deterred each from overt armed intervention. Aware that neither the American public nor America's traditional allies would support another Korea and that the resources needed for a global commitment were limited, the Eisenhower administration resisted the temptation to intervene in Indochina. Similar considerations restrained the Beijing leaders: the urgency of domestic construction, the reluctance of the Soviet Union to support the Viet Minh, and probably the fear of offending the world opinion made any thought of military intervention almost impossible.

When the Geneva Accords were signed, the crisis temporarily relaxed. Nevertheless, the legacy of mutual misunderstanding as well as the pattern of mutual deterrence determined that neither Washington nor Beijing had adequately defined their commitments to Southeast Asia. The potential for danger and an uncertain future were embodied in the fact that Beijing's material assistance to the Viet Minh, which Washington hoped to discourage, continued throughout the early 1970s, and a Washington-led regional security organization (SEATO), which Beijing tried to prevent, materialized at the end of the crisis. The settlement in Indochina paved the way for another but much bigger conflict later. But now tension was mounting in the Taiwan Strait.

141. George and Smoke, *Deterrence in American Foreign Policy,* pp. 259–61.

[7]

The First Taiwan Strait Crisis,
1954–1955

Shortly after the cessation of hostilities in Korea and Indochina, Beijing initiated a major crisis in the Taiwan Strait. On 3 September 1954,
the PLA artillery force bombarded Jinmen (Quemoy), an offshore island under Chinese Nationalist control. Alarmed at an impending
danger of Chinese Communist invasion of Jinmen and other KMT-held
offshore islands, the Eisenhower administration immediately put the
U.S. Pacific Fleet on alert. Once again, the People's Republic and the
United States were brought into direct confrontation. Why did Beijing
authorities decide to take the offensive? How did Washington officials
view the CCP's open challenge to the "status quo"?

I

Western commentators often describe the 1954–55 Taiwan Strait incident as a "crisis."[1] The terms "Taiwan Strait Crisis" and "Jinmen-
Mazu [Matsu] Crisis" have been perpetuated in textbooks and in
scholarly studies of post-World War II international relations. The Chinese, however, never considered the incident a "crisis" in that sense.
Wei ji, the Chinese equivalent of "crisis," means both "dangerous situation" and "opportunity." It can also imply a situation that emerges
unexpectedly and may get out of control. In this sense, the Taiwan
Strait incident of 1954–55 was no crisis. The Chinese leaders planned

1. One typical example of this view is Kalicki, *The Pattern of Sino-American Crises,*
pp. 120–59.

and initiated the incident, and it was never out of their control. They decided to take military action in the Strait primarily because they saw a potential danger and an opportunity to prevent that danger developing further.

Since taking power, the CCP leadership had been concerned about the threat of U.S. military action from the Taiwan Strait. They perceived that threat within the framework of the "three-front" concept, which assumed that the Untied States would be most likely to invade China from the Korean peninsula, the Taiwan Strait, or French Indochina. The Korean War ended in July 1953. A cease-fire was agreed to in Indochina in July 1954. It seemed that a relaxation of the tension between Beijing and Washington lay ahead. The Chinese did not view the situation in the Far East that way. As Zhou Enlai explained later, "Following the 1953 [Korean] cease-fire, the years of 1954 and 1955 saw tension mount along the Taiwan Strait. The entire world situation was put on hold."[2] Wang Bingnan, China's principal negotiator in the Sino-American talks in the 1950s, also recalled that although the cease-fire agreements eased tensions in Korea and Indochina, the CCP Central Committee was still quite sensitive about the situation in the Taiwan Strait. The Chinese leaders believed that the United States would neither easily swallow its military "defeat" in Korea, nor accept a diplomatic setback in Indochina. The next act of American imperialism, the Central Committee concluded, might be to expand the military conflict onto the mainland from the Taiwan Strait, "either to take revenge or start a new war."[3]

U.S. Taiwan policy, as the CCP leaders saw it, was part of a long-term scheme to encircle China. Lin Meiqing, an analyst in the Ministry of Foreign Affairs, wrote in May 1954 that "the essence of the U.S. Far Eastern policies is to establish a military bloc for aggression in the Pacific area, and to build American military bases in Asia. The main objective of these policies is to encircle the People's Republic of China, maintaining a continuous threat of military attack to [China's] mainland." Lin listed a number of indications of this policy, among these Vice-President Richard Nixon's call for "a perimeter military alliance in Asia"—including Turkey, Iran, Pakistan, Taiwan, Indochina, and Japan—during his October 1953 trip to the Far East; Assistant Secretary of State Walter Robertson's testimony to Congress in early 1954 that, in his words, "the US will maintain an unrestricted control in the Far East in order to have a continuous threat of attack on Red China"; and re-

2. Zhou Enlai, "Some Fundamental Issues Concerning Economic Construction, Report to the Second Session of the Eighth CCP Central Committee," 10 November 1956, in SWZ, p. 236.

3. *Wang Bingnan Memoirs*, pp. 22–29.

tired JCS chairman Omar N. Bradley's article, "Our Navy in the Far East," in the October 1953 issue of American Geography, "which outlined the U.S. strategy of a chain-of-islands defense in the Western Pacific region." Lin argued that Japan and the Philippines were the ends of this chain-of-islands defense line, to which Taiwan and the Taiwan Strait were of indispensable strategic value. He asserted that "the United States will turn these island into beachheads for its continuous expansion in the east." Moreover, Lin claimed that the United States sought to turn Thailand and Pakistan into strategic "strongholds to encircle Southwestern China and Soviet Asian territory."[4] Two very detailed maps of U.S. military bases and alliances in the Asian-Pacific area accompanied this analysis.[5]

Dulles's alliance-building activities in Asia during 1953–54 did nothing to allay China's fear of strategic encirclement. Even before the formation of the Southeast Asian Treaty Organization (SEATO) in early September 1954, Zhou Enlai explicitly stated in a major foreign affairs report to the Central People's Government Council (dated 11 August) that the purpose of SEATO was to encircle the People's Republic of China. Zhou anticipated that Dulles would next "form a northeast Asian counterpart" to SEATO, with Japan, Taiwan, and South Korea.[6] An article in the Renmin Ribao summarized the official Chinese position as follows: The American government "seeks to link up these two military blocs [in the Southeast and Northeast Asia] to form a hostile encirclement of China and to tie the Asian countries together with the Syngman Rhee clique and Chiang Kai-shek gangsters as tools for U.S. aggression against China."[7]

Why did the United States need these military alliances? Zhou Enlai explained to the First National People's Congress on September 23 1954 that Washington had four objectives: first, to split the Asian nation-states from each other and "ensure that Asians would fight Asians" in the name of containing "communist expansion"; second with those alliances, "to interfere with and intervene in the national [liberation] movements in Southeast Asia whenever it wants to"; third, to "grab as much of the strategic materials produced by these countries

4. Lin Meiqing, "The U.S. Policy to Encircle the New China and Threaten the Peace of Asia," Shijie Zhishi, 5 May 1954, pp. 11–12.

5. Wang Ji, "A Map of U.S. Military Bases in the Asia-Pacific Region," Shijie Zhishi, 5 May 1954, p. 13; Zhu Yulian, "A Map of Newly Planned U.S. Military Aggression in Southeast Asia," ibid., p. 14.

6. Zhou Enlai, "Report on Foreign Affairs to the Central People's Government Council," 11 April, 1954, in Taiwan Wenti Wenjian Huibian, ed. Editorial Division, Shijie Zhishi, pp. 110–11.

7. Wu Zhuan, Commentary, Renmin Ribao, 8 August, 1954, p. 3.

as possible"; and fourth, to "legalize" present and future U.S. military actions in the name of "defending these areas."[8]

Of all these, the PRC leadership was alert to a possible "U.S.-Taiwan military alliance." As early as late July 1954—nearly five months before the Dulles-Yeh secret talks that created the U.S.-Taiwan alliance—China suspected that preparations for such an agreement were under way. The Chinese noted General James Van Fleet's three visits to Taiwan between April and July, and especially his and Ambassador Karl Rankin's statements on a mutual security treaty between the United States and Taiwan. *Renmin Ribao* claimed (in a 23 July editorial) that Van Fleet's and Rankin's statements proved a conspiracy between Taipei and Washington and clearly indicated "America's hostility toward the Chinese people."[9] The *Shijie Zhishi* on 5 August insisted that Van Fleet's visits to Taiwan , were part of the Eisenhower administration's "aggressive plot" in the Far East. Such an alliance, *Shijie Zhishi* explained, would serve Washington's two main purposes: first, it would stand as "an important chain" for the future creation of an "anti-Communist military bloc in the Pacific," guaranteeing the realization of the American policy of "Asians fighting Asians"; and second, it would directly contribute to Washington and Taipei's "ultimate goal of conquering the mainland . . . in the name of containing the spread of communism in Asia." Together with the military alliances with Japan and South Korea, the United States would then form a "Northern Pillar" in the Asia-Pacific region against China.[10] According to Wang Bingnan's reminiscences, the CCP leaders at the July Central Committee meeting generally accepted these judgments. They believed that the U.S. Taiwan alliance would make the U.S. occupation of Taiwan seem legal and turn the island into a staging area for military strikes against the Chinese mainland.[11]

The Chinese leaders found evidence to support their views in Eisenhower's increasing military assistance to Chiang Kai-shek. In late August 1954, Lin Meiqing noted that "in four years (1950–54), Washington has already provided Chiang with one billion dollars of military aid, excluding $80 million which was initially designated for French Indochina but shifted to Chiang after the Geneva Accord." Citing from Eisenhower's report to Congress on the "Mutual Security Program" from July through December of 1953, Lin emphatically

---

8. Zhou Enlai, "Report on the Work of the Government to the First Session of the First National People's Congress," *Xinhua Yuebao*, 23 September 1954, p. 88.

9. "We Must Liberate Taiwan," 23 July 1954, *Renmin Ribao*, pp. 3–4.

10. Yang Xueshuen, "Van Fleet's Conspiratorial Provocations in Asia," *Shijie Zhishi*, 5 August 1954, p. 13.

11. *Wang Bingnan Memoirs*, p. 22.

pointed out that the priority of U.S. military aid to Taiwan for 1954 was upgrading the KMT Air Force with jet fighters. The first shipment of three *Lightning* jet fighters had already arrived on Taiwan, and some F-80 bombers were on the way. These aircraft, the study asserted, would greatly increase the offensive capability of the KMT Air Force, which was already equipped with one hundred *Lightnings*. In addition, the White House had congressional permission to deliver twenty-five warships to the KMT Navy, the first of which had arrived in Taiwan on 4 August 1954. Moreover, the size of the U.S. Military Assistance Advisory Group (MAAG) in Taiwan was greatly expanded in 1953–54. The study noted that the MAAG consisted of "only 54 persons before 1954, now is increased to 750, and will be enlarged to 1,500 soon, with the mission to train KMT soldiers to be more combat effective." Consequently, "Chiang will be able to intensively rebuild his military offensive capability and greatly increase his military disturbance on our southeast coastal areas under the protection of the [US] Seventh Fleet." Lin's study concluded that "increased U.S. military activities in the Taiwan area undoubtedly aim at turning Taiwan into its military base for attacking China."[12]

The PRC leadership did not believe that the United States or the KMT supported by U.S. military forces would take immediate military action, but it did see a threat in the U.S. commitment to defending the Taiwan Strait. It thus insisted that something had to be done and the sooner, the better. This position was stated as early as 23 July 1954, when Mao Zedong called Zhou Enlai, then en route back from the Geneva Conference, to express his great concern:

In order to *break up* the collaboration between the United States and Chiang Kai-shek, and keep them from joining together militarily and politically, we must announce to our country and to the world the slogan of liberating Taiwan. It was improper of us not to raise this slogan in a timely manner after the cease-fire in Korea. If we were to continue dragging our heels now, we would be making a serious political mistake.[13]

Soon after Zhou's return, the CCP Politburo met to discuss China's policy toward Taiwan. The Politburo endorsed Mao's concerns and resolved that the CCP must immediately and publicly proclaim its

12. Lin Meiqing, "The Sins of the U.S. Invasion in Taiwan," *Shijie Zhishi*, 5 September 1954, pp. 8–9.
13. Cited in He Di, "The Evolution of the PRC Policy toward the Offshore Islands, 1954–58" (Beijing: Institute of American Studies, Chinese Academy of Social Sciences, 1987 [unpublished]), pp. 7–8 [emphasis added].

intention to liberate Taiwan to deter the United States from forming a military and political alliance with Chiang.[14]

The *Renmin Ribao* editorial "We Must Liberate Taiwan" on 23 July 1954 marked the beginning of a massive propaganda campaign. Marshal Zhu De, commander-in-general of the PLA, then addressed the public on Army Day (1 August), stressing China's resolve to liberate Taiwan and claiming that the PLA was determined to fulfill this task.[15] In late August and early September, in his reports to the Central People's Government Council and the National People's Congress, Zhou Enlai repeatedly emphasized that the liberation of Taiwan had become official policy. The Chinese press publicized Zhou's reports with an explicit warning that any "attempt to 'occupy' or 'neutralize' or make Taiwan 'independent' will be unacceptable to the Chinese people and will definitely encounter the Chinese people's opposition."[16]

China's action might have provoked a vigorous KMT or U.S. reaction. But Mao Zedong believed that a short-term belligerency—if well controlled—would be the best deterrent to a long-term or potential threat. He considered U.S. imperialists too arrogant to see reason unless "driven into a tight corner."[17] Mao, following Sun Tze, decided that "the best strategy of war is to destroy the adversary's strategy before it is put into effect." In his judgment, proclaiming the liberation of Taiwan would demonstrate to Washington that any military alliance with Chiang could lead to war with China, which, Mao believed, the United States could not afford, and for which the United States was not yet ready.

Mao was optimistic that the PRC no longer feared the United States. His optimism came from what he considered China's military success in Korea. Addressing Korean War veterans in the fall of 1953, he claimed the following:

> Each of the various arms—the army, the air force, the navy, the infantry, the artillery corps, the anti-aircraft defense units, the signal corps, as well as the medical corps, the logistical corps, etc.—have all actually fought U.S. aggressor troops. This time we really felt out the U.S. armed forces. . . . We fought with them for thirty-three months, and we have become thoroughly acquainted with them. U.S. imperialism is not such an awesome thing, it is just what it is, and that's all.

14. *Wang Bingnan Memoirs,* p. 23.
15. "We Must Liberate Taiwan," *Renmin Ribao,* 23 July 1954, reprinted in *Xinhua Yuebao,* August 1954, pp. 1–2; Zhu De, "The Speech for the Army Day," 1 August, 1954, p. 8.
16. Zhou Enlai, "Report on Foreign Affairs to the Central People's Government Council," pp. 10–11; and "Report on the Work of Government to the First Session of the First People's Congress," 23 September 1954, p. 88.
17. Mao Zedong, in SWM 5:116.

Mao continued, "If the U.S. imperialists refuse to postpone their new aggressive war and say they want to fight, we will make use of the [experience] to deal with them."[18] Significantly, Mao based this confidence on the maxim by Sun Tze: "Know the enemy and know yourself, and you can fight a hundred battles with no danger of defeat [*Zhibi zhiji baizhan budai*]."[19]

The Chinese leadership also believed that the Soviet Union would support China's actions in the Taiwan Strait more actively than it had in Korea, yet in 1953 and 1954 the Kremlin was unstable because of Stalin's death and uncertainty over his successor. Mao was primarily concerned that the new leader—whoever he might be—would continue the Soviet commitment to China's security and economic construction.[20] The prospects of Sino-Soviet cooperation were more encouraging than ever in the spring of 1954. Moscow made several substantial offers, including the complete transfer of Soviet shares in four Sino-Soviet mining ventures in Xinjiang (Sinkiang) province, transfer of all the equipment of the Soviet naval bases at Lushun (Port Arthur), and a promise of Soviet assistance both in materials and personnel for up to fifteen more projects. By the early fall, the Chinese leaders generally felt that they could count on Soviet support in the Taiwan Strait.[21]

It is interesting that CCP leaders were anxious to seize the offshore islands held by the KMT. The PLA had prepared to attack these islands much earlier. In the summer of 1952, Chen Yi, commander of the East China Military Region, assigned his chief of staff, Zhang Aiping, to design plans for seizing the offshore islands. Zhang urged that the offshore islands be taken before the United States could occupy them. He argued that, although the six KMT divisions on the six main offshore islands assisted by twelve warships posed no great threat, the United States with its Seventh Fleet might take these islands and use them as stepping-stones in expanding the Korean conflict to China's coast.[22] The Central Military Commission seriously considered Zhang's proposal. Mao Zedong approved it late that year. But when the Korean truce was signed, the CMC suspended planning for the attack against

18. Mao Zedong, "Speech on the Victory in Resist US Aggression and Aid Korea Movement," 21 September 1953, in Kau and Leung, *The Writings of Mao Zedong*, p. 386.

19. Division of War Theories, Chinese Academy of Military Sciences, ed., *Sun Tze Bingfa Xinzhu* (Beijing, 1977), p. 3.

20. Mao's talk with Liu Xiao, Chinese ambassador to Moscow, in Liu Xiao, *Chushi Sulian Banian* (Beijing, 1986), pp. 3–4 [hereafter cited as *Liu Xiao Memoirs*].

21. Ibid., p. 126. Liu, however, wrongly recalled that Khrushchev visited China in October 1954. There was no such visit, unless it was a secret one.

22. Nie Fengzhi, ed., *Sanjun Huizhan Donghai* (Nanjing, 1986), pp. 26 and 38 [hereafter cited as *Nie Fengzhi Memoirs*].

The Taiwan Strait area

the offshore islands on the ground that any resumption of large-scale military action would turn world opinion against China.[23]

In January 1954, the East China Military Command (ECMC) suggested resuming preparations for attacking the offshore islands. The first target, they decided, should be the Dachen Islands, consisting of Yijiangshan (I-chiangsan), Upper and Lower Dachen, and a few small islands, where the KMT had one regular division, six teams of special forces, and ten naval vessels, which threatened the East Zhejiang coast. The ECMC planned an amphibious attack of infantry, navy, and air forces to wipe out the KMT troops there once and for all. Mao, Zhu De, and Peng Dehuai approved the plan and ordered that military preparations be intensified immediately. As a preliminary action, the PLA forces landed on the Dongji Island on 15 May and turned it into a forward staging area.[24]

The ECMC soon noted a vigorous U.S. response. On the morning of 1 June 1954, the ECMC telephoned Deputy Chief of Staff Su Yu to report that eight to twelve naval vessels of the U.S. Seventh Fleet had conducted an anti-amphibious maneuver exercise off the Dachen Islands. The U.S. Air Force had increased its overflights, and the KMT had reinforced its complement with another regiment of regulars. General Su immediately reported to Mao, Zhu De, and Liu Shaoqi, and pointed out that the U.S. "imperialists" were openly challenging the PLA. He recommended observing, but not attacking the U.S. force, and retaliating "resolutely" to any KMT attack. In his reply on the following day, Mao concurred completely: "We shall never be the first to open fire on U.S. troops, and [we] will only maintain a defensive position there so that we should avoid direct conflict [with the United States] to the best of our ability."[25]

At the end of June the situation was unchanged. The CMC then authorized the ECMC to bombard the Dachen Islands with naval and air forces in early July. This bombardment was, as the CMC order put it, to demonstrate that "the Chinese people will never yield to imperialist

---

23. Ibid., p. 38. General Ye Fei, then commander-in-chief of the Fujian Military Region, recalls that his forces had spent the entire Korean War period building coastal defenses. After the war was over, he considered attacking Jinmen, Mazu, and finally Taiwan. In 1953, Ye proposed a seaway connecting Xiamen with the Fujian mainland to facilitate troop movement. Chen Yi supported Ye's proposal and with Mao's final approval, the seaway project was started in late July 1953 and completed in October 1954 (*Ye Fei Memoirs*, pp. 616–34).

24. *DDZGJSGZ* 1:255–56.

25. The ECMC's telephone report, 1 June 1954, is enclosed in Su Yu to Mao, Liu Shaoqi, and Zhu De, 1 June 1954, in *JGYLMWG* 4:495 n.2; Mao to Su Yu, 2 June 1954, ibid., p. 495.

pressure."[26] The Chinese leaders had no intention of provoking the U.S. troops. In mid-July, the CMC drafted an instruction to restrain the operations of People's Navy and Air Force in the Southeast China Sea. Mao added: "At present, our [naval and air force] escort operations are intended to prevent KMT piracy. As long as no self-defense is necessary, any offensive actions against foreign warships and airplanes are forbidden." The CMC emphasized that violation of this order would be "punished severely."[27] The CMC further specified that only if the U.S. Navy or Air Force initiated an attack on PLA positions were the Chinese soldiers to "consider striking back if this involves no grave risks."[28]

Meanwhile, the PLA's preparations for an attack on the offshore islands intensified. In late July, the Central Military Commission established a Zhedong (East Zhejiang) Front Command, and named Zhang Aiping commander with full authority over the infantry, naval, and air forces in Zhejiang and Fujian Provinces.[29] At the first Zhedong Front Command meeting, Zhang proposed seizing Yijiangshan before attacking Dachen, not only to bring the PLA assault forces even closer to Dachen before an actual attack and to get within artillery range of the objective, but also—since the KMT considered Yijiangshan the "gate" of the Dachen defense zone—to inflict serious political and psychological damage on the "enemy." More important, he noted, was the prospect that, with the PLA so near, the KMT Forces might retreat to Taiwan without fighting. If that were to happen, the PLA was to seize all the offshore islands immediately. To seize Yijiangshan, Zhang designated one infantry regiment plus one battalion as the main attacking force, with one long-range artillery regiment, one anti-aircraft artillery regiment, two rocket-gun battalions, sixty-six air force squadrons, and the Sixth Fleet in support. He was confident that this joint amphibious operation would succeed.[30]

Mao cautioned his commanders against overoptimism. He still worried about possible U.S. military action. On 24 July he ordered Peng Dehuai to "summon the commanders of the East China Military Command and the Fujian, Zhejiang, and Shanghai military regions to Beijing so that [we can] carefully and thoroughly consider the plan [for the attack on Yijiangshan and Dachen]." He considered at least thirty, if not forty, days of preparation absolutely essential for such

26. *DDZGHJ*, p. 209.
27. Mao's reaction on the CMC's instructions concerning escort operations, 23 July 1954, in *JGYLMWG* 4:520.
28. *DDZGJSGZ* 1:256–57.
29. *Nie Fengzhi Memoirs*, pp. 4 and 38.
30. Ibid., pp. 40–41.

operations.[31] When he was informed by the Air Defense Command of increased overflights by U.S. aircraft of the Dachen Islands, Mao ordered Peng on 21 August not to allow an offensive if U.S. warships and aircraft were in the area.[32]

It seems, though, that Beijing authorities were determined to test the United States. In late August, the Central Military Commission authorized the Zhedong Front Commander Zhang Aiping to prepare an attack on Dachen but to start by assaulting Yijiangshan, and to shell Jinmen to cover the offensive.[33] The PLA artillery in Fujian began shelling Jinmen on 3 September. The Zhedong Front Command canceled the amphibious attack, but during the next two months, its ground, naval, and air forces trained intensively on coordinated landing operations.[34]

The artillery bombardment of Jinmen explicitly challenged the status quo in the Taiwan Strait. The CCP leaders intended to demonstrate China's strength and China's determination to challenge the U.S. commitment to the KMT, and hoped to eliminate the Nationalist troops on the Yijiangshan-Dachen islands, if this could be accomplished without large-scale military conflict with U.S. forces. They understood that accomplishing these objectives would depend on how Washington responded.

II

In his memoirs, Eisenhower acknowledged that the bombardment of Jinmen "did not come as a complete surprise." He also recalled that the following nine months threatened to split the United States from "nearly all its allies, and seemingly carry the country to the edge of war."[35] The general feeling of the administration was that Beijing's military action against the offshore islands, along with its propaganda about "liberating Taiwan," posed an immediate threat to U.S. security interests.

The Eisenhower administration's perception of this threat was shaped by its policy toward the Chinese Nationalists. When Eisenhower took office in January 1953, the Taiwan question was an important legacy from his predecessor. Truman's order sending the Seventh Fleet to patrol the Taiwan Strait in June 1950 had clearly excluded the

---

31. Mao to Peng Dehuai, 24 July 1954, in *JGYLMWG* 4:520.
32. Mao to Peng Dehuai, 21 August 1954, in *JGYLMWG* 4:533.
33. *Nie Fengzhi Memoirs*, p. 41.
34. *DDZGJSGZ* 1:258–61; *DDZGHJ*, pp. 212–15; *DDZGKJ*, pp. 320–23.
35. Eisenhower, *The White House Years: Mandate for Change*, pp. 459 and 462.

offshore islands. Truman had sought to limit the scope and objective of the military aid provided Chiang by stipulating that it should be confined to maintaining "internal security," and that KMT forces trained and equipped by the United States were not to be sent to the offshore islands for operations against the mainland.[36]

Shortly after taking office, Eisenhower "unleashed Chiang," largely to pressure the Chinese Communists to accept an armistice in Korea. As early as 31 March 1952, John Foster Dulles had pointed out that since Chiang's forces in Taiwan were symbolically important to "ardent anti-communists in Asia and in the US," the United States could exploit this force to "halt the actual warfare in Korea."[37] Clearly, Eisenhower was not dramatically changing Truman's Taiwan policy.

The Chinese Nationalists hailed the "unleashing" order as a wise step, long overdue. They believed that the United States was ready for more vigorous anti-communist offensives, and they even hoped for a third world war, which would increase the chance of their return to the mainland.[38] They wasted no time. Immediately after Eisenhower's "unleashing" order, Wellington Koo, Chiang's ambassador to Washington, went to see John M. Allison, assistant secretary of state for Far Eastern affairs, for a clarification of Eisenhower's intentions. He explicitly indicated a strong desire to secure a U.S. military commitment to the offshore islands as a basis for future offensive operations against the mainland.[39] Moreover, during a meeting with Senator Alexander Smith, Ambassador Rankin, and others in late November 1953, Chiang Kai-shek himself impatiently criticized the U.S. containment policy as too negative. For him, "the only solution for Asia and the whole world, is to go to the heart of the matter and drive the Communists out of China." Chiang claimed that "supporting the Nationalist government's attempt to return to the mainland is the only way [for the United States] out of this imbroglio."[40]

The Eisenhower administration, however, did not change its Taiwan policy in 1953. The fleet did not stop patrolling the Strait after the "unleashing" order, and in April Dulles ordered Ambassador Rankin to

36. Cited in George and Smoke, *Deterrence in American Foreign Policy*, pp. 268–69.

37. Dulles, "Policy Paper on Formosa," 31 March 1952, John Foster Dulles Papers, Box 60, Seeley Mudd Library, Princeton University. For more about Eisenhower's "unleashing" order, see Chapter 6.

38. U.S. Embassy in Taipei to the State Department, 6 February 1953, Department of State (SD), Decimal Files, "The Republic of China, 1950–1954," Record Group (RG) 59, 794.00 (W)/2–265, General Records of the Department of State, Diplomatic Branch, National Archives.

39. Wellington Koo, "Notes of Conversation with John M. Allison," 2 February 1953, V. K. Wellington Koo Papers, Box 187, Butler Library, Columbia University.

40. Rankin to Dulles, 30 November 1953, Karl Lott Rankin Papers, Box 22, Seeley Mudd Library, Princeton University.

obtain Chiang's pledge not to attack the mainland.[41] During that summer, CCP–KMT fighting occurred over the Dongshan Islands, resulting in a miserable defeat and heavy casualties for the KMT forces. Chiang and his foreign minister, George Yeh, requested the Seventh Fleet protect all the Nationalist-held offshore islands. Local U.S. officials supported Chiang's request. Dulles opposed extending the fleet's responsibility to the offshore islands because this would "severely constrain future options [on Taiwan] for U.S. diplomacy."[42]

The administration revised its Taiwan policy in late 1953. NSC 146/2, "U.S. Objectives and Courses of Action with Respect to Formosa and the Chinese Nationalist Government," explicitly recognized that keeping Taiwan independent and non-communist was essential to U.S. security in the Far East. It also proposed that military pressure in the Taiwan Strait could deter the Chinese Communists from releasing "their defense forces for build-up elsewhere," and that the KMT forces "constitute the only visible source of manpower for extensive guerrilla operations in China and for possible invasion of the mainland, should developments such as overt Chinese Communist intervention in Indochina or a renewed aggression in Korea, make large-scale U.S. action against China necessary." Claiming that simply denying these islands to the PRC would be insufficient, the NSC recommended the effective incorporation of "Formosa and the Pescadores within U.S. Far East defense positions by taking all necessary measures to prevent hostile forces from gaining control thereof, even at grave risk of general war, and by making it clear that the United States will so react to any attack." The NSC study added, however, that the United States should pursue these goals, to defend Nationalist territory and to raid Chinese Communist territory and commerce, "without committing U.S. forces, unless Formosa or the Pescadores are attacked." The NSC suggested continuing military assistance to Taiwan beyond Fiscal Year 1954 to ensure that KMT forces:

(1) without U.S. air, naval, and logistic support, would be able to undertake more active raids against the Communist mainland and seaborne commerce with Communist China; (2) without US air, naval, and logistic support, but to an even greater extent with such support, would continue to represent a threat to Communist China and add significantly to the strategic reserves potentially available to the free world in the Far East;

41. Dulles to Rankin, 13 April 1953, Decimal Files, SD794A.5/4–1353; Rankin to Dulles, 16 April 1953, ibid., SD794A.5/4–1653.

42. Wellington Koo, "Conversation with Walter Robertson," 29 July 1953, Koo Papers, Box 187; Rankin to Dulles, 24 July 1953, Decimal Files, SD794A.00(W)/7–2453; Dulles to Wilson (secretary of defense), 17 August 1953, ibid., 794A.5/8–1753.

(3) while not alone able successfully to defend Formosa or initiate large-scale amphibious operations against the mainland of China, would with U.S. air, naval and logistic support, have an increased capability for the defense of Formosa and be able to initiate such large-scale amphibious operations.[43]

Clearly, the NSC proposed a much more vigorous Taiwan policy than the United States had ever had before. The United States was to make a full commitment to the defense of Taiwan, including the offshore islands, and strengthen the KMT forces as U.S. strategic assets against Communist expansion in Asia.

Military strategists strongly supported this proposal. One of its elements was the "Van Fleet concept." General Van Fleet asserted that the United States could not afford the "almost two million men and . . . 25 billion dollars per year" he estimated it would take to save Asia. Based on his experience in Korea, Van Fleet worked out a formula that would "let the Asians save themselves" with U.S. military training and equipment. This formula, he argued, was particularly workable in Taiwan: "$300,000,000 American aid to Chiang—only a little more than the cost of one American division per year—has produced 21 anti-Communist Chinese divisions, plus two air groups."[44]

Meanwhile, the U.S. military advisors on Taiwan pushed to strengthen the KMT offensive capability. The MAAG pointed out in February that a program such as the KMT offensive military capability was desirable because "such forces are to be employed in large-scale flanking movements and diversions against the mainland, possibly in connection with other allied courses of action." These officials argued that "the maximum utilization must be made of ChiNat's [Chinese Nationalists] offensive operations against the mainland which are in support of U.S. military objectives with respect to Chi-Coms [Chinese Communists]."[45]

Ranking policymakers in Washington accepted the idea that the United States might need to use KMT forces to inhibit the Communist Chinese from renewing hostilities elsewhere. In early 1954, both the

43. NSC 146/2, "U.S. Objectives and Courses of Action with Respect to Formosa and the Chinese Nationalist Government," 5 November 1953, in *FRUS: 1952–1954*, 14:307–8, and 318–19. NSC 146/2 also placed the third option subject to review by the Department of Defense (p. 306).

44. Van Fleet, "Twenty-Five Divisions for the Cost of One," 20 January 1954. OS/China, January–August 1954, Records of JCS Chairman Arthur Radford, Modern Military Records Branch, National Archives. Eisenhower sent this paper to Radford without indicating his own opinion.

45. MGGE 400, "Chinese Proposal for Augmental Forces: NGRC 'Kai' Plan," 20 February 1954, CCS 381 Formosa (11–8–48), Section 14, RG 218, Records of the JCS, Modern Military Records Branch, National Archives.

State Department and the Joint Chiefs of Staff agreed that KMT forces could support U.S. military operations against Communist-held Hainan Islands in the event of renewed aggression in Korea. Secretary of Defense Wilson had reservations, but Dulles and Admiral Radford clearly concurred. Eisenhower, too, indicated his interest, "because it looked as though this was the kind of operation which might be successfully done."[46] A few months later, administration officials also considered having the KMT attack the Chinese Communists from the Taiwan Strait to deter PRC military intervention in Indochina. At a meeting with Eisenhower on 24 March 1954, Dulles proposed that "it might be preferable to slow up the Chinese Communists in Southeast Asia by harassing tactics from Formosa and along the sea cost which would be more readily within our natural facilities than actually fighting in Indochina." As Dulles noted, "The President indicated his concurrence with this general attitude."[47]

Nevertheless, maintaining the military strength of Taiwan as a U.S. strategic asset was one thing, but Chiang's war to recover the mainland was another matter. This became a focal issue in the KMT's efforts to bring about a bilateral Mutual Security Treaty with the United States. After the French collapse at Dien Bien Phu in May 1954, the Eisenhower administration started to work on a South and Southeast Asian multilateral security treaty, seeking in part to guarantee the U.S. and allied long-term commitment to the defense of Asia. The proposed pact would include seven other nations—Britain, France, Australia, New Zealand, Pakistan, Thailand, and Philippines—but not Taiwan. The KMT immediately suspected that the United States might change its policy toward Taiwan. "If the Philippines, which is situated near to Formosa, is included," KMT ambassador Koo told the State Department in late April, "there is no reason why Formosa should not be included." Koo stressed that East Asia was much more strategically important than Southeast Asia: East Asian anti-Communist nations could directly attack the coastal front of Communist China, whereas Southeast Asia would have great difficulty establishing an offensive anti-Communist front.[48] One month later, Chiang expressed the same theme to Secretary of Defense Wilson and General Van Fleet, during their visit to Taiwan. He strongly proposed an East Asian alliance, including the United States, South Korea, Japan, and Taiwan, stressing a

46. Notes of NSC meeting, "Analysis of Possible Courses of Action in Korea," 11 January 1954, Eisenhower Papers, Whitman File, NSC Series, Box 5, Eisenhower Library.

47. Memorandum of conversation with the president, 24 March 1954, in *FRUS: 1952–54*, 14:396–97.

48. Notes of a conversation with Everett F. Drumright, 29 April 1954, Koo Papers, Box 191.

bilateral military pact between Taiwan and the United States as a "prerequisite."[49]

Walter Robertson, the assistant secretary of state for Far Eastern affairs, supported Chiang's appeal. He considered it desirable at that moment to raise the morale of the Nationalists and to treat them as legitimate members of the U.S. "system of alliances in the Pacific."[50] Ambassador Rankin supported Robertson's view. Rankin did not consider a mutual security treaty or a Pacific pact premature.[51] The pro-Chiang group in Congress also picked up on this issue. Congressman Walter H. Judd told Wellington Koo in July that he could not understand Dulles's reluctance and boasted that Congress would strongly support a military alliance with Taiwan. Senator Knowland showed his sympathy for this KMT initiative as well.[52]

Neither Eisenhower nor Dulles supported the KMT initiative. On several occasions, Dulles mentioned "unfortunate" problems that could not be easily solved. First, such a treaty might either "check Chinese [Nationalist] operations against the mainland Communists" or "get [the United States] directly involved . . . in those operations," which the United States could by no means politically or strategically afford.[53] Second, the scope of such a treaty would be difficult to define. Would it apply to Taiwan and the Pescadores, or the Nationalist-held offshore islands, or even the mainland? Since the KMT claimed sovereignty over all of these territories, the United States might lose its freedom of action in the event of a CCP-KMT conflict.[54] Third, the timing for such a treaty was diplomatically unfavorable. Dulles worried that signing such a treaty at that time would be misunderstood, especially by Britain and France, who had expected tensions to decrease after the Geneva talks. Eisenhower agreed completely. He considered a mutual security alliance with Taiwan "too big a commitment of U.S. prestige and forces."[55]

---

49. Memorandum by Rankin, 29 May 1954, Decimal Files, SD794A.oo(W)/5–2954.

50. Note of conversation with Robertson, 13 December 1953, Koo Papers, Box 187; Robertson to Dulles, 5 February 1954, in *FRUS: 1952–1954*, 14:367–68; memorandum by McConaughy, "Remarks of the Secretary of State Regarding Proposed China—U.S. Security Pact," 27 February 1954, ibid., pp. 368–70.

51. Rankin to Dulles, 15 February 1954, Rankin Papers, Box 23; Rankin, 26 August 1954, personal note, ibid.

52. Note of conversation with Walter H. Judd, 16 July 1954, Koo Papers, Box 191; note of conversation with William Knowland, 17 July 1954, ibid.

53. Memorandum by McConaughy, undated [May 1954], in *FRUS: 1952–1954*, 14:423.

54. Memorandum by Dulles, 18 June 1954, Decimal Files, SD611.94A/6–1854; note of conversation with Dulles, 18 June 1954, Koo Papers, Box 191.

55. Memorandum by McConaughy, "Remarks of the Secretary of State," 27 February 1954, p. 369; conference with the president, 23 May 1954, Dulles Papers, White House Memorandum Series, Box 1, Eisenhower Library.

For those reasons, the Eisenhower administration was not prepared to sign a security treaty with Taiwan at that point. On the way back from Manila in early September 1954, Dulles visited Taiwan and explicitly discouraged Chiang from seeking a security pact with the United States. He pointedly stated that current U.S. protective operations regarding Formosa were covered by an executive order, and that with a security treaty President Eisenhower would not feel free to act in the event of a Chinese Communist attack on Taiwan. So he suggested that Chiang should "think twice before changing the present situation."[56]

It seemed that the United States might have to defend Taiwan when the Chinese Communists began to shell Jinmen on 3 September 1954. On the following day, a State Department special intelligence report listed five possible objectives behind Communist China's action: (1) to take a further step toward achieving its goals in the Far East in the light of its recent success in Indochina; (2) to seize the offshore islands to ensure the security of coastal traffic between Burma and North China, which had been greatly hampered by the recent Nationalist blockade; (3) to head off a U.S. commitment to the defense of the offshore islands, by taking the islands "before any such guarantee was put into effect"; (4) to seize some of the offshore islands to "lend credence to their current threats to invade Taiwan or as a preliminary to such an invasion"; and (5) "to aggravate differences between the U.S. and its allies, . . . and possibly *deter* the US from extending a long-range commitment to Chiang Kai-shek."[57]

The State Department did not see Communist China's bombardment of the offshore islands as a prelude to an attack on Taiwan. It argued that the Communists were not then capable of taking over Taiwan, despite the transfer of experienced combat forces from Korea to the Fujian coast. The State Department considered the PLA not yet competent in "major joint amphibious operations" and assessed the likelihood of Moscow's active support for large-scale Chinese military action as low. The study noted that "in the past three weeks, the Chinese Communists 'liberation' theme has been given prominent treatment in the leading Moscow papers, but without independent commentary."[58]

Higher-ranking officials concurred in this analysis. "It does not seem," Secretary of State Dulles argued, "that any all-out ChiCom assault is likely in the near future because of (a) early adverse weather

56. Minutes, NSC meeting, 12 September 1954, in *FRUS: 1952–1954*, 12:905–6.
57. SNIE 100–4–54, "The Situation with Respect to Certain Islands off the Coast of Mainland China," 4 September 1954, in *FRUS: 1952–1954*, 14:567–68 [emphasis added].
58. Ibid., pp. 565 and 566.

conditions, and (b) uncertainty as to U.S. actions."[59] Allen Dulles, director of the Central Intelligence Agency, reported that that "the Chinese Communist Navy was of negligible strength," but, referring to warnings from the British Joint Intelligence Committee, added that more evidence was needed "to determine whether the Chinese Communist bombardment of Quemoy was a propaganda feature designed to embarrass the Manila negotiations on SEATO, or actually portended a Chinese Communist attempt to seize these islands."[60]

But administration officials did believe that if the Communist Chinese seized Jinmen or Mazu, U.S. prestige and the U.S. strategic position in Asia would be at stake. On 4 September Dulles cabled Washington from Manila emphasizing that the "loss of Quemoy would have grave psychological repercussions and lead to mounting Communist actions against deteriorating anti-Communist morale . . . [resulting in] chain of events which could gravely jeopardize entire [US] offshore position."[61] Radford, representing the JCS, also showed his concern over this danger. He explicitly told State Department officials on 7 September that Communist Chinese control of Jinmen or Mazu would "represent a political and psychological blow to the US prestige in the Far East generally and would demoralize the Chinese Nationalists in Taiwan." At a 9 September NSC meeting, when asked by Vice-President Nixon how much U.S. prestige was involved, Radford's response was "100%."[62] Although Eisenhower voiced reservations over the military-strategic importance of the offshore islands and the feasibility of defending them, he admitted that Jinmen was psychologically important and that whether the United States would commit to defend them was an important question.[63] He later explained that "the psychological effect in the Far East of deserting our friends on Formosa would risk a collapse of Asiatic resistance to the Communists."[64] For him, "with international communism having thus penetrated the island barrier in the Western Pacific," the Communist Chinese would be "in a position to threaten the Philippines and Indonesia immediately and directly, [and] all of us would soon be in far worse trouble than we are now."[65]

59. Memorandum by Dulles, 12 September 1954, in *FRUS: 1952–1954*, 14:611–12.
60. Minutes, NSC meeting, 9 September, in *FRUS: 1952–1954*, 12:584–85.
61. Dulles to the Department of State, 4 September 1954, in *FRUS: 1952–1954*, 12:560.
62. Memorandum by Murphy, 7 September 1954, in *FRUS: 1952–1954*, 12:576; minutes, NSC meeting, 9 September 1954, p. 585.
63. Minutes, NSC meeting, 12 September 1954, p. 616.
64. Eisenhower to Winston Churchill, 25 January 1955, Eisenhower Papers, Whitman-DDE-Diary, Box 5, "January 1955 <1>," Eisenhower Library.
65. Eisenhower to Alfred M. Gruenther, 1 February 1955, Eisenhower Papers, Whitman-DDE-Diary, Box 6, "February 1955 <2>," Eisenhower Library.

Pentagon strategists insisted that losing the offshore islands would bring Taiwan directly under Chinese Communist military threat. Army Chief of Staff General Matthew Ridgway argued on 11 September that the defense of the offshore islands was "substantially related to the defense of Formosa." Possession of these islands, in his view, would afford the Communists "unrestricted and unimpeded use of their best harbor south of Shanghai from which could be launched an amphibious attack against Formosa and the Pescadores."[66] For Radford, Jinmen was of the greatest military importance, "because Amoy [the Xiamen peninsula two miles from Jinmen] is the best staging area for an attack on Formosa." He further pointed out in a 12 September NSC meeting that with the control of Jinmen, "Communist China would have been able to build up air forces in the Amoy area which might have kept us from our aerial reconnaissance."[67]

It is clear that even though Washington officials did not believe that the Communist Chinese shelling would lead to an attack on Taiwan, they were certain that a Chinese seizure of Jinmen or Mazu would immediately damage U.S. prestige in the region and threaten U.S. security interests in the long run. It was generally agreed that the United States would have to react to this challenge. How did the Eisenhower administration respond to this threat?

III

Before the shelling had begun, the Eisenhower administration had agreed upon a principle for dealing with Communist China. NSC 5429 of August 1954 stated that the United States was to "put its relations with Communist China on the same footing as those with the Soviet Union." To this end, the United States would "*make clear* to Communist China [its] determination to attack Communist China only if it commits armed aggression."[68] The administration applied that principle to the issue of the offshore islands at that point and Taiwan in the future.

As early as late May 1954, Eisenhower had considered employing U.S. military counterthreats in the Taiwan Strait to deter Communist Chinese military action against the offshore islands. He suggested "that elements of the U.S. Seventh Fleet, such as destroyers, or light carriers and possibly a cruiser, visit the Dachen and other islands held

66. Radford to Wilson, 11 September 1954, in *FRUS: 1952–1954*, 14:603.
67. Minutes, NSC meeting, 12 September 1954, pp. 616–17.
68. NSC 5429, "Review of U.S. Policy in the Far East," 4 August 1954, in *FRUS: 1952–1954*, 14:516–17 [emphasis added].

by the ChiNat, make calls on these islands and perhaps stay for a few days." The president believed that "this *show* of US strength would make our position clear." Five days later, he further pointed out at the 27 May 1954 NSC meeting that these visits were meant to "make a show of strength that might *deter* the Chinese Communists from attacking these islands."[69] On 1 July, the president also explained to Wellington Koo that the recent patrol by the Seventh Fleet around the Dachen Islands was intended to be "observed by the Chinese Communists." He assured Koo that "there would undoubtedly be other U.S. naval patrols in the vicinity of the offshore islands."[70] In a late August press conference, Dulles mentioned for the first time in public the likelihood of a U.S. military commitment to the defense of the offshore islands. These islands "might from a military standpoint be so intimately connected with the defense of Formosa that the military would be justified in concluding that the defense of Formosa comprehended a defense of these islands," because they had "radar equipment and early-warning devices . . . which were related to the defense of Formosa."[71]

But Communist China's bombardment of Jinmen proved that attempts at deterrence merely by showing force did not work. Robertson pointed out on 4 September that Communist China's artillery attack on Jinmen, "despite the 7th Fleet's demonstration off the Dachen Islands and Secretary Dulles' public warning that an attack on GRC-held offshore islands might provoke U.S. military intervention, makes it clear that threat of U.S. intervention can not be relied upon to deter Communist attacks on these islands." He argued that "some more positive action by the U.S. is necessary if these islands are not to be swallowed up by the Communists one by one and if a significant defeat for U.S. policy in the area is to be avoided." Robertson recommended that the administration provide logistic support for Nationalist forces defending these islands and openly deploy U.S. naval and air forces to maintain the sea and air supply lines between Taiwan and the islands under attack. These preliminary responses would, as Robertson put it, "enable the US naval and air force to attack and destroy [the] enemy's naval [vessels] and aircraft in the vicinity of the attacked islands, . . .

69. Dulles memorandum, conference with the President, 22 May 1954, Dulles Papers, White House Memorandum Series, Box 1, "Meetings with the President—1954<3>," Eisenhower Library; minutes, NSC meeting, 27 May 1954, in *FRUS: 1952–1954*, 14:433–34 [emphasis added].

70. Memorandum by McConaughy, 1 July 1954, in *FRUS: 1952–1954*, 14:487.

71. Memorandum by Henry Suydam, chief of the News Division, "Dulles" Remarks at a Press Conference," 24 August 1954, in *FRUS: 1952–1954*, 14:562n. 1.

[thus] providing scope for inflicting such severe *punishment* on the enemy's naval and air strength committed to the attack as to significantly impair his chances of success."[72]

Pentagon strategists supported Robertson's proposal for punishing Communist China as well as preempting further attack by deploying U.S. naval and air forces. Speaking for the majority of the JCS, Admiral Radford not only recommended permitting KMT planes to bomb inland China as a retaliation, but also advised that if the Chinese Communists responded by trying to occupy Jinmen, the United States should send its own planes "into the fray." He explained to Secretary of Defense Wilson on 11 September that "if we fail to resist this aggression, we commit [ourselves] to progressive loss of free world strength to local aggression until or unless all-out conflict is forced upon us."[73]

Robertson's proposal, however, was not popular among other Washington officials. They believed that defending these offshore islands was not possible in the long run and would draw the United States into a larger conflict with Communist China. Secretary of Defense Wilson explicitly objected to military involvement in Chiang's war. At the 9 September NSC meeting he asserted that "to defend [Jinmen] successfully the US would have to attack mainland China," or at least to silence the shore batteries and sink the junks. The secretary of defense strongly opposed a war with Communist China over these "doggoned little islands." For him, a war with China would be hard to contain because the PLA "could accept substantial attrition of their forces, and therefore, force us to expand the war."[74] Eisenhower was also aware how vulnerable Jinmen was to mainland artillery assault and how difficult it was for U.S. naval vessels to maneuver between these islands and the mainland. He knew that direct U.S. involvement could lead to another world war because, as he put it, "if we attack China, we are not going to impose limits on our military actions as in Korea." The general feeling was that if it was to be war, then better with the Soviet Union than with China.[75]

Direct U.S. involvement in the defense of the offshore islands would also entail political problems. As Wilson put it, "it would be extremely

72. Robertson to Smith, 4 September 1954, in *FRUS: 1952–1954*, 14:562 [emphasis added].

73. Minutes, NSC meeting, 9 September 1954, pp. 583–95; Radford to Wilson, 11 September 1954, pp. 598–600.

74. Minutes, NSC meeting, 9 September 1954, pp. 588–89; minutes, NSC meeting, 12 September 1954, pp. 616–17.

75. Minutes NSC meeting, 12 September 1954, p. 617; telephone call, Eisenhower to Smith, 6 September 1954, Eisenhower Papers, Whitman-DDE-Diary, Box 4, "Telephone Conversations Series," Eisenhower Library.

difficult to explain . . . why, after refusing to go to war with Communist China over Korea and Indochina, we were perfectly willing to fight over these small islands."[76] A special intelligence study dated 4 September confirmed that allies of the United States would consider such action "ill-advised and provocative," and that the direct involvement of U.S. armed forces would sharpen the fundamental differences in Far East policy between the United States and such countries as Britain and India. It would also cause uneasiness in Japan, because of the increased likelihood of a general war in the Far East.[77] Eisenhower clearly showed his concern over the "possibility of driving a wedge between ourselves and our principal European allies, especially Britain" in this case. Dulles was afraid that U.S. military action in the Strait "would alienate world opinion and gravely strain our allies, both in Europe and with ANZUS."[78] The secretary of state was also worried about "a sharply divided Congress and nation, if the Executive sought to use his authority to order U.S. forces to defend Jinmen or Dachen," since it would be hard to persuade Congress and the American public that these offshore islands were essential to U.S. security interests. Eisenhower agreed with Dulles because "his letters from the farm areas . . . constantly say don't send our boys to war. . . . [I]t will be a big job to explain to the American people the importance of these islands to US security."[79]

In the following two months, the administration ordered a number of measures intended to *avoid* direct U.S. involvement. Publicly, Washington condemned the communist threat and emphasized its support for the defense of Taiwan and the Pescadores, but never clearly stated whether Jinmen and the other offshore islands were included.[80] Administration officials were still searching for ways to achieve maximum deterrence against Communist China without immediately and directly committing U.S. armed forces.

One way was to compel the Chinese Communists to stop shelling Jinmen and to dissuade them from seizing the offshore islands by exerting diplomatic—not military—pressure. Dulles suggested a UN resolution calling for a cease-fire. He considered this a stone aimed at several birds. First, it would bring world opinion onto the side of the

76. Minutes, NSC meeting, 9 September 1954, p. 588.
77. SNIE 100-4-54, 4 September 1954, p. 611.
78. Eisenhower to Smith, 8 September 1954, in *FRUS: 1952–1954*, 14:577; memorandum by Dulles, 12 September 1954, p. 611.
79. Memorandum by Dulles, 12 September 1954, p. 611; minutes, NSC meeting, 12 September 1954, p. 621.
80. Minutes, NSC meeting, 12 September 1954, p. 623; minutes, NSC meeting, 24 September 1954, in *FRUS: 1952–1954*, 14:659–60; Cutler to Dulles, 26 September 1954, ibid., pp. 661–62.

United States and portray Communist China as "an international out-cast." Dulles wanted to portray the situation as "not purely domestic" but also as "a threat to international peace," and wanted international support for "provisional measures" if necessary. Second, appealing for a UN resolution would help regain support from allies that was then lacking. Projecting a prudent and cool image before the world would avert criticism by cautious allies. And if the Chinese Communists re-fused to accept the UN resolution, Dulles thought, the United States would be able to revive cooperation among its allies and friendly na-tions on the issues of PRC admission to the UN, and on a trade em-bargo against Communist China. Third, presenting the issue to the UN would "put a serious strain on Soviet-ChiCom relations." Dulles asserted that the Soviet Union would encounter a dilemma; if it sup-ported Communist China, Moscow's "peace offensive would be gravely impaired"; but if it failed to do so, dissatisfaction in Beijing would be hard to avoid. In either case, the Chinese Communists would have hard feelings toward Moscow.[81] Without much difficulty, the United States convinced New Zealand to propose such a UN res-olution in late September.[82]

Meanwhile, the Eisenhower administration began to consider a mu-tual security treaty with Chiang. Walter Robertson argued in early Oc-tober that such a treaty was "the best means of *deterring* a Communist attack against Formosa." It would immediately clarify the U.S. inten-tion to defend Taiwan. Robertson pointed out that Communist China's recent propaganda suggested that there existed certain "room for doubt that an attack on Formosa will result in bringing into action all U.S. forces necessary for defense of that territory," because "Formosa remains the only territory in the Pacific island-chain not covered by such a [mutual security] treaty." Moreover, the treaty's approval by Congress would show American determination to counter further Communist Chinese military action in the Strait.[83]

The question whether such a treaty would commit the United States to defending the offshore islands remained open. Robertson argued, "it can be reiterated that a number of [the offshore] islands may be so intimately connected with the defense of Formosa that the military

81. Memorandum by Dulles, 12 September 1954, pp. 611–13; minutes, NSC meeting, 12 September 1954, pp. 619–20; memorandum of conversation by Key, 4 October 1954, in *FRUS: 1952–1954*, 14:677–80.

82. Dulles to Washington, 27 September 1954, Dulles Papers, Telephone Calls Series, Box 3, "Telephone Memos. September–October 1954 <2>," Eisenhower Library; mem-orandum by Dulles, 5 October 1954, Dulles Papers, White House Memorandum Series, ibid.

83. Robertson to Dulles, 7 October 1954, in *FRUS: 1952–1954*, 14:706–7 [emphasis added].

would be justified in concluding that the defense of Formosa comprehended the defense of these islands."[84] But Dulles insisted on not clar-
ifying in the treaty but on maintaining "doubt in the minds of the
Communists as to how the U.S. would react to an attack on the offshore islands." He wanted to "fuzz up" the language of the treaty
specifying U.S. obligations and to "leave open to U.S. determination
whether or not to construe an attack on the offshore islands as an attack on Formosa itself."[85] Apparently, Dulles thought that such a tactic
of ambiguity would keep the Chinese Communists guessing about
U.S. intentions toward defending the offshore islands, and the situation of uncertainty would eventually deter the Chinese Communists
from taking unexpected risks.[86]

The Mutual Defense Treaty between the United States and Taiwan
was eventually signed on 5 December, 1954. The United States had
committed itself to oppose an armed attack on Taiwan, the Pescadores,
and "such other territories as may be determined by the mutual agreement." One of the main objectives of this language, Robertson explained, was that "the U.S. did not want to encourage the Communist
Chinese to think they could seize additional territories without serious
risk."[87]

Nevertheless, in late 1954 the situation in the Taiwan Strait continued to deteriorate, and turned for the worse at the start of 1955. On 10
January, a hundred aircraft from the mainland raided the Dachen Islands; on 19 January, Communist Chinese forces overran a thousand
KMT troops (including eight Americans) on the Yijiangshan Islands
and started an extensive military buildup opposite Jinmen and
Mazu.[88] It became apparent to the Eisenhower administration that neither the UN resolution nor the mutual defense treaty seemed to have
deterred the PRC. The tactic of ambiguity had weakened the deterrent. "Doubts as to our intentions were having a bad effect," Dulles
admitted on 19 January, "it was in many quarters assumed that we
would defend the [offshore] islands, and our failure to do so indicated
that we were running away when actual danger appeared."[89] A few
days later, Dulles further explained at a NSC meeting that leaving U.S.
intentions unclear would now create "a greater risk." The U.S. policy
of obscuring its public stand to confuse the enemy might mislead the

84. Robertson to Dulles, 25 August 1954, in *FRUS: 1952–1954*, 14:549.
85. Minutes, NSC meeting, 2 November 1954, in *FRUS: 1952–1954*, 14:828–29.
86. For how Dulles used the tactic of ambiguity, see Gaddis, *The Long Peace*, p. 135.
87. Ibid., pp. 135–36.
88. Gordon H. Chang, "To the Nuclear Brink: Eisenhower, Dulles, and the Quemoy/
Matsu Crisis," *International Security* (Spring 1988): 135.
89. Memorandum by Dulles, 19 January 1955, in *FRUS: 1955–57*, 2:42. Also see Gaddis, *The Long Peace*, p. 136.

Chinese Communists into believing that United States would not fight for any of the offshore islands. Dulles thus suggested that the administration should request Congress to grant to the president the *explicit* power to extend the defense to the "related areas," not specified in a mutual defense treaty, such as Jinmen and Mazu.[90] Eisenhower endorsed Dulles's suggestion and sent a special request to Congress on 24 January 1955. Four days later, without much debate, Congress passed the Formosa Resolution, authorizing the president to deploy armed forces to protect Taiwan, the Penghus, and "related positions and territories of that area now in friendly hands."[91] Although the resolution's language regarding the offshore islands was much more explicit than the administration's previous statements, none of these islands was yet specified.

To back up this commitment, administration officials saw nuclear threats as an effective way to end the crisis without widening hostilities. Eisenhower, Dulles, and Pentagon strategists had on several occasions discussed threatening to use nuclear weapons in the Taiwan Strait in 1954,[92] but it was not until March 1955 that employing such weapons was seriously considered. On 6 March, on his return from the Far East, Dulles told Eisenhower that the critical situation in the Taiwan Strait would require "drastic measures" such as "the use of atomic missiles." Eisenhower "thoroughly agreed with this" and directed Dulles to state in a nationally televised speech on 8 March that the administration considered nuclear weapons "interchangeable with the conventional weapons" in the U.S. military arsenal.[93]

Eisenhower and Dulles felt that the extension of U.S. nuclear deterrence over the Taiwan Strait needed explicit domestic political support if it was to work. The president asserted that the Chinese Communists knew "that we, in our democracy, are honestly devoted to peace and by instinct and training abhor the thought of mass destruction and attacks that would necessarily involve helpless people," and that the Chinese thus did not fear such threats. On 10 March, Dulles pointed out that the NSC should take "urgent steps to create a better public

90. Minutes, NSC meeting, 20 January 1955, Eisenhower Papers, Whitman File, NSC Series, Box 6, "NSC Summaries of Discussion, 1955," Eisenhower Library.

91. Memorandum by Dulles, "The Meeting with Congressional Leaders," 20 January 1955, Dulles Papers, White House Memorandum Series, Box 2, "White House Memo: Formosa Straits<2>," Eisenhower Library.

92. Minutes, NSC meeting, 25 August 1954, in *FRUS: 1952–1954*, 14:519; Dulles to John M. Allison, 20 August 1954, ibid., pp. 545–46; Radford to Wilson, 11 September 1954, pp. 598–610. Also see Betts, *Nuclear Blackmail and Nuclear Balance*, pp. 55–57.

93. Memorandum by Dulles, "Meeting with the President," 6 March 1955, Dulles Papers, White House Memorandum Series, Box 6, "Meetings with the President, 1955 <4>," Eisenhower Library. Also see Gaddis, *The Long Peace*, p. 136.

climate for the use of atomic weapons by the U.S. if we found it necessary to intervene in the defense of Formosa."[94] For this purpose, Eisenhower himself told a press conference on 16 March that he could see no reason why atomic weapons should not be employed "just exactly as you would use a bullet or anything else." Dulles also explained to Senator Walter George that "the missiles we had in mind had practically no radioactive fall-out and were entirely local in effect."[95] The main purpose of educating the American public to accept the use of nuclear weapons, Eisenhower recalled later, was to "have some effect in persuading the Chinese Communists of the strength of our determination."[96]

Meanwhile, military strategists started to prepare contingency plans for the use of nuclear missiles in the Taiwan Strait. In late March, General Curtis LeMay, commander of the Strategic Air Command, reported that B-36 bombers stationed in Guam were prepared "to deal with any eventuality involving Communist China."[97] Admiral Robert Carney, chief of naval operations, then leaked to the press that the United States had actual plans to conduct an all-out attack on China, and even mentioned that a general war with China would start on 15 April.[98] Policy Planning Staff director Robert Bowie further recommended that the administration announce that it would "from time to time" drop nuclear bombs on Jinmen and Mazu if the Communist Chinese attempted to capture them.[99] With all these actions, as a CIA report confirmed in late April, "There may be a *show* [of nuclear determent] for calculated impact and effect."[100]

But whatever the intentions of their strategists, Eisenhower and Dulles were merely considering deterring the Communist Chinese from further aggression; they hoped to avoid using nuclear weapons. In March, in a meeting at the White House, Eisenhower stressed that

94. Eisenhower to Winston Churchill, 25 January 1955, Eisenhower Papers, Whitman-DDE-Diary, Box 5, "January 1955 <1>," Eisenhower Library.

95. Minutes, NSC meeting, 10 March 1955 in *FRUS: 1955–1957*, 2:347; memorandum by Dulles, "Conference with the President," 7 March 1955, Dulles Papers, White House Memorandum Series, Box 3, "Meetings with the President 1955 <1>," Eisenhower Library; Eisenhower Press conference, 16 March 1955, *Public Papers: 1955*, p. 332; memorandum of conversation with George by Dulles, 7 March 1955, in *FRUS: 1955–57*, 2:337.

96. Eisenhower, *The White House Years: Mandate for Change*, p. 477. For how Eisenhower and Dulles tried to educate the American people about nuclear weapons, see Gaddis, *The Long Peace*, p. 137.

97. Cited in Chang, "To the Nuclear Brink," p. 112.

98. Telephone call, Eisenhower to Dulles, 28 March 1955, Eisenhower Papers, Whitman-DDE-Diary, Box 9, "Phone Calls, January–July 1955," Eisenhower Library.

99. Memorandum by J. W. Hanes, "Meeting with Dulles, Hoover, and Others," 28 March 1955, in *FRUS: 1955–57*, 2:409–13.

100. Telephone call, General Goodpaster to Dulles, 30 April 1955, Dulles Papers, Telephone Calls Series, Box 10, Eisenhower Library [emphasis added].

the objective of threatening to use nuclear weapons was "to delay [a Chinese Communist] attack in strength on Quemoy and Matsu, without thereby provoking [such an] attack."[101] In a meeting with top State Department advisers, Dulles suggested threatening "generalized" attack with both conventional and nuclear weapons aimed at China's "great POL dumps (petroleum, oil, and lubricants)" and its communication and rail lines if Jinmen and Mazu were attacked. Dulles calculated that if the Chinese knew that this would be the U.S. reaction, they might not attack.[102] In early April, he also suggested stationing "with public knowledge" U.S. units possessing "atomic capability" on Taiwan. Eisenhower accepted Dulles's suggestion and added that "the aircraft squadron we presently have there could be increased to a wing [of nuclear capability] . . . We could station some additional anti-aircraft artillery for the protection of fields, . . . we could also station there a couple of regiments of Marines." All these forces, Eisenhower argued, would be "visible evidence to all that the United States is irrevocably committed to the defense of Formosa."[103] There is, however, no indication whether the U.S. Air Force squadron stationed on Taiwan was ever equipped with nuclear components during this period.

Administration officials, though, were still trying to avoid the moment of decision between war and retreat in event that deterrence failed. To this end, Dulles recommended a withdrawal combined with a naval blockade. He wanted to persuade Chiang to evacuate the offshore islands, and then to blockade the five hundred miles of Chinese coast along the Taiwan Strait with elements of the Seventh Fleet and the Fifth Air Force already in the area. The blockade, Dulles argued, would hinder the Chinese Communists from building up their supplies and facilities for an attack against Taiwan, which they could not easily accomplish overland because of rough terrain.[104] Such a policy, in effect, was a U.S. retreat from its commitment to the offshore islands to its original policy of defending just Taiwan. On 20 April, with the president's approval, Radford and Robertson left for Taipei to inform

101. Telephone call, Eisenhower to Dulles, 28 March 1955, Eisenhower Papers, Whitman-DDE-Diary, Box 5, "Phone Calls, January–July, 1955<2>," Eisenhower Library; memorandum by Cutler, "Eisenhower Meeting with Dulles and Other Advisers," 11 March 1955, in *FRUS: 1955–57*, 2:358–60.

102. Memorandum by Hanes, "Meeting with Dulles, Hoover, and Others," 28 March 1955, pp. 409–15.

103. Memorandum by Dulles "Conversation with the President," 17 April 1955, in *FRUS: 1955–57*, 2:492; Eisenhower to Dulles, 3 April 1955, Dulles Papers, White House Memorandum Series, Box 2, "Position Papers on Offshore Islands, April–May, 1955<5>," Eisenhower Library.

104. Memorandum by Dulles, "Conversation with the President," 17 April 1955, pp. 492–93.

Chiang of the plan. When Chiang refused to entertain such an idea of reducing his forces on the islands, Robertson firmly told him that the United States would not assist him in defending them.[105]

Whatever the effect of U.S. deterrence, Zhou Enlai announced at the Bandung Conference on 23 April that China wanted no war with the United States, and that he was willing to negotiate to reduce tensions in the Taiwan area. Dulles found this a "significant" response. On 26 April, seizing this chance to escape the predicament, Dulles agreed to talk with Beijing about a cease-fire. That eased tensions in the Taiwan Strait. Then on 27 April Dulles congratulated himself on the success of his deterrence strategy at a meeting with Senators Hickenlooper, Knowland, and Smith: "We have worked very hard to produce . . . the result" that had inhibited Communist China's intentions "to follow a Pacific raw belligerent course."[106] How true was this?

IV

In the months following the shelling of Jinmen on 3 September 1954, decision-making in Beijing was primarily circumspect. The CCP leaders patiently awaited changes, and the initial stage of the Jinmen bombardment only lasted for twelve days. The United States did not retreat during a one-week pause (16–21 September). Shelling resumed on 22 September, the day the UN Security Council met to discuss the crisis in the Taiwan Strait. Nevertheless, there was no indication that the Chinese leaders were planning to attack Jinmen or Mazu through the end of 1954. The Zhedong Front Command concentrated on seizing Dachen during this period.[107] The PRC leadership still sought only to dissuade the United States from committing itself to the defense of the offshore islands and Taiwan by demonstrating that any such commitment would risk provoking an immediate military conflict with China.

One of the PRC's effective deterrents was the Sino-Soviet Military Alliance of 1950. The Moscow-Beijing relationship at the time, however, was rather subtle, and certain suspicions existed, particularly in Mao's mind. Indeed, only shortly before, Mao had dismissed Gao Gang, who was openly pro-Soviet. But Mao clearly indicated his determination to maintain close ties with Moscow and to exploit the al-

105. Robertson to Dulles, 25 April 1955, in *FRUS: 1955–57*, 2:510, 512, and 516. Concerning whether the United States would require Chiang to evacuate the offshore islands, see Gaddis, *The Long Peace*, pp. 138–39.

106. Memorandum by Dulles, 27 April 1955, in *FRUS: 1955–57*, 2:527. Also see Chang, "To the Nuclear Brink," p. 117.

107. *DDZGJSGZ* 1:259–61.

liance in pressing the United States. During the Jinmen shelling, negotiations were already under way in Beijing between CCP and Soviet leaders regarding the withdrawal of Soviet armed forces stationed in Lushun, Northeast China, provided for in a 1950 agreement. But the Chinese leaders now offered to postpone the withdrawal and to keep the Soviet troops there "for some years." The Soviet Union had no objection to this offer. On 16 September, the Ministry of Foreign Affairs, announcing the Sino-Soviet agreement on extending Soviet army and navy emplacements in Lushun, explicitly stated that "as our history has already told us, Dalian [Dairen] and Lushun have always been the bridgehead of imperialist invasions of the Far East." The Chinese press also stressed that the willingness of Soviet armed forces to assist in defending China's coast demonstrated to the world "the Soviet government's respect for our nation's independence and honor, and its unquestionable loyalty to the brotherly alliance between our two countries."[108]

From 29 September to 13 October, upon Beijing's invitation, Nikita Khrushchev led a Soviet delegation to China for the celebration of the fifth anniversary of the founding of the People's Republic. Khrushchev's visit was given a tremendous amount of publicity in Beijing. It is still unknown whether Mao and Khrushchev talked about Soviet assistance in the event of a U.S. counterattack in the Taiwan Strait, but after Khrushchev left for home, Mao, on behalf of the CCP leaders who visited an exhibition of Soviet achievements in economy and culture, inscribed that "we are proud to have such a powerful ally, [and] the might of the Soviet Union is an important factor in striving for world peace and human progress."[109] In early November, Mao also telegraphed the Kremlin leader, reaffirming that "the great alliance between China and the Soviet Union increasingly reveals its extraordinarily great role in promoting the common prosperity of the two countries' security and defending the peace in the Far East."[110] Later that year, the CCP Chairman instructed Liu Xiao, PRC ambassador to Moscow, to inform Khrushchev that China would "sincerely consult the Soviet Union in the matters of foreign policies, and in

108. Editorial, "To Develop the Strongest Possible Sino-Soviet Alliance," *Renmin Ribao*, 16 September 1954, reprinted in *Xinhua Yuebao*, October 1954, p. 117.

109. "Chairman Mao's Inscription Expressing Gratitude to the Soviet Union," 25 October 1954, in Kau and Leung, *The Writings of Mao Zedong*, pp. 492–93. Khrushchev remembered agreeing "to send military experts, artillery, machine guns, and other weapons in order to strengthen China" (Nikita Khrushchev, *Khrushchev Remembers: The Last Testament* [Boston, 1974], p. 246). There is, however, no Chinese evidence for this.

110. Mao Zedong, "Letter to the Delegation of the USSR," 12 October 1954, in Kau and Leung, *The Writings of Mao Zedong*, p. 479; Mao's telegram to the USSR, 6 November 1954, ibid., p. 497.

return would like to have as much Soviet support as possible."[111] In his 14 February 1955 telegram to Moscow, Mao went further, stating that U.S. aggression in the Taiwan area threatened China, but that "from now on, in life and in practice, this [alliance] treaty's great force and boundless brilliance will be further exhibited."[112]

Despite the Chinese pressure, the United States signed a mutual defense treaty with the KMT on 2 December, 1954. Beijing was furious. On 8 December Zhou Enlai denounced this "open aggression" and warned that the United States would have to accept the consequences of signing such a treaty.[113] Chinese authorities then considered launching the Yijiangshan offensive as a preliminary assault against Dachen. Meanwhile, the CMC directed the Zhedong Front Command to intensify bombardment of Dachen to "make it clear that the Chinese Government and people firmly stand against the [U.S. Taiwan] treaty of aggression."[114] The Chinese leaders believed that an escalation of military action at this point would be of great significance.

Nevertheless, the Chinese leaders did not mean to provoke—and actually tried to avoid—a general conflict with the United States. Still uncertain of whether the United States would actually assist Chiang in defending all of the offshore islands, they decided to attack Yijiangshan, a nearly unnoticeable offshore island, to probe U.S. intentions. On 11 December Mao recommended postponing the assault because of U.S. maneuvers off the Zhejiang coast.[115] The Central Military Commission also took the precaution of ordering that no attacking forces should engage Americans in that area. The Zhedong Front Command, too, emphasized in its instructions to all the forces the "seriousness of this issue" and the importance of not provoking the United States. The instructions provided a number of rules guiding military engagements in order to avoid any direct contact with U.S. armed forces. General Nie Fengzhi, then air force commander of the East China Military region, recalls ordering his pilots not to engage any U.S. planes without express and prior approval from the Zhedong Front Command headquarters.[116]

The authorities in Beijing proceeded with the attack on Yijiangshan with extreme caution. On 16 January 1955, the field commanders scheduled a landing operation for 18 January. But on 17 January, CMC

---

111. *Liu Xiao Memoirs*, pp. 6–7.
112. Mao's telegram to Moscow, 12 February 1955, in Kau and Leung, *The Writings of Mao Zedong*, pp. 519–20.
113. Speech of Premier Zhou Enlai, 8 December 1954, *Taiwan Wenti Wenjian Huibian*, pp. 164–65.
114. *DDZGJSGZ* 1:61; *Nie Fengzhi Memoirs*, p. 50.
115. Mao Zedong to Peng Dehuai, 11 December 1954, *JGYLMWG* 4:627.
116. *Nie Fengzhi Memoirs*, pp. 12 and 38.

chief of staff Luo Ruiqing ordered the Zhedong Front Command to postpone the attack until success was certain. General Zhang Aiping requested that the CMC reconsider. He insisted that the U.S. naval force in the Strait would not react vigorously even if the PLA attacked Yijiangshan. He argued that "since we adopted the policy of not provoking the Americans, the United States has been restricting its activities. . . . It will probably continue acting that way. In fact, the U.S. Navy evacuated the Dachen area in mid-November." As Zhang remembers, Mao discussed his request thoroughly with Defense Minister Peng Dehuai and Chen Geng, then deputy chief of staffs for combat operations, and finally agreed with Zhang. As a result, the attack began on schedule. The PLA seized the small island within twenty-four hours.[117]

After taking Yijiangshan, the PLA secured their positions and rested for one week. Their next target was the Dachen Islands. Once again, the Central Military Commission sent urgent instructions to the field commanders to postpone the scheduled attack on Dachen. The leaders in Beijing worried that "the shifting international political situation" might not favor China's escalation of military conflict, and that movements of the Seventh Fleet in the Strait indicated that the United States might intervene directly. Worried about the prospect of engaging the Seventh Fleet, the Chinese central leadership decided to hold the attack on Dachen, pending further changes in the situation.[118]

Taking no further action, the Zhedong Front Command headquarters received reports in early February that U.S. forces were helping the KMT evacuate Dachen. When he learned that the KMT troops were withdrawing from Dachen, Zhang Aiping requested from the CMC on 5 February permission to attack Dachen immediately, because "it is better to strike while the 'iron' is still hot." The CMC denied Zhang's request on the grounds that, with U.S. elements assisting the KMT evacuation, any attack on Dachen would inevitably involve Americans. Mao twice instructed Minister of Defense Peng that the Zhedong Front Command should just "let the enemy evacuate safely." The field commanders then held off until the KMT had left, and, on 14 February, occupied the empty islands. This brought the Yijiangshan-Dachen campaign to an end.[119]

The CCP leaders now found themselves at a crossroads: they had to either continue assaulting other offshore islands one by one, or stop

117. *DDZGJSGZ* 1:264–65. Also see Zhou Peide, "The Joint Rear Services of the Army, Navy, and Air Force in the Liberation of Yijiangshan," *Junshi Shilin*, April 1990, pp. 49–51.

118. *Nie Fengzhi Memoirs*, p. 57.

119. Mao Zedong to Peng Dehuai, 2 February 1955, *JGYLMWG* 5:23; Mao to Peng Dehuai, 14 March 1955, ibid., p. 51. Also see *DDZGJSGZ* 1:270–71.

and seek a diplomatic solution to the conflict in the Taiwan Strait. Available materials suggest that Beijing chose diplomacy in the spring of 1955. A major concern was the greatly increased likelihood of direct U.S. intervention if the PLA continued its attacks on other offshore islands, including Jinmen and Mazu. Eisenhower's special request to Congress on 24 January and the consequent Formosa Resolution reinforced their fear. An analysis in the 29 January issue of *Shijie Zhishi* pointed out that the Eisenhower administration had, for the first time, clearly expressed its military commitment not only to Taiwan and Penghu but also to the KMT-held offshore islands. The *Shijie Zhishi* noted that Congress had given Eisenhower "the special authority" to implement such a commitment and that U.S. armed forces were actually preparing preemptive strikes against Chinese seaports and airfields by "re-employing and strengthening the KMT forces."[120] Clearly, the immediate and conceivable danger of U.S. military action had deterred the Chinese leadership from attacking the other offshore islands.

More important, Beijing authorities worried that the United States might use atomic weapons against China. Zhou Enlai claimed in late January that the United States was "brandishing atomic weapons" in an attempt to maintain its position on Taiwan. In April, he accused the Eisenhower administration of "openly boasting of nuclear missiles as conventional weapons and preparing for nuclear war." The Chinese press clearly noted the *Washington Star*'s report on 22 January that "the Seventh Fleet was equipped with tactical nuclear bombs and any action to attack Taiwan would have to go through [them] first." A *Shijie Zhishi* analysis also indicated that it was "not an accident" that Dulles, speaking at a press conference on 15 March, Eisenhower on 16 March, and Vice-President Richard Nixon on 17 March, all mentioned the possibility of using nuclear weapons wether to "stop the PLA's action of liberating Taiwan" or "to fight a war against China in the Far East."[121]

It is interesting to note that this was the first time the PRC leadership had taken the U.S. nuclear threat seriously. Throughout the spring of 1955, CCP leaders had repeatedly stressed that "we are not afraid of atomic bombs but we don't want a nuclear war." In his 28 January talk with Carljohan Sundstrom, Finland's first ambassador to China, Mao specially commented on the possibility that the United

120. Zhang Minyang, "We Shall Not Allow Any Intervention in the Taiwan Straits," *Shijie Zhishi*, 5 February 1955, pp. 6–7.
121. Zhou's statement is cited in Tan Wenrui, "Oppose the U.S. Preparation for Atomic War," *Renmin Ribao*, 16 January 1955, also cited in John Wilson Lewis and Xue Litai, *China Builds the Bomb* (Stanford, 1988), p. 37; Zhou Enlai, "Speech at the Asian-African Convention," 19 April 1955, in *SWZ*, p. 148. Also see "The United States Is Bluffing," *Shijie Zhishi*, 5 April 1955, p. 2.

States sought an atomic war in the Taiwan Strait. He asserted that "we do not want [such a] war" but "if anybody commits aggression against us, we'll resolutely strike back." Mao claimed that "we have a population of 600 million, and a territory of 9.6 million square kilometers, . . . [and with] little bit of atomic weapons, . . . the United States cannot annihilate the Chinese people." But he also explicitly admitted that "busting a hole in the Earth [by U.S. atomic weapons] . . . might be a matter of significance to the solar system."[122]

Beginning to fear the threat of nuclear war, the CCP leaders called for preparations against possible U.S. nuclear attack. On 12 February, Guo Moruo, the chairman of the Sino-Soviet Friendship Organization, spoke to the Chinese public on the issue of nuclear war. Guo went to considerable length to tell the nation that U.S. nuclear weapons should not be feared because "our land is so vast and our industry is in such an initial stage that nuclear weapons would not hurt us" and "our ally, the Soviet Union, already has both atomic and hydrogen bombs, as well as long-range strategic bombers, which can be used to retaliate against U.S. use [of nuclear weapons] against China." But at the same time, Guo warned against being overoptimistic because imperialists such as the United States were illogical and unpredictable—"mad dogs [that] may jump over a wall."[123] On 31 March, although he insisted that there was no such thing as an invincible weapon, Mao warned other party leaders to "think in terms of and prepare for the worst . . . to study intensively how to deal with the nuclear age." Mao believed that "if we are prepared beforehand, . . . the atomic and hydrogen bombs the imperialists use to scare us will not be that terrifying."[124]

To the Chinese leaders, U.S. nuclear weapons may not have been "an empty threat." They were evidently not sure how willing Moscow would be to retaliate for a U.S. nuclear strike against China, nor were they certain how willing the Chinese people would be to face the risk of massive destruction. It is interesting, however, that Mao's concern about the U.S. nuclear threat forced him to consider building China's own atomic bomb shortly after the crisis was over.[125] Two conclusions

122. Mao Zedong, "The Atomic Bomb Cannot Frighten the Chinese People," 28 January 1955, in Kau and Leung, *The Writings of Mao Zedong*, p. 516.

123. Guo Moruo, "To Strengthen Peace and to Reduce the Threat of Nuclear War," *Xinhua Yuebao*, 22 February 1955, pp. 1–5.

124. Mao Zedong, "Concluding Remarks at the National Conference of the CCP," 31 March 1955, in Kau and Leung, *The Writings of Mao Zedong*, p. 540, and "Outlines of the Concluding Speech at the National Congress of the CCP," 31 March 1955, in *JGYLMWG* 5:72.

125. For the initial planning of China's nuclear project, see Lewis and Xue, *China Builds the Bomb*, pp. 37–39. Lewis and Xue also argue that the start of the nuclear project

can be reasonably drawn here: Mao, having felt the threat of U.S. nuclear attack, began to realize the real power of such weapons and, unable to secure any commitment from Moscow for a nuclear
counterattack in the event of a U.S. nuclear strike at China, decided
that China therefore needed to build its own nuclear weapons.

A combination of factors—a limited initial objective, the concern
about provoking a large-scale military conflict with the United States,
and the fear of U.S. nuclear counterattack—eventually led the CCP
leaders to look for a diplomatic solution to the tensions in the Taiwan
Strait. On 23 April, Zhou Enlai announced at the Bandung Conference
that "the Chinese people do not want a war with the United States.
The Chinese government is willing to sit down with the U.S. government to discuss the question of relaxing tensions in the Far East, and
especially the question of decreasing tensions in the Taiwan area."[126]
The Eisenhower administration responded on 13 July, via the British
embassy in Beijing, that the United States was willing to meet at
Geneva. The PRC soon accepted this proposal, thus ending the crisis
in the Taiwan Strait.

V

The Taiwan Strait crisis of 1954–55 is an example of the People's Republic's "tension policy" or "coercive diplomacy" in dealing with a situation of perceived U.S. threat and an opportunity to inhibit it.

Consistently bound by the "three-front" concept, the Chinese leaders jumped to a conclusion that increased U.S. military activity in the
Taiwan Strait in the spring of 1954 indicated a possible U.S. invasion.
The perceived threat, however, was not real. The Eisenhower administration had in fact sought first to compel the PRC to stop fighting in
Korea and then to deter the Chinese forces from intervening in Indochina. Beijing obviously mistook U.S. actions to prevent conflict for
preparations to open them.

Seeing the United States as invariably hostile, the CCP leaders
tended to "read" American policies in Asia in terms of imperialist aggression: Van Fleet's concept of "Letting Asians Save Asia" was interpreted as "Letting Asians Fight Asians." Dulles's effort to build
alliances for regional defense in the Asia-Pacific area was seen as prep-

---

was, in part, a result of Beijing's "great concern about the possible American use of nuclear weapons against China" in early 1955 (p. 37).

126. Premier Zhou's Announcement at Bandung on 23 April 1955, *Renmin Ribao*, 24
April 1955, p. 1.

aration for the strategic encirclement of China, the U.S.-Taiwan security treaty, which had been a KMT inihative, was mistaken as evidence of U.S. intentions to turn Taiwan into an U.S. military base for a future invasion of China. The PRC leadership failed to see that Chiang had tried to trap a reluctant U.S. government into defending Taiwan and the offshore islands, and that the United States never intended to support Chiang's war to regain the mainland.

Moreover, unable to understand the differences within the Eisenhower administration, the Chinese leaders could not determine whose policy proclamations were valid. For instance, they never doubted that General Van Fleet's opinions represented Eisenhower's. They took it for granted that Walter Robertson spoke for Dulles.

Certainly as significant was Beijing's belief that by providing offensive weapons to Taiwan, the Eisenhower administration had endorsed Chiang's war efforts. It was true that U.S. military strategists had considered strengthening the KMT with a view to using it as a U.S. asset to contain Communist expansion in Asia. But there is no indication that by equipping the KMT forces with such offensive weapons as *Lightning* jet fighters and naval vessels, the Eisenhower administration intended to support the KMT in war to recover the mainland.

To head off this danger, Beijing once again took belligerent actions. The Chinese leaders believed that the Eisenhower administration could be brought to terms as it had been in Korea and Indochina, but they could not be certain how Washington might react and thus sought to "let their thunder sound louder than real rain" to minimize the risk of war.

U.S. documentary evidence leaves no doubt that Washington officials clearly understood Beijing's limited objectives. Nevertheless, the Eisenhower administration, concerned that a Communist Chinese seizure of any of the KMT-held offshore islands would threaten U.S. prestige, found itself unable to ignore the PRC's open challenge to the status quo. But no one in the administration ever seriously questioned this reasoning. Ironically, after Yijiangshan and the Dachen Islands fell to the PRC, the question of damage to U.S. prestige did not arise.

The pattern of the Sino-American confrontation in this case again indicates mutual deterrence: the PRC tried to deter the United States from committing itself to the defense of Taiwan, and the Eisenhower administration attempted to deter the Chinese Communists from seizing Jinmen, Mazu, and Taiwan in the future. Each side, however, practiced deterrence strategy differently. Beijing expected that short-term, controlled belligerence would show its resolve and capability, whereas Washington strategists stressed the show of force and a political willingness to use that force without really taking action. In retrospect, neither side accomplished its purposes. Beijing's actions in effect only assisted the KMT in securing a mutual security pact with Washington, which reconfirmed the U.S. commitment to the defense of Taiwan and the offshore islands. Washington's tactic of ambiguity did not deter the PRC but rather encouraged the Communist commanders to seize Yijiangshan and Dachen.

The Chinese forces would have tried to take Jinmen, Mazu, and the other offshore islands if Beijing leaders had not been concerned about the nuclear threat. Evidently, the Chinese leadership for the first time took the U.S. nuclear threat seriously, although more substantial evidence is needed to specify the extent to which the PRC leadership identified the threat and understood its implication. It would be interesting to know why the U.S. nuclear threat impressed the Chinese this time, but not before, and why Beijing began to realize the importance of these weapons in standing up to the powerful opponents. A recent study of Beijing's nuclear policy shows that a nuclear education program by China's nuclear scientists during this period made the Chinese leadership more aware of the danger of nuclear weapons. Mao finally came to believe in the bomb's military value.[127] Shortly after— in fact, in just a few years—Beijing would again want to prove its powerful status and resolute determination to the United States as well as the world in the Taiwan Strait.

127. Lewis and Xue, *China Builds the Bomb,* pp. 36–45.

[8]

The Second Taiwan
Strait Crisis, 1958

Why did the People's Republic of China shell the offshore islands of Jinmen and Mazu again in August of 1958? The traditionalists argue that the Chinese leaders, particularly Mao Zedong, "needed" an external adventure to make a point to back up such domestic policies as the suppression of dissent, the Great Leap Forward Campaign, and the mass militia movement. The revisionists argue that Mao felt greatly threatened by U.S. actions in the Middle East, Southeast Asia, and Taiwan, and that the bombardment was simply a response to the external threat in the Taiwan Strait. Another explanation is possible if one places Beijing's policymaking, once again, in the context of the Chinese understanding of "crisis," namely, as danger and opportunity.

I

After the crisis of 1954–55, the Chinese leaders had come to believe in a potential if not imminent danger in the Taiwan Strait. By early 1958, they perceived a significant change in the Eisenhower administration's strategic thinking from an emphasis on massive nuclear retaliation to the possibility of limited or local nuclear war. Such a change, Beijing feared, meant that Washington might be less restricted in using tactical nuclear weapons to protect its interests in a local crisis, and that "bold" U.S. action in the Far East was much more likely. An expert on U.S. strategy in the Ministry of Foreign Affairs pointed out at the end of 1957 that Washington had started to prepare for such a change as early as the previous spring, when Secretary of Defense Charles Wilson told Congress that the administration distinguished "between all-out nuclear weapons and nuclear weapons with military feasibility for local or limited war." Henry Kissinger's new book, *Nuclear Weapons and Foreign Policy*, the analyst believed, (Kissinger was noted as a special counsel to the JCS) laid down "a theoretic basis for developing limited nuclear war strategy for local conflicts." This U.S. policy specialist also found that Dulles had endorsed such a strategy in his article in the October 1957 issue of *Foreign Affairs*, stressing "the possibility of less and less relying on the deterrence of massive retaliation."[1] The same specialist explicitly warned in early 1958 that the United States, realizing the difficulty involved with massive retaliation, had begun to shift to a strategy of "a limited but actual use of nuclear weapons."[2] The 19 January 1958 editorial of *Renmin Ribao* noted that in his budget request to Congress, Eisenhower asked for "an increase of $1.3 billion for military expenditure, . . . [of which] the primary proportion will be spent on building missiles and tactical nuclear weapons."[3]

The U.S. decision to deploy tactical nuclear weapons to Taiwan seemed to confirm this perceived change in U.S. strategic thinking. The intelligence came to Beijing two months before the State Department announced on 7 May 1957 the planned deployment of Matador surface-to-surface tactical nuclear missiles to Taiwan. In a 5 March report on his trip to several Asian and European countries, Zhou Enlai mentioned that Washington was planning to spend $25 million to build more air force bases in Taizhong (T'ai-chung), and to deploy nuclear missiles there as well. Zhou asserted that the United States "aims at increasing the tension in the Taiwan area."[4] A spokesman of the Ministry of Foreign Affairs pointed out on 12 May that the U.S. decision to deploy nuclear weapons on Taiwan "not only reveals the warlike nature of America's policy to deploy nuclear weapons everywhere around the world, but indicates a U.S. conspiracy to turn Taiwan into a nuclear base against China."[5]

China's concern about U.S. nuclear missiles grew during 1958. An analysis of U.S. China policy, appearing in the 15 July issue of *Renmin*

1. Gi Nong, "The U.S. Military Strategy Is at Stake," *Shijie Zhishi*, 5 December 1957, pp. 12–13.
2. Gi Nong, "The Power Politics Is Facing a Dead-End: Current U.S. Military Strategy," *Shijie Zhishi*, 20 January 1958, pp. 10–11.
3. Editorial, "Where Is the United States Heading?" *Renmin Ribao*, 19 January, 1958, reprinted in *Xinhua Yuebao*, April 1958, pp. 178–79.
4. Zhou Enlai, "Report on the Visit to Eleven Countries," *Renmin Ribao*, 5 March 1957, p. 10. The intelligence concerning U.S. missile deployment came from CCP sources in Taiwan. Off-the-record interview.
5. "The Announcement of the Ministry of Foreign Affairs to Protest U.S. Deployment of Nuclear Weapons on Taiwan," *Xinhua Yuebao*, 12 May 1957, p. 89.

Ribao, maintained that "the U.S. Defense Department announced in April that a study is being undertaken on setting up intermediate ballistic missiles in the Far East, with Taiwan and South Korea the first priority. The first test-firing of such missiles already took place in May." This analysis then asserted that the United States was no longer "bluffing the Chinese people" but was actually "speeding up its preparations for a nuclear war against China."[6] Moreover, the CCP press network clearly regarded U.S. military activities in South Korea as part of this scheme. As a *Renmin Ribao* commentary pointed out in January, the United States had transformed two of its regular divisions into five special units equipped with nuclear missiles. U.S. forces, it noted, had conducted a joint maneuver with South Korean forces simulating a nuclear offensive near the Thirty-Eighth Parallel, which, the analysis found, had been the largest military activity there since the truce of 1953. The study cited Syngman Rhee's recent announcements on several occasions that "the matter is not whether South Korea would accept U.S. nuclear weapons but how soon these weapons can be deployed."[7]

According to Chinese press reports KMT and U.S. military activity in the Taiwan Strait increased suddenly. As a *Renmin Ribao* analysis noted, the KMT now had 100,000 soldiers on Jinmen and Mazu islands, including six infantry divisions supported by 380 pieces of heavy artillery. A number of high-ranking U.S. officers had recently visited Taiwan and the offshore islands, the KMT had conducted intensive training in offensive maneuvers in the Taiwan Strait under the supervision of these American officers, and the Nationalists had greatly intensified their propaganda leaflet drops over the mainland coastal areas, their sabotage missions, reconnaissance overflights, and air and naval clashes. Moreover, the analysis pointed out that in May, the Eisenhower administration had authorized the establishment of a U.S.-Taiwan Defense Command, consisting in seventeen units (both civilian and military) on Taiwan. Vice-Admiral Austin K. Doyle, the commander of this new organization, had encouraged the KMT troops by stating in July that "the task you bear to counterattack the mainland will achieve an absolute success."[8]

The Chinese leaders also saw sudden changes in U.S. diplomatic attitudes toward China as further evidence of hostile intentions. They believed that the Sino-American ambassadorial talks at Geneva had

6. Xiao Yuan, "The U.S. Conspiracy to Invade Taiwan through the Sino-American Talks," *Xinhua Yuebao,* 15 July 1958, pp. 34–36.
7. Editorial, "Watch for U.S. War Preparations," *Renmin Ribao,* 31 January 1958, p. 176.
8. Xiao Yuan, "The U.S. Conspiracy to Invade Taiwan," pp. 34–35. Also see *DDZGJSGZ,* 1:382–85.

come to a halt in late 1957 mainly due to the United States's refusal to elevate the talks to a higher level for the resolution of more substantial Sino-American conflicts. After U. Alexis Johnson, the main negotiator for the United States, was transfered to Bangkok in December 1957, the Eisenhower administration failed to send a replacement. This, in China's view, closed the door to further dialogue. A *Renmin Ribao* commentary concluded "that Washington has no sincere intention to seek a peaceful solution to the conflict in the Taiwan area."[9] A public statement of the Ministry of Foreign Affairs even asserted that the United States sought to use the ambassadorial talks to cover up its real intentions to occupy Taiwan permanently.[10] The CCP press also found evidence in the State Department's memorandum of 11 August, that the United States had resumed "tough diplomacy" toward China. *Renmin Ribao* published the entire text of the memorandum five days later, and its special editorial pointed out that Washington's tough diplomacy was part of its scheme to occupy Taiwan and the offshore islands permanently.[11]

The PRC leadership was very concerned about the possibility that the United States might control Taiwan permanently. A commentator for the *Shijie Zhishi* pointed out in May 1958 that "the United States has desired to perpetuate its control over Taiwan in order to legitimate its occupation, as well as to maintain a constant threat to the vital areas of China, thus intensifying the situation in the Far East."[12] Earlier, in a report to the State Council, Zhou Enlai even accused the United States of seeking to turn Taiwan into another Hawaii.[13] In his February speech to the fifth meeting of the Central People's Government Council, Zhou further noted that the recent focus of the U.S. China policy was to make "two Chinas" a reality. The Eisenhower administration, he explained, was in a dilemma: on the one hand, it realized that the PRC could not possibly be kept out of the international community forever; but on the other hand, it could hardly sacrifice its control over Taiwan. Therefore, as Zhou concluded it, Washington's solution to this dilemma was to project the existence of two Chinas.[14]

9. *DDZGWJ*, p. 104.
10. An Announcement by the Ministry of Foreign Affairs, 12 April 1958, *DWGXWJ* 5:88–89.
11. Editorial, "The Old Tones of U.S. Aggression Should Fade Away," *Renmin Ribao*, 16 August 1958, reprinted in *Xinhua Yuebao*, August 1958, pp. 49–50.
12. Feng Jinfu, "To Resolutely Crush the U.S. Two-Chinas Conspiracy," *Shijie Zhishi*, 3 March 1958, pp. 4–6.
13. Zhou Enlai, "Report on the Visit of Eleven Countries," p. 2.
14. Zhou Enlai, "Our Foreign Policy and the Current International Situation," *Shijie Zhishi*, 10 February 1958, pp. 39–40.

There is still no evidence that the Chinese leaders believed in an immediate threat from the United States in the spring of 1958, but they evidently perceived that any further deterioration of the situation in the Taiwan Strait could be dangerous. In early 1957, Mao Zedong had warned ranking CCP leaders that the United States now favored using military force in places like Japan and Taiwan, but opposed using military force in the Middle East. On 27 May 1958 he explained to the Eighth Party Congress that the biggest danger today was "the existence of the possibility of war [with the imperialists] and the disintegration [of the socialist camp]," and he called upon China to prepare for both.[15] The Party Congress resolved to "by all means keep alert, [because] the United States is still actively making war threats, and preparing for a new war . . . to the point of directly using military force to suppress the national liberation movement."[16]

To meet this perceived threat, the CCP leadership went beyond simply waiting and preparing. In late May, Mao insisted that "Dulles looks down upon us [because] we have not yet completely shown and proven our strength." The best way to deal with the fearsome U.S. imperialists, he asserted, was to "*demonstrate* our boldness."[17] As Mao later recalled, the decision to shell Jinmen and Mazu was based upon the thesis of "ghost's fear," which he had articulated from *Liaozhai Zhiyi*, a collection of traditional Chinese ghost stories. "All the stories in the novel tell us only one truth," Mao explained, "that is, do not be afraid of ghosts. The more you fear them, . . . the more likely it is that they will eat you up."[18]

Indeed, the Chinese leaders were confident that the international situation was favorable to China. On several occasions, Mao expressed his belief that "the East wind is over the West wind," implying that the strength of the socialist camp had become superior to that of the imperialist.[19] By early 1958, he was certain that the Moscow-led socialist camp was more united than before. In 1956–58, Beijing had consistently supported Khrushchev's domestic and foreign policies simply for the sake of unity. Marshall Zhu De and Deng Xiaoping headed a

15. Mao's talks with some provincial CCP leaders, January 1957, *MSXWS*, part 1, p. 82; Mao's speeches at the Eighth Party Congress, 17–23 May 1958, ibid., part 1, pp. 216–17.

16. Resolution of the Eighth Party Congress, 25 May 1958, *DWGXWJ* 5:140–41.

17. Mao's speech at the Eighth Party Congress, 23 May 1958, *MSXWS*, part 1, p. 217 [emphasis added].

18. Mao's speech at the Sixteenth Supreme Conference for State Affairs, 15 April 1959, *MSXWS*, part 1, p. 290.

19. *Liu Xiao Memoirs*, p. 57. In his visit to Moscow in 1957, Mao stressed the East Wind blowing over the West Wind at his meeting with the Chinese students at Moscow State University, 17 November 1957 (ibid.).

high-ranking delegation to attend the Soviet Twentieth Party Congress in February 1956. When Zhu and Deng reported to Mao that Khrushchev was going to launch a campaign to criticize Stalin, Mao immediately instructed them to stay but not to comment on the criticism of Stalin.[20] Later at the Enlarged CCP Central Committee meeting, Liu Shaoqi explained that Khrushchev's criticism of Stalin would result in some contradictions among the socialist countries, but "we should try our best to reconcile these contradictions."[21] During the anti-Soviet riots in Poland and Hungary in 1956, Mao dispatched Liu and Deng to Moscow to mediate the "internal conflicts among the socialist countries"; however, Liu and Deng told the Kremlin leaders explicitly that the CCP understood and supported Khrushchev's policy of suppression.[22]

In addition, Zhou Enlai visited the leaders of East Germany, Poland, and Hungary between 7 and 17 January 1957, trying further to mediate the conflicts between these countries and the Soviet Union. Although the contents of Zhou's meetings with these leaders are unknown, the outcome of the ten-day visit, Zhou told the Kremlin leaders, was "very constructive."[23] After defeating Malenkov and Molotov in June, Khrushchev sent Mikoyan to Beijing to seek China's acknowledgement. Mao announced his complete support for Khrushchev when he visited the Soviet Union in November for the fortieth anniversary ceremony of the October Revolution. During his stay in Moscow, Mao met many East European leaders, including Gomulka of Poland and Kardelj of Yugoslavia, and attempted to persuade them to accept Moscow's leadership of the international socialist movement. As Ambassador Liu Xiao remembered, Mao was pleased with the agreements he reached with these leaders.[24]

As unity among the socialist countries became more pronounced, the CCP leaders believed that the split in the U.S.-led Western camp was getting wider. "One of the biggest troubles [for the United States] today," Mao told the Eighth Party Congress in May, "is the fighting within the imperialist bloc; because the more the United States expands its influence, the more trouble it has either with the old imperialists such as Britain and France or with the indigenous countries such as Algeria, Indonesia, Egypt, Lebanon, and the Latin American countries."[25] He asserted that no one in the Western bloc wanted a war

20. Ibid., p. 17.
21. Ibid., p. 21.
22. Ibid., pp. 23–25.
23. Ibid., pp. 31–39.
24. Ibid., pp. 49, and 58–59.
25. Mao's speech at the Eighth Party Congress, 17 May 1958, *MSXWS*, part 1, p. 197.

with the Soviet Union or China at this point; "but many are afraid that the United States would make trouble around the world that will eventually involve them into an unfavorable war."[26] Therefore, Mao saw a good opportunity to exploit the difficulties between the United States and its allies and the neutral states. He claimed that "now that the United States has adopted a policy of 'brinkmanship,' we will counter them also by forcing them into the brink of war." Because pressures from its allies and other countries would be so tremendous, Washington would have either to back down or fight alone.[27] Moreover, the countries fighting against the United States for their independence would welcome and support China's bold action to counter the United States, simply because, in Mao's words, "once we tie down the United States, its pressure on these countries will automatically decrease."[28]

The Chinese leadership was optimistic also because Sino-Soviet military deterrents in the Far East seemed to have been strengthened. Khrushchev had invited the Chinese to attend the 1955 Warsaw Pact conference. Mao sent Peng Dehuai, then minister of national defense. Peng talked with Khrushchev twice in Moscow about military cooperation between the two countries. At one meeting, Khrushchev lectured Peng on the strength of Soviet advanced weaponry, especially on long-range strategic bombers and guided nuclear missiles, which, he stressed, could be used to help the Chinese. He also ensured Peng that "Russia's powerful Navy and Air Force in the Far East can be at Chinese disposal at any time." The Soviet leader further claimed that since the Warsaw Pact was not only for the defense of Europe but for the Far East as well, some measures had to be taken to incorporate China into this defense system. With a strong Sino-Soviet military cooperation in the Far East, Khrushchev believed, the United States would hesitate before risking war against either China or the Soviet Union. Peng was very pleased with the offer, and presented a copy of "China's Strategic and Military Planning in the Far East" to the Kremlin leader for Soviet review.[29] Mao also seemed to be pleased with Khrushchev's offer and in November 1957, let Peng lead another military mission to Moscow that included almost all the top commanders of the Chinese Army, Navy, Air Force, Artillery Force, and Logistic services. When Khrushchev met the Chinese generals, he reconfirmed

---

26. Mao's speech at the Fifteenth Supreme Conference for State Affairs, 5 September 1958, *MSXWS*, part 1, p. 233.
27. Mao's speech at the Zheng Zhou meeting (an enlarged CCP Central Committee Meeting), 3 February 1959, *MSXWS*, part 2, p. 43.
28. Mao's speech at the Fifteenth Supreme Conference for State Affairs, 5 September 1958, p. 240.
29. *Liu Xiao Memoirs*, pp. 10–13.

his offer, and directed Marshal Georgii K. Zhukhov to discuss details of Sino-Soviet military cooperation.[30]

At this time, Mao really counted on Soviet assistance, and particularly on the Soviet modern technology that "the selfish imperialists would have never provided."[31] The technology most impressive and most desired was certainly that of nuclear weapons. The Chinese leaders had begun to feel the necessity of possessing the atomic bomb during the first Taiwan Strait crisis in 1955. At an enlarged meeting of the CCP Secretariat called on 15 January 1955 to discuss the possibility of starting a nuclear weapons program, Mao pointed out that "in the past . . . there had not been enough time for us to pay attention to this matter [of nuclear weapons]. . . . Now, it is time . . ."[32] In April 1956, Mao proclaimed to the enlarged Politburo meeting that China would build an atomic bomb and stated explicitly that "in today's world, if we don't want to be bullied by others, we should have atomic bombs by all means." He thus ordered that China would "as its first priority, build atomic bombs, missiles, long-range delivery systems, and strategic bombers, . . . rather than concentrate on conventional weapons and munitions."[33]

Beijing authorities understood that they would have to have Soviet assistance. Formal negotiations began in March 1956, and a protocol was signed five months later that stated that the Soviet Union would supply the materials and the technology for the Chinese to construct a nuclear power plant. Apparently, this did not satisfy the Chinese desire to have a bomb immediately. In September 1957, Marshal Nie Rongzhen, the vice-premier in charge of military and nuclear industries, led a mission to Moscow to procure more substantial assistance. Nie's trip resulted in another Sino-Soviet protocol in October, in which the Soviets agreed to provide a training model of an atomic bomb and related equipment; however, the details were not settled until August 1958.[34]

It is interesting that Moscow seemed anxious to incorporate China's coastal defenses into its Far Eastern defense system. On 18 April 1958, in a letter to Peng Dehuai, Marshal Radion I. Malinovskii, Soviet minister of defense, suggested "jointly" building a powerful long-wave radio station linking the Chinese Navy with the Soviet Navy in the Far

30. Ibid., pp. 60–61.

31. Mao's instructions at the Conference of National Industry and Commerce, 8 December 1956, *MSXWS*, part 1, p. 63.

32. Guo Fuwen, "China's Sun," *Zuoping Yu Zhengming*, February 1988, p. 3. Also see Lewis and Xue, *China Builds the Bomb*, p. 39.

33. Lewis and Xue, *China Builds the Bomb*, pp. 2–3. Also see Tu Shouer, "Contribute to My Motherland Quietly," *Renmin Ribao—Haiwai ban*, 12 June 1991, p. 2.

34. *DDZGHGY*, pp. 19–22.

East. Malinovskii made it clear that the Soviet Union would provide the technology and most of the money needed.[35] On 21 July, Soviet ambassador to Beijing Pavel F. Iudin met Mao Zedong, and also proposed on behalf of Khrushchev establishing a joint navy with China "for a common defense in the Far East." Iudin explained that the Siberian coast was not appropriate for the new Soviet nuclear submarines, and that China had better "harbor conditions for our advanced submarines to demonstrate their strength."[36]

The Chinese leaders were pleased with these offers, but they were sensitive to the possibility that the Soviet Union might eventually control China militarily. They wanted to be sure that China would have complete authority over both the radio station and the joint submarine fleet. On 12 June, Peng telegraphed Malinovskii stressing that China welcomed the Soviet offers, but insisting that China would only accept technological assistance.[37] Mao also said to Iudin: "First of all, we have to make it clear that we will build [the station and the fleet] by ourselves and only with your assistance." At another meeting with the Soviet ambassador, Mao explicitly stated that "the Soviet Union's request for building a joint submarine fleet is a political issue involving China's autonomy." He lectured Iudin that "if you want to talk about political conditions [of assisting us in building the fleet], we will never accept [your request]. . . . You may accuse me of being nationalist, but I then can accuse you of bringing Russia's nationalism over to China's coast."[38]

This dispute was, however, not settled until Khrushchev's visit to Beijing on 31 July 1958. The Soviet leader accommodated the CCP's concerns by confirming that the Soviet Union would only provide loans and technology for building the radio station, of which China would have complete ownership. Khrushchev also explained to Mao that Moscow had never intended to establish a joint submarine fleet in China, that Iudin had passed the wrong message thus resulting in a misunderstanding.[39] The conflict in the Sino-Soviet relationship appeared to be resolved.

At this point, Beijing's military leaders seemed to have believed that they were capable of handling military affairs on their own and an active defense policy would improve China's strategic position. Since

---

35. Letter, Malinovskii to Peng Dehuai, 19 April 1958, cited in *DDZGWJ*, p. 112.
36. Minutes, Mao-Iudin meeting, 21 July 1958, in *DDZGWJ*, p. 113. Mao clearly stated that "first of all we ought to establish a principle, that is, we will be mainly responsible to the program only with your assistance."
37. Peng to Soviet Ministry of National Defense, 12 June 1958, in *DDZGWJ*, p. 113.
38. Minutes, Mao-Iudin meeting, 21 July 1958, in *DDZGWJ*, p. 114.
39. Record of Khrushchev-Mao meeting, 31 July 1958, in *DDZGWJ*, p. 114. Khrushchev explained to Mao that it was Iudin's idea to build a joint fleet.

September 1954, Peng Dehuai, as vice-chairman of the CMC and the first minister of national defense, had been in charge of China's military affairs. Given his experience in the Korean War, he held that an active defense would be the best national security policy for China. At an enlarged CMC meeting in March 1956, Peng explained that "China will remain defensive strategically as long as no general war breaks out, but our defense has to be active and forward—not passive and inactive." Mao endorsed Peng's position. In January 1957, the CMC instructed that "PLA's military preparations for future anti-aggression war must be based on the active defense strategy." To this end, the General Staff Department organized a large-scale military maneuver to test how the Chinese command could best coordinate with that of the Soviet and North Korean forces in the event of U.S. armed attack in East Asia. The PLA also held several anti-amphibious exercises along China's coasts.[40] Reporting to the Third Session of the National Defense Commission on 16 July 1958, Peng further explained that "the main objective of our active defense is to apply [short-term] belligerence to prevent general war [*yizhan zhizhan*]." Peng recalled that China's intervention in the Korean War was an active defense that prevented the United States from invading China.[41]

Mao stressed the particular importance of an active defense in reducing military threat in the Taiwan Strait. In his view, as long as it remained "up to the United States to determine when and how to launch the war," China had lost the initiative in defending China's security. Moreover, the fear of war made it hard to mobilize the full strength of the Chinese people to carry out domestic construction. Therefore, he argued that "we now should firmly make up our mind that if war will come sooner or later, let us fight it first and then carry out our [domestic] construction."[42] For Mao, the best way to gain the initiative was to involve the United States in a situation of local tension at China's choice. This became the essence of his "hanging rope" concept: the United States was expanding around the world at the cost of its own resources; therefore each place that the United States controlled would "add one rope hanging around its neck"; and each time it became involved in local tension, it "will leave the ends of the rope to the hands of the other side, enabling it to pull the rope and hang the United States at its own will." Mao calculated that "the United States is roped over Taiwan and probably Jinmen and Mazu, too, . . . but it

40. Peng Dehuai's speech to the CMC meeting, March 1956, cited in *DDZGJSGZ* 1:45. For the PLA military preparations, see ibid., pp. 45–46.

41. Peng Dehuai, "Report on Military Construction," 16 July 1957, in *PJSWX*, pp. 587–91.

42. Mao's speech at the Supreme State Conference, 5 September 1958, pp. 236–37.

only has so many troops, which are spread all over the world, and I really don't know how they can manage a war with us [over Jinmen and Mazu]." Mao also estimated that "in order to avoid a war with us, America has to find a way out. How? The only way is to withdraw the 110,000 [KMT] troops from Jinmen and Mazu as they did for Dachen in 1955."[43]

In considering the attack on Jinmen and Mazu, Mao and the other leaders admitted the risk of a U.S. counterattack but maintained that the risk could be minimized if China would aim at a limited and flexible objective. As early as late 1957, Mao began considering bombarding Jinmen or Mazu again. He considered the time to be right, in terms of both world opinion and China's military capability. On 18 December he directed the Air Force Command to prepare to deploy units into Fujian. Meanwhile, the CMC authorized the Fujian Military Command to make operational plans for the attack on the offshore islands. Commanders Han Xianchu and Ye Fei soon worked out a plan and submitted it to the General Staff Department on 27 April. The CMC approved the plan and directed Han and Ye to proceed to military preparations right away. Nevertheless, Beijing authorities remained cautious and waited through the spring of 1958 for the best time to act.[44]

When the United States became militarily involved in the Lebanon crisis in mid-July, tension in the Taiwan Strait suddenly increased. The Fujian Military Command reported to the CMC on 17 July that the KMT had put its armed forces on alert and increased air reconnaissance along the Fujian-Guangdong coast. That evening Defense Minister Peng Dehuai discussed the movement of all the naval and air forces assigned for the Jinmen/Mazu attack to the Fujian front. That same night, Mao called a Politburo meeting at Beidaihe, the Beijing authorities' summer resort, to discuss the military situation in the Taiwan Strait. Mao pointed out that the time had come to bombard Jinmen and Mazu. "Jinmen and Mazu are Chinese territories," he explained, "if we shell these islands to punish the KMT troops, it will only involve China's internal affairs, and should not provide any excuse for [U.S.] military intervention." But this action, Mao asserted, "will pin down the U.S. imperialist [and] prove that China supports the national liberation movements in the Middle East with not only words but also deeds." To this end, he directed the planned artillery bombardment and the deployment of two air force divisions to Shantou and Liancheng in case of counterattack. The CMC also directed the Fujian

43. Mao's speech at the Supreme State Conference, 5 September 1958, pp. 237–39.
44. Mao to the Air Force Command, 18 December 1957, cited in *DDZGJSGZ* 1:385; Air Force Command to Mao, January 1958, ibid., p. 386; Han Xianchu and Ye Fei to the General Staff Department, 27 April 1958, ibid., p. 387.

Military Command to impose a naval blockade to cut KMT supply lines between Taiwan and Jinmen and Mazu.[45] Still, in all this there is no indication that Beijing authorities had planned to attack Taiwan at that point or to seize Jinmen or Mazu.

It is interesting that Mao suggested considerable caution in timing the military action. According to the General Staff Department schedule, the Fujian Military Command was to begin the bombardment on 25 July. Although an unexpected storm delayed the deployment, all the attacking forces were poised on the morning of 26 July, but Mao suddenly decided to postpone the attack. At 10:00 P.M., 27 July, he wrote to Peng Dehuai explaining:

I couldn't sleep [last night]. I got to thinking about this military action. It is appropriate to postpone the attack on Jinmen for a few days. [Let's] wait and see how the situation will change during this period. If the enemy keeps its forces there, we won't strike them; even if their forces evacuate, we will still wait. Only if the enemy attacks us with no reason, [we will] then counterattack. [I anticipate that] it will take some time to resolve the Middle East crisis. We thus have a lot of time and why do we have to be in a hurry? It will be a wonderful timing [for us to take the action] if the enemy assaults Zhangzhou, Shantou, Fuzhou, or Hangzhou. What do you think of it? Can you discuss this with some comrades? It is always to our advantage if we give priorities to politics and consider [military actions] over and again. "To press to the finish without letup [*yigu zuoqi*]" often results in careless planning and action. I have repeatedly experienced this and frequently made miscalculations. . . . We must adhere to the principle of fighting no battles of no assured success.[46]

Mao was concerned that world opinion would condemn Beijing and decided to try diplomacy first and belligerency second [*xianli houbing*]. On 30 June, the Ministry of Foreign Affairs formally requested that Washington resume the ambassadorial talks within fifteen days. Mao recalled in early 1959 that "the United States did respond . . . but deliberately delayed for two days. We were ready to start the bombardment, so we ignored the reply and, therefore, we bombed Jinmen for a justified reason."[47]

Nevertheless, Beijing authorities did not intend to engage U.S. forces and wanted to avoid provoking U.S. intervention. At a 17 July CMC combat operations meeting, Peng Dehuai explicitly directed that

45. Minutes of CMC combat operation meeting, 17 July 1958, in *DDZGJSGZ*, 1:387. Also see *Ye Fei Memoirs*, pp. 649 and 656–57.
46. Letter, Mao to Peng Dehuai, 27 July 1958, in *MJSWXNBB*, p. 364.
47. Mao's speech at the Sixteenth Supreme Conference for State Affairs, p. 290.

contact with U.S. forces be avoided.[48] On 21 August, briefing Mao, Peng, and Lin Biao on the military preparations, Ye Fei reported that he had gathered three artillery divisions (one had been moved from Indochina) and one tank brigade for the bombardment. Mao then asked: "You are going to use so much shellfire and have you ever considered that you might hit the Americans there?" When Ye replied affirmatively, Mao "pondered deeply over this matter" and asked Ye again: "Can you try to avoid hitting the Americans?" Ye Fei did not think so. Lin Biao then suggested instructing Wang Bingnan in Warsaw to leak the plan to shell the islands to Washington. Mao rejected Lin's proposal "because telling the Americans would mean to inform Taiwan."[49]

Beijing waited for three weeks. To the CCP leaders' disappointment, the KMT troops did not attack the Fujian-Guangdong coast or evacuate Jinmen or Mazu, and Chiang's propaganda machine continued to threathen to recover the mainland by military means. On 20 August, Mao made up his mind and directed the Fujian Military Command to "attack the KMT troops on Jinmen (not Mazu) with a concentrated, surprising, and extensive artillery shellfire and at the same time, blockade [the strait surrounding Jinmen and Mazu]." Still, he ordered no landing operation. "After being hit by us for a period of time," Mao explained, "the enemy might consider either evacuating from Jinmen/Mazu or putting up a last-ditch resistance there. Whether we attack these islands will depend on how the military situation changes. One step at a time."[50] With this order, the Fujian Military Command began a massive bombardment on Jinmen at 5:30 P.M., 23 August. Altogether 459 pieces of heavy artillery fired at the KMT defense positions, and more than 80 naval vessels (mostly torpedo boats), 200 jet fighters, and 6 anti-aircraft artillery regiments were poised to encounter the expected KMT counterattack and possible U.S. intervention.[51]

II

Two factors proved almost equally important in determining how the Eisenhower administration would react to the Chinese bombardment of Jinmen: U.S. official perception of Beijing's intentions as related to U.S. security interests, and the actual decision-making process

---

48. Peng's speech at the CMC combat operation meeting, 17 July 1958, *DDZGJSGZ* 1:387.
49. *Ye Fei Memoirs*, pp. 654–56.
50. Mao's instruction to the CMC, 20 August 1958, cited in *DDZGJSGZ* 1:394.
51. Ibid., pp. 394–95.

that led to the U.S. response. In the literature on the 1958 Taiwan Strait crisis, little has been written in the light of recently available archival material on how Washington decided to respond.[52]

The Eisenhower administration's previous perception of Communist China's objectives in the Far East shaped its understanding of Beijing's military action at this time. The first crisis confirmed that Communist China was the most dangerous power in Asia and a continuous threat to U.S. interests in the Far East.[53] Robert R. Bowie, assistant secretary of state for policy planning, further explained in June 1957:

> a. Communist China is hostile to the United States; has acted and prob-ably will continue to act in ways which are . . . adverse to US interests;
> b. Communist China is a solid partner of the Soviet Union and an active agent of international Communism;
> c. US moves toward accommodation to the Communist Chinese regime will not have significant effect on the character of the regime or its relation to Russia and international Communism;
> d. Any move by the US which appears to be in the direction of accommo-dation to the Chinese Communists will:
> (1) increase the prestige of the Chinese Communists; (2) have unsettling effects in Taiwan; and (3) dispose the Asian friends of the US to move to-ward closer and possibly dangerous relationships with the Chinese Communists.[54]

At no point in 1955–58 did administration officials see any need to revise this belief. In its China policy reassessment of early 1957, the Far Eastern Bureau of the State Department reconfirmed its rationale and recommended no change in U.S. policy toward China.[55] Dulles, at his San Francisco speech on 28 June, openly expressed the conviction that "nothing could be more dangerous than for the United States to op-erate on the theory that if hostile and evil forces do not quickly or readily change, then it is we who must change to meet them." He char-

52. For previous studies, see Don E. Kash, "United States Policy for Quemoy and Matzu," *Western Political Quarterly* 2 (December 1963): 912–23; Marian D. Irish, "Public Opinion and American Foreign Policy: The Quemoy Crisis of 1958," *Political Quarterly* 31 (1960): 151–62; John Wilson Lewis, "Quemoy and American China Policy," *Asian Survey* 2 (March 1962): 12–19; John R. Thomas, "Soviet Behavior in the Quemoy Crisis of 1958," *Orbis* 6 (April 1962): 38–64; and Allen S. Whiting, "Quemoy 1958: Mao's Miscalcula-tions," *China Quarterly* 63 (September 1975): 263–70.

53. See NSC 5429/5, "Current U.S. Policy toward the Far East," 22 December 1954, and NSC 5502, "U.S. Policy toward the Government of the Republic of China," 15 June 1955, in *FRUS: 1955–57*, 2:2–5, 9–11, 24–25, and 30–34.

54. Bowie to Dulles, 19 June 1957, in *FRUS: 1955–57*, 3:545.

55. Paper prepared by Robert McClintock of the PPS, 31 December 1957, in *FRUS: 1955–57*, 3:660–61.

acterized the relationship between the United States and the PRC as "a state of semi-warfare."[56]

An important part of the Eisenhower administration's policy toward Communist China was to reinforce U.S. military deterrence in the Taiwan Strait. In the fall of 1957, Eisenhower and Dulles had strongly opposed decreasing the U.S. military commitment to Taiwan, despite the fact that the KMT capabilities had greatly improved and that domestic opinion favored lower military expenditure. They in particular opposed dissuading the KMT from hoping for a return to the mainland, although they believed such a possibility was very small. Dulles believed that taking away from the Nationalists that hope would end U.S. influence in the Far East. Upon their insistence, NSC 5723, dated 4 October 1957, reconfirmed the continuation of the U.S. military commitment to Taiwan.[57]

The administration considered deploying to Taiwan one U.S. tactical missile squadron equipped with TM-61C (Matador) missiles with nuclear warheads. Admiral Felix B. Stump, the commander-in-chief of the Pacific Fleet, and Ambassador Karl Rankin had requested these missiles as early as the spring of 1956. They argued that "the presence [of] this unit on Taiwan would have substantial psychological value . . . [since] Matador would provide effective means [to] counterattack mainland airfields in event of Communist strikes on Taiwan."[58] The first Matador missiles scheduled for deployment on Taiwan arrived at Xinzhu (Hsin-chu) airfield on 6 May 1957, along with supporting equipment and an operating crew of thirty-five personnel. On the same day, the U.S. Embassy in T'ai-pei confirmed the arrival of this missile unit in a press release.[59]

Meanwhile, the military strategists were seeking ways to use the KMT's military potential to enhance American nuclear deterrence in the Far East. In late 1957, Admiral Stump proposed to "rotate elements of atomic capable fighter bombers, all-weather interceptor, and tactical reconnaissance squadrons" from other U.S. Air Force bases in the Pacific to Taiwan with sufficient frequency to support contingency war

56. Address by Dulles in San Francisco, 28 June 1957, in *FRUS: 1955–57*, 3:558–73.

57. Dulles to the Embassy in Taipei, 30 August 1956, in *FRUS: 1955–57*, 3:425; memorandum of conversation, 27 February 1957, ibid., p. 470; Robertson to Dulles, 6 March 1957, ibid, pp. 493–94; U. Alexis Johnson to the State Department, 15 May 1957, note 4, ibid., p. 522; Lay to the NSC, 9 September 1957, ibid., pp. 593–99; NSC 5723, "U.S. Policy toward Taiwan and the Government of the Republic of China," 4 October 1957, ibid., pp. 619–23.

58. Stump to Carney, chief of naval operations, 28 January 1956, *FRUS: 1955–57*, 3:283–84.

59. Rankin to the State Department, 4 May 1956, *FRUS: 1955–57*, 3:356–57. Current evidence leaves unclear how many missiles the United States actually deployed on Taiwan.

plans.[60] In early 1958 the Joint Chiefs of Staff produced "eight proposals for equipping the Chinese [Nationalist] armed forces with guided missiles and for training Chinese personnel . . . in the use of missiles with nuclear warheads in case of need." The JCS also thought it "desirable" to equip "five [KMT] brigades."[61] The State Department apparently concurred. In February 1958, acting assistant secretary for Far Eastern affairs Howard P. Jones wrote to the Pentagon, agreeing that the strengthening of the KMT forces "would have not only a military but also a political impact" as far as the U.S. positions in East and Southeast Asia were concerned.[62] Dulles also thought in August that "flights of F-100s atomic capable bombers to Taiwan should be continued regularly . . . [because these are] useful psychological move[s]."[63]

In addition, the administration insisted on tough diplomacy to prevent Communist China from gaining political prestige. There is reason to argue that when the Eisenhower administration decided to return to Geneva for ambassadorial talks, it did not expect as much as the PRC leadership wanted to accomplish. To U.S. officials, the talks were nothing but a temporary convenience to discuss Korean POW issues and to respond to world and domestic pressures. "The talks are not a conclusive factor in preventing a Chinese Communist attack on Taiwan or the offshore islands," Walter P. McConaughy, the director of the office of Chinese affairs, pointed out in late 1956, "the major deterrent is the presence of powerful American armed forces. The second important deterrent is the Chinese Communist desire to maintain a peaceful posture before the world."[64] Dulles considered any result of the talks that might lead to U.S. recognition of the PRC or to U.S. endorsement of UN membership for the PRC unacceptable. "The strongest single motivation of the [Communist] Chinese in their international conduct," Dulles explained, "was a desire to be treated like everyone else; . . . [therefore] the US unwillingness to concede to them in this had been the greatest *sanction* upon them which we held."[65] It was for that rea-

60. Stump to the chief of naval operations, 19 November 1957, CCS 381 Formosa (11–8–48), Section 33, Records of the JCS, Box 146, RG 218, Modern Military Records Branch, National Archives; executive message from CNO to CINCPAC, 6 March 1958, ibid., Section 35.

61. Maxwell Taylor, Army chief of staff, to Wilson, 17 March 1958, CCS 381 Formosa (11–8–48), Section 34. Records of the JCS, Box 147, RG 218, Modern Military Records Branch, National Archives.

62. Howard D. Jones to Mansfield D. Sprague, 18 February 1958, Department of State (SD) General Records: 1955–59, Records Group (RG) 59, Box 3923, 793.00/2-1858, Diplomatic Branch, National Archives.

63. Dulles to Embassy in Taipei, 2 August 1958, General Records, Box 3924, SD 793.00/8-258.

64. McConaughy to Robertson, 1 October 1956, in *FRUS: 1955–57*, 3:433.

65. Memorandum of conversation, State Department, 12 February 1957, in *FRUS:*

son that the State Department preferred in late 1957 to suspend the talks indefinitely.

It is interesting that during this period the Eisenhower administration had been concerned about the defense of the KMT-held offshore islands. As early as the spring of 1955, the administration established a Watch Committee to observe developments in the Taiwan Strait on a daily basis. Apparently this committee had kept the top authorities well informed. In early 1956, Dulles described the military situation in the Taiwan Strait to British foreign minister Selwyn Lloyd in quite impressive detail: he mentioned several new jet airfields built by the Chinese Communists, and two new railroads connecting Xiamen and Fuzhou that were under construction and would be ready for use by the end of that year.[66]

But during this period, the predominant opinion in Washington was that immediate Chinese action was unlikely. From a military point of view, U.S. military strength in the Strait was sufficient to deter any Communist Chinese aggression. Intelligence analysts estimated that Communist China, although it possessed the capability to attack any one of the offshore islands, would not do so because the United States might defend these islands "with its own forces or react in strength elsewhere."[67] Ranking officials seemed to have accepted that although the Chinese Communists were capable of artillery interdiction on any one of the offshore islands, large-scale amphibious operations were unlikely due to the presence of the Seventh Fleet. Also, from a political point of view, they believed that "the opportunities for the Chinese Communists to improve their international position by maintaining a peaceful posture might make them indisposed to gamble on a military effort in the Taiwan area." Dulles explained to Lloyd that all the Chinese efforts to get into the UN and to exploit neutral sentiments "would be jeopardized by a military adventure."[68]

Nevertheless, Eisenhower and Dulles strongly overruled the idea of either withholding possible involvement of U.S. armed forces to defend

---

1955–57, 3:477–78 [emphasis added].

66. Memorandum of conversation, State Department, 31 January 1956, in *FRUS: 1955–57*, 3:286–90.

67. NIE 13-56, "Chinese Communist Capability and Probable Courses of Action throughout 1960," 5 January 1956, in *FRUS: 1955–57*, 3:230–34. This estimate was reconfirmed by SNIE 100-4-56, "Possibility of Chinese Communist Military Action against Certain Offshore Islands," 10 April 1956, ibid., pp. 340–41, and NIE 13-57, "Communist China through 1961," 19 March 1957, ibid., pp. 497–510.

68. Memorandum of conversation, White House, 31 January 1956, in *FRUS: 1955–57*, 3:293–94. Also see note 2, p. 294; minutes, NSC meeting, 26 June 1957, ibid., pp. 554–56; memorandum of conversation, State Department, 31 January 1956, pp. 288–89; SNIE 100-4-56, 10 April 1956, pp. 340–41.

the offshore islands or persuading Chiang to evacuate them.[69] But what if the United States should be dragged into Chiang's war of return to the mainland? Administration officials in fact were sensitive to the danger of fighting Chiang's war, particularly in 1957 when the KMT started to issue a flurry of statements proclaiming its determination to return. The KMT, as two U.S. intelligence reports estimated, might take offensive actions on the grounds that (1) its military capability was at its peak and soon would decline if not used at this point; (2) recent riots in the mainland made it "politically ripe" for an immediate offensive; (3) world pressure for accepting the Beijing government would soon compel the United States to withhold its military commitment or even sacrifice Taiwan; and (4) the Nationalists, though they might not initiate an attack, would seize on limited provocation by the Communists as an excuse for an all-out counterattack.[70] Local officials also reported that the KMT's military preparations supported its public rhetoric, given increased training activities for amphibious or airborne attack and for mountain and jungle fighting. The U.S. Air Attaché in Taipei reported in April that the KMT Air Force had the capability to attack targets on the mainland with group-size task forces and to airdrop one regiment on the mainland. Even worse, "such actions could be taken unilaterally [and] unknown to American observers." If that happened, the United States would be forced to choose between watching Chiang destroy himself or going to war with Communist China.[71]

Dulles was aware of the danger. In late 1957 and early 1958, he and Walter S. Robertson had tried hard to prevent the KMT from taking provocative actions against the mainland. In their several meetings with KMT defense minister Yu Dawei [Yu Tai-wei] in Washington and with Chiang Kai-shek in Taiwan, they stressed the impracticability of the KMT's intention to fight for return to the mainland. Particularly because of this concern, the NSC staffs rejected Chiang's proposal of March 1958 for a joint U.S.-KMT military maneuver on the ground that "the situation is not yet ripe."[72] Clearly, during this period, although

69. Minutes, NSC meeting, 2 October 1957, in *FRUS: 1955–57*, 3:611–19.

70. SNIE 43-57, "Likelihood of Military Action by the Government of the Republic of China," 9 April 1957, in *FRUS: 1955–57*, 3:515–19; NIE 43-257, "The Prospects for the Government of Republic of China," 27 August 1957, ibid., pp. 585–653.

71. Embassy in Taipei to the State Department, 5 March 1957, General Records, Box 3924, SD793.5.

72. Doyle to U.S. military offices in Taipei, "U.S. Policy toward ChiNat Offensive Actions," 3 December 1957, in *FRUS: 1955–57*, 3:645–48; memorandum of conversation, State Department, 9 December 1957, ibid., pp. 653–57; memorandum of conversation, State Department, 14 March 1958, General Records, Box 3928; NSC Operation Coordinating Board, "Report on Taiwan," 16 April 1958, Office of Chinese Affairs Records, Diplomatic Branch, National Archives.

the Eisenhower administration considered strengthening KMT military capabilities and assisting the KMT in defending the offshore islands, it never intended to encourage Chiang to attack the mainland, and actually attempted to restrict the KMT from any provocative action.

In early August 1958, however, reports from American observers in Taiwan indicated a suddenly intensified situation in the Taiwan Strait with the Chinese Communists noticeably increasing their military activities. On 8 August, newly appointed ambassador to Taiwan Everett F. Drumwright informed Dulles that the Communist Chinese forces in the coastal airfields of the Xiamen area were on alert, which suggested the beginning of "a new problem and a new phase" of the military conflict in the area. Their next step, he anticipated, would be the "interdiction of offshore islands and control of the Strait." Two days later, Drumwright reported clashes between Nationalist and Communist jet fighters, but predicted that an immediate and direct attack on Taiwan was "unlikely."[73] On August 23, massive Communist shelling of Jinmen suddenly started, but this was not a total surprise to Washington.

Administration officials believed that the Soviet Union might be testing U.S. resolve. Alert to the possibility of a Mao-Khrushchev conspiracy, they suspected that the crisis had developed because the Communist leaders "have concluded to choose this moment to make trouble in the Far East." As the U.S. observers in Hong Kong reported it, "nuclear weapons and Taiwan might be specific subjects [of the meeting]."[74] Dulles also expressed his judgement to Eisenhower on 12 August that perhaps the Chinese Communists and the Soviets together were "probing to see whether Soviet possession of ballistic missiles is softening our resolve anywhere." He believed that "the Communist bloc might now be pushing all around the perimeter . . . [to test] our resolution."[75] On another occasion, Dulles told Eisenhower that the Mao-Khrushchev meetings would mean the start of a "Soviet war of nerves, . . . [to see if] we were weakening at any point."[76]

73. Drumwright to Dulles, dispatch no. 133, 5 August 1958, General Records, Box 3924, SD793.00/8–558; Drumwright to Dulles, dispatch no. 147, 7 August 1958, ibid., SD793.00/8–758. Also see Leonard H. Gordon, "U.S. Opposition to the Use of Force in the Taiwan Straits, 1954–62," *Journal of American History* 72 (December 1985): 644.

74. Plecher to Dulles, dispatch no. 198, General Records, Box 3924, SD793.00/8–458.

75. Memorandum of conversation with the president, 14 August 1958, Eisenhower Papers, Whitman-DDE-Diary, Box 21, "August 1958, Staff notes <2>," Eisenhower Library. Also see memorandum by Dulles, 12 August 1958, Dulles Papers, Box 7, White House meetings, "Meetings with the President <8>," Eisenhower Library.

76. Memorandum by Dulles, 3 August 1958, Dulles Papers, Box 7, White House Meetings, "Meetings with the President, July-December, 1958 <9>," Eisenhower Library.

Military advisers confirmed that the shelling of Jinmen was part of Moscow's response to the Lebanon crisis. At a White House meeting on 8 August, Donald A. Quarles, deputy secretary of defense, pointed out that "Khrushchev's visit to Peiping may have been designed to prepare a diversionary activity [in the Far East] in case the USSR got more directly involved in the Middle East."[77] Admiral Arleigh A. Burke, chief of naval operations, further speculated that the Communist Chinese action was the possible outcome of a deal between Mao and Khrushchev, in which "Mao supported [the] USSR's foreign policy in the Middle East, [and] Mao was granted more of a free hand in Asiatic affairs."[78] Eisenhower was convinced that "Khrushchev . . . may have concluded that the reopening of the offshore island issue might divert the attention of the world from Lebanon to the Far East and show that Communism was still on the offensive."[79]

In spite of all these calculations, administration officials generally agreed that the Chinese Communists probably had a limited objective and that their actions would depend on how the United States reacted. The Chinese Communists, as Washington officials predicted it, would first focus on the interdiction of the offshore islands, and then launch a massive attack to seize one or more of the islands if the United States did not show a strong and immediate military commitment to their defense; they might expect to go further in their long-hoped attack on Taiwan after the seizure of the offshore islands. Apparently, Washington officials anticipated that the most the Chinese Communists might want to achieve immediately was to seize one or two offshore islands. Once again, disagreements emerged in Washington regarding the extent to which the loss of these offshore island would hurt U.S. security interests in the Western Pacific. At different times, Eisenhower, the Joint Chiefs, and CIA analysts had all reconfirmed their previous belief that these offshore islands had "no military-strategic value."[80]

Others, however, insisted that the value of these offshore islands was more psychological or political than military. The "chain reaction" or "prestige value" concept that had dominated the administration's

77. Memorandum of meetings with the secretary, 8 August 1958, General Records, Box 3924, "Taiwan Straits," SD793.00/8–828.

78. Office of chief of naval operations to assistant secretary of state for Eastern Asian affairs, 12 September 1958, General Records, Box 3976, SD794A.5/9–258.

79. Eisenhower, *The White House Years: Waging Peace*, p. 294.

80. Drumwright to Dulles, dispatch no. 133, 5 August 1958, General Records, Box 3924, SD793.00/8–558; Drumwright to Dulles, dispatch no. 147, 7 August 1958, ibid., SD793.00/8–758; Smith to Dulles, "The Offshore Islands," 15 August 1958, ibid., SD793.00/8–558; Herter to Dulles, "Recommended Warnings to Peiping against Attacking the Offshore Islands," 15 August 1958, ibid., SD793.00/8–1558; memorandum of conversation with the president, 12 August 1958, Dulles Papers, White House Meetings, Box 7, "Meetings with the President <9>," Eisenhower Library.

perception of threat in the 1954–55 crisis continued to shape strategic thinking. Robertson wrote to Dulles on 20 August, expressing his concern that the fall of the offshore islands would greatly endanger U.S. prestige in Asia. "Small countries along the Sino-Soviet periphery would wonder if they, too, might be considered expendable by the United States when the heat was really on." Robertson further pointed out that if the United States allowed the Chinese Communists to seize the offshore islands, "the Communists would be confirmed in their view that the exercise of military power and threat pay off handsome dividends."[81] On 26 August, Admiral Stump more explicitly stated to the JCS that "the psychological factors outweigh the pure military ones in this case. . . . [Because] these islands are symbolic in the eyes of neutral and friendly Asian nations."[82]

From the very beginning, Dulles stressed that the United States ought to take both the strategic value and political importance of the offshore islands into consideration, particularly in a crisis situation. At a State-Defense meeting in August, he noted that "unlike the situation in late 1954, the offshore islands are now sufficiently integrated with Taiwan [that] . . . an attack on the offshore islands would now constitute an attack on Formosa itself." He also explained to Eisenhower that "the connection from a political and psychological standpoint had become such that I thought now it would be quite dangerous to sit by while the ChiComs [Chinese Communists] took Quemoy and Matsu."[83] Dulles succeeded in convincing Pentagon strategists to accept his domino theory—that losing the offshore islands to the Chinese Communists would "produce a cumulating rollback effect [that] would have serious repercussions on the Philippines, Japan, and other friendly countries of the Far East and Southeast Asia." Thus, Dulles created the appearance of independent agreement and used that consensus as the basis for the U.S. response to the crisis.[84]

Administration officials all found it desirable that the United States should further mount military counterthreats in the Taiwan Strait to the point of persuading the Communist Chinese either to back down

81. Robertson to Dulles, 20 August 1958, General Records, Box 3924, SD793.00/8–2058.

82. CINCPAC to JSC, 26 August 1958, CCS 381 Formosa (11–8–48), Section 37, Records of the JCS, Box 147, RG 218.

83. Memorandum of meetings with the secretary, 8 August 1958, General Records, Box 3924, "Taiwan Straits," SD793.00/8–828; memorandum of conversation with the president, 12 August 1958, Dulles Papers, White House Memorandum Series, Box 7, "Meetings with the President <8>," Eisenhower Library.

84. Summary of an estimate, 4 September 1958, Dulles Papers, White House Memorandum Series, Box 7, "Meetings with the President, July–December 1958 <7>," Eisenhower Library; Dulles to Harold Macmillan, 4 September 1958, ibid.

or withhold further aggression.[85] The administration, in effect, intended both to *compel* Beijing to stop shelling Jinmen and to *deter* the PLA from taking further action. But how to hit these two birds with one stone apparently remained a problem. First, Dulles urged sending out a clear "warning" signal immediately so that U.S. commitment to the defense of the offshore islands "could not be misunderstood."[86] How to send out this warning became the focus of the State-JCS meeting of 15 August. The conferees concluded that "an effective confidential diplomatic channel" might be more appropriate than "an explicit public statement or declaration" and recommended that Dulles convey "informally and verbally to Gromyko or Menshikov" the U.S. intention to intervene if the Chinese Communists attacked the offshore islands.[87] Under Secretary of State and Chairman of the Operations Coordinating Board Christian A. Herter found "some disadvantages" with the proposal; Dulles himself did not like the idea either. On 27 August, Dulles telephoned Herter that "he was giving serious consideration to the . . . idea of acting through some other suitable third party." Herter noted that Dulles perhaps thought of going through India.[88]

The next question was what to warn with. On 25 August, JCS Chairman General Nathan F. Twining and Admiral Burke suggested to Herter that a U.S. warning should not only convey to the Chinese Communists what the KMT could do in response and what would involve the United States, but should also let them know that the United States was preparing "for any eventuality for defending the offshore islands from Communist seizure, which may include the use of tactical nuclear missiles." Deputy Assistant Secretary of State for Far Eastern Affairs J. Graham Parsons opposed such a "pointed warning." He thought it "unwise, too early and going too far." To him, a warning at this point "should be tailored to the situation."[89]

In spite of all these differences, Eisenhower finally authorized Dulles to send out a warning on 14 September in the form of a public statement that was ambivalent on U.S. intentions regarding the offshore islands. It clearly stated that the president would not hesitate to use force to defend Taiwan, "if he judges that the circumstances make this

85. Policy paper by Dulles, 4 September 1958, Eisenhower Papers, International Series, Box 10, "Formosa 1958 <2>," Eisenhower Library.

86. Memorandum of meetings with the secretary, 8 August 1958, General Records, Box 3924, "Taiwan Straits," SD793.00/8–1158.

87. Herter to Dulles, "Recommended Warnings to Peiping against Attacking the Off-shore Island," 15 August 1958, General Records, Box 3924, SD793.00/8–1558.

88. Memorandum of telephone conversation between Dulles and Herter, 27 August 1958, General Records, Box 3924, SD793.00/8–2758.

89. Twining and Burke's proposal is enclosed in J. Graham Parsons to Herter, 25 August 1958, General Records, Box 3976, SD794a.5/8–2558.

necessary," and "that the security and protecting of Quemoy and Matsu have increasingly become related to the defense of Taiwan." The statement hinted that the United States had not yet given up its intention to solve the Taiwan problem by peaceful means, implying that the administration might agree to resume the Sino-American ambassadorial talks.[90] Dulles was vague in his public warning, partly because of his political concern that an explicit commitment to the defense of the-offshore islands might turn out to be unnecessary, unpopular, or too costly.[91]

Administration officials seemed to have understood that deeds were at least as important as words for the sake of reinforcing U.S. deterrence. Pentagon strategists proposed making nuclear counterthreats. Before the shelling started, Assistant Secretary of Defense Quarles had suggested that "even with the U.S. presence in the Strait an effort of the Chinese Communists to control the Strait could not be stopped unless the mainland air bases themselves were bombed with atomic bombs."[92] On 15 August, a JCS military plan, being also discussed by both the State Department and the CIA, recommended "an initial test of Communist intentions by a U.S. nuclear strike against a relatively small number of coastal air bases. . . . If this does not cause the Communist to desist, a progressive expansion of nuclear strikes deep into mainland China should follow." Such a progressive expansion, the JCS suggested, would "involve first targeting against the ChiCom air bases at Lungchi and Lung-Tien [in Fujian], and then against the ChiCom military structure in accordance with war plans."[93]

The JCS proposal was in accord with the U.S. nuclear strategy of early 1958. At this point, Pentagon strategists had concluded that it was necessary to be able to respond flexibly to local crises. NSC 5810 of May 1958 described ideal nuclear deterrence as based on strategic nuclear weapons as a "shield" and tactical nuclear missiles and conventional forces as a "spear." Now that the United States could "deter, defeat, or hold local aggression . . . from broadening into general war," the NSC paper stressed, "a deterrent would cease to be a deterrent if the enemy came to believe that we had lost our will to use it."[94]

90. Statement by Dulles, 4 September 1958, Eisenhower Papers, Cental Files, Box 856, Eisenhower Library.

91. See George and Smoke, *Deterrence in American Foreign Policy*, pp. 379–81.

92. Memorandum of meetings with the secretary, 8 August 1958, General Records, Box 3924, "Taiwan Straits," SD793.00/8–858.

93. Smith to Dulles, "The Offshore Islands," 15 August 1958, General Records, Box 3924, SD793.00/8–1558; briefing prepared by the Strategic Division, JSC, 15 August 1958, CCS 381 Formosa (11–8–48), Section 37, Records of the JCS, Box 147, RG 218.

94. Minutes, NSC meeting, 1 May 1958, Eisenhower Papers, Whitman file, NSC Series, Box 10, Eisenhower Library.

Certainly, the Taiwan Strait conflict seemed to be the kind of crisis that called for the United States to demonstrate its will to exercise a flexible response capability.

Military proposals for the actual use of nuclear weapons, however, met a vigorous challenge within the administration. CIA director Allen W. Dulles told Secretary of State Dulles that his recent intelligence estimate on the possible effect of use of nuclear weapons indicated that "there would be a grave risk of a Communist nuclear response, [which] would entail a general war with the USSR."[95] Robertson also feared "probable Communist nuclear retaliation against our position in Taiwan, Okinawa or elsewhere." Preferring "a gradual series of counters . . . to dissuade [the enemy] from further aggression," Robertson proposed first challenging the Chinese Communists in the air or on the sea while assisting a KMT resupply, and then bombing the airfields in the Xiamen area with conventional bombs if that failed. He recommended using nuclear weapons only if the conventional bombing failed, and then only "low-yield nuclear bombing of selected targets in Fukian [Fujian]," and insisted that every option "be supported by parallel diplomatic efforts."[96] J. Graham Parsons was concerned about the "predominant Free World reaction" to a U.S. use of nuclear weapons in the Strait. He told Under Secretary of State Herter on 27 August that he would like to see "time-phased military measures which would serve progressively to deter the Chinese Communists from attacking the offshore islands." To this end, he recommended conventional military action.[97]

Dulles endorsed gradually escalating the U.S. military response, beginning with non-nuclear means. Talking to Herter on 27 August, he expressed the view that Robertson's proposal might be the best way to do this. At a State-Defense joint meeting of 3 September, Dulles further explained that the key to deterring the Chinese Communists was to convince them of U.S. *readiness* to use nuclear weapons rather than actually using them. The next day, he gave the two reasons he doubted the feasibility of using nuclear weapons: (1) "there would be strong popular revulsion against the United States in most of the world"; and (2) there would exist a great possibility of "a more extensive use of nuclear weapons and even a risk of general war."[98]

95. Allen W. Dulles to Secretary of State Dulles, 15 August 1958, General Records, Box 3924, SD793.00/8–1558.

96. Robertson to Dulles, 20 August 1958, General Records, Box 3924, SD793.00/8–2058.

97. Parsons to Herter, 27 August 1958, General Records, Box 3924, SD793.00/8–2758.

98. Memorandum of telephone conversation with the secretary, 27 August 1958, General Records, Box 3924, SD793.00/8–2758; Minutes, State Department meeting, 3 Septem-

Eisenhower did not believe that the United States should use nuclear weapons in this case. In early August, he suggested considerable caution when he directed the CIA to estimate the consequences of a U.S. nuclear strike deep into China. At a meeting with his top national security advisers on 29 August, he made it clear that "since we do not wish to outrage world opinion, the administration perhaps had better reserve the use of nuclear weapons." Eisenhower even expressed his reservation about using U.S. conventional forces to defend the offshore islands. He was concerned that the U.S. naval escort of a KMT resupply effort might be engaged by Communist Chinese forces, which would escalate to U.S. direct intervention. Therefore, he would only agree to escort the KMT ships in "international waters." But Eisenhower stressed that he had no objection to "Chiang striking back at the ChiComs as long as it would not drag us into attacking Peiping and the whole of China." One of his main concerns was that because "the Orientals can be very devious, they would then call the tune."[99]

Probably under the influence of Eisenhower and Dulles, administration officials finally agreed to implement a graduated commitment starting with conventional forces. To this end, the administration ordered the U.S. forces in the Pacific to stay alert in case they were needed for the defense of the offshore islands. On 29 August, Eisenhower authorized the Seventh Fleet "to escort and protect China [KMT] resupply ships." At the same time, the JCS directed the Navy "to sail [the] Essex [aircraft carrier] and 4 DD's [destroyers] from [the] Mediterranean through the Suez Canal to augment the 7th Fleet units." The JCS also placed on alert a squadron of fifteen B-47s on Guam in case they were needed to launch an atomic attack against mainland targets.[100] But in early September, the Joint Chiefs admitted that "U.S. participation in the defense of the offshore islands and Taiwan will probably be of a gradually increasing degree and therefore, conventional weapons will probably be used initially."[101]

ber 1958, ibid., SD793.00/9–358; Policy paper summary by Dulles, 4 September 1958, Dulles Papers, White House Memorandum Series, Box 7, "Meetings with the President, July–December 1958 <7>," Eisenhower Library.

99. Smith to Dulles, 15 August 1958, General Records, Box 3924, SD793.00/8–1558; Memorandum of conversation with the president, 29 August 1958, Eisenhower Papers, Whitman-DDE-Diary, Box 21, "Staff Notes, August 1958 <2>," Eisenhower Library.

100. Army circular telegram, 947046, JSC, 25 August 1958, Department of State, Office of Chinese Affairs Records, Diplomatic Branch, National Archives; Navy telegram 6342, CINCPACFLT to COMSEVENTHFLT, 25 August 1958, ibid.; JSC to COMTAIWANDEF-COM, 25 August 1958, CCS 381 Formosa (11–4–48), Section 37, Records of the JCS, Box 147, RG 218; minutes, State Department meeting, 25 August 1958, General Records, Box 3924, SD793.00/8–2558.

101. JSC decision on JCS 2118/110, 6 September 1958, CCS 381 Formosa (11–8–48), Section 38, Records of the JCS, Box 147, RG 218.

The Seventh Fleet escort action began on 7 September. By then, the United States had assembled six carriers with five hundred warplanes. The *demonstration* of U.S. military counterthreats as an initial response to the Communist Chinese bombardment of Jinmen was therefore accomplished.

III

In the first week of September the Beijing-Washington military confrontation in the Taiwan Strait reached its peak. The United States had already demonstrated—and acted upon—its military commitment to the defense of the KMT-held offshore islands. The Chinese leaders became very concerned about the immediate U.S. reponse.

When Dulles's warning was released on 4 September, it was immediately translated and passed around at the meeting of the Supreme State Council in Beijing.[102] As a footnote to the statement, the Ministry of Foreign Affairs attached to it a summary of recent U.S. deployments in the Taiwan Strait, clearly pointing out that "the United States has decided to dispatch a large number of naval and air forces from the Mediterranean and its mainland to reinforce the Seventh Fleet." The summary further estimated that the entire U.S. forces there would include seven aircraft carriers, three LTS, forty destroyers and twenty warships, plus the U.S. Forty-sixth Air Division, one jet unit of the U.S. Fifth Air Division, and the U.S. First Marine Air Division already stationed on Taiwan and in the Philippines. In addition, the report noted, a series of "secret meetings" involving the U.S. State Department, the Defense Department, and the JCS recently held in Washington indicated that the Eisenhower administration had already proceeded with actual military planning for large-scale actions.[103] It is interesting that the Ministry of Foreign Affairs estimate did not mention the possibility of a U.S. nuclear strike.

This information convinced the Chinese leaders that the situation in the Taiwan Strait was serious. On the night of 3 September, Mao ordered the Fujian Military Command to cease shelling Jinmen for three days to see how the United States and the KMT would react.[104] During

102. "Dulles's Statement of Aggression," 7 September 1958, reprinted in *Xinhua Yeubao*, September 1958, p. 16.

103. Statement of the Ministry of Foreign Affairs, "Current Situation Estimate Concerning the Taiwan Area," 5 September 1958, reprinted in *Shijie Zhishi*, September 1958, p. 18.

104. Mao's instruction to the Fujian Military Command, 3 September 1958, cited in *DDZGJSGZ* 1:400.

a three-day Supreme State Council meeting (5–8 September), Mao Ze-dong repeatedly expressed his concern that war seemed to be imminent, although he claimed that "the East wind will prevail over the West wind" in the long run. Mao explained that since "a bourgeois monopoly still exists in the world, I am afraid that such a monopoly may be reckless of consequences and risk a war against us." It is interesting that it was Mao who explicitly anticipated at the meeting that if the United States decided to launch an attack against China, it would "probably be a nuclear strike." Nevertheless, in spite of the danger, the CCP Chairman did not want to retreat at this point. Instead, he called upon the whole country to "fully prepare for an anti-aggression war." It is still unknown to what extent Mao regarded a U.S. nuclear attack as imminent, but he was serious in wanting to prepare for such a worst case. "We will arm our people," he instructed, "we will arm hundreds of thousand of people now and arm a thousand thousands in the future; each province will also produce conventional weapons, such as rifles and machine guns."[105]

At this critical juncture, Beijing warned the United States against military intervention in the Taiwan Strait. Zhou Enlai proclaimed on 4 September that China's territorial waters extended to twelve nautical miles and "no foreign military aircraft or naval vessels are allowed to enter our territorial sky and sea without Chinese goverment's permit." Two days later, Zhou made another public statement and warned more explicitly that "if the United States continues to interfere in [China's internal affairs] and to invade [China's territories] to impose war upon the Chinese people, it must prepare to bear all the serious consequences that its [aggressive] action may lead to." The next day, the spokesman of the Ministry of Foreign Affairs issued a "serious warning" against the U.S. Navy escorting the KMT supply vessels to Jinmen.[106]

Meanwhile, the CCP leadership considered resuming the Sino-American ambassadorial talks. In late August and after a careful deliberation, Mao called back Ambassador Wang Bingnan, who had served as the main negotiator with the Americans at Geneva. At a CCP Politburo meeting of 2 September, Mao asked Wang to brief the Politburo members on the ambassadorial talks and stressed that it might be possible to resume them soon. As Wang recalled, all the leaders agreed that China should try to reopen the only channel of direct dialogue with Washington. Mao then instructed Premier Zhou to see to it that the Ministry of Foreign Affairs "drafts a new policy paper to

105. Mao's speech at the Fifteenth Supreme Conference for State Affairs, 5 September 1958, pp. 231–37.
106. *DDZGWJ*, pp. 105–6.

guide the resumption of Sino-American negotiations as soon as possible."[107] A few days later, Mao introduced the Politburo's decision on the resumption of the talks to the Supreme State Council meeting and received unanimous agreement. On 6 September, in his five-point policy statement regarding the Strait crisis, Zhou announced that his government was "ready to accept the U.S. offer of early August to resume the Sino-American ambassadorial talks."[108]

It seemed that Beijing leaders understood not only the importance of firmness but also that of prudence and flexibility. Now that the massive shelling of Jinmen had raised tensions, they believed, any further military action would probably risk general war, which China did not wish. In late August, field commander Han Xianchu proposed an air strike on Jinmen. Mao Zedong rejected Han's proposal on the grounds that such an action could involve possible air battle with the U.S. Air Force in the area.[109] Also on 7 September, when PLA radar identified the U.S. Navy escorting KMT supply vessels, Mao authorized shelling "the KMT vessels only and not the Americans." In his instruction to Ye Fei, Mao made it clear that "only Beijing has the authority to decide when to fire." It is interesting that, as soon as the PLA opened fire, U.S. naval vessels quickly moved away. Four days later, the U.S. Navy escorted another convoy to Jinmen. Zhou Enlai ordered immediate fire at the KMT vessels. Again, the Americans ran to the high seas right away. The Chinese leaders were pleased to find out that the United States was not prepared to engage the PLA forces.[110]

Undoubtedly, the Chinese leaders were not ready to cease military activities at this time, especially under U.S. military pressure. They were still hoping that the United States would eventually compel the KMT to evacuate Jinmen or Mazu or both. On 8 September, Mao pointed out that the Eisenhower administration had two grave difficulties in this case: first, world opinion, including that of its allies and other neutral countries, and American domestic opinion, would "request it to get out of the offshore islands"; and second, the United States was not ready for fighting general war against China, because, as he put it, a general war would require many more troops than the United States could raise or afford. He thus anticipated that "the United States had a way of disengaging from the Korean War and,

107. *Wang Bingnan Memoirs*, p. 24.
108. Mao's speech on current world situation at the Supreme Conference for State Affairs, 6 September 1958, *Renmin Ribao*, 7 September 1958, p. 1; Zhou Enlai's announcement on the situation in the Taiwan Strait, 6 September 1958, *Xinhua Yuebao*, September 1958, pp. 15–16.
109. *Ye Fei Memoirs*, pp. 663–64.
110. *DDZGJSGZ* 1:402–3. Also see *Ye Fei Memoirs*, pp. 658–62.

now, I think that they also have a way of getting out of Jinmen and Mazu. How? They will have to remove the 110,000 KMT troops from there."[111]

The CCP leaders also expected that the resumed ambassadorial talks would play a significant role in persuading Washington to disengage from the Taiwan Strait, or at least reaching a peaceful solution to the Taiwan question. Before Ambassador Wang left for Warsaw, Mao instructed him to "use more sincere persuasion than harsh criticism this time in the negotiation." "For instance," Mao told Wang, "you can tell them that the United States is a strong power but China is not too weak, and ask them why a powerful country like theirs should fight with us 600 million Chinese people over these tiny islands." Mao in particular stressed that Wang should avoid "expressing ourselves in a tough and harsh way as we did in the Panmunjom Truce talks so as to avoid hurting their feelings." The CCP Chairman wanted Wang to make it clear that "both the Chinese and the American people belong to glorious nations and there is no reason why we should not be friendly to each other." Zhou also wrote to Wang instructing him to be "active but flexible" this time. In accordance with all these instructions, Wang declared in Warsaw on 15 September that China, although determined to liberate Jinmen and Mazu, was willing to go along with a peaceful solution to the Taiwan question.[112]

Appearing to be as flexible as possible, Mao at the same time insisted on demonstrating China's resolution and readiness to counter U.S. war plans. To ensure that his call for mass mobilization was seriously put into effect, he took an inspection trip to the East China provinces in mid-September. Speaking to a press conference on 29 September, Mao expressed a determination to rapidly increase the production of steel and to rearm the people. "The imperialists are threatening us," he averred, "so we should *threaten them back* and even on a greater scale; and if our country is fully mobilized, the imperialists could not expect to seize one inch of our land even if they invade us."[113] Moreover, throughout September, Beijing's press propaganda network repeatedly stressed the theme that "no one likes to sleep next to someone who snores," implying that China would not tolerate the presence of U.S. military forces so close to its coastal border.[114]

111. Mao's speech at the Fifteenth Supreme Conference for State Affairs, 8 September 1958, pp. 238–39.

112. *Wang Bingnan Memoirs*, p. 25.

113. Commentary, "Chairman Mao's Important Speeches in September," *Hongqi*, October 1958, pp. 1–2 [emphasis added].

114. Ibid., p. 2.

Nevertheless, the situation became more complicated when the Soviet Union became involved. The CCP leadership had not informed Moscow of its decision to shell Jinmen beforehand.[115] Only when the bombardment actually started did the PLA Chief of Staff tell the Soviet military advisers in China of the CCP's decision. The Chinese leaders had never intended to let the Soviet Union play any role in their military action. During Khrushchev's three-day visit to China (31 July–2 August, 1958), the Soviet leader spent most of his time lecturing the Chinese on his vision of international communist movements. Concerning future cooperation within the socialist camp, Khrushchev envisioned that China would become the major agricultural base and supply other socialist countries, and would, in return, obtain industrial products from the Soviet Union or other Eastern European countries. He even sought to persuade Mao not to build nuclear weapons and to leave China's defense to the Soviet Union.[116] The Kremlin leader also showed his concern about the mounting tension in the Taiwan Strait and warned that increased U.S. military activity in the area might lead to "a dangerous situation." The CCP leaders had the impression that Khrushchev feared that China's resumption of attacks on the offshore islands would result in the U.S. Seventh Fleet's counterattack, which might develop into a larger scale conflict. Suggesting that the Chinese leaders consider accepting a "two-Chinas" status quo, Khrushchev implied that Beijing would be on its own against the United States if Chinese forces attacked the offshore islands or Taiwan.[117] The Chinese leadership had reason deliberately to keep its decision to bombard the offshore islands from Moscow.

When the bombardment started, Khrushchev sent Andrei A. Gromyko to Beijing. Arriving on 6 September, Gromyko expressed Moscow's concern that China's military action might trigger a general conflict between the Soviet Union and the United States in the Far East. Gromyko later recalled that in their discussion about a possible U.S. attack on China as a result of mounting tensions in the Taiwan Strait, Mao had told him that the Chinese would react according to the principle of "blade against blade." Chinese forces would evacuate the peripheries of China to let U.S. forces enter China's heartland. Once they were deep within Chinese territory, the Soviet Union then should help the Chinese retaliate "with all the possible means." Gromyko noted that he told Mao that "the scenario of war described by you cannot meet a positive response by us." But according to recently released

115. *Liu Xiao Memoirs*, p. 72.
116. Ibid., pp. 72–73. Also see Guo Fuwen, "China's Sun," pp. 2–3.
117. *Liu Xiao Memoirs*, p. 73.

Chinese sources, Mao and Zhou made it clear to Gromyko (1) that China's bombardment was intended mainly to "punish the KMT" and "pressure the United States not to pursue a 'two-Chinas' policy"; (2) that China had no intention to attack Taiwan; and (3) that China would be fully responsible for the Taiwan problem, and if it "came out disastrously," China would bear it alone and would not "pull the Soviet Union into the water." There is no evidence, a recent study even asserts, that Mao expressed himself as Gromyko recorded in his memoir; the CCP Chairman may have only said that "it's getting so hot, and we want to force Eisenhower to take a shower."[118]

Rather unexpectedly to the Chinese leaders, Khrushchev acted on his own initiative. On 7 September, he warned Eisenhower in a letter that an attack on China would mean an attack on the Soviet Union, and clearly stated that any U.S. nuclear strike on China's mainland would result in Soviet nuclear retaliation. The Soviet leader also urged the United States to resume negotiations.[119] This Soviet policy was truly different from Moscow's stand prior to the crisis. There is as yet no evidence from the Chinese side why the Kremlin did this. A few days later, Khrushchev called in Chinese ambassador Liu Xiao to talk about "how the Soviet Union can further help China." Once again, the Soviet leader showed his concern that U.S. brinkmanship in the Taiwan Strait might lead to a larger conflict in the Far East. He repeatedly urged Liu to report back to Beijing that "the Soviet Politburo has already decided to strengthen the Soviet Air Force in the Far East for the purpose of effectively deterring the U.S.-KMT naval forces from attacking China."[120]

Moscow expressed its intention to extend Soviet deterrence over the Taiwan Strait; nevertheless, in a personal letter to Khrushchev two weeks later, Mao firmly rejected Khrushchev's offer. He told the Soviet leader that the situation was well under control. He also predicted that the United States was not ready for a general war with China or the Soviet Union, but that even if it was, China was fully prepared and would not need any Soviet assistance. When Ambassador

118. Andrei A. Gromyko, *Memoirs* (New York, 1989), pp. 251–52. Also see, Philip Taubman, "Gromyko Says Mao Wanted Soviet A-Bomb Used on G.I.'s," *New York Times*, 22 February 1988, pp. 1 and 6–7; minutes, Mao-Gromyko talks, (undated) September 1958, cited in *DDZGWJ*, p. 115. After reading Gromyko's memoirs, Chinese officials have denied that Mao made the proposal as Gromyko described it in his memoirs (Wei Shiyan, "Gromyko's Recollection of His Talk with Chairman Mao on the Taiwan Strait Crisis Is Not True," in *Xinzhongguo Waijiao Fengyun*, pp. 135–38). Without seeing the original records of Mao-Gromyko talks, one cannot assess the accuracy of either Gromyko's or the Chinese versions.

119. Letter, Khrushchev to Eisenhower, 7 September 1958, *DDZGWJ*, pp. 115–16.

120. *Liu Xiao Memoirs*, pp. 62–63.

Liu presented Mao's letter to Khrushchev, the Soviet leader responded that "the Chinese comrades may know better than we do on the Taiwan Strait situation."[121]

There is still no evidence to explain why Mao did not accept Khrushchev's proposal to extend deterrence over the Taiwan Strait. He might have been concerned that if the Soviet forces were allowed to defend China's coast, Moscow would be able to increase its control over China's military affairs and Beijing might lose its freedom of action on the Taiwan issue.[122] Or, Mao may have been confident that the situation in the Taiwan area would not get out of control. With or without Soviet extended deterrence, the Chinese leaders were certain that they were capable of managing the crisis. How, then, did the Eisenhower administration decide to respond?

IV

By late September, the situation in the Taiwan Strait had become a stalemate: the United States remained committed to defending the offshore islands without escalating the conflict, and Beijing still demonstrated no sign of retreat from its shelling of the islands. Under these circumstances, Washington decision makers felt an urgent need to reconsider U.S. policy if an extended conflict in the Taiwan Strait was to be avoided.

What did the Chinese Communists intend? At a State-JCS-Defense joint meeting on 20 September, Washington officials outlined three possibilities: (1) the Chinese Communists might attempt to seize the offshore islands; (2) they might try a Berlin-type blockade to impose a limited but sustained military presence on Jinmen for political and diplomatic gains; and (3) they might (as they had in 1954–55) gradually reduce their efforts to the point of relative quiet in the face of a U.S. counterthreat. The analysts concluded that the last two options seemed to be more likely.[123]

---

121. Ibid., pp. 63–65.

122. There are two different arguments on this point. One view is that Moscow never intended to support Beijing as it had expected. See Alice L. Hsieh, *Communist China's Strategy in the Nuclear Era* (Englewood Cliffs, N.J., 1962), pp. 179–30. Another view is that Beijing did not really expect more from the Soviet Union because Mao's objective was limited. See Morton H. Halperin and Tang Tsou, "The 1958 Quemoy Crisis," in *Sino-Soviet Relations and Arms Control*, ed. M. H. Halperin (Cambridge, Mass., 1963), pp. 265–304.

123. State Department Memorandum, 20 September 1958, General Records, Box 3925, SD793.00/9–2058. Also see Robertson to Dulles, 25 September 1958, ibid., SD793.00/9–2558.

Apparently, administration officials believed that the strategy of deterrence had worked. An intelligence report of 18 September suggested that the presence of U.S. forces "probably made Peiping (and Moscow) realize more fully than before that any attempt to seize the offshore islands by force runs a serious risk of drawing the U.S. into direct hostility," and thus, the Chinese expectations to invade the islands "have undoubtedly faded if not disappeared."[124] Concerning the Soviet warnings, the Eisenhower administration believed that although the Soviet Union had made the strongest expression of support for Communist China since 1949, the Soviet action was more a political show than a military deterrent. They noted especially that the Soviets had not gone on alert, as they had during the Suez crisis in 1956, nor had they made any other unusual preparations. "Khrushchev apparently hoped," Dulles pointed out, "to create an atmosphere favorable to Moscow and Peiping for further diplomatic moves."[125] In addition, administration officials were almost certain that the Chinese Communists intended to exploit political and diplomatic gains rather than take military risks. Dulles explained, "This was a war of nerves tactic, . . . [by which] the ChiComs might prolong the interdiction of Quemoy, avoiding direct assault with the view to gaining political advantage in the UN."[126]

What action, then, should the United States take to end the crisis as soon as possible? Administration officials first considered how to respond to Beijing's initiative to reopen the ambassadorial talks. When commenting on Chinese Communist intentions in this initiative, Ambassador Drumwright congratulated Dulles, speculating that Zhou Enlai's offer was the result of the "deterrence effect" of Dulles's warning statement of 4 September. Hugh S. Cumming, Jr., an intelligence analyst in the State Department, also believed that the Communist Chinese had been dissuaded from taking any military action against the offshore islands.[127] Pleased with the result, Dulles pointed out in a phone conversation with Robertson that Communist China's initiative in resuming the talks could be exploited. The United States would have no support anywhere, the secretary of state felt, unless it

124. DDS R&A report, 18 September 1958, General Records, Box 3920, SD790003. Also see Eisenhower, *The White House Years: Waging Peace*, p. 303.

125. Hugh S. Cumming, Jr., to Dulles, 10 September 1958, General Records, Box 3924, SD793.00/9–758; DSS R&A report, 18 September 1958, ibid., SD790003; minutes, State-JCS meeting, 20 September 1958, ibid., SD793.00/9–2058.

126. Memorandum of conversation between Dulles and Sir Harold Caccia, 12 September 1958, General Records, Box 3925, SD793.00/9–1258; minutes, State-Defense meeting, 12 September 1958, ibid., SD793.00/9–1258.

127. Drumwright to Dulles, 7 September 1958, General Records, Box 3924, SD793.00/9–758; Hugh S. Cumming, Jr., to Dulles, 6 September 1958, ibid., SD793.00/9–658.

openly welcomed the Communist Chinese offer; the reopening of diplomatic contacts would also be useful in minimizing the military risk in the Taiwan area. At a cabinet meeting on 6 September, Eisenhower endorsed Dulles's proposal to resume the talks with the Chinese Communists. Five days later, the president declared to the public that the U.S. ambassador to Poland had been instructed to resume talks with Beijing's ambassador to Poland.[128]

Nevertheless, the Eisenhower administration still did not believe that the ambassadorial talks would persuade the Chinese Communists to retreat—not even to achieve a reasonable *quid pro quo*. An intelligence analysis on the possible outcome of the talks explicitly asserted that Communist China would go nowhere because "there is no indication in the statement that Peiping's position in discussions of the Taiwan Strait situation would be in any respect different from the position it took in the Geneva Ambassadorial talks."[129] Dulles also thought that it was a "fair guess" that the Chinese Communists would not change their positions. "The talks," he estimated, "might then break off or we might then get down to realities, although past experience inspired little hope that we would get beyond the old Communist jargon and stonewalling."[130]

Without much hope, administration officials decided to pursue a no-compromise policy toward the ambassadorial negotiations. One concern was that any compromise would damage U.S. prestige among its allies and friends. "If by our action we were to give the world the impression that we were afraid of the Communists and were falling back in the face of their threat," Dulles explained to British ambassador Sir Harold Caccia on 12 September, "the whole free world defense structure in the Far East would collapse."[131] Another concern, as many U.S. officials in Taiwan expressed it, was that the KMT would certainly not cooperate with any deal that the United States might make with the Chinese Communists.[132] Probably because of these concerns, the Joint

---

128. Telephone call by Robertson, 6 September 1968, Dulles Papers, Telephone Conversation Series, Box 9, Eisenhower Library; Statement at the White House, 6 September 1958, ibid.; Eisenhower's address of September 4 was referred to in Joint Strategic Survey Council's report to JCS, 5 September 1958, CCS 381 Formosa (11–8–48), Section 39, Records of the JCS, Box 147, RG 218.

129. Cumming to Dulles, 6 September 1958, General Records, Box 3924, SD793.00/9–658.

130. Minutes, State-Defense meeting, 12 September 1958, General Records, Box 3924, SD793.00/9–1258.

131. State Department memorandum, 12 September 1958, General Records, Box 3925, SD793.00/9–1285.

132. Drumwright to Dulles, 7 September 1958, General Records, Box 3924, SD793.00/9–758; memorandum of conversation of Dulles and George Yeh, 13 September 1958, ibid., Box 3925, SD793.00/9–1358.

Chiefs stressed as their proposed guidelines for the negotiations "not to agree to commence negotiation until a cease-fire has been effected; not to agree to a reduction of military strength in the Taiwan Strait area pending results of the negotiation; to maintain the principle of inseparability of territory presently held by the Republic of China; . . . not to [agree upon] any arrangements which would prejudice the rights of the Republic of China."[133] Apparently, the U.S. insistence on the return of the status quo in the Strait was far from what the PRC expected to achieve. As a result, the ambassadorial talks, as Robertson told Dulles, were "getting into the frustrating ruts of the Geneva talks."[134]

Although it adopted a no-compromise policy at the diplomatic level, the administration wanted to restrict any military activities that might be too provocative. KMT actions such as air offensives against the mainland artillery fields, leaflet raids, and interference with shipping and overflights would be unacceptable as far as U.S. political and diplomatic positions were concerned.[135] They also felt that the U.S. convoy activities were potentially provocative. J. Graham Parsons told Dulles that it might be provocative to convoy up to the three-mile limit, which he thought at least left the Chinese Communists "a plausible protest before world opinion for resuming fire." Parsons recommended that the United States cancel all escort activities, allow "no U.S. vessels or planes . . . within twenty miles of the China coast," and persuade the KMT "that the supply mission would not carry military equipment but only food, medical supplies and other necessities."[136] Pentagon strategists, however, worried that without U.S. naval escorts, the KMT resupply efforts would be almost impossible. They were also afraid that once the United States quit escorting the convoys, the morale of the KMT forces on the islands would plummet. So the Joint Chiefs argued that "largely for psychological reasons, . . . the convoy should continue at the level of 300 tons per

133. Joint Chiefs of Staff to Wilson, "Possible Negotiations with the Chinese Communists," enclosed in JSC report, 15 September 1958, CCS 381 Formosa (11–8–48), Section 39, Records of the JCS, Box 148, RG 218.

134. Robertson to Dulles, 25 September 1958, General Records, Box 3925, SD793.00/9–2558.

135. Dulles to Drumwright, 7 September 1958, General Records, Box 3924, SD793.00/9–758; Parsons to Dulles, 7 September 1958, ibid., Box 3976, SD794.A5/9–758; Chief of Naval Operations (CNO) to CINCPACFLT, 8 September 1958, CCS 381 Formosa (11–8–48), Section 38, Records of the JCS, Box 148, RG 218; Parsons to Herter, 19 September 1958, General Records, Box 3925, "Taiwan Crisis: Where Do We Go From Here?" SD793.00/9–1858.

136. Memorandum by Parsons, 7 September 1958, General Records, Box 3576, SD794A.5/9–758; Parsons to Herter, 19 September 1958, General Records, Box 3925, "Taiwan Crisis: Where Do We Go From Here?" SD793.00/9–1828.

day."[137] Dulles also found it necessary to continue U.S. escort activity and supported the JCS proposal.[138]

Washington officials knew that the KMT would not easily go along with a policy of caution. There was a possibility that the Chinese Nationalists might undertake a unilateral counteroffensive or large-scale retaliation against mainland targets. In mid-September, American officials in Taiwan began to suspect that the Nationalists were "planning something big." Examining the military potential and objectives of the KMT, the Operations Coordinating Board in Washington also considered it likely that the KMT might act boldly.[139] Eisenhower was also very concerned. He complained to his national security aides that the State Department seemed to be "doing nothing to convert Chiang to flexibility." Probably under this pressure, Dulles felt it imperative to do something "to place the Nationalist force in defensible terrain, . . . and to induce better [Nationalist] understanding of the military realities."[140] Dulles then instructed Ambassador Drumwright to keep reminding Chiang that the United States opposed any unilateral offensive against the mainland.[141] In late September, when Chiang planned to attack the mainland in retaliation for extensive shelling of Dadan and Erdan, two small islands near Jinmen, U.S. naval officials immediately warned him of the futility of the action and reiterated U.S. opposition.[142]

By early October, the Eisenhower administration's general policy lines had become clear: at the diplomatic level, it maintained a tough attitude of no concessions; at the military, it restricted its commitment to conventional and nonprovocative acts. Believing that the Chinese Communists would not escalate the crisis, Washington decision

137. Minutes, State-Defense meeting, 12 September 1958, General Records, Box 3925, SD793.00/9–1258; minutes, State-JCS meeting, 20 September 1958, ibid., SD793.00/9–2058.

138. Minutes, State-JCS meeting, 20 September 1958, General Records, Box 3925, SD793.00/9–2058. Also see telephone call to Arthur H. Dean, 25 September 1958, Dulles Papers, Telephone Conversation Series, Box 9, Eisenhower Library; telephone call to Richard M. Nixon, 25 September 1958, ibid.

139. Navy telegram 3509, 14 September 1958, Department of State, Office of Chinese Affairs Records; Drumwright to Dulles, 15 September 1958, 611.93, ibid.; Navy telegrams 5705, 5728, CINCPAC to JCS, 22 September 1958, ibid.

140. Memorandum of conversation with the president, 11 September 1958, Dulles Papers, White House Memorandum Series, Box 7, "Meetings with the President, July-December, 1958," Eisenhower Library; telephone call to the president at Newport, 22 September 1958, Telephone Conversation Series, Box 13, ibid.; minutes, State-Defense meeting, 20 September 1958, General Records, Box 3925, SD793.00/9–2058.

141. Memorandum of conversation of Dulles and George Yeh, 13 September 1958, General Records, Box 3925, SD793.00/9–1358.

142. Navy telegram 6154, CINCPAC to JCS, 23 September 1958, Department of State, Office of Chinese Affairs Records; Navy telegram 6165, COMTAIWANDEFCOM to CINCPAC, 25 September 1958, ibid., Navy telegram 7567, 27 September 1958, ibid..

makers in effect expected that maintaining both diplomatic and military pressure would somehow deter the Chinese Communists from seizing the offshore islands and compel them to cease the shelling—although not many people in the administration had ever clearly distinguished between the two objectives.

At the same time, the Chinese leadership also reconsidered its policy toward the Taiwan question and the offshore islands in particular. In assessing what the United States might do next, Mao Zedong considered three possibilities. First, the United States might simply continue its military commitment to the offshore islands in order to achieve an eventual de facto cease-fire. Second, it could compel Chiang Kai-shek to withdraw from the offshore islands in exchange for a long-term U.S. commitment to the defense of Taiwan. And third, the United States, if it failed to persuade Chiang to withdraw, might even forcibly remove the KMT forces from the islands to Taiwan. Mao worried that either of the last two possibilities would lead to the realization of two Chinas, which would render the prospect of removing U.S. military threat in the Taiwan area indefinitely remote. Further, Mao asserted, to let the United States "disengage from the troublesome" offshore islands would in effect enable it to strengthen its military position in the Taiwan Strait. He also believed that capturing the offshore islands would mean their loss as a convenient instrument of China's "tension policy" to compel the United States to respect the Beijing government and to prevent Washington's permanent control of Taiwan. Mao therefore decided that it would be wise to tie both the United States and the KMT down on these small islands, which "will make it easier for us to solve the problem of Taiwan, Jinmen, and Mazu once and for all in the future."[143] When the CMC informed the Fujian Military Command of Mao's instruction to decrease the artillery assault on Jinmen, the field commanders did not understand why Chairman Mao made such a decision. They calculated that the KMT defense on Jinmen was so severely devastated that it could not sustain itself for long.[144]

Indeed, the Chinese leaders had given up on taking the offshore islands in the near future, but they insisted on decreasing military activities against Jinmen gradually, expecting that the United States would hang back. On 6 October, Mao announced a unilateral seven-day cease-fire.[145] In addition, the CCP leaders used their propaganda

---

143. Mao's instructions to the Fujian Military Command, 5 October 1958, cited in *DDZGJSGZ* 1:409–10.

144. *Ye Fei Memoirs*, pp. 665–66.

145. Mao, "A Message to Our Compatriots," 6 October 1958, in *MJSWXNBB*, pp. 365–66.

network to repeat messages to the Eisenhower administration about Chinese intentions to de-escalate the crisis. Stressing that the cease-fire was only temporary, an editorial in *Renmin Ribao* in early October suggested that whether China resumed the bombardment would depend on the United States, but it also made it clear that China's cease-fire was not "a trick" prior to a larger offensive.[146]

The Chinese leaders were not disappointed when the Eisenhower administration ordered U.S. convoy activity halted. Beijing then proclaimed on 13 October, the last day of its seven-day cease-fire, that the PLA would hold its fire for another two weeks, but "if the United States resumes its escort of the KMT into the Jinmen area, the interdiction will resume immediately."[147] Nevertheless, as the Taiwan Strait quietened down, the CCP leadership began to stress that it would never accept any solutions that could result in two Chinas. Both Zhou Enlai and Vice-Premier Chen Yi, then in charge of foreign affairs, expressed China's position that the United States had to withdraw from the Taiwan Strait before there could be a peaceful solution to the Taiwan question. They implied that anything short of this, such as a reduction of KMT force ratios or demilitarization of the offshore islands, would not be acceptable.[148]

Up to this point, Beijing's willingness to relax tension were manifest; however, the Chinese leaders were still uncertain as to how the United States might respond. On 20 October, Dulles announced that he would visit Taiwan. The CCP leadership decided to resume shelling Jinmen. Although the action was based on an excuse that one U.S. escort vessel had ventured near the island on 19 October, it was in fact an attempt to pressure Dulles by reminding him that the crisis was not yet over. What came out of Dulles's visit, however, was encouraging news to the Beijing authorities. Dulles announced that the KMT would renounce the use of force against the mainland and that the United States was willing to talk with the PRC government over the Taiwan question. The Chinese leaders immediately responded by announcing that the PLA would bombard the offshore islands only on even dates

146. Editorial, "Let Us See How They React," *Renmin Ribao*, 6 October 1958, reprinted in *Xinhua Yuebao*, October 1958, pp. 19–20.

147. An announcement by the Ministry of Foreign Affairs, *Renmin Ribao*, 8 October 1958, reprinted in *Xinhua Yuebao*, October 1958, p. 16; Peng Dehuai, "Order for Another Two-Week Cease-Fire on Jinmeng," ibid., 13 October 1958, p. 16.

148. "Premier Zhou Talks with Six Japanese Delegates on the Taiwan Question," *Renmin Ribao*, 8 October 1958, reprinted in *Xinhua Yuebao*, October 1958, pp. 10–17; Vice-Premier Chen Yi's speech at the Celebration of East Germany's National Day, ibid., 8 October 1958, pp. 18–19; editorial, "No Talks on Cease-Fire: Disengage as Soon as Possible," ibid., 11 October 1958, pp. 19–20; Xinhua Press Agency commentary, "The U.S. Insists on Aggressive Policy and the 'Two-Chinas' Conspiracy," ibid., 8 October 1958, pp. 20–22.

and would not target airfields, seaports, or vessels, but still on the condition of no U.S. convoying.[149] Apparently, the CCP authorities believed that their policy of "tension" had worked and probably would work in the future with the United States.

Communist China's 6 October cease-fire resulted in at least temporary relief in Washington. Two days later, Dulles met with his aides to "discuss future moves in the Taiwan Strait." Assistant Secretary of State for Policy Planning Gerald C. Smith proposed that the United States should induce the KMT to evacuate the offshore islands. The Chinese Communists, he asserted, might now return to the *status quo ante* in the belief that world opinion would now shift in favor of the PRC. Smith proposed letting the Communists have the offshore islands, but putting "into effect the . . . two-China policy, which is abhorrent to Peiping." Dulles, however, did not like the idea, because he believed that "any loss or retreat from the offshores, [from] even Da Tan [Dadan] and Er Tan [Erdan], would be played up as a retreat" and damage the Nationalists.[150]

In effect, the Eisenhower administration was in a dilemma. On the one hand, the political pressure from the allies and the American public increasingly criticized U.S. "overreactions" to threats against the offshore islands and would only accept the defense of Taiwan and the Penghu. On the other, Chiang stubbornly opposed abandoning the offshore islands and accepting the two-Chinas concept.[151] The Eisenhower administration decided to reduce the KMT garrison on the offshore islands. On 7 October, Eisenhower instructed Dulles to make it clear to Chiang that the United States *might* assist the KMT troops to carry out its return policy in the event of internal riots on the mainland *if* the KMT would reduce its forces on the offshore islands now. The president explained to Dulles that this was "a tactical approach" to induce Chiang's acceptance.[152] At a State Department meeting on 18 October, the secretary of state tried to convince his aides that the

---

149. Peng Dehuai, "The Order to Resume Fire on Jinmen and Its Sea Area," *Renmin Ribao*, 20 October 1958, reprinted in *Xinhua Yuebao*, October 1958, pp. 48–49, and "Another Message to Our Taiwanese Compatriots," ibid., 25 October 1958, p. 49. Also see *DDZGJSGZ* 1:414–17.

150. Minutes, State Department meeting, 8 October 1958, General Records, Box 3926, SD793.00/10–858.

151. Memorandum of conversation, 23 September 1958, Dulles Papers, White House Memorandum Series, Box 7, "Meetings with the President, July–December 1958 <6>," Eisenhower Library; memorandum of conversation with the president, 30 September 1958, Eisenhower Papers, Whitman-DDE-Diary, Box 22, "Staff notes, September 1958," Eisenhower Library; minutes, State Department meeting, 8 October 1958, General Records, Box 3926, SD793.00/10–858.

152. Eisenhower to Dulles, 7 October 1958, Eisenhower Papers, Whitman-DDE-Diary, Box 22, "DDE dictates, October 1958," Eisenhower Library.

president's solution was the only way to retain domestic support and secure Chiang's cooperation.[153]

Pentagon strategists backed this idea with the understanding that military deterrence in the Strait would not be weakened. They agreed that this proposal was a good strategy for avoiding the concentration of KMT forces on the small islands, which might become a "big military liability" for the United States. General Twining recommended having Chiang renounce the use of force as a way of returning to the mainland unless an anti-Communist revolution occurred there. The administration seemed unanimously to have accepted the idea of inducing the KMT to withdraw part of its forces from the offshore islands and to renounce the use of force in effecting the return to the mainland. In return, the United States would further strengthen the KMT military forces, particularly their amphibious lift capability.[154] The objective was to reinforce military counterthreats in the Taiwan Strait by concentrating the KMT forces on Taiwan. Administration officials in particular calculated that the increase of the KMT amphibious lift capability would suggest to the Chinese Communists that the KMT could not only resupply and reinforce the offshore islands but also that the KMT forces were increasingly prepared to attack the mainland in the event of Communist expansion in Korea or Southeast Asia.[155]

Eisenhower sent Dulles to Taiwan to ensure that the Chinese Nationalists understood this policy. Dulles went to Taiwan despite the resumption of Chinese Communist shelling of Jinmen on 20 October; and, after a three-day conference, with a promise to increase U.S. military assistance to the KMT, Dulles successfully convinced Chiang to renounce the use of force in his return policy and to agree to remove fifteen to twenty thousand soldiers from Jinmen and Mazu.[156] This, in effect, paved the way toward a gradual relaxation of the military conflict in the Taiwan Strait.

Still, although interests in the area appeared to be more clearly defined, the entire structure and situation of the Sino-American confrontation there remained unchanged, given the garrison of eighty thousand on the offshore islands, the increased U.S. commitment to

153. Minutes, State Department meeting, 10 October 1958, General Records, Box 3926, SD793.00/10–1058.

154. Ibid.

155. Personal note by Dulles, 13 October 1958, Dulles Papers, personal files, Seeley Mudd Library, Princeton University; JCS 2118/123, "Force-level Requirements on the Offshore Islands <U>," 22 December 1958, p. 958, CCS 381 Formosa (11–8–48), Section 40, Records of the JCS, Box 148, RG 218.

156. Minutes, State-Defense meeting, 20 October 1958, p. 6, General Records, Box 3926, SD793.00/10–1058; JCS to Wilson, 27 October 1958, pp. 963–70, CCS 381 Formosa (11–8–48), Section 41, Records of the JCS, Box 148, RG 218.

the defense of Taiwan and the Penghu, and shelling from the mainland every other day.

V

Why did Beijing and Washington confront each other at the risk of war in the Taiwan Strait for the second time, only a few years after the first Strait Crisis? There is no simple answer to this question; nevertheless, each side once again perceived the other as a threat and once again took action to neutralize that threat. Perhaps this pattern can explain the origins of the crisis.

Although Beijing felt an increasing threat in the Taiwan Strait, none of the leaders was certain of how and when that perceived threat would become a reality. Acting upon the "worst case" assumption, the CCP authorities felt it imperative to proceed with a policy of preemption. But this time, they overestimated the opportunity for success and miscalculated the role of belligerency. Mao expected the United States to force Chiang to evacuate Jinmen and Mazu. That, however, turned out to be wishful thinking. Beijing tried to punish the KMT and intimidate the United States. Instead, the United States and Taiwan reacted vigorously, which made large-scale hostilities much more likely.

During this period, Mao saw the socialist camp—particularly with the endorsement of Khrushchev by the Eastern European countries—as much stronger than the capitalist, which, on the contrary, was thought to be full of internal difficulties. But the Taiwan Strait crisis of 1958 marked a turning point in the Sino-Soviet relationship. Mao generally counted on Soviet strategic deterrence in the event of war with the United States, but the Kremlin wanted to incorporate China into its own global defense system in order to place the seemingly reckless Beijing regime under its control. This caused Mao to suspect Khrushchev's intentions. In addition, Beijing's effort to keep the Soviets from interfering in the crisis was counterproductive in the long term. The mutual distrust and estrangement that developed weakened the Sino-Soviet alliance considerably.

After visiting the United States in September 1959, Khrushchev abruptly decided to visit Beijing. On 2 October, he and Mao talked for seven hours but could hardly agree with each other. Khrushchev insisted that China's bombardment of the offshore islands had "created a big problem for the Soviet Union, because while the United States clearly supported Chiang Kai-shek, we then announced to support you, thus leaving the impression that we were initiating general war against the United States." Khrushchev demanded that the CCP renounce the use of force against Taiwan and recognize its independence. Khrushchev's attitude further convinced Mao and other leaders that Moscow intended to accommodate U.S. imperialism at China's expense. The CCP leaders began to realize that China could not rely any longer on the Soviet extended deterrence unless it was prepared to sacrifice its own sovereignty and national interests.[157]

Actually aiming at a limited and flexible objective in shelling Jinmen, Beijing authorities had made it look as though they were seeking a much broader purpose—the "liberation" of Taiwan. This apparent confusion put China in an unfavorable position. Neutrals were worried about Beijing's challenge to the status quo in the Strait. Even the Soviets feared that if Beijing leaders really meant what they said, a general war in the Far East had a high probability. Further, even if Washington did not believe that Beijung aimed at attacking Taiwan at that point, the administration could exploit support either from the American public or from its allies for vigorous U.S. reactions simply by condemning Beijing's aggressive intentions.

The Eisenhower administration was no better at managing this crisis. After the first Strait crisis, it seemed to have believed firmly that Communist China was and would continue to be the major threat to U.S. security interests in Asia. There is reason to argue that Washington's understanding of an ongoing "semi-war" between the United States and China was inadequate. The Eisenhower administration regarded the reinforcement of U.S. military deterrence in the area as the only reasonable response to the Communist Chinese challenge. But what if the KMT authorities had managed to project U.S. deterrence into a threat of offensive operations? Evidently, Washington did little—or could do little—to prevent the KMT from doing exactly that. The result was that Beijing saw all U.S. commitments to the defense of Taiwan and the offshore islands as evidence of U.S. intent to back the KMT fight to regain the mainland. Consequently, U.S. efforts to strengthen military deterrence in the Taiwan Strait had misleading effects on the Chinese Communists, who took preparation of counterthreats for evidence of aggression.

Clearly, at the outbreak of the crisis, U.S. officials mistook Communist China's anxiety to defend its border for an aggressive strategy backed by Moscow. It is now clear that the Soviet Union hardly played any role and China's actions had nothing to do with a "Khrushchev-Mao conspiracy" or an "international Communist scheme." But even

---

157. *DDZGWJ*, pp. 115–16. A few years later, Khrushchev told the Chinese to destroy the records on his meeting with Mao on 2 October 1958. The Chinese refused firmly because it was "evidence of Khrushchev's conspiracy to control China" (ibid., pp. 115–16).

when Washington was sure that the Communist Chinese bombardment was for a limited objective, the influence of the established "domino" or "prestige" concept interfered with the management of the crisis.

Responding to the Communist Chinese challenge, Washington miscalculated the effect of "tough diplomacy." U.S. officials believed that an image of no-compromise at the diplomatic level would finally bring Beijing to terms. They calculated that a U.S. effort to stop the PRC replacing the KMT in the United Nations would serve that purpose. They never understood the mentality of Chinese Communist leaders who were extremely proud of themselves as revolutionaries and took "face" and self-pride very seriously. Chinese leaders treated U.S. diplomatic pressure with obvious emotion. Clearly, the rigidity of U.S. officials produced not retreat, but even harder feelings in Beijing.

[9]

Misperception and Mutual Deterrence

The Sino-American confrontation of 1949–58 was characterized by mutual deterrence. Each side perceived the other as the aggressor—potential or immediate—and itself as defender. Neither side, however, realized that it could be misperceiving the other's motives.

Neither side had the aggressive intentions that the other feared. The Truman and Eisenhower administrations never intended to invade Communist China, whether from Korea, the Taiwan Strait, or Indochina. Washington's decision to dispatch the Seventh Fleet was made to neutralize the Taiwan Strait. Suggestions to expand the Korean hostilities into China were made more to inhibit Chinese intervention than from any serious intention to invade that country, and even that plan had gone nowhere. The same thing happened later in Indochina and the Taiwan Strait. U.S. military involvement was escalated to deter Chinese intervention and to prevent these areas from falling under Beijing's control. Washington consistently restrained the Chinese Nationalists from taking offensive action against the mainland rather than encouraged them to do so.

The CCP leadership, after seizing power in China, had never intended to upset the status quo in Asia by force for the purpose of eliminating U.S. influence there or spearheading a Kremlin-led Communist expansionist movement. "Leaning" toward the Soviet Union was a way to defend China's security. Military intervention in Korea was an effort to restore the status quo rather than to assist the North Koreans in liberating the whole peninsula. The PRC provided the Viet Minh with military assistance to secure a buffer zone along a vulnerable border rather than to expand international communism into that region.

Despite having never given up the goal of liberating Taiwan, the CCP leadership regarded the Taiwan issue as an extension of China's civil war rather than as an international conflict. From Beijing's perspective, a military assault against the offshore islands or even Taiwan was never defined as a challenge to the status quo.[1] Nevertheless, Washington and Beijing constantly practiced deterrence against each other both in immediate encounters and long-term defensive measures.

These efforts at mutual deterrence made it difficult to resolve bilateral conflicts. China and the United States learned little from each other during these confrontations. On the contrary, each side's defensive actions seem to have intensified the other's perception of its adversary's hostility. The Chinese leaders never fully understood that U.S. military commitments in the Taiwan Strait, the Korean peninsula, and French Indochina were defensive. U.S. officials never understood that China's alliance with the Soviet Union, its armed intervention in Korea, its military assistance to the Viet Minh, and its artillery assaults against the offshore islands were motivated by a deep fear of U.S. invasion. This pattern of confrontation never escalated into general war, but was sufficiently deeply rooted to be sustained for another fifteen years after the second offshore-islands crisis.

I

Both short- and long-term consequences of Sino-American mutual deterrence are apparent, but contemporary deterrence theory provides no satisfactory analytical framework for explaining how and why the two countries evolved this relationship.[2] I believe that it is possible, using new historical sources, to refine deterrence theory to make it more relevant to this problem.

Sino-American confrontation during the 1950s grew out of the earliest manifestations of the Cold War in Asia. East Asian regional instability in the post-World War II period almost guaranteed Sino-American hostility; in retrospect, the Yalta settlements for post-war

1. When I interviewed Wang Bingnan in October 1989, he told me that the Ministry of Foreign Affairs had never been responsible for the issue of Taiwan. Throughout the 1950s, the East China Military Command was fully responsible for the liberation of Taiwan, and was under direct control of Mao and the Central Military Commission.

2. In recent debate about deterrence theories, neither defenders of rational deterrence theory nor its critics satisfactorily discuss mutual deterrence or deterrence from both perspectives. See Achen and Snidal, "Rational Deterrence Theory and Comparative Case Studies"; George and Smoke, "Deterrence and Foreign Policy"; Jervis, "Rational Deterrence"; Lebow and Stein, "Rational Deterrence Theory"; and George W. Downs, "The Rational Deterrence Debate," *World Politics* 31 (January 1989): 225–38.

East Asia had little chance to survive. To end the civil war in China, the United States tried to achieve a coalition government in order to guarantee U.S. influence in that country. But heavy responsibilities in Europe, the feeble character of Chiang's regime, and the dynamism of the Chinese Communists rendered America's intentions irrelevant. The Truman administration then wanted to disengage from support-ing Chiang. But U.S. domestic politics prevented doing this openly and promptly. Continued U.S. support to the Chinese Nationalists convinced the CCP leaders that the U.S.-Chiang connection would never cease. Believing that an enemy's friend was not trustworthy, the CCP leadership decided to "lean over" to the Soviet Union, America's number-one opponent. The establishment of a Communist China and the Sino-Soviet military alliance thus tilted the balance of power in East Asia, heightening suspicions on both sides.

Mutual suspicions soon paved the way for bilateral hostilities when the Korean War broke out. In the spring of 1950, neither Beijing nor Washington anticipated fighting each other directly over Korea; but in the end they did just that. Optimism growing out of military successes lured the UN forces across the Thirty-Eighth parallel to "roll back" Communism. A strong sense of insecurity and determination to stand up against western powers drove Beijing authorities to send a large number of troops across the Yalu River to "teach the U.S. aggressors a bloody lesson." Despite the fact that the Chinese "volunteers" and the UN troops fought a standstill in Korea, the Chinese leaders gained confidence in confronting the United States. Whenever they perceived a potential—often uncertain—danger of U.S. military action in Asia, they would challenge it. They thus felt it not only desirable but also justifiable to initiate crises in Indochina and the Taiwan Strait. The Ko-rean War also caused a catalytic reaction in the U.S. policy toward East Asia. It forced the United States to commit itself to a forward defense of the Asian rimland, and thus to abandon plans for merely defending the islands and sea lanes of the Western Pacific. Washington officials came to view Communist China as the most dangerous enemy in Asia. Consequently, the bitter legacy of Korea added fuel to the flames of Sino-American confrontation. Distrustful of and hostile toward each other, both Washington and Beijing felt a strong compulsion to view incidents suggesting a potential danger as important tests of strength and of their resolve to defend their respective security interests.

Efforts by regional leaders to manipulate China and the United States contributed significantly to the Sino-American confrontation. Both Chiang Kai-shek and Syngman Rhee sought to defend and ex-pand their political positions. Chiang not only wanted to survive on Taiwan, but he also expected to regain control of the mainland. Rhee intended to rule all of Korea. Both were aware that they could accomplish their objectives only with U.S. support. To this end, the KMT and the ROK tired hard to form strong military and political ties with Washington. They succeeded in committing the United States to defend Taiwan and South Korea and, more important, they created the impression that Washington would support their military actions against the Communists. On the Communist side, much the same thing happened with Kim Il-sung and Ho Chi Minh. As soon as the CCP succeeded in China, the North Koreans and the Vietnamese Communists began to work on obtaining China's (as well as Russia's) support. Regarding Communist China as the more important ally in Asia, both North Korea and the Viet Minh sought to convince the world that their struggles for national liberation were directly linked to that of the People's Republic. Therefore, Beijing leaders believed that Washington was directing Chiang, Rhee, and even the French in Indochina to initiate hostilities. At the same time U.S. officials believed that Kim and Ho were implementing Beijing's (as well as Moscow's) expansionist plans.

In tracing the origins of the Sino-American confrontation, no one can ignore the effect of the post–World War II East-West conflict, China's civil war, and the outbreak of fighting in Korea.[3]

II

History, though, does not reveal its secrets easily. Mutual misperceptions and miscalculations made the Sino-American conflict the result of a remarkable accumulation, over time and space, of erroneous judgments by each side about the other.

Any nation's understanding of an adversary's intentions, of its own responses, and probably outcomes reflects the mental processes of its leaders. These processes, however, often embody both reality and distortion. Neither U.S. nor Chinese policymakers succeeded in avoiding distorted judgments. Why? My proposition is that culture-bound perceptions of and behavior by each country confused important aspects of their strategic thinking. Being "culture-bound" is the inability to put aside one's cultural attitude and imaginatively respond to perceived

3. Standard studies on the Cold War in Asia include Tang Tsou, *America's Failure in China;* Akira Iriye, *The Cold War in Asia: A Historical Introduction* (Englewood Cliffs, N.J., 1974); Kalicki, *The Pattern of Sino-American Crises;* Warren I. Cohen, *America's Response to China: An Interpretative History of Sino-American Relations,* 2d ed. (New York, 1980); John G. Stoessinger, *Nations in Darkness: China, Russia and America,* 4th ed. (New York, 1986); Tucker, *Patterns in the Dust,* Harding and Yuan, *Sino-American Relations;* and Chang, *Friends and Enemies: The United States, China and the Soviet Union.*

challenges from the perspectives of the other.[4] Policymakers in China and the United States had studied each other very little. Each group neglected the possibility that cultural differences between the two countries might be reflected in very different styles of strategic thinking. No one from either country realized that such differences might lead decision makers, consciously or subconsciously, to evade reality. The unfortunate result was to intensify the predicaments, tensions, and conflicts they feared.

To "know the enemy" is a cardinal and almost universally accepted tenet of strategy. But strategists frequently pay no attention to the danger of "knowing" the enemy in an ethnocentric fashion. Cultural differences are manifest and identifiable. They include, as Ken Booth puts it, "different modes of thought, implicit and explicit behavioral patterns and social habits, identifiable symbols and signals for acquiring and transmitting knowledge, . . . and particular ways of adapting to the environment and solving problems."[5] Since culture is basic to politics, society, and history, it would be a great surprise if culture did not play an important role in shaping strategy.

China and America are nations of distinctively different cultural backgrounds. Geopolitically, China is a land power, whereas the United States has long seen itself as a maritime state. China has struggled against constant foreign invasions over the past two centuries, but America has been relatively free from such dangers. The military and strategic thought of Sun Tze has dominated Chinese thinking about war for centuries, whereas American strategists are more familiar with the Clausewitzian "political philosophy of war." Few would deny that, as Booth gently puts it, "individual qualities of intellect and character occur more frequently and are more highly valued in one nation than the other."[6]

The problem was not that the United States and China had different cultures, but rather that each nation's leaders ignored that fact. This incomplete understanding proved critical at several points of Sino-American confrontation between 1949 and 1958.

Defining Security Interests

China and the United States shared no common conception of national security interests. There were two important elements in

---

4. Ken Booth, a pioneer of strategic culture studies, uses the term "ethnocentric." See his *Strategy and Ethnocentrism* (New York, 1979), pp. 13–19. I, however, prefer the term "culture-bound."
5. Ibid., p. 14.
6. Ibid., p. 16.

America's geopolitical calculations during the postwar period. First, the United States, as an insular power that had developed very substantially in isolation from the conflicts of Europe, instinctively harbored the belief that security was possible as long as oceanic isolation and sea lines of communications were guaranteed; therefore, the American defense system in the Asia-Pacific region focused largely on opposing any possible adversary's control of the sea.[7] Second, having become a superpower after the war, the United States tended to consider that defending world peace, containing communism, and protecting non-communist countries ware its responsibility. Its role in protecting the "free world" would, in turn, lead its policymakers to regard U.S. prestige as a vital interest. A good example can be seen in Washington's calculations regarding defense of the offshore islands: the United States acted to protect its prestige to the point of risking war over some islands of negligible military value.

By contrast, the Chinese had defined security interests in terms of border security and national autonomy. China's status as a land power, its bitter experience of foreign intervention, and its traditional self-image of being at the center of the universe dictate that the Chinese defense establishment would focus on physical survival and national autonomy. The CCP leaders certainly demonstrated strong nationalistic inclinations. Most of them had been involved in the "May Fourth" movement (a major anti-foreign campaign in the early 1900s) and had fought against Japan. Regarding pre-1949 China as a "semicolony," they felt an intense need to construct a new China free of foreign control and foreign influence. Thus, to the Chinese leaders, national sovereignty is even more important than territorial integrity. Even when they trusted the Soviet Union to protect China's security, Mao and his associates remained alert to the Soviet-Union's growing influence over China's military, economic, and political affairs. The CCP's sensitivity to any possibility of foreign interference, international disdain, and outside control had far-reaching implications.

Neither U.S. officials nor Chinese leaders understood how the other nation formulated its interests. Historical lessons had taught the Chinese leaders that China's coast was vulnerable to foreign invasions. Thus they tended to overreact to perceived threats to China's coastal security. Without understanding why the United States had emphasized a chain-of-islands defense and the security of sea lanes in the Pacific, the Beijing authorities mistook the rearming of Japan, the stationing of U.S. troops in the Philippines, and, later, U.S. military

7. Colin S. Gray, *The Geopolitics of Super Power* (Lexington, Ky., 1988), p. 58. Also see Gaddis, *The Long Peace*, pp. 72–103.

commitments to Korea, Taiwan, and French Indochina as indications of a plot against China first and the Soviet Union second. With the historical role of British Royal Navy in mind, the Chinese leaders regarded American efforts to maintain bases and sea-lane communications in the Pacific as preparations for offensive action against the Asian continent.

On the other hand, U.S. strategists could not understand why the Chinese should be so worried about China's coast. From their perspective, China's security should be most vulnerable in the north, given Russia's long-standing desire to dominate Xinjiang (Sinkiang) and North China (Manchuria). When the PRC kept challenging the United States along China's periphery in the east and southeast, Washington officials assumed that the Chinese Communists were spearheading a Kremlin-led communist expansion into the rest of Asia. Korea was a good example. At first, Washington did not anticipate Chinese intervention because China's interests did not seem to be involved there. But the Chinese did intervene, and U.S. officials quickly concluded that the Soviet Union was behind their actions.

Perceiving External Threats

Neither Beijing nor Washington paid sufficient attention to how the other perceived external threat. Nations of different power positions and historical experience tend to see threats differently. Having twice intervened in world wars to stop aggression, the United States after 1945 took the protection of international peace as its primary responsibility. One strong element in American thinking about global security was what later became known as the "domino" theory. It was the fear of political and psychological damage to major interests if peripheral interests were lost to opponents. In Asia, this view became evident with U.S. intervention to save South Korea in order to avoid losing Japan. It then became an inescapable equation that, as John Lewis Gaddis puts it: "If the loss of South Korea would be psychologically devastating, why not South Vietnam? Why not Quemoy and Matsu?"[8]

The Chinese leaders, however, seemed never to have understood the "domino" logic in U.S. threat perception. The CCP news network often asked why the United States was reacting so vigorously when its own territory was by no means at stake. In Chinese eyes, a rearmed

8. Cited from John Lewis Gaddis, "Introduction: The Evolution of Containment," in *Containing the Soviet Union: A Critique of U.S. Policy,* ed. Terry L. Deibel and John Lewis Gaddis (Washington, D.C., 1987), pp. 2–3.

Japan would only increase the danger of hostilities in East Asia and the Pacific, which threatened both China and the United States, but Korea and Indochina under communist rule did not threaten U.S. security by any "reasonable" standard.

The Chinese leaders, sensitive to border security, tended to perceive U.S. intentions as hostile on the basis of its military presence. As they saw it, any increase in U.S. military commitments in the Asia-Pacific region entailed an increase in the threat to China's territory. That was why they were so apprehensive about the U.S. Marines in Qingdao in 1949, the interposition of the Seventh Fleet in the Taiwan Strait, the UN advance toward the Yalu, the possibility that the United States might replace the French in Indochina, the prospect of a U.S.-Taiwan alliance treaty in 1954, and the development of U.S. tactical nuclear missiles on Taiwan in 1958. U.S. officials did not understood this emphasis in the CCP's threat identification. They often wondered why the Chinese Communists should be worried about the presence of U.S. armed forces that were merely for defensive purposes. They failed to see that Beijing authorities mistook the U.S. containment policy in Asia for an effort to encircle China.

Communication and Understanding

According to mass communication theory, effective social communication depends on how much the senders of messages share knowledge and experiences with receivers.[9] China and America share little in this regard, and their leaders know each other only on the basis of very brief, limited contacts. It should not be surprising, then, that Sino-American communication in this period was very much open to errors.

When the policymakers of the two states perceived each other, they started with national self-images. Probably the most rigid self-image was that held by imperial China, which the CCP leaders evidently inherited: the conception that foreign barbarians were by no means trustworthy. Based on their limited experience in dealing with the Americans, the CCP leaders came to believe that they should not trust the "Meiguolao" (American devils). They claimed that Marshall had cheated them in his mediation effort in 1946, that Truman had lied on the Taiwan question in early 1950, that MacArthur had tried to fool them in Korea, and that Eisenhower and Dulles had conspired to

9. For this point, I benefited from discussion with my wife, Chen Ni, who has a Ph.D. in international communications. She recommended David K. Berlo's *Process of Communication: An Introduction to Theory and Practice* (New York, 1960), pp. 106–31.

occupy Taiwan. Mao had clearly concluded by the spring of 1949 that the United States, as a new imperialist nation, was unpredictable and untrustworthy. (It is interesting, that Sino-Soviet relations deteriorated in a similar manner. Mao never truly trusted Stalin and was even more suspicious of Khrushchev. Neither Stalin nor Khrushchev ever trusted Mao.)

Traditionally, despite their admiration of Chinese culture, Americans had come to regard the Chinese as wards in their own country, and as heathens to be civilized. They tenaciously refused to see that nationalism and communism in China had been cast in the same anti-Western mold. The failure of Marshall mission, the myth of the "loss" of China, and finally Chinese intervention in Korea had strengthened America's conviction that China under communist rule was a hostile and menacing power. Unable to understand Communist Chinese nationalist feelings and anti-foreign intentions, U.S. officials usually ended up vacillating between self-deception and disenchantment.

The Nature of Policymaking

Alongside the role of self-image, ignorance of differences in decision-making systems blocked effective mutual understanding. The American political system is based on pluralism. Policy making concerning national security and the allocation of resources has always involved congressional debate, bureaucratic struggle, and public discussion. Very often, the executive authorities do not have to follow—and do not—what Congress proposes. By contrast, China's centuries-old hierarchical processes have survived into the Communist era. Particularly with regard to national security policies, only a small core of key decision makers are involved, usually with the top man having the final authority. Chinese leaders *were* relatively free from domestic challenge and had always controlled the mass media.

These differences were obvious, but neither the Chinese leaders nor Washington officials seem to have acknowledged them. Each tended to assess the other's decision making on its own terms. The CCP leadership frequently took public statements by pro-Chiang senators and congressmen, China lobbyists, and such public figures as General MacArthur and Admiral Cooke as reflections of official U.S. policy. Announcements from the White House were seen as a "smoke screen." Moreover, the Chinese never distinguished between the various "audiences" to which Washington policymakers had to appeal. They interpreted administration messages aimed at the American public as having been designed for their own consumption (for example, Acheson's White Paper, Eisenhower's "honorable peace," the rhetoric

[276]

of "rolling back the Communists," and even the Formosa Resolution). Taking U.S. imperialism for granted, the Chinese leaders tended to rule out the possibility that Washington might seek to constrain its allies, or that U.S allies might be able to manipulate the United States in defending their interests. To them, America's dealings with its allies seemed like schemes of aggression and expansion, examples being the deployment of the Seventh Fleet into the Taiwan Strait and the U.S.-Taiwan defense treaty.

In the United States, things went in the opposite direction. Washington officials paid little attention to what the CCP's press, radio, or ranking officials were saying. To them, these comments were just propaganda, and thus not reliable as a means of detecting Beijing's real intentions. Evidently, the Truman administration never took seriously Lu Dingyi's article of 1948 (actually drafted by Mao), Li Tao's announcement of 1949, Nie Rongzhen's talks with Panikkar in late September of 1950, Song Qingling's and Guo Moruo's warning's against U.S. military commitment to the defense of the Taiwan Strait in 1954–55, Peng Dehuai's statements (drafted by Mao) in 1958, and many editorials of *Renmin Ribao* in which the CCP leaders often discussed policy and strategy. U.S. officials were not aware that the Chinese leaders liked to send out messages through public statements. Moreover, always constrained themselves by domestic politics, U.S. policymakers never understood the possibility that China's decision making might have relatively little to do with its domestic problems. A good example was the Truman administration's underestimation of the likelihood of China's intervention in Korea because, as Washington calculated, the Chinese Communists had too many domestic difficulties to intervene in Korea.

III

From a narrowly military point of view, culture-bound concepts of deterrence are not necessarily dysfunctional. The experience of Sino-American mutual deterrence, however, suggests that during the period 1949–58, China and the United States did not share a common calculus of deterrence.

Thinking about War

"Strategic theories have their roots in philosophies of war, which are invariably ethnocentric," Ken Booth points out. "National strategies are the immediate descendants of philosophies of war."[10] American strategists generally accepted the Clausewitzian concept that war was a continuation of politics, and that policymakers would go to war for political interests. The Chinese have other views of war. The most important one is that of the *Sun Tze Bingfa* [Sun Tze's *Art of War*], which in general taught that states would go to war for moral reasons as well as for political interests.[11]

These two strategic traditions evidently influenced the Chinese and American officials. As good students of Sun Tze, Mao and other CCP military leaders tended to judge military conflicts by moral standards. If a state acquired *Dao* (justice or moral strength), it would eventually win; if not, it was doomed to defeat.[12] Mao was not afraid of engaging in the military conflict in Korea because he believed that it was a just war against aggression; nor did he fear possible U.S. nuclear attack because he assumed that any such U.S. action would offend the *Dao* and result in defeat. In the early 1960s, Mao explained: "Who is afraid of whom in today's world? It is the U.S. imperialists who are afraid of the peoples [of the world]. Those who have acquired the 'dao' will have support from the [mass] majority, whereas those who have lost the 'dao' will have no one's support [*dedao duozhu shidao guazhu*]. U.S. imperialism is doomed to defeat. This historical trend is irresistible."[13]

U.S. decision makers, however, did not understand the moral dimension to Chinese thinking about confrontation. In assessing the likelihood of Chinese intervention in Korea, they assumed that no Chinese political interests would be endangered if Manchuria was not attacked; thus, they believed that China would have nothing to gain by pulling the Soviet chestnut out of the fire. Neither did U.S. officials understand why Beijing should support the Viet Minh. They assumed that China's only possible rationale for doing so was to bring Indochina under its control. Judging Chinese intentions only in terms of political interests, Washington decision makers underestimated the weight of moral factors in Chinese military considerations.

---

10. Booth, *Strategy and Ethnocentrism*, p. 73.

11. *Sun Tze Bingfa Xinzhu*, pp. 3–5.

12. Mao was very fond of Sun Tze's *Art of War*. He liked to read it and encouraged others to read it several times (Gong Yuzhi and Xiang Xianzhi, eds., *Mao Zedong De Dushu Shenghuo* [Beijing, 1987], p. 261). Marshal Liu Bocheng, the president of the Chinese Military Academy in the 1950s, held that Sun Tze's *Art of War* should be the main textbook for the course entitled "Science of Campaigns," which he himself taught (General Tao Hanzhang, Yuan *Sun Tze's Art of War: The Modern Chinese Interpretation*, trans. Yuan Shibing [New York: 1987], pp. 8–9).

13. Mao Zedong, *Mao Zhuxi Yulu* (Beijing, 1968), p. 234.

Dealing with Crisis

The American concept of "crisis" differs from the Chinese. Having developed largely in isolation from international rivalries, Americans believed that peace was the normal and universally desired condition of mankind. Washington policymakers thus insisted that since war was abnormal, any conflict that might develop into war should be avoided or resolved.[14]

U.S. strategists also viewed crisis as a dangerous situation and conceived of it in a strictly negative sense. During the period 1948–58, no U.S. president welcomed the outbreak of crises in Asia. Whenever tensions occurred in that region, Washington would attempt either to deter its adversaries from further challenging the status quo or to compel them to back away. American crisis-management methods therefore primarily responded to and aimed at resolving—rather than initiating and escalating—crisis situations. Although the Truman administration decided to send military forces into Korea, that decision was made primarily to localize the conflict and to prevent it from developing into a global war.

The Chinese approach to crisis is different. First, the Chinese tend to view crisis dialectically. The term "crisis" in Chinese stands for a situation [*shi*] embodying both danger [*wei*] and opportunity [*ji*]. Mao Zedong stressed that all crisis situations were dialectical in terms of their strong and weak points, their advantages and disadvantages, their danger and opportunity. He believed that these elements could be transformed into their opposites under certain circumstances.[15] Thus, Mao and other leaders considered any crisis to be both negative and positive, believing that a dangerous situation could be turned to advantage.

Second, the Chinese emphasize grasping "major contradictions" to resolve crisis. Since everything was composed of major and minor factors, Mao taught, "it is always the primary and key factor that is decisive, . . . so one should never be misled by complicated minor factors."[16] According to this logic, it was disadvantageous to strike out in all directions or to fight a war on two or more fronts; it was important to identify the major danger and neglect the minor one. When the CCP seized power in China, its leaders believed that imperialist intervention was the major threat to their rule, not the increase of Soviet influence in China. When UN forces intervened in Korea, Chinese

---

14. Gray, *The Geopolitics of Super Power*, p. 58.
15. Tao, *Sun Tze's Art of War*, pp. 28–29.
16. Ibid., p. 29.

leaders regarded Korea as the primary danger, rather than the Taiwan Strait or Indochina. After the truce in Korea, Taiwan became the most important issue on the CCP's agenda. But Washington officials did not understand the shifting emphasis in the Chinese policies regarding Sino-American tensions.

Third, the Chinese regard the use—not merely the demonstration—of force as an important means of crisis management. Sun Tze taught: "To win one hundred victories in one hundred battles is not the acme of skill. To subdue the enemy without fighting is the supreme excellence." But his principle of field operations stresses taking preemptive action to obtain strategic advantage.[17] Its essence is to take short-term military action [*fabin*] to prevent the enemy from launching general war [*famou*]. Mao and other CCP leaders perfectly understood this principle. Their decision to intervene in Korea, their diplomacy of tension regarding the Taiwan Strait, and Mao's "rope around the neck" concept all reflected this Chinese calculation that short-term belligerency would serve as a means of general deterrence.

Defining Counterthreats

American understanding of counterthreats differs from the Chinese. The United States had been involved in both world wars, the bitterest of modern conflicts. U.S. commanders invariably stressed the importance of modern military technology. They admired a modern navy and an air force equipped with advanced technologies. In calculating deterrence strategy, U.S. strategists tend to regard military killing capacity as the key to deterrence. It was generally accepted that as long as one possessed potent killing power and was politically free to use it to inflict punishment, deterrence would be successfully attained. MacArthur had relied then on superior UN air power to deter the Chinese from intervening militarily in Korea. Eisenhower had stressed the role of nuclear retaliation in preventing the Communists from renewing hostilities in Korea. Washington strategists had three times dispatched the U.S. navy into the Taiwan Strait to deter Beijing from seizing Taiwan and the offshore islands.

The Chinese, however, understand counterthreats in subtler terms. Sun Tze's *Art of War* told of five strategic assets crucial to deterrence. "(1) The Moral Law; (2) Heaven; (3) Earth; (4) The Commander, [and] (5) Method and discipline."[18] In short, proper morale, the best timing, the most favorable positioning, domestic harmony, and the fighters'

---

17. Ibid., p. 15.
18. *Sun Tze Bingfa Xinzhu*, pp. 1–2.

virtues of wisdom, sincerity, benevolence, courage, and discipline are the main components of counterthreats. As a firm believer in Sun Tze, Mao claimed on several occasions that one's success in preventing a war was not determined by military weapons but by the masses who operated them. Although the Chinese leaders recognized the superiority of American weapons, they considered the United States strategically weak in several aspects, including the lack of domestic support, the low morale of its military forces, and an excessively extended defense line. They believed that as long as China demonstrated internal harmony and resolve to resist foreign invasions, the United States would not risk general war against it.

Calculations regarding the utility of nuclear weapons in particular reflected this difference. American strategists believe that the credibility of nuclear deterrence lay in its massive killing capability. But the killing power of these weapons, in the Chinese eyes, is not a decisive factor of deterrence. Sun Tze wrote that "the elements of the art of war are first, the measurement of space; second, the estimation of quantities; third, strategic calculation; fourth, strength comparison; and fifth, chances of victory." As he stressed, the most important factors are land space and population size.[19] Mao followed the same calculation: the United States, even with nuclear weapons, could not conquer China, a country of vast land and huge population. The Chinese leaders thus commented that, even if the United States might kill several million people with its nuclear weapons, it could not seize all of China. They assumed that China's history of always denying final victory to the foreign invader would prevent the United States from using nuclear weapons against China. It is, however, important to note that frequent U.S. exercises in nuclear deterrence seemed gradually to have convinced Mao and other CCP leaders that the atomic bomb was a real tiger. The leaders learned more about nuclear technology and strategy and began to take the U.S. nuclear threat seriously. More important, believing that the bomb was needed to assure China's security, the PRC leadership started building its own nuclear weapons in 1955. Mao made it clear at the enlarged politburo meeting in April 1956 that "in today's world, if you don't want to be bullied by others, we should have atomic bombs by all means."[20]

Calculating Cost and Gain

Chinese and Americans weigh differently the costs and gains of deterrence strategy. American leaders have greater difficulty than

---

19. Ibid., pp. 35–36; and Tao, *Sun Tze's Art of War*, p. 102.
20. Guo Fuwen, "China's Sun," *Zuoping Yu Zhengming*, February 1988, p. 3.

Chinese accepting the human costs of military conflict. Therefore, in defending U.S. security interests, they tend to prefer methods of deterrence—even if they would require huge material costs—to actual fighting that might involve human losses. The strategies of "massive retaliation," "brinkmanship," and "flexible response" reflect this American tradition.

The Chinese, however, differentiate much less than the Americans between human and material costs. Traditional Chinese ideology of warfare clearly encourages the Chinese people to fight and die for a holy and moral cause. The CCP leaders seemed to have consistently believed in the necessity of sacrificing human lives to gain a final victory. Mao in particular stressed the relationships between short-term belligerency and long-term security, and between sacrifice and a general victory. The CCP leaders were thus much less constrained than their American counterparts in taking military actions, because they never had to be seriously concerned about the human sacrifices. They were proud of their courage in confronting American imperialism; they believed that the costs sustained were worthy, given that China had glorified itself by showing no timidity when challenged by a great power.

IV

In the final analysis, each side saw a devil in its foe. Each vividly perceived its own terrible fear of the other, but neither could experience the other's fear or even understand why it should be so nervous. The battleground was thus established for tragic encounters; a spiral of Hobbesian fear was set in motion, creating the Sino-American mutual deterrence relationship.

One must avoid the temptation to exaggerate the role of an explanatory insight, in this case, the effect of culture-bound misperceptions and miscalculations. Nevertheless, the lack of mutual understanding and the uncompromising determination to have things done in their own ways were significant factors in bringing about the mutual deterrence relationship between the United States and the People's Republic of China. National characters and styles do differ in terms of how threats are perceived and strategies calculated, particularly between countries of entirely different cultural backgrounds.

Therefore, I believe, Ken Booth's warning of 1979 is still relevant today: "The construction of a rational strategic model as a tool for thinking about the world is a dangerous distortion. . . . Civilian strategists

[282]

and policy planners need to 'retool' in order to take account of ethno-centric bias."[21] I have demonstrated, I hope, that the pursuit of cultural and strategic relativism might be a liberating experience for both de-terrence theorists and professionals.

21. Booth, *Strategy and Ethnocentrism*, pp. 17–18.

Bibliography

MATERIALS IN CHINESE

Primary Sources

Chen Yun. *Chen Yun Wenxuan: 1926–1949* [Selected Works of Chen Yun: 1926–1949]. Beijing: Renmim Press, 1984.
——. *Chen Yun Wenxuan: 1949–1956* [Selected Works of Chen Yun: 1949–1956]. Jiangsu: Renmim Press, 1984.
Li Xiannian. *Li Xiannian Wenxuan: 1935–1988* [Selected Works of Li Xiannian: 1935–1988]. Beijing: Renmin Press, 1989.
Liu Shaoqi. *Liu Shaoqi Xuanji* [Selected Works of Liu Shaoqi]. Vol. 2. Beijing: Renmin Press, 1985.
Mao Zedong. *Mao Zedong Sixiang Wansui* [Long Live Mao Zedong Thought]. Beijing: unpublished collection, 1967.
——. *Mao Zedong Xuanji* [Selected Works of Mao Zedong]. Vols. 4 and 5. Beijing: Renmin Press, 1977.
——. *Mao Zedong Junshi Wenxuan—Neibuban* [Selected Military Works of Mao Zedong, edition for internal circulation]. Beijing: Jiefangjun Zhanshi Press, 1981.
——. *Jianguo Yilai Mao Zedong Wengao: 1949.9–1950.12* [Mao Zedong's Manuscripts since the Foundation of the PRC: September 1949–December 1950]. Vol. 1. Beijing: Zhongyang Wenxian Press, 1987.
——. *Jianguo Yilai Mao Zedong Wengao: 1951.1–1951.12* [Mao Zedong's Manuscripts since the Foundation of the PRC: January 1951–December 1951]. Vol. 2. Beijing: Zhongyang Wenxian Press, 1988.
——. *Jianguo Yilai Mao Zedong Wengao: 1952.1–12* [Mao Zedong's Manuscripts since the Foundation of the PRC: January–December 1952]. Vol. 3. Beijing: Zhongyang Wenxian Press, 1989.
——. *Jianguo Yilai Mao Zedong Wengao: 1953.1–1954.12* [Mao Zedong's Manuscripts since the Foundation of the PRC: January 1953–December 1954]. Vol. 4. Beijing: Zhongyang Wenxian Press, 1990.
——. *Jianguo Yilai Mao Zedong Wengao: 1955.1–12* [Mao Zedong's Manuscripts since the Foundation of the PRC: January–December 1955]. Vol. 5. Beijing: Zhongyang Wenxian Press, 1991.

Peng Dehuai. *Peng Dehuai Junshi Wenxuan* [Selected Military Works of Peng De-huai]. Beijing: Zhongyang Wenxian Press, 1988.

Wang Jiaxiang. *Wang Jiaxiang Xuanji* [Selected Works of Wang Jiaxiang]. Bei-jing: Renmin Press, 1989.

Zhou Enlai. *Zhou Enlai Xuanji* [Selected Works of Zhou Enlai]. Vol. 2. Beijing: Renmin Press, 1984.

——— . *Zhou Enlai Tongyi Zhanxian Wenxuan* [Selected Works of Zhou Enlai on the United Front]. Beijing: Renmin Press, 1984.

Zhu De. *Zhu De Xuanji* [Selected Works of Zhu De]. Anhui: Renmin Press, 1983.

Memoirs, Oral History, and Official Documentation

Bo Yibo. *Ruogan Zhongda Juece yu Shijian de Huigu* [My Recollections of Decision Making on Several Important Policies and Events]. Vol. 1. Beijing: Zhong-gong Zhongyang Dangxiao Press, 1991.

Chai Chengwen. *Banmendian Tanpan* [The Panmunjom Negotiations]. Beijing: Jiefangjun Press, 1989.

Chen Geng. *Chen Geng Riji* (Xu) [Diary of General Chen Geng, Continued]. Beijing: Zhan Shi Press, 1982.

Cheng Zihua. *Cheng Zihua Huiyilu* [Memoirs of Chen Zihua]. Beijing: Jiefangjun Press, 1987.

Dangdai Zhongguo Series. *Dangdai Zhongguo Haijun* [China Today: The People's Navy]. Beijing: Zhongguo Shehui Kexue Press, 1987.

——— . *Dangdai Zhongguo Hegongye* [China Today: Nuclear Industry]. Beijing: Zhongguo Shehui Kexue Press, 1987.

——— . *Dangdai Zhongguo Waijiao* [China Today: Diplomacy]. Beijing: Zhongguo Shehui Kexue Press, 1987.

——— . *Dangdai Zhongguo Jundui De Junshi Gongzhuo* [China Today: The Military Affairs of the Chinese Army]. 2 Vols. Beijing: Zhongguo Shehui Kexue Press, 1989.

——— . *Dangdai Zhongguo Kongjun* [China Today: Air Force]. Beijing: Zhongguo Shehui Kexue Press, 1989.

——— . *Kangmei Yuanchao Zhanzheng* [China Today: The War to Resist U.S. Ag-gression and Aid Korea]. Beijing: Zhongguo Shehui Kexue Press, 1990.

Division of Central Archives and Manuscripts, ed. *Song Qingling Nianpu* [The Chronicle of Song Qingling]. Beijing: Zhongyang Wenxian Press, 1986.

——— . *Zhu De Nianpu* [The Chronicle of Zhu De]. Beijing: Renmin Press, 1986.

——— . *Zhou Enlai Nianpu: 1898–1949* [The Chronicle of Zhou Enlai]. Beijing: Zhongyang Wenxian Press, 1989.

Division of Military History, Chinese Academy of Military Sciences, ed. *Zhong-guo Renmin Jiefangjun Zhan Shi* [The War History of the People's Liberation Army]. Vol. 3. Beijing: Junshi Kexue Press, 1987.

——— . *Zhongguo Renmin Jiefangjun Liushinian Dashiji: 1927–1987* [Records of Im-portant Events of the People's Liberation Army from 1927 to 1987]. Beijing: Junshi Kexue Press, 1988.

——— . *Zhongguo Renmin Zhiyuanjun Kangmei Yuanchao Zhan Shi* [The War His-tory of the Chinese People's Volunteers in the War to Resist the United States and Assist Korea]. Beijing: Junshi Kexue Press, 1988.

Dong Jiwu, *Rongma Chunqiu* [My Years in the Military]. Beijing: Jiefangjun Press, 1986.

Du Ping. *Zhai Zhiyuanjun Zhongbu* [My Years at CPV Headquarters]. Nanjing: Jiefangjun Press, 1989.

Editorial Division of *Shijie Zhishi*, ed. *Taiwan Wenti Wenjian Huibian* [A Collection of Materials Concerning the Taiwan Issue]. Beijing: Shijie Zhishi Press, 1957.

——. *Zhongmei Guanxi Ziliao Huibian* [A Collection of Materials Concerning Chinese-American Relations]. Beijing: Shijie Zhishi Press, 1957.

——. *Zhonghua Renmin Gongheguo Duiwai Guanxi Wenjian Ji: 1949–1950* [A Collection of Documents of Foreign Relations of the PRC]. Vol. 1. Beijing: Shijie Zhishi Press, 1957.

——. *Zhonghua Renmin Gongheguo Duiwai Guanxi Wenjian Ji: 1951–1953* [A Collection of Documents of Foreign Relations of the PRC]. Vol. 2. Beijing: Shijie Zhishi Press, 1958.

——. *Yindu Zhina Wenti Wenjian Huibian, 1955–57* [Collection of Documents Concerning Indochina]. Beijing: Shijie Zhishi Press, 1959.

He Fang. October 1988. Institute of American Studies, Chinese Academy of Social Sciences. Beijing (oral history).

Hoang Van Hoan. *Canghai Yisu: Hoang Van Hoan Geming Huiyilu* [Hoang Van Hoan's Revolutionary Reminiscences]. Beijing: Jiefangjun Press, 1987.

Hong Xuezhi. *Kangmei Yuanchao Zhanzheng Huiyi* [Recollections of the War to Resist U.S. Aggression and Aid Korea]. Beijing: Jiefangjun Wenyi Press, 1990.

Huang Daoxia, Dia Zhou, and Yu Zhan. eds. *Zhonghua Renmin Gongheguo Sishinian Dashi Ji: 1949–1989* [Records of the Important Events of the People's Republic of China from 1949 to 1989]. Beijing: Guangming Ribao Press, 1989.

Huang Hua. "My Contacts with Leighton Stuart in the Early Days after the Liberation of Nanjing." In *Xinzhongguo Waijiao Fengyun* [Winds and Clouds of New China's Diplomacy], ed. Division of Diplomatic History, Ministry of Foreign Affairs, pp. 22–31. Beijing: Shijie Zhishi Press, 1990.

Li Jukui. *Li Jukui Huiyilu* [Memoirs of Li Jukui]. Beijing: Jiefangjun Press, 1986.

Li Shenzhi. *Yafei Huiyi Riji—Rineiwa Huiyi Tongxun* [Diary of the Asian-African Conference—Newsletters of the Geneva Conference]. Beijing: Zhongguo Xinwen Press, 1986.

Li Weihan. *Huiyi yu Yanjiu* [Recollections and Analyses]. Vol. 2. Beijing: Zhongyang Dangshi Ziliao Press, 1986.

Liu Bocheng. *Liu Bocheng Huiyilu* [Memoirs of Liu Bocheng]. Vol. 3. Shanghai: Renmin Press, 1988.

Liu Xiao. *Chushi Sulian Banian* [My Eight Years as Ambassador to the Soviet Union]. Beijing: Zhongyang Dangshi Ziliao Press, 1986.

Ma Lie. October 1988. Institute of American Studies, Chinese Academy of Social Sciences. Beijing (oral history).

Nie Fengzhi, ed. *Sanjun Huizhan Donghai* [The Three Armies Fighting in East China Sea]. Nanjing: Jiefangjun Press, 1986.

Nie Rongzhen. *Nie Rongzhen Huiyilu* [Nie Rongzhen Memoirs], Vol. 2. Beijing: Jiefangjun Press, 1984.

Peng Dehuai. *Peng Dehuai Zishu* [Personal Recollections of Peng Dehuai]. Beijing: Jiefangjun Press, 1982.

Pi Dingjun. *Pi Dingjun Riji* [Diary of Pi Dingjun]. Beijing: Jiefangjun Press, 1986.

Shi Zhe. "With Chairman Mao in the Soviet Union." In *Ren Wu* [Biographical Studies], May 1988, pp. 3–24.

Tian Weiben. October 1988. *Zhonggong Zhongyang Dang Xiao* [Central University of the CCP]. Beijing (oral history).

Wang Bingnan. *Zhongmei Huitan Jiunian Huigu* [Nine Years of Sino-American Diplomacy in Retrospect]. Beijing: Zhijie Zhishi Press, 1985.

Wang Bingnan. October 1988. Beijing (oral history).

Wu Xiuquan. *Zhai Waijiaobu Banian de Jingli, 1950.1–1958.10* [My Eight Years in the Ministry of Foreign Affairs: January 1950–October 1958]. Beijing: Shijie Zhishi Press, 1983.

——. *Zhai Zhonglianbu Banian, 1958.10–1966.12* [My Eight Years in the Ministry of Central Unification]. Beijing: Zhongyang Dangshi Ziliao Press, 1983.

Xiao Hua. *Jianku Suiyue* [Those Difficult Years]. Shanghai: Wenyi Press, 1983.

Xiao Jingguang. *Xiao Jingguang Huiyilu* [The Memoirs of Xiao Jingguang]. Beijing: Jiefangjun Press, 1987.

"Xinghuo Liaoyuan" Editorial Division, ed. *Jiefangjun Jiangling Zhuan* [The Chronicle of PLA Senior Generals]. Vol. 1. Beijing: Jiefangjun Press, 1984.

——. *Jiefangjun Jiangling Zhuan* [The Chronicle of PLA Senior Generals]. Vol. 3. Beijing: Jiefangjun Press, 1986.

——. *Jiefangjun Jiangling Zhuan* [The Chronicle of PLA Senior Generals]. Vol. 7. Beijing: Jiefangjun Press, 1988.

Xu Xiangqian. *Lishi De Huigu* [To Recall the History]. Vol. 2. Beijing: Jiefangjun Press, 1987.

Yang Dezhi. *Wei Le Heping* [For the Sake of Peace]. Beijing: Changzheng Press, 1987.

Yao Xu. October 1988. Guofang Da Xue [University of National Defense]. Beijing (oral history).

Ye Fei. *Ye Fei Huiyilu* [Ye Fei Memoirs]. Beijing: Jiefangjun Press, 1988.

Newspapers and Periodicals

Dagongbao [Great Justice Daily]. 29 August 1949.

Dongbei Ribao [Northeast China Daily]. 20 July 1950 to 7 November 1950.

Hongqi Zhazhi [Journal of Red Flag]. 1 January 1958 to 30 December 1958.

Jiefang Ribao [The Liberation Daily]. 4 January 1947 to 19 February 1950.

Renmin Ribao [People's Daily]. 1 July 1949 to 20 October 1958.

Renmin Ribao—Haiwai Ban [People's Daily—Oversea Edition]. 12 June 1991.

Shijie Zhishi [World Knowledge]. July 1950 to September 1958.

Wen Huibao [Collected Literature]. 10 August 1949 to 2 March 1950.

Xinhua Yuebao [New China Monthly]. 14 March 1949 to October 1958.

Xue Xi [Studies]. September 1949 to August 1950.

Books

Chen Xiaolu. *Yuanshuai Waijiaojia* [A Marshal and A Diplomat]. Beijing: Jiefangjun Wenyi Press, 1985.

Deng Chao. *Meidi Junshi Shang De Ruodian* [The Military and Strategic Weaknesses of U.S. Imperialism]. Beijing: Shijie Zhishi Press, 1950.

Division of CCP Central Archives and Manuscripts, ed. *Zhou Enlai Zhuan, 1898–1949* [Biography of Zhou Enlai]. Beijing: Renmin Press, 1989.

——. *Zhonggong Dangshi Fengyun Lu* [Records of the Winds and Clouds of the CCP History]. Beijing: Renmin Press, 1990.

Division of War Theories, Chinese Academy of Military Sciences. Ed. *Sun Tze Bingfa Xinzhu* [A New Interpretation of Sun Tze's *Art of War*]. Beijing: Zhonghua Shuju, 1977.

Gong Yuzhi, and Xiang Xianzhi. *Mao Zedong de Dushu Shenghuo* [Mao Zedong's Reading]. Beijing: Sanlian Books, 1986.

Hoang Van Hoan. *Yuezhong Zhandou Youyi De Shishi Burong Waiqu* [The Reality of Sino-Vietnamese Friendship in Fighting Ought not to Be Distorted]. Beijing: Renmin Press, 1979.

——. *Yuezhong Youhao yu Li Sheng de Bei Pan* [The Sino-Vietnamese Friendship and Li Sheng's Betrayal]. Beijing: Renmin Press, 1983.

Huang Zhen. *Hu Zhiming Yu Zhongguo* [Ho Chi Minh and China]. Beijing: Jiefangjun Press, 1987.

Lin Baye. *Xuexi Mao Zedong Junshi Zhuzuo Zhong De Zhexue Sixiang* [Philosophical Thoughts in Mao Zedong's Military Thinking]. Tianjin: Renmin Press, 1982.

Lu Zhikong. *Waijiao Ju Bo* [A Great Authority in Diplomacy]. Henan: Renmin Press, 1989.

Mu Xin. *Chen Geng Dajiang* [Senior General Chen Geng]. Beijing: Xinhua Press, 1985.

The Museum of Chinese People's Military Revolutions, ed. *Peng Dehuai Yuanshuai Fengbei Yongcun* [The Unforgettable Achievements of Marshal Peng Dehuai]. Shanghai: Renmin Press, 1985.

——. *Liu Shaoqi Daxing Chaizhao Ji* [Colored Photography of Liu Shaoqi]. Beijing: Renmin Press, 1986.

——. *Ming Jiang Su Yu* [Su Yu: A Famous Senior General]. Beijing: Xinhua Press, 1986.

Pan Jijiong. *Meidi Yuanzi Waijiao De Pochan* [The Failures of "Atom" Diplomacy for U.S. Imperialism]. Shanghai: Xin Zhishi Press, 1950.

——. *Yuanzineng Wenti Shang De Liangtiao Daolu* [The Two Lines Concerning the Issue of Nuclear Energy]. Shanghai: Xin Zhishi Press, 1955.

Xie Yixian. *Zhongguo Waijiao Shi, 1949–1979* [Chinese Diplomatic History, 1949–1979]. Zhengzhou: Henan Renmin Press, 1988.

Xu Peilan, and Zheng Pengfei. *Chen Geng Jiangjun Zhuan*. Beijing: Jiefangjun Press, 1988.

Xu Yan. *Diyici Jiaoliang* [The First Encounter]. Beijing: Zhongguo Guangbo Dianshi Press, 1990.

Yao Xu. *Cong Yalujiang Dao Banmendian* [From the Yalu River to Panmunjom]. Beijing: Renmin Press, 1980.

Ye Yumen. *Heixue: Chubing Chaoxian Jishi* [Black Snow: Historical Records of Chinese Military Intervention in Korea]. Beijing: Zuojia Press, 1989.

Zi Zhongyun. *Meiguo Duiwai Zhengce de Yuanqi yu Fazhan, 1945–1950* [The Origins and Evolution of U.S. Policy toward China, 1945–1950]. Chongqing: Chongqing Press, 1987.

Articles

Bao Mingrong. "When Was the Strategy of Mobile Warfare in Korea Made?" *Tangshi Yanjiu Ziliao* [Studies and Materials of the Party History], March 1987, pp.18–21.

CCP Central Committee. "The Current Situation and Our Tasks in 1949" (8 January 1949). *Wenxian Yu Yanjiu* [Materials and Studies], October 1984, pp. 1–3.

Deng Shusheng. "The China Policy of Franklin D. Roosevelt." *Lishi Yanjiu* [Historical Studies], December 1985, pp. 10–19.

"Footnote to the *Selected Works of Chen Yun: 1949–1956*." *Wenxian Yu Yianjiu*, February 1982, p. 11.

Guo Fuwen. "China's Sun." *Zuoping yu Zhengming* [Literature and Commentary], February 1988, pp. 3–5.

He Di. "The Development of the CCP's Policy toward the United States, 1945–49." *Lishi Yanjiu*, June 1987, pp. 15–33.

——— . "The Evolution of PRC Policy toward the Offshore Islands, 1945–58." Beijing: Institute of American Studies, Chinese Academy of Social Sciences, 1987 (unpublished).

"How to Perceive the Intentions of the United States." In *Shishi Souce* [Handbook on Current Affairs], pp. 29–37. Beijing: Sanlian Press, 1950.

Hu Changshui. "The Formation of the Concept That Imperialism Is a Paper Tiger." *Tangshi Yanjiu Ziliao*, July 1988, pp. 16–18.

Huang Xiangping. "The Evolution of the Slogan 'Catching Up with Britain and America' in the Late 1950s." *Tangshi Yanjiu Ziliao*, April 1988, pp. 21–26.

Li Ke. "The Chinese Military Advisory Group in the Struggle to Resist France and Aid Vietnam." *Junshi Lishi* [Military History], March 1989, pp. 26–29.

Liu Liyun. "China's Mountains." *Xinhua Wenzhai* [Abstracts of New China's Literature], August 1987, pp. 136–39.

Qi Dexue. "An Important Decision by the Chinese People's Volunteers." *Tangshi Yanjiu Ziliao*, March 1987, pp. 18–21.

Sun Baosheng. "Mao Zedong Anticipated the U.S. Landing at Inchon." *Junshi Shilin* [Studies of Military History], October 1990, p. 13.

Tao Wenzhao. "President Truman's China Policy and General Marshall's Mission in China." *Lishi Yanjiu*, January 1986, pp. 40–48.

Tian Weiben. "The Meeting at Xiao He, July 1947." *Dangshi Zhengji Tongxun* [Newsletter of Collected CCP History Materials], July 1957, pp. 21–24.

Wang De. "Mao Zedong and Zhou Enlai Wanted to Visit the United States in 1944–45." *Mao Zedong Sixiang Yanjiu* [Studies of Mao Zedong Thought], February 1982, pp. 7–11.

Wang Funian. "A Summary of the Negotiations on the Korean Cease-Fire." *Tangshi Yanjiu Ziliao*, June 1983, pp. 2–12.

Wang Jianwei. "The U.S. Policy toward China, 1948–50." *Lishi Yanjiu*, November 1986, pp. 34–45.

Xia Yan. "From Hong Kong to Shanghai." *Renmin Wenxue* [People's Literature], January 1988, pp. 46–47.

Xiong Huayuan. "Zhou Enlai and the Asian-African Conference." *Tangshi Wenhui* [Collection of Studies on the Party's History], May 1987, pp. 4–8.

Xue Qi. "An Important Strategic Decision by the CPV." *Dangshi Yanjiu* [Studies of the History of the CCP], May 1985, pp. 60–61.

Yao Xu. "The Wisdom of Deciding to Resist the United States and Assist Korea." *Tangshi Yanjiu Ziliao*, October 1980, pp. 5–14.

——— . "Peng Dehuai's Great Contribution to the War to Resist the United States and Assist Korea." *Tangshi Yanjiu Ziliao*, January 1982, pp. 2–12.

Yu Zhan, and Zhang Guangyou. "On Whether Stalin Ever Persuaded Us Not to Cross the Yangtze River." In *Xinzhongguo Waijiao Fengyun*, ed. Division of Diplomatic History, Ministry of Foreign Affairs, pp. 15–21. Beijing: Shijie Zhishi Press, 1990.

Yuan Ming. "The Nature of Truman's China Policy Shown in a Debate from 1947 to 1948." *Lishi Yanjiu,* January 1985, pp. 37–45.

—— . "The Concept in U.S. Policy toward China around the Founding of the PRC." *Lishi Yanjiu,* June 1987, pp. 24–33.

Zhai Qiang. "The China Lobby and President Truman's China Policy, 1947–49." *Lishi Yanjiu,* May 1986, pp. 37–45.

Zhang Baijia. "Comments on the Seminar on the History of Sino-American Relations, 1945–1955." *Lishi Yanjiu,* June 1987, pp. 34–53.

—— . "The Policies of the KMT and the CCP toward the United States, 1937–45." *Lishi Yanjiu,* June 1987, pp. 3–14.

Zhang Yimin. "The Evolution of Mao Zedong's Idea of 'Resisting Revisionism.' " *Tangshi Yanjiu Ziliao,* February 1986, pp. 33–40.

Zhang Yisheng. "The Revolutionary Friendship between Premier Zhou and Chairman Ho." *Yingu Zhina Yanjiu* [Studies of Indochina], March 1981, pp. 12–25.

Zhou Peide. "The Joint Rear, Services of the Army, Navy, and Air Force in the Liberation of Yijiangshan." *Junshi Shilin,* April 1990, pp. 49–51.

Zi Zhongjun. "U.S. Policy toward Taiwan around the Founding of the PRC." *Guoji Wenti Yanjiu* [Studies of International Affairs], March 1982, pp. 34–42.

MATERIALS IN ENGLISH

Manuscript Sources

Dulles, John Foster. Papers. Dwight D. Eisenhower Library.

—— . Papers. Seeley Mudd Library, Princeton University.

Eisenhower, Dwight D. Papers. Dwight D. Eisenhower Library.

Kennan, George F. Papers. Seeley Mudd Library, Princeton University.

Koo, Wellington V. K. Papers. Butler Library, Columbia University.

Rankin, Karl Lott. Papers. Seeley Mudd Library, Princeton University.

Smith, H. Alexander. Papers. Seeley Mudd Library, Princeton University.

U.S. Army. Staff Records. Modern Military Records Branch, National Archives.

U.S. Department of State. Decimal Files. Diplomatic Branch, National Archives.

—— . General Records, 1955–59. Diplomatic Branch, National Archives.

—— . Office of Chinese Affairs Records. Diplomatic Branch, National Archives.

—— . Office of Intelligence and Research Records. Diplomatic Branch, National Archives.

U.S. Joint Chiefs of Staff. Records. Modern Military Records Branch, National Archives.

U.S. National Security Council. Records. Modern Military Records Branch, National Archives.

Published Documents

Public Papers of the Presidents: Dwight D. Eisenhower, 1953–1961, Washington, D.C.: U.S. Government Printing Office, 1960–1961.

Bibliography

Public Papers of the Presidents: Harry S. Truman, 1945–1953. Washington, D.C.:
U.S. Government Printing Office, 1961–66.
U.S. Department of Defense. United States–Vietnam Relations, 1945–1967. Wash-
ington, D.C.: U.S. Government Printing Office, 1971.
U.S. Department of State. Department of State Bulletin.
——— .Foreign Relations of the United States.
——— . United States Relations with China, with Special Reference to the Period 1944–
1949 [China White Paper]. Washington, D.C.: U.S. Government Printing Of-
fice, 1949.

Books

Acheson, Dean. Present at the Creation: My Years in the State Department. New
York: W. W. Norton, 1969.
Adams, Sherman. First Hand Report: The Inside Story of the Eisenhower Adminis-
tration. New York: Harper & Row, 1961.
Art, Robert J., and Kenneth N. Waltz, eds. The Use of Force: International Politics
of Foreign Policy. 2d ed. Lanham, Md.: University Press of America, 1983.
Berlo, David K. The Process of Communication: An Introduction to Theory and Prac-
tice. New York: Holt, Rinehart, and Winston, 1960.
Betts, Richard K. Nuclear Blackmail and Nuclear Balance. Washington, D.C.: The
Brookings Institution, 1987.
Billings-Yun, Melanie. Decision against War: Eisenhower and Dien Bien Phu, 1954.
New York: Columbia University Press, 1988.
Blair, Bruce G. Strategic Command and Control: Redefining the Nuclear Threat.
Washington, D.C.: The Brookings Institution, 1985.
Blum, Robert M. Drawing the Line: The Origins of the American Containment Policy
in East Asia. New York: W. W. Norton, 1982.
Booth, Ken. Strategy and Ethnocentrism. New York: Holmes and Meier, 1979.
Borg, Dorothy, and Waldo Heinrichs, eds. Uncertain Years: Chinese-American Re-
lations, 1947–1950. New York: Columbia University Press, 1980.
Braken, Paul J. The Command and Control of Nuclear Forces. New Haven: Yale Uni-
versity Press, 1983.
Brodie, Bernard. Strategy in the Missle Age. Princeton: Princeton University
Press, 1959.
Buhite, Russell D. Soviet-American Relations in Asia, 1945–1954. Norman: Uni-
versity Press of Oklahoma, 1981.
Caridi, Ronald J. The Korean War and American Policies: The Republican Party as a
Case Study. Philadelphia: University of Pennsylvania Press, 1968.
Chang, Gordon H. Friends and Enemies: The United States, China, and the Soviet
Union, 1948–1972. Stanford: Stanford University Press, 1990.
Cimbala, Stephen J. Extended Deterrence: The United States and NATO Europe.
Lexington, Mass.: Lexington Books, 1987.
Clausewitz, Carl von. On War. Edited and translated by Peter Paret and
Michael Howard. Princeton: Princeton University Press, 1976.
Cohen, Warren I. America's Response to China: An Interpretative History of Sino-
American Relations. 2d ed. New York: Columbia University Press, 1980.
Cumings, Bruce. The Origins of the Korean War: Liberation and the Emergence of
Separate Regimes, 1945–1947. Princeton: Princeton University Press, 1981.
——— . The Origins of the Korean War. Vol. 2, The Roaring of the Cataract, 1947–1950.
Princeton: Princeton University Press, 1990.

Dallek, Robert. *The American Style of Foreign Policy: Cultural Politics and Foreign Affairs.* New York: Oxford University Press, 1983.

Deibel, Terry L., and John Lewis Gaddis, eds. *Containing the Soviet Union: A Critique of U.S. Policy.* Washington D.C.: Pergamon-Brassey, 1987.

Dobbs, Charles M. *The Unwanted Symbol: American Foreign Policy, the Cold War, and Korea, 1945–1950.* Kent, Ohio: Kent State University Press, 1981.

———. *The United States and East Asia since 1945.* Lewiston: N.Y.: E. Mellen Press, 1990.

Eisenhower, Dwight D. *The White House Years: Mandate for Change, 1953–1956.* Garden City, N.Y.: Doubleday, 1963.

———. *The White House Years: Waging Peace, 1957–1961.* Garden City, N.Y.: Doubleday, 1965.

Foot, Rosemary. *The Wrong War: American Policy and the Dimensions of the Korean Conflict, 1950–1953.* Ithaca: Cornell University Press, 1985.

———. *A Substitute for Victory: The Politics of Peacemaking at the Korean Armistice Talks.* Ithaca: Cornell University Press, 1990.

Gaddis, John Lewis. *Strategies of Containment: A Critical Appraisal of Postwar American National Security Policy.* New York: Oxford University Press, 1982.

———. *The Long Peace: Inquiries into the History of the Cold War.* New York: Oxford University Press, 1987.

George, Alexander L., and Richard Smoke. *Deterrence in American Foreign Policy: Theory and Practice.* New York; Columbia University Press, 1974.

Gray, Colin S. *The Geopolitics of Super Power.* Lexington: University Press of Kentucky, 1988.

Gromyko, Andrei A. *Memoirs.* Foreword by Henry A. Kissinger; translated by Harold Shukman. New York: Doubleday, 1989.

Gurtov, Melvin, and Byong-Moo Huang. *China under Threat: The Politics of Strategy and Diplomacy.* Baltimore: Johns Hopkins University Press, 1980.

Halperin, Morton H. *Nuclear Fallacy: Dispelling the Myth of Nuclear Strategy.* Cambridge, Mass.: Ballinger, 1987.

Hamby, Alonzo L. *Beyond the New Deal: Harry S. Truman and American Liberalism.* New York: Columbia University Press, 1973.

Harding, Harry, and Yuan Ming, eds. *Sino-American Relations, 1945–1955: A Joint Reassessment of a Critical Decade.* Wilmington, Del.: Scholarly Resources, 1989.

Heald, Morrell, and Lawrence S. Kaplan, *Culture and Diplomacy: The American Experience.* Westport, Conn: Greenwood Press, 1977.

Holsti, Ole R. *Crisis, Escalation, War.* Montreal: McGill-Queen's University Press, 1977.

Hsieh, Alice L. *Communist China's Strategy in the Nuclear Era.* Englewood Cliffs, N.J.: Prentice-Hall, 1962.

Hughes, Emmett John. *The Ordeal of Power: A Political Memoir of the Eisenhower Years.* New York: Atheneum, 1963.

Huth, Paul K. *Extended Deterrence and the Prevention of War.* New Haven: Yale University Press, 1988.

Immerman, Richard H., ed. *John Foster Dulles and the Diplomacy of the Cold War.* Princeton: Princeton University Press, 1990.

Iriye, Akira. *The Cold War in Asia: A Historical Introduction.* Englewood Cliffs, N.J.: Prentice-Hall, 1974.

Iriye, Akira, and Warren I. Cohen, eds. *The United States and Japan in the Postwar World.* Lexington: University Press of Kentucky, 1989.

James, D. Clayton. *The Years of MacArthur: Triumph and Disaster, 1945–1964*. Boston: Houghton Mifflin, 1985.

Jervis, Robert. *Perception and Misperception in International Politics*. Princeton: Princeton University Press, 1976.

——, ed. *Dominoes and Bandwagons: Strategic Beliefs and Great Power Competition in the Eurasian Rimland*. New York: Oxford University Press, 1991.

Jervis, Robert, Richard Ned Lebow, and Janice Gross Stein, eds. *Psychology and Deterrence*. Baltimore: Johns Hopkins University Press, 1985.

Kahn, E. J., Jr. *The China Hands: America's Foreign Service Officers and What Befell Them*. New York: Penguin Books, 1976.

Kahn, Herman. *On Thermonuclear War*. Princeton: Princeton University Press, 1960.

Kalicki, J. H. *The Pattern of Sino-American Crises: Political and Military Interactions in the 1950s*. New York: Cambridge University Press, 1975.

Kaplan, Lawrence S., Denise Artaud, and Mark R. Bubin, eds. *Dien Bien Phu and Franco-American Relations, 1954–1955*. Wiliminston, DL.: Scholarly Resources, 1990.

Kau, Michael Y. M., and John K. Leung, eds. *The Writings of Mao Zedong, 1949–1976*. Vol. 1, *September 1949–October 1955*. Armonk, N.Y.: M. E. Sharpe, 1986.

Kaufman, Burton I. *The Korean War: Changes in Crisis, Credibility, and Command*. New York: Knopf, 1986.

Kennan, George F. *American Diplomacy, 1900–1950*. Chicago: University of Chicago Press, 1951.

——. *Memoirs: 1925–1950*. Boston: Little, Brown, 1967.

——. *Memoirs: 1950–1963*. Boston: Little, Brown, 1972.

Khrushchev, Nikita S. *Khrushchev Remembers: The Last Testament*. Edited and translated by Strobe Talbott. Boston: Little, Brown, 1974.

Khrushchev, Sergei. *Khrushchev on Khrushchev: An Inside Account of the Man and His Era*. Edited and translated by William Taubman. Boston: Little, Brown, 1990.

Larson, Deborah Welch. *Origins of Containment: A Psychological Explanation*. Princeton: Princeton University Press, 1985.

Lebow, Richard Ned. *Between Peace and War: The Nature of International Crisis*. Baltimore: Johns Hopkins University Press, 1981.

Lewis, John Wilson, and Xue Litai. *China Builds the Bomb*. Stanford: Stanford University Press, 1988.

Liu Shaoqi. *On Internationalsim and Nationalism*. Peking: Foreign Languages Press, 1949.

MacDonald, Callum A. *Korea: The War before Vietnam*. New York: The Free Press, 1986.

Mao Tse-tung. *Selected Military Writings of Mao Tse-tung*. Peking: Foreign Languages Press, 1963.

——. *Selected Works of Mao Tse-tung*. 4 vols. Peking: Foreign Languages Press, 1965.

——. *Quotations from Chairman Mao Tse-tung*. Peking: Foreign Languages Press, 1966.

Mayers, David Allan. *Cracking the Monolith: U.S. Policy against the Sino-Soviet Alliance, 1949–1955*. Baton Rouge: Louisiana State University Press, 1986.

Mearsheimer, John J. *Conventional Deterrence*. Ithaca: Cornell University Press, 1983.

Morgan, Patrick M. *Deterrence: A Conceptual Analysis.* Beverly Hills, Calif.: Sage, 1983.

Neustadt, Richard E., and Ernest R. May. *Thinking in Time: The Uses of History for Decision-Makers.* New York: The Free Press, 1986.

Osgood, Robert E. *Limited War: The Challenge to American Strategy.* Chicago: University of Chicago Press, 1956.

Panikkar, Kavalam M. *In Two Chinas: Memoirs of a Diplomat.* London: George Allen, 1955.

Peng Dehuai. *Memoirs of a Chinese Marshal: The Autobiographical Notes of Peng Dehuai, 1898–1974.* Peking: Foreign Languages Press, 1984.

Rotter, Andrew J. *The Path to Vietnam: Origins of the American Commitment to Southeast Asia.* Ithaca: Cornell University Press, 1987.

Schaller, Michael. *The American Occupation of Japan: The Origins of the Cold War in Asia.* New York: Oxford University Press, 1985.

——— . *Douglas MacArthur: The Far Eastern General.* New York: Oxford University Press, 1989.

——— . *The United States and China in the Twentieth Century.* 2d ed. New York: Oxford University Press, 1990.

Schelling, Thomas C. *The Strategy of Conflict.* Cambridge: Harvard University Press, 1960.

——— . *Arms and Influence.* New Haven: Yale University Press, 1966.

Shimshoni, Jonathan. *Israel and Conventional Deterrence.* Ithaca: Cornell University Press, 1988.

Snyder, Glenn. *Deterrence and Defense.* Princeton: Princeton University Press, 1961.

Spence, Jonathan D. *The Search for Modern China.* New York: W. W. Norton, 1990.

Steinbruner, John D. *The Cybernetic Theory of Decision.* Princeton: Princeton University Press, 1974.

Stoessinger, John G. *Nations in Darkness: China, Russia, and America.* 4th ed. New York: Random House, 1986.

Stolper, Thomas. *China, Taiwan, and the Offshore Islands.* Armonk, N.Y.: M. E. Sharpe, 1985.

Stueck, William Whitney, Jr. *The Road to Confrontation: American Policy toward China and Korea, 1947–1950.* Chapel Hill: University of North Carolina Press, 1981.

Tang, Tsou. *America's Failure in China, 1941–1950.* Chicago: University of Chicago Press, 1963.

Tao Hanzhang. *Sun Tze's Art of War: The Modern Chinese Interpretation.* Translated by Yuan Shibing. New York: Sterling Publishing, 1987.

Tucker, Nancy Bernkopf. *Patterns in the Dust: Chinese-American Relations and the Recognition Controversy, 1949–1950.* New York: Columbia University Press, 1983.

Whiting, Allen S. *China Crosses the Yalu: The Decision to Enter the Korean War.* New York: Macmillan, 1960.

——— . *The Chinese Calculus of Deterrence.* Ann Arbor: University of Michigan Press, 1975.

Articles

Achen, Christopher H., and Duncan Snidal. "Rational Deterrence Theory and Comparative Case Studies." *World Politics* 41 (January 1989): 143–69.

Betts, Richard K. "Conventional Deterrence: Predictive Uncertainty and Policy Confidence." *World Politics* 37 (January 1985): 153–79.

Brody, Richard A. "Deterrence Strategy: An Annotated Bibliography." *Journal of Conflict Resolution* 4 (December 1960): 443–57.

Chang, Gordon H. "To the Nuclear Brink: Eisenhower, Dulles, and the Quemoy/Matsu Crisis." *International Security* 12 (Spring 1988): 96–123.

Cohen, Warren I. "Conversations with Chinese Friends: Zhou Enlai's Associates Reflect on Chinese-American Relations in the 1940s and the Korean War." *Diplomatic History* 11 (Summer 1987): 283–89.

Dingman, Roger. "Atomic Diplomacy during the Korean War." *International Security* 13 (Winter 1988/89): 61–89.

Downs, George W. "The Rational Deterrence Debate." *World Politics* 31 (January 1989): 225–38.

Ellsberg, Daniel. "The Crude Analysis of Strategic Choice." *American Economic Review* 21 (May 1961): 472–78.

Foot, Rosemary. "Nuclear Coercion and the Ending of the Korean Conflict." *International Security* 13 (Winter 1988/89): 99–112.

Gaddis, John Lewis. "New Conceptual Approaches to the Study of American Foreign Relations: Interdisciplinary Perpectives." *Diplomatic History* 14 (Summer 1990): 405–23.

George, Alexander L., and Richard Smoke. "Deterrence and Foreign Policy." *World Politics* 41 (January 1989): 170–82.

Glaser, Charles. "Why Even Good Defenses May Be Bad." *International Security* 9 (Fall 1984): 47–70.

Goldstein, Steven M. "Chinese Communist Policy toward the United States: Opportunities and Constraints, 1944–1950." In *Uncertain Years: Chinese-American Relations, 1947–1950*, ed. Dorothy Borg and Waldo Heinrichs, pp. 235–78. New York: Columbia University Press, 1980.

Gordon, Leonard H. "U.S. Opposition to the Use of Force in the Taiwan Straits, 1954–1962." *Journal of American History* 72 (December 1985): 578–646.

Halperin, Morton H., and Tang Tsou. "The 1958 Quemoy Crisis." In *Sino-Soviet Relations and Arms Control*, ed. Morton H. Halperin, pp. 265–304. Cambridge: Harvard University Press, 1963.

Herring, George C., and Richard H. Immerman. "Eisenhower, Dulles, and Dienbienphu: 'The Day We Didn't Go to War' Revisited." *Journal of American History* 41 (September 1984): 343–63.

Hunt, Michael. "Mao Tse-tung and the Issue of Accommodation with the United States." In *Uncertain Years: Chinese American Relations, 1947–50*, ed. Dorothy Borg, and Waldo Heinrichs, pp. 185–234. New York: Columbia University Press, 1980.

———. "Internationalizing U.S. Diplomatic History: A Practical Agenda." *Diplomatic History* 15 (Winter 1991): 1–12.

Huntington, Samuel. "Conventional Deterrence and Conventional Retaliation in Europe." *International Security* 8 (Winter 1983–84): 32–56.

Huth, Paul K. "Extended Deterrence and the Outbreak of War." *American Political Science Review* 82 (Spring 1988): 423–43.

Huth, Paul, and Bruce Russett. "What Makes Deterrence Work? Cases from 1900 to 1980." *World Politics* 36 (January 1984): 496–526.

———. "Deterrence Failure and Crisis Escalation." *International Studies Quarterly* 32 (May 1988): 29–45.

——— . "Testing Deterrence Theory: Rigor Makes a Difference." *World Politics* 42 (July 1990): 466–501.

Immerman, Richard H. "The United States and the Geneva Conference of 1954: A New Look." *Diplomatic History* 14 (Winter 1990): 43–66.

Irish, Marian D. "Public Opinion and American Foreign Policy: The Quemoy Crisis of 1958." *Political Quarterly* 31 (1960): 151–62.

Jervis, Robert. "Deterrence Theory Revisited." *World Politics* 31 (January 1979): 289–324.

——— . "Rational Deterrence: Theory and Evidence." *World Politics* 41 (January 1989): 183–207.

Jervis, Robert, Richard Ned Lebow, and Janice Gross Stein. "Beyond Deterrence." *Journal of Social Issues* 43 (Winter 1987): 21–41.

——— . "Deterrence: The Elusive Dependent Variable." *World Politics* 42 (April 1990): 336–69.

Kaplan, Morton. "The Calculus of Nuclear Deterrence." *World Politics* 11 (Fall 1958): 20–43.

Kash, Don E. "United States Policy for Quemoy and Matsu." *The Western Political Quarterly* 2 (December 1963): 912–23.

Kaufmann, William W. "Limited War." *In Military Policy and National Security,* ed. William W. Kaufmann. Princeton: Princeton University Press, 1956.

Lebow, Richard Ned, and Janice Gross Stein. "Rational Deterrence Theory: I Think, Therefore I Deter." *World Politics* 41 (January 1989): 208–24.

Lepingwell, John. "The Laws of Combat? Lanchester Reexamined." *International Security* 12 (Summer 1987): 89–127.

Levy, Jack S. "Misperception and the Cause of War." *World Politics* 36 (October 1983): 79–99.

——— . "The Offensive-Defensive Balance of Military Technology: A Theoretical and Historical Analysis." *International Studies Quarterly* 28 (June 1984): 219–38.

Lewis, John Wilson. "Quemoy and American China Policy." *Asian Survey* 2 (March 1962): 12–19.

Nalebuff, Barry. "Rational Deterrence in an Imperfect World." *World Politics* 43 (April 1991): 313–35.

Nye, Joseph S., Jr., and Sean M. Lynn-Jones. "International Security Studies: A Report of a Conference on the State of the Field." *International Security* 12 (Spring 1988): 11.

Rosenberg, David Alan. "The Origins of Overkill: Nuclear Weapons and American Strategy, 1945–1960." *International Security* 7 (Spring 1983): 3–71.

Russett, Bruce. "Pearl Harbor: Deterrence Theory and Decision Theory." *Journal of Peace Research* 4, no. 2 (1967): 89–105.

Sagan, Scott. "1914 Revisited: Allies, Offense, and Instability." *International Security* 12 (Fall 1987): 151–75.

Schaller, Michael. "Securing the Great Crescent: Occupied Japan and the Origins of Containment in Southeast Asia." *Journal of American History* 39 (September 1982): 392–414.

Stein, Arthur A. "When Misperception Matters." *World Politics* 34 (July 1982): 505–26.

Stein, Janice Gross. "Extended Deterrence in the Middle East: American Strategy Reconsidered." *World Politics* 39 (April 1987): 326–52.

Steinbruner, John D. "National Security and the Concept of Strategic Stability." *Journal of Conflict Resolution* 22 (September 1978): 411–28.

Thomas, John R. "Soviet Behavior in the Quemoy Crisis of 1958." *Orbis* 6 (April 1962): 38–64.

Whiting, Allen S. "Quemoy 1958: Mao's Miscalculations." *China Quarterly* 63 (September 1975): 263–70.

Wohstetter, Albert. "The Delicate Balance of Terror." *Foreign Affairs* 37 (January 1959): 211–34.

Zagare, Frank C. "Rationality and Deterrence." *World Politics* 42 (January 1990): 238–60.

Index

Library of Congress Cataloging-in-Publication Data

Zhang, Shu Guang.
  Deterrence and strategic culture : Chinese-American
confrontations, 1949–1958 / Shu Guang Zhang.
    p. cm. — (Cornell studies in security affairs)
  Includes bibliographical references and index.
  ISBN 0-8014-2751-7
  1. United States—Foreign relations—China. 2. China—Foreign relations—United
States. 3. United States—Foreign relations—1945–1953. 4. United States—
Foreign relations—1953–1961. 5. China—Foreign relations—1949–1976.
  I. Title. II. Series.
E183.8.C5Z43 1992
327.73051—dc20   92-52777